Readings in
Eastern Religions

Second Edition

Edited by

Harold Coward
Ronald Neufeldt
and
Eva K. Neumaier

Wilfrid Laurier University Press

We acknowledge the financial support of the Government of Canada through the Book Publishing Industry Development Program for our publishing activities.

Library and Archives Canada Cataloguing in Publication

Readings in eastern religions / [compiled and edited by] Harold Coward, Ronald Neufeldt and Eva K. Neumaier. — 2nd ed.

ISBN-13: 978-0-88920-435-5
ISBN-10: 0-88920-435-7

1. China — Religion. 2. Japan — Religion. 3. India — Religion. 4. Religions.
I. Coward, Harold G., 1936–   II. Neufeldt, Ronald W. (Ronald Wesley), 1941–
III. Neumaier-Dargyay, E.K. (Eva K.), 1937–

BL1055.R42 2007   294   C2007-905780-X

CONTENTS

TEN

New Religions • 379

ACKNOWLEDGEMENTS

THE EDITORS WISH TO THANK GERRY DYER for her careful typing and correcting of the original manuscript. Gratitude is also due to Brian Henderson and his staff at Wilfrid Laurier University Press for their work on the second edition. Not only has the book been nicely published but from the beginning those working on the book at the Press have imbibed of its spirit.

All of us hope that this book will introduce its readers to the depth and richness of the source scriptures of the Eastern religions.

INTRODUCTION

THIS ANTHOLOGY WAS ORIGINALLY DEVELOPED for use in the introduction to Eastern Religions in the Department of Religious Studies at the University of Calgary. The existing anthologies did not suit the structure of our introductory course, so our intention with this volume was to create a volume that served our purposes and addressed a number of concerns regarding existing anthologies. The concerns we had then are still relevant and so are repeated here.

Given the drastic rise in the costs of printing and publication, most anthologies have become too expensive for students in introductory courses. In part this is a function of the size of most available anthologies. To be sure, there are relatively inexpensive anthologies available for a tradition like Hinduism or a country like India. Generally speaking, however, anthologies covering South and East Asia tend to be large and expensive.

Frequently, anthologies attempt to cover too much territory. Consequently, the excerpts provided are much too short to give a proper flavour of the excerpted text or the particular development it is supposed to represent. This becomes a serious problem in the case of stories that are meant to be told as much as possible in their entirety. The evocative power of a story simply does not come through well in the case of short excerpts, nor does the flavour of a text for that matter. While the approach of many short excerpts may provide better coverage of the broad sweep of a tradition, it does not provide a good sense of texts, stories, or even specific development within a tradition.

Too frequently, anthologies are governed by a bias towards doctrinal materials or, as students might put it, dry teachings. This is, we think, a peculiarly Western bias in religious studies. Traditions are much more colourful and gripping than an emphasis on doctrinal elements alone would suggest. There are, after all, colourful stories and anecdotes that present the heart of a tradition at least as well as the sermonic, discourse, and philosophical aspects of a tradition. And stories are much more memorable and gripping.

The arrangement of the excerpts is both chronological and thematic. It has been our experience that a thematic arrangement alone is not particularly good for students at the introductory level. It seems that religious developments as seen through primary texts are more memorable and understandable if they can be seen or read within a historical framework. Harold Coward was responsible for the sections on Hinduism and Jainism, Eva K. Neumaier prepared the Buddhist selections, and Ronald Neufeldt the readings for Sikhism and the Chinese and Japanese traditions.

The chapters themselves are designated by traditions. The first chapter, on Hinduism, includes excerpts from texts such as the *Samhitas, Brahmanas, Upanishads, Laws of Manu, Bhagavad Gita, Ramayana, Devi-Mahatmyam,* and medieval poet-saints, emphasizing topics such as creation, death, sacrifice, *dharma,* the Absolute, and knowledge of the Absolute. An excerpt on Hindu ethics and *dharma* has been added to this second edition.

The second chapter is devoted to the lengthy story of the son of Mriga, taken from the *Jaina Sutras* in order to illustrate concerns central to Jainism— the misery or frustration of life when seen correctly, and the vows necessary for liberation from repeated cycles of misery.

The third chapter, devoted to Buddhist developments, is systematically arranged according to the refuge formula (Buddha, doctrine, community). Each topic is illustrated through excerpts taken from Hinayana and Mahayana sources, thus making the change in doctrinal ideas clear. Excerpts are taken from the Pali Canon, the Mahayana Canon in its Tibetan and Chinese version, and the commentarial works by Buddhist masters of India, Tibet, and the Far East. Furthermore, the development of Buddhist thought in Tibet is illustrated through selections from the *Tibetan Book of the Dead,* the "pastoral" writings of Tibetan monk-scholars, and tantric sources.

Chapter 4 is devoted to the Sikh tradition, highlighting the *Adi Granth,* in particular the hymns of Guru Nanak, the founder of Sikhism, whose teachings were and still are the formative influence for Sikh beliefs. The second edition includes an excerpt from the Sikh Rahit Maryada, a document dating from 1950.

Chapters 5, 6, 7, and 8 deal with religious developments in China. Chapter 5, on *Early Chinese Thought*, includes selections from *The Book of Odes*, The *Book of History*, and the *Yijing/I Ching*. Chapter 6, on Confucian thought, emphasizes the *Analects, Mencius, Xunzi/Hsuntzu*, and later neo-Confucian developments. Chapter 7 emphasizes philosophical and religious Daoism/ Taoism, in particular the thought of *Laozi/Lao tzu, Zhuangzi/Chuangtzu,* and *Gehong/Ko Hung*. For the second edition we have added an excerpt from Ge Hong/Ko Hung to represent developments in religious Daoism. Chapter 8 deals with the thought of Mao Zedong/Mao tse Tung, emphasizing his hope for a future without evil. The chapter on Mao Zedong has been renamed "Chinese Communist Thought," and includes an expansion of the material on Mao.

Chapters 9 and 10 deal with Japan. Chapter 9, on Shinto developments, deals with early mythology, early institutions and rituals, medieval Shinto, Shinto revival, and the disestablishment of Shinto. Chapter 10 highlights two developments, Tenrikyo and Sokka Gakkai, in the so-called "new religions" phenomenon in twentieth-century Japan.

Throughout the anthology, a concerted effort has been made to present more than the usual short excerpts. That is, as much as is possible, larger excerpts have been offered in the hope that the students will get a better feel for significant developments within traditions. We are well aware that this means something is lost with respect to offering students an idea of the over-all breadth of a tradition.

As much as is possible, doctrinal elements have been combined with story in the hope that the traditions will come alive for the students, in the sense that the teachings will be seen more as live options rather than museum pieces that are no longer relevant for today's world. It is hoped that this collection will aid students to enter, at least partially, into the traditions presented.

In putting the first edition together, it had been our hope that this anthology would prove useful beyond the context of our own courses. This hope, it seems, was a realistic one. Thus, this second edition. A number of changes have been made, however. The first edition lacked a section on Ch'an/Zen developments. These have been added to the second edition. In the case of Daoism, the first edition included only Laozi and Zhuangzi. In this edition we have added excerpts from the writings of Ge Hong, representing the central concerns of so-called religious Daoism. Also in this second edition we have expanded the introductions that appeared in the first edition and have added new introductions in order to provide a better sense of the context for the excerpts and a better sense of historical developments.

THE SACRED LANGUAGES OF THE EAST, Sanskrit, Pali, Tibetan, Chinese, and Japanese—to name only those relevant to this collection of texts—are written in scripts that are different from the Roman alphabet. In order to render words of these languages using Western equipment such as word processors, a system was created that permitted an accurate transformation of the indigenous characters into Roman characters. This process is called transliteration, or romanization. As most Asian scripts use more than twenty-four letters, additional signs—diacritical marks—are added to a normal Roman letter to indicate that in this combination the letter carries another connotation. This method is necessary when working with the original languages.

A novice student of Eastern religions, however, will be confused by the complexity of this system. Therefore a simplified form of transliteration was adopted in this book. There are no diacritical marks. Instead, the consonants are given in a form that allows an English-speaking person to come to an approximately correct pronunciation without difficulty. The vowels should be pronounced like the vowels in Italian: a like the u in *but*, o like o in *nor*, u like oo in *roof*, i like i in *give*, e like e in *better*, ai like y in *my*, au like ow in *shower*. The reader will note that in the case of the section on Chinese traditions two systems of transliteration are used, the Pinyin and the Wade-Giles. In most instances the Pinyin spelling is given first, followed by the Wade-Giles. The older system, the Wade-Giles, is, however, left intact in the excerpts.

Hinduism

ONE

Hinduism

Scripture in Hinduism

HINDUISM IS FOUNDED UPON A SCRIPTURE that is judged to be essential to the realization of release, or *moksa*, the Hindu parallel to salvation. The Hindu scriptures are held to be without beginning—just as in the Hindu view the whole of the universe has existed without beginning as a series of cycles of creation going backward into time infinitely. Although the Hindu scripture is spoken anew at the beginning of each cycle of creation, what is spoken is identical with the scripture that had been spoken in all previous cycles, without beginning. The very idea of an absolute point of beginning for either creation or the scripture is simply not present in Hindu thought. A close parallel to this Hindu notion of the eternal presence of scripture is perhaps found in the Christian idea of *logos*, especially as expressed in the New Testament Gospel of John 1:1, "In the beginning was the Word, and the Word was with God, and the Word was God."

According to many Hindus, their basic scripture, the Veda, is authorless. The idea of an authorless scripture is logically consistent with the claim of its eternality, in that the identification of an author would indicate a historical point of beginning. Another consideration is that authors are human and thus capable of error. Being authorless, it is argued, therefore safeguards Hindu scripture from the possibility of human error. Some Hindu schools explicitly rule out the suggestion of God as the author of scripture, since God is seen by some scholars as being a human personification and thus also open to error. While most Hindus are satisfied to think of their scripture as in some sense identified with or authored by God, one school, the Purva-Mimamsa, goes to the extreme of denying the existence of God as author to ensure that the errorless nature of scripture cannot be called into question. If even God is open to question as author, certainly humans cannot be seen as composers of scripture. The *rsis*, or seers, identified as speakers of particular Vedas, are understood to be mere channels through which the transcendent word passes to make itself available to humans at the start of each creation cycle. Thus the same *rsis* are said to speak the Vedas in each cycle of creation, and the very language in which the Vedas are spoken—Sanskrit—is itself held to be divine.

For the Hindu, the spoken or chanted scripture of the tradition is the Divine Word (*Daivi Vak*) descending and disclosing itself to the sensitive soul. The "sensitive soul" was the seer, or *rsi*, who had purged himself of ignorance, rendering his consciousness transparent to the Divine Word. The *rsi* was not the author of the Vedic hymn but, rather, the seer of an eternal, authorless truth. The *rsi's* initial vision is of the Veda as one, which is then broken down and spoken as the words and sentences of scripture. In this Vedic idea of revelation there is no suggestion of the miraculous, or supernatural. The *rsi*, by the progressive purifying of consciousness through the practices of yoga, had simply removed the mental obstructions to the revelation of the Divine Word. While the Divine Word is inherently present within the consciousness of all, it is the *rsis* who first reveal it and in so doing make it available to help others achieve the same experience. The spoken Vedic words of the *rsis* act powerfully upon us to purify our consciousness and give to us that same full spiritual vision of the unitary Divine Word that the *rsi* first saw. This is *moksa*, the enlightenment experience, the purpose for which Hindu scriptures exist. Once the direct experience of the Divine Word is realized, the manifested forms (i.e., the words and sentences of the Veda) are no longer needed. The Vedic words and sentences function only as a "ladder" to raise one to the direct, intuitive experience of the complete Divine Word. Once the full enlightenment or *moksa* experience is achieved, the "ladder of scripture" is no longer needed; it is, however, useful for teaching others who have not yet reached release. This Hindu idea that scripture can and indeed must be eventually transcended is heresy to other religions such as Judaism, Christianity, and Islam. For them, human limitations are such that even the most saintly person would get only part way up the ladder of scripture (Torah, Bible or Qur'an) and could never completely transcend scripture in the sense that most Hindus accept.

In addition to offering release, or *moksa*, Hindu scriptures, together with the Hindu legal texts, the Dharma Shastras, offer ethical guidance for the living of our worldly lives. After examining the various categories of Hindu scriptures, our consideration of Hinduism will conclude with an exposition of Hindu ethics written by the contemporary scholar Vasudha Narayanan, who offers a woman's reading of the key ethical, or *dharma* (legal), texts relating to duties required of all humans, food, and cooking regulations, duties of the various caste groups, moral paradigms in the Hindu epics, and finally legal obligations relating to abortion and the new reproductive technologies. With her reflections, Vasudha Narayanan brings to our readings on Hinduism a contemporary ethics engagement from the perspective of a leading woman scholar in the religion.

With this basic introduction to the ways most Hindus approach their scripture, let us sample some of the basic Hindu texts. The dates given are from the perspective of modern critical scholarship. From the traditional Hindu perspective, such dating makes little sense since, as outlined above, the Divine Word the scripture manifests is held to be eternal and authorless. The Veda is divided into three layers. The Samhitas, or original hymns, spoken by the *rsis* (dated from 1500 to 900 BCE), the Brahmanas, or priestly commentaries, on the original hymns (dated from 1000 to 800 BCE), and the Upanishads, or philosophical commentaries, composed by teachers in forest communities to bring out the philosophical meanings of the original hymns (dated from 800 to 500 BCE).

Samhitas

The four Veda Samhitas ("collection of hymns") are a primary source of Hindu literature. These four—the Rigveda Samhita, the Yajurveda Samhita, the Samaveda Samhita, and the Atharvaveda Samhita—have had a seminal influence on the religious, social, and cultural life of the Indian subcontinent. In the view of some modern scholarship, the Samhitas are thought to reflect the religious perception of the Aryans, who entered northwest India as conquerors around 1500 BCE, or earlier. Other scholars hold that the Aryans were native to India, first living in the Himalayan region and later migrating southward. Hindus identify the Samhitas as *sruti* ("learning which is heard"), and believe that the knowledge contained in them was directly revealed to ancient seers, or *rsis*, who in turn began the earthly transmission of this knowledge. Three other, mostly later, bodies of literature can also be regarded as *sruti*: the Brahmanas, the Aranyakas, and the Upanishads. Together the four collections comprise what is often referred to as "Vedic literature."[1]

Rigveda

The Rigveda is the oldest of the Samhitas. Thought to have been composed between 1500 and 900 BCE, it is largely an anthology of poems addressed to various gods. While several forms of literature later drew their inspiration from the Rigveda, as well as from the other Samhitas, the importance of the text itself eventually came to rest principally in its ritual function, in which its lines were recited by priests as part of the liturgy.[2] While some modern scholars see these hymns as essentially polytheistic—in praise of many different gods—traditional Hindu scholars see the hymns to different deities as manifestations of the many different aspects, or faces, of the one Divine Reality, *Brahman*.

▼ CREATION

1   There was neither non-existence nor existence then; there was neither the realm of space nor the sky which is beyond. What stirred? Where? In whose protection? Was there water, bottomlessly deep?

2   There was neither death nor immortality then. There was no distinguishing sign of night nor of day. That one breathed, windless, by its own impulse. Other than that there was nothing beyond.

3   Darkness was hidden by darkness in the beginning; with no distinguishing sign, all this was water. The life force that was covered with emptiness, that one arose through the power of heat.

4   Desire came upon that one in the beginning; that as the first seed of mind. Poets seeking in their heart with wisdom found the bond of existence in non-existence.

5   Their cord was extended across. Was there below? Was there above? There were seed-placers; there were powers. There was impulse beneath; there was giving forth above.

6   Who really knows? Who will here proclaim it? Whence was it produced? Whence is this creation? The gods came afterwards, with the creation of this universe. Who then knows whence it has arisen?

7   Whence this creation has arisen—perhaps it formed itself, or perhaps it did not—the one who looks down on it, in the highest heaven, only he knows— or perhaps he does not know.

(*Creation Hymn* 10.129)[3]

1   The Man has a thousand heads, a thousand eyes, a thousand feet. He pervaded the earth on all sides and extended beyond it as far as ten fingers.

2   It is the Man who is all this, whatever has been and whatever is to be. He is the ruler of immortality, when he grows beyond everything through food.

3   Such is his greatness, and the Man is yet more than this. All creatures are a quarter of him; three quarters are what is immortal in heaven.

4 With three quarters the Man rose upwards, and one quarter of him still remains here. From this he spread out in all directions, into that which eats and that which does not eat.

5 From him Viraj was born, and from Viraj came the Man. When he was born, he ranged beyond the earth behind and before.

6 When the gods spread the sacrifice with the Man as the offering, spring was the clarified butter, summer the fuel, autumn the oblation.

7 They anointed the Man, the sacrifice born at the beginning, upon the sacred grass. With him the gods, Sadhyas, and sages sacrificed.

8 From that sacrifice in which everything was offered, the melted fat was collected, and he made it into those beasts who live in the air, in the forest, and in villages.

9 From that sacrifice in which everything was offered, the verses and chants were born, the metres were born from it, and from it the formulas were born.

10 Horses were born from it, and those other animals that have two rows of teeth; cows were born from it, and from it goats and sheep were born.

11 When they divided the Man, into how many parts did they apportion him? What do they call his mouth, his two arms and thighs and feet?

12 His mouth became the brahmin; his arms were made into the warrior, his thighs the people, and from his feet the servants were born.

13 The moon was born from his mind; from his eye the sun was born. Indra and Agni came from his mouth, and from his vital breath the wind was born.

14 From his navel the middle realm of space arose; from his head the sky evolved. From his two feet came the earth, and the quarters of the sky from his ear. Thus they set the worlds in order.

15 There were seven enclosing-sticks for him, and thrice seven fuel-sticks, when the gods, spreading the sacrifice, bound the Man as the sacrificial beast.

16 With the sacrifice the gods sacrificed to the sacrifice. These were the first ritual laws. These very powers reached the dome of the sky where dwell the Sadhyas, the ancient gods.

(Hymn of Man 10.90) [4]

1 The sage, our father, who took his place as priest of the oblation and offered all these worlds as oblation, seeking riches through prayer, he entered those who were to come later, concealing those who went before.

2 What was the base, what sort of raw matter was there, and precisely how was it done, when the All-Maker, casting his eye on all, created the earth and revealed the sky in its glory?

3 With eyes on all sides and mouths on all sides, with arms on all sides and feet on all sides, the one God created the sky and the earth, fanning them with his arms.

4   What was the wood and what was the tree from which they carved the sky and the earth? You deep thinkers, ask yourselves in your own hearts, what base did he stand on when he set up the worlds?

5   Those forms of yours that are highest, those that are lowest, and those that are in the middle, O All-Maker, help your friends to recognize them in the oblation. You who follow your own laws, sacrifice your body yourself, making it grow great.

6   All-Maker, grown great through the oblation, sacrifice the earth and sky yourself. Let other men go astray all around; let us here have a rich and generous patron.

7   The All-Maker, the lord of sacred speech, swift as thought—we will call him today to help us in the contest. Let him who is the maker of good things and is gentle to everyone rejoice in all our invocations and help us.

1   The Father of the eye, who is wise in his heart, created as butter these two worlds that bent low. As soon as their ends had been made fast in the east, at that moment sky and earth moved far apart.

2   The All-Maker is vast in mind and vast in strength. He is the one who forms, who sets in order, and who is the highest image. Their prayers together with the drink they have offered give them joy there where, they say, the one dwells beyond the seven sages.

3   Our Father, who created and set in order and knows all forms, all words, who all alone gave names to the gods, he is the one to whom all other creatures come to ask questions.

4   To him the ancient sages together sacrificed riches, like the throngs of singers who together made these things that have been created, when the realm of light was still immersed in the realm without light.

5   That which is beyond the sky and beyond this earth, beyond the gods and the Asuras—what was that first embryo that the waters received, where all the gods together saw it?

6   He was the one whom the waters received as the first embryo, when all the gods came together. On the navel of the unborn was set the one on whom all creatures rest.

7   You cannot find him who created these creatures; another has come between you. Those who recite the hymns are glutted with the pleasures of life; they wander about wrapped up in mist and stammering nonsense.

(*The All-Maker* 10.81, 82) [5] ▲

▼ DEATH

1 The one who has passed beyond along the great, steep straits, spying out the path for many, the son of Vivasvan, the gatherer of men, King Yama—honour him with the oblation.

2 Yama was the first to find the way for us, this pasture that shall not be taken away. Where our ancient fathers passed beyond, there everyone who is born follows, each on his own path.

3 Matali made strong by the Kavyas, and Yama by the Angirases, and Brihaspati by the Rikvans—both those whom the gods made strong and those who strengthen the gods: some rejoice in the sacrificial call, others in the sacrificial drink.

4 Sit upon this strewn grass, O Yama, together with the Angirases, the fathers. Let the verses chanted by the poets carry you here. O King, rejoice in this oblation.

5 Come, Yama, with the Angirases worthy of sacrifice: rejoice here with the Vairupas, sitting on the sacred grass at this sacrifice. I will invoke Vivasvan, who is your father.

6 Our fathers, the Angirases, and the Navagvas, Atharvans, and Brihgus, all worthy of soma—let us remain in favour with them, as they are worthy of sacrifice, and let them be helpful and kind.

7 [To the dead man] Go forth, go forth on those ancient paths on which our ancient fathers passed beyond. There you shall see the two kings, Yama and Varuna, rejoicing in the sacrificial drink.

8 Unite with the fathers, with Yama, with the rewards of your sacrifices and good deeds, in the highest heaven. Leaving behind all imperfections, go back home again; merge with a glorious body.

9 [To demons] Go away, get away, crawl away from here. The fathers have prepared this place for him. Yama gives him a resting place adorned by days, and waters, and nights.

10 [To the dead man] Run on the right path, past the two brindled, four-eyed dogs, the sons of Sarama, and then approach the fathers, who are easy to reach and who rejoice at the same feast as Yama.

11 Yama, give him over to your two guardian dogs, the four-eyed keepers of the path, who watch over men. O King, grant him happiness and health.

12 The two dark messengers of Yama with flaring nostrils wander among men, thirsting for the breath of life. Let them give back to us a life of happiness here and today, so that we may see the sun.

13 For Yama press the soma; to Yama offer the oblation; to Yama goes the well-prepared sacrifice, with Agni as its messenger.

14 Offer to Yama the oblation rich in butter, and go forth. So may he intercede for us among the gods, so that we may live out a long lifespan.

15 Offer to Yama, to the king, the oblation most rich in honey. We bow down before the sages born in the ancient times, the ancient path-makers.

16 All through the three soma days he flies to the six broad spaces and the one great one. *Trishtubh, gayatri*, the metres—all these are placed in Yama.

(Yama and the Fathers 10.14)[6]

1   Do not burn him entirely, Agni, or engulf him in your flames. Do not consume his skin or his flesh. When you have cooked him perfectly, O knower of creatures, only then send him forth to the fathers.

2   When you cook him perfectly, O knower of creatures, then give him over to the fathers. When he goes on the path that leads away the breath of life, then he will be led by the will of the gods.

3   [To the dead man] May your eye go to the sun, your life's breath to the wind. Go to the sky or to earth, as is your nature; or go to the waters, if that is your fate. Take root in the plants with your limbs.

4   [To Agni] The goat is your share; burn him with your heat. Let your brilliant light and flame burn him. With your gentle forms, O knower of creatures, carry this man to the world of those who have done good deeds.

5   Set him free again to go to the fathers, Agni, when he has been offered as an oblation in you and wanders with the sacrificial drink. Let him reach his own descendants, dressing himself in a life-span. O knower of creatures, let him join with a body.

6   [To the dead man] Whatever the black bird has pecked out of you, or the ant, the snake, or even a beast of prey, may Agni who eats all things make it whole, and soma who has entered the brahmins.

7   Gird yourself with the limbs of the cow as an armour against Agni, and cover yourself with fat and suet, so that he will not embrace you with his impetuous heat in his passionate desire to burn you up.

8   [To Agni] O Agni, do not overturn this cup that is dear to the gods and to those who love soma, fit for the gods to drink from, a cup in which the immortal gods carouse.

9   I send the flesh-eating fire away. Let him go to those whose king is Yama. Carrying away all impurities. But let that other, the knower of creatures, come here and carry the oblation to the gods, since he knows the way in advance.

10 The flesh-eating fire has entered your house, though he sees there the other, the knower of creatures; I take that god away to the sacrifice of the fathers. Let him carry the heated drink to the farthest dwelling-place.

11 Agni who carries away the corpse, who gives sacrifice to the fathers who are strengthened by truth—let him proclaim the oblation to the gods and to the fathers.

12 [To the new fire] Joyously would we put you in place, joyously would we kindle you. Joyously carry the joyous fathers here to eat the oblation.

13 Now, Agni, quench and revive the very one you have burnt up. Let kiyamba, pakadurva, and vyalkasha plants grow in this place.

14 O cool one, bringer of coolness; O fresh one, bringer of freshness; unite with the female frog. Delight and inspire this Agni.

(The Funeral Fire 10.16)[7]

1 If your spirit has gone to Yama the son of Vivasvan far away, we turn it back to you here to dwell and to live.

2 If your spirit has gone to the sky or to the earth far away, we turn it back to you here to dwell and to live.

3 If your spirit has gone to the four-cornered earth far away, we turn it back to you here to dwell and to live.

4 If your spirit has gone to the four quarters of the sky far away, we turn it back to you here to dwell and to live.

5 If your spirit has gone to the billowy ocean far away, we turn it back to you here to dwell and to live.

6 If your spirit has gone to the flowing streams of light far away, we turn it back to you here to dwell and to live.

7 If your spirit has gone to the waters, or to the plants, far away, we turn it back to you here to dwell and to live.

8 If your spirit has gone to the sun, or to the dawns far away, we turn it back to you here to dwell and to live.

9 If your spirit has gone to the high mountains far away, we turn it back to you here to dwell and to live.

10 If your spirit has gone to this whole moving universe far away, we turn it back to you to dwell and to live.

11 If your spirit has gone to distances beyond the beyond, far away, we turn it back to you to dwell and to live.

12 If your spirit has gone to what has been and what is to be, far away, we turn it back to you to dwell and to live.

(A Spell to Turn Back the Departing Spirit 10.58)[8] ▲

▼ **SACRIFICE**

1 Wake up with one mind, my friends, and kindle the fire, you many who share the same nest. I call Dadhikra and Agni and the goddess Dawn, all joined with Indra, to help you.

2 Make your thoughts harmonious; stretch them on the loom; make a ship whose oars will carry us across; make the weapons ready and set them in place; drive the sacrifice forward, my friends.

3 Harness the plough and stretch the yoke on it; sow the seed in the prepared womb. And if the hearing of our song is weighty enough, then the ripe crop will come nearer to the scythes.

4 The inspired poets who know how to harness the plough and stretch the yokes on either side to win favour among the gods.

5 Make the buckets ready and fasten the straps well. We want to draw water from the fountain that is easy to draw water from, flowing freely, inexhaustible.

6 I draw water from the fountain whose buckets are in place, with good straps, easy to draw water from, freely flowing and inexhaustible.

7 Keep the horses happy and you will win the stake. Make your chariot into the vehicle of good fortune. Drink at the fountain that has soma-vats for buckets, a pressing-stone for its wheel, a consecrated goblet for its casing; this is the fountain where men drink.

8 Make an enclosure, for this is a drink for men. Stitch the breast-plates thick and broad. Make iron forts that cannot be breached; make your goblet strong so that nothing will flow out.

9 I turn toward our case here your sacrificial attention, gods, your divine thought that is disposed toward sacrifice and worthy of sacrifice. Let the great cow give us milk in thousands of streams of milk, as if she were walking in a meadow.

10 Pour the tawny one into the lap of wood; carve it with knives made of stone. Embrace it all around with ten girths; yoke the draught animal to the two shafts.

11 The draught animal is pressed tight between the two shafts, like a man in bed with two women. Stand the tree up in the wood; sink the well deep without digging.

12 The penis, men, take the penis and move it and stick it in to win the prize. Inspire Indra, Nishtigri's son, to come here to help us, to come eagerly to drink soma.

(*The Sacrificial Priests* 10.101)[9]

1 Mitra, Varuna, Aryaman the active, Indra the ruler of the Ribhus, and the Maruts—let them not fail to heed us when we proclaim in the assembly the heroic deeds of the racehorse who was born of the gods.

2 When they lead the firmly grasped offering in front of the horse that is covered with cloths and heirlooms, the dappled goat goes bleating straight to the dear dwelling of Indra and Pushan.

3 This goat for all the gods is led forward with the racehorse as the share for Pushan. When they lead forth the welcome offering with the charger, Tvashtri urges him on to great fame.

4   When, as the ritual law ordains, the men circle three times, leading the horse that is to be the oblation on the path to the gods, the goat who is the share for Pushan goes first, announcing the sacrifice to the gods.

5   The invoker, the officiating priest, the atoner, the fire-kindler, the holder of the pressing-stones, the reciter, the priest who prays—fill your bellies with the well-prepared, well-sacrificed sacrifice.

6   The hewers of the sacrificial stake and those who carry it, and those who carve the knob for the horse's sacrificial stake, and those who gather together the things to cook the charger—let their approval encourage us.

7   The horse with his smooth back went forth into the fields of the gods, just when I made my prayer. The inspired sages exult in him. We have made him a welcome companion at the banquet of the gods.

8   The charger's rope and halter, the reins and bridle on his head, and even the grass that has been brought up to his mouth—let all of that stay with you even among the gods.

9   Whatever of the horse's flesh the fly has eaten, or whatever stays stuck to the stake or the axe, or to the hands or nails of the slaughterer—let all of that stay with you even among the gods.

10   Whatever food remains in his stomach, sending forth gas, or whatever smell there is from his raw flesh—let the slaughterers make that well done; let them cook the sacrificial animal until he is perfectly cooked.

11   Whatever runs off your body when it has been placed on the spit and roasted by the fire, let it not lie there in the earth or on the grass, but let it be given to the gods who long for it.

12   Those who see that the racehorse is cooked, who say, "It smells good! Take it away!" and who wait for the doling out of the flesh of the charger—let their approval encourage us.

13   The testing fork for the cauldron that cooks the flesh, the pots for pouring the broth, the cover of the bowls to keep it warm, the hooks, the dishes—all these attend the horse.

14   The place where he walks, where he rests, where he rolls, and the fetters on the horse's feet, and what he has drunk and the fodder he has eaten—let all of that stay with you even among the gods.

15   Let not the fire that reeks of smoke darken you, nor the red-hot cauldron split into pieces. The gods receive the horse who has been sacrificed, worshipped, consecrated, and sanctified with the cry of "Vashat!"

16   The cloth that they spread beneath the horse, the upper covering, the golden trappings on him, the halter and the fetters on his feet—let these things that are his own bind the horse among the gods.

17   If someone riding you has struck you too hard with heel or whip when you shied, I make all these things well again for you with prayer, as they do with the oblation's ladle in sacrifices.

18 The axe cuts through the thirty-four ribs of the racehorse who is the companion of the gods. Keep the limbs undamaged and place them in the proper pattern. Cut them apart, calling out piece by piece.

19 One is the slaughterer of the horse of Tvashtri; two restrain him. This is the rule. As many of your limbs as I set out, according to the rules, so many balls I offer into the fire.

20 Let not your dear soul burn you as you go away. Let not the axe do lasting harm to your body. Let no greedy, clumsy slaughterer hack in the wrong place and damage your limbs with his knife.

21 You do not really die through this, nor are you harmed. You go to the gods on paths pleasant to go on. The two bay stallions, the two roan mares are now your chariot mates. The racehorse has been set in the donkey's yoke.

22 Let this racehorse bring us good cattle and good horses, male children and all-nourishing wealth. Let Aditi make us free from sin. Let the horse with our offering achieve sovereign power for us.

(The Sacrifice of the Horse 1.162)[10] ▲

▼ **DEVAS**

1 Pray to Agni, the household priest who is the god of the sacrifice, the one who chants and invokes and brings most treasure.

2 Agni earned the prayers of the ancient sages, and of those of the present, too; he will bring the gods here.

3 Through Agni one may win wealth, and growth from day to day, glorious and most abounding in heroic sons.

4 Agni, the sacrificial ritual that you encompass on all sides—only that one goes to the gods.

5 Agni, the priest with the sharp sight of a poet, the true and most brilliant, the god will come with the gods.

6 Whatever good you wish to do for the one who worships you, Agni, through you, O Angiras, that comes true.

7 To you, Agni, who shine upon darkness, we come day after day, bringing our thoughts and homage.

8 To you, the King over sacrifices, the shining guardian of the order, growing in your own house.

9 Be easy for us to reach, like a father to his son. Abide with us, Agni, for our happiness.

(I Pray to Agni 1.1)[11] ▲

▼

1 Let me now sing the heroic deeds of Indra, the first that the thunderbolt-wielder performed. He killed the dragon and pierced an opening for the waters; he split open the bellies of mountains.

2 He killed the dragon who lay upon the mountain; Tvashtri fashioned the roaring thunderbolt for him. Like lowing cows, the flowing waters rushed straight down to the sea.

3 Wildly excited like a bull, he took the soma for himself and drank the extract from the three bowls in the three day Soma ceremony. Indra the generous seized his thunderbolt to hurl it as a weapon; he killed the first-born of dragons.

4 Indra, when you killed the first-born of dragons and overcame by your own magic the magic of the magicians, at that very moment you brought forth the sun, the sky, and dawn. Since then you have found no enemy to conquer you.

5 With his great weapon, the thunderbolt, Indra killed the shoulderless Vritra, his greatest enemy. Like the trunk of a tree whose branches have been lopped off by an axe, the dragon lies flat upon the ground.

6 For, muddled by drunkenness like one who is no soldier, Vritra challenged the great hero who had overcome the mighty and who drank soma to the dregs. Unable to withstand the onslaught of his weapons, he found Indra an enemy to conquer him and was shattered, his nose crushed.

7 Without feet or hands he fought against Indra, who struck him on the nape of the neck with his thunderbolt. The steer who wished to become the equal of the bull bursting with seed, Vritra lay broken in many places.

8 Over him as he lay there like a broken reed the swelling waters flowed for man. Those waters that Vritra had enclosed with his power—the dragon now lay at their feet.

9 The vital energy of Vritra's mother ebbed away, for Indra had hurled his deadly weapon at her. Above was the mother, below was the son; Danu lay down like a cow with her calf.

10 In the midst of the channels of the waters which never stood still or rested, the body was hidden. The waters flow over Vritra's secret place; he who found Indra an enemy to conquer him sank into long darkness.

11 The waters who had the Dasa for their husband, the dragon for their protector, were imprisoned like the cows imprisoned by the Panis. When he killed Vritra he split open the outlet of the waters that had been closed.

12 Indra, you became a hair of a horse's tail when Vritra struck you on the corner of the mouth. You, the one god, the brave one, you won the cows; you won the soma; you released the seven streams so that they could flow.

13 No use was the lightning and thunder, fog and hail that he had scattered about, when the dragon and Indra fought. Indra the generous remained victorious for all time to come.

14 What avenger of the dragon did you see, Indra, that fear entered your heart when you had killed him? Then you crossed the ninety-nine streams like the frightened eagle crossing the realms of earth and air.

15   Indra, who wields the thunderbolt in his hand, is the king of that which moves and that which rests, of the tame and of the horned. He rules the people as their king, encircling all this as a rim encircles spokes.

(The Killing of Vritra 1.32)[12] ▲

▼

1   The generations have become wise by the power of him who has propped apart the two world-halves even though they are so vast. He has pushed away the dome of the sky to make it high and wide; he has set the sun on its double journey and spread out the earth.

2   And I ask my own heart, "When shall I be close to Varuna? Will he enjoy my offering and not be provoked to anger? When shall I see his mercy and rejoice?"

3   I ask myself what that transgression was, Varuna, for I wish to understand. I turn to the wise to ask them. The poets have told me the very same thing: "Varuna has been provoked to anger against you."

4   O Varuna, what was the terrible crime for which you wish to destroy your friend who praises you? Proclaim it to me so that I may hasten to prostrate myself before you and be free from sin, for you are hard to deceive and are ruled by yourself alone.

5   Free us from the harmful deeds of our fathers, and from those that we have committed with our own bodies. O king, free Vasishtha like a thief who has stolen cattle, like a calf set free from a rope.

6   The mischief was not done by our own free will, Varuna; wine, anger, dice, or carelessness led me astray. The older shares in the mistake of the younger. Even sleep does not avert evil.

7   As a slave serves a generous master, so would I serve the furious god and be free from sin. The noble god gave understanding to those who did not understand; being yet wiser, he speeds the clever man to wealth.

8   O Varuna, you who are ruled by yourself alone, let this praise lodge in your very heart. Let it go well for us always with your blessings.

(Varuna Provoked to Anger 7.86)[13] ▲

Atharvaveda

The Atharvaveda is the most recently compiled Samhita, dating back to approximately 900 BCE Its general tone differs from that of the Rigveda because it frequently addresses the daily needs of ordinary people. This collection of hymns contains many magical formulations and prayers used for cures, as love charms, and for long life.[14]

The following selection describes the cosmological attributes of the brahmachari, who, in the mundane world, was a person dedicated to Brahman and to the study of the Samhitas. It can be noted that in later times, brahmacharya came to denote the first stage of a holy life, characterized by the study of Vedic texts and by the practice of celibacy.[15]

▼   The brahmachari travels animating the two hemispheres; the gods become like-minded in him. He sustains earth and heaven; he fills his teacher with fervor.

The fathers, the god-folk and all the gods collectively follow the brahmachari; the six thousand three hundred and thirty-three Gandharvas went after him. He fills all the gods with fervor.

When the teacher accepts the brahmachari as a disciple, he treats him as an embryo within his own body. He carries him for three nights in his belly; when he is born, the gods assemble to see him....

Born prior to Brahman, clothing himself in heat, the brahmachari arose with his fervor. From him were born Brahmahood, the highest Brahman, and all the gods together with immortality.

The brahmachari goes forth, kindled by sacred fire-sticks, clothing himself with black-antelope skin, consecrated, long-bearded. Within one single day does he go from the eastern to the northern ocean; having gathered together the worlds, he fashions them repeatedly.

The brahmachari, begetting Brahman, the waters, the world, Prajapati [lord of creatures], the most exalted one, creative force, having become an embryo in the womb of immortality, indeed, having become Indra, has shattered the demons.

The preceptor fashioned both these hemispheres, the wide and the deep, namely, earth and heaven. These two the brahmachari protects with his fervor; in him the gods become like-minded....

Through brahmacharya, through fervor, a king protects his kingdom. A teacher through brahmacharya seeks a brahmachari for his student.

Through brahmacharya a maiden finds a young husband. Through bramacharya a steer or horse strives to obtain food.

Through brahmacharya, through fervor, the gods dispelled death. Through brahmacharya Indra brought heaven to the gods.
Plants, past and future, trees, the year and the seasons were all born from the brahmachari.

Animals of the earth and those of heaven, wild and domestic, wingless and winged, were all born from the brahmachari....

The brahmachari fashioned these things on the back of the waters. He stood in the sea performing austerities. When he has performed ritual ablution, he shines extensively over the earth, brown and ruddy.

(*Brahmachari* 11.5.1–8, 17–26)[16] ▲

Brahmanas—The Shatapatha Brahmana

Sacrifice, in the early Indian traditions, was thought to have the vital function of generating the power needed to maintain universal order.[17] Through their elaborate explanation and systematization of the four Veda Samhitas, the Brahmanas became essential manuals for performing the complex rituals and sacrifices of this period. Composed between 900 and 700 BCE, these texts provide valuable information on the activities of the priesthood and are a rich source of myth and legend.[18]

The concern of the Brahmanas both to detail a ritual's proper execution and to establish its scriptural basis is evident in the following passage from the Shatapatha Brahmana.

▼ FOURTH BRAHMANA

The Agnihotra or Morning and Evening Libations; and the Agny-Upasthana, or Homage to the Fires

1   Prajapati alone, indeed, existed here in the beginning. He considered, "How may I be reproduced?" He toiled and performed acts of penance. He generated Agni from his mouth; and because he generated him from his mouth, therefore Agni is a consumer of food: and, verily, he who thus knows Agni to be a consumer of food, becomes himself a consumer of food.

2   He thus generated him first of the gods; and therefore [he is called] Agni, for agni [they say] is the same as agri. He, being generated, went forth as the first; for of him who goes first, they say that he goes at the head. Such, then, is the origin and nature of that Agni.

3   Prajapati then considered, "In that Agni I have generated a food-eater for myself; but, indeed, there is no other food here but myself, whom, surely, he would not eat." At that time this earth had indeed been rendered quite bald; there were neither plants nor trees. This, then, weighed on his mind.

4   Thereupon Agni turned towards him with open mouth; and he [Prajapati] being terrified, his own greatness departed from him. Now his own greatness is his speech: that speech of his departed from him. He desired an offering in his own self, and rubbed [his hands]; and because he rubbed [his hands], therefore both this and this [palm] are hairless. He then obtained either a butter-offering or a milk-offering; but, indeed they are both milk.

5   This [offering], however, did not satisfy him, because it had hairs mixed with it. He poured it away [into the fire], saying, "Drink, while burning!" From it plants sprang: hence their name "plants." He rubbed [his hands] a second time, and thereby obtained another offering, either a butter-offering or a milk-offering; but, indeed, they are both milk.

6   This [offering] then satisfied him. He hesitated: "Shall I offer it up? shall I not offer it up?" he thought. His own greatness said to him, "Offer it up!" Prajapati was aware that it was his own [sva] greatness that had spoken [aha] to him; and offered it up with "svaha!" This is why offerings are made with svaha! Thereupon that burning one [viz., the sun] rose; and then that blowing one [viz., the wind] sprang up; whereupon, indeed, Agni turned away.

7   And Prajapati, having performed offering, reproduced himself, and saved himself from Agni, death, as he was about to devour him. And, verily, whosoever, knowing this, offers the agnihotra reproduces himself by offspring even as Prajapati reproduced himself; and saves himself from Agni, death, when he is about to devour him.

8   And when he dies, and when they place him on the fire, then he is born [again] out of the fire, and the fire only consumes his body. Even as he is born from his father and mother, so is he born from the fire. But he who offers not the agnihotra, verily, he does not come into life at all: therefore the agnihotra should by all means be offered.

9   And as to that same birth from out of doubt, when Prajapati doubted, he, while doubting, remained steadfast on the better [side], insomuch that he reproduced himself and saved himself from Agni, death, when he was about to devour him: so he also who knows that birth from out of doubt, when he doubts about anything, still remains on the better [side].

10 Having offered, he rubbed [his hands]. Thence a vikankata tree sprung forth; and therefore that tree is suitable for the sacrifice, and proper for sacrificial vessels. Thereupon those [three] heroes among the gods were born, viz. Agni, that blower [Vayu], and Surya: and, verily, whosoever thus knows those heroes among the gods, to him a hero is born.

11 They then said, "We come after our father Prajapati: let us then create what shall come after us!" Having enclosed [a piece of ground], they sang praises with the gayatri stanza without the "hin": and that [with] which they enclosed was the ocean; and this earth was the praising-ground.

12 When they had sung praises, they went out towards the east, saying, "We [will] go back thither!" The gods came upon a cow which had sprung into existence. Looking up at them, she uttered the sound "hin." The gods perceived that this was the hin of the saman [melodious sacrificial chant]; for heretofore [their song was] without the hin, but after that it was the [real] saman. And as this same sound hin of the saman was in the cow, therefore the latter afford the means of subsistence; and so does he afford the means of subsistence whosoever thus knows that hin of the saman in the cow.

13 They said, "Auspicious, indeed, is what we have produced here, who have produced the cow: for truly, she is the sacrifice, and without her no sacrifice is performed; she is also the food, for the cow, indeed, is all food."

14 This [word "go"], then, is a name of those [cows], and so it is of the sacrifice: let him, therefore, repeat it, [as it were] saying, "Good, excellent!" and, verily, whosoever, knowing this, repeats it, [as it were] saying, "Good, excellent!" with him those [cows] multiply, and the sacrifice will incline to him.

15 Now, Agni coveted her: "May I pair with her?" he thought. He united with her, and his seed became that milk of hers: hence, while the cow is raw that milk in her is cooked [warm]; for it is Agni's seed; and therefore also, whether it be in a black or in a red [cow], it is ever white, and shining like fire, it being Agni's seed. Hence it is warm when first milked; for it is Agni's seed.

16 They [the men] said, "Come, let us offer this up!" "To whom of us shall they first offer this?" [said those gods]. "To me!" said Agni. "To me!" said that blower [Vayu]. "To me!" said Surya. They did not come to an agreement; and not being agreed, they said, "Let us go to our father Prajapati; and to whichever of us he says it shall be offered first, to him they shall first offer this." They went to their father Prajapati, and said, "To whom of us shall they offer this first?"

17 He replied, "To Agni: Agni will forthwith cause his own seed to reproduce, and so you will be reproduced." "Then to thee," he said to Surya; "and what of the offered [milk] he then is still possessed of, that shall belong to that blower [Vayu]!" And, accordingly, they in the same way offer this [milk] to them till this day: in the evening to Agni, and in the morning to Surya; and what of the offered [milk] he then is still possessed of, that, indeed, belongs to that blower.

18 By offering, those gods were produced in the way in which they were produced, by it they gained that victory which they did gain: Agni conquered this world, Vayu the air, Surya the sky. And whosoever, knowing this, offers the *agnihotra*, he, indeed, is produced in the same way in which they were then produced, he gains that same victory which they then gained; indeed, he shares the same world with them, whosoever, knowing this, offers the *agnihotra*. Therefore the *agnihotra* should certainly be performed.

(*The Satapatha Brahmana, Agnihotra* II, 1.4.1–18) [19] ▲

Upanishads

The Upanishads are the last collection of texts (circa 700 BCE) which can be classified as *sruti* in the Hindu tradition. Discussion of ritual, so central to the Brahmanas, becomes an issue of diminished importance in the Upanishads; some even go so far as to criticize the sacrificial tradition. Usually written as forest dialogues between teacher and student, they are the first Vedic texts to present liberation (*moksa*) from the world as a religious goal. [20] The Upanishads are generally speculative in tone. Each expounds upon one of the four Samhitas, rethinking the basic notions of the earlier text. Because they are usually regarded as the last development of Vedic religious thought, the Upanishads are often referred to as Vedanta, or "the end of the Veda."[21]

▼ **BRIHAD ARAN YAKA UPANISHAD**

Concerning Sacrificial Worship and Its Rewards

1   Janaka, [king] of Videha, sacrificed with a sacrifice at which many presents were distributed. Brahmans of the Kurupancalas were gathered together there. In this Janaka of Videha there arose a desire to know which of these brahmans was the most learned in scripture. He enclosed a thousand cows. To the horns of each ten padas [of gold] were bound.

2   He said to them: "Venerable brahmans, let him of you who is the best brahman drive away these cows."

Those brahmans durst not.

Then Yajnavalkya said to his pupil: "Samashravas, my dear, drive them away."

He drove them away.

The brahmans were angry. "How can he declare himself to be the best brahman among us?"

Now there was Ashvala, the hotri-priest of Janaka, [king] of Videha. He asked him: "Yajnavalkya, are you now the best brahman among us?"

He replied: "We give honor to the best brahman. But we are really desirous of having those cows."

Thereupon Ashvala, the hotri-priest, began to question him.

3   "Yajnavalkya," said he, "since everything here is overtaken by death, since everything is overcome by death, whereby is a sacrificer liberated beyond the reach of death?"

"By the hotri-priest, by fire, by speech. Verily, speech is the *hotri* of sacrifice. That which is this speech is this fire, is the *hotri*. This is release [*mukti*], this is complete release."

4   "Yajnavalkya," said he, "since everything here is overtaken by day and night, since everything is overcome by day and night, whereby is a sacrificer liberated beyond day and night?" "By the adhvatyu-priest, by the eye, by the sun. Verily, the eye is the adhvaiyu of sacrifice. That which is this eye is yonder sun, is the adhvaiyu. This is release, this is complete release."

5   "Yajnavalkya," said he, "since everything here is overtaken by the waxing and waning moon, by what means does a sacrificer obtain release from the waxing and waning moon?"

"By the udgatri-priest, by the wind, by breath. Verily, breath is the *udgatri* of the sacrifice. That which is this breath is wind, is the *udgatri*. This is release, this is complete release."

6   "Yajnavalkya," said he, "since this atmosphere does not afford a [foot] hold, as it were, by what means of ascent does a sacrificer ascend to the heavenly world?"

"By the brahman-priest, by the mind, by the moon. Verily, the mind is the brahman of the sacrifice. That which is the mind is yonder moon, is the brahman. This is release, this is complete release." Thus [concerning] liberation. Now the acquirements.

7   "Yajnavalkya," said he, "how many Rig verses will the hotri make use of today in this sacrifice?"

"Three."

"Which are those three?"

"The introductory verse, the accompanying verse, and the benediction as the third."

"What does one win by these?"

"Whatever there is here that has breath."

8   "Yajnavalkya," said he, "how many oblations will the adhvaryu pour out today in this sacrifice?"

"Three."

"Which are those three?"

"Those which when offered flame up, those which when offered flow over, those which when offered sink down."

"What does one win by these?"

"By those which when offered flame up, one wins the world of the gods, for the world of the gods gleams, as it were. By those which when offered flow over, one wins the world of the fathers, for the world of the fathers is over, as it were. By those which when offered sink down, one wins the world of men, for the world of men is below, as it were."

9   "Yajnavalkya," said he, "with how many divinities does the brahman protect the sacrifice on the right today?"

"With one."

"Which is that one?"

"The mind. Verily, endless in the mind. Endless are the all-gods. An endless world he wins thereby."

10 "Yajnavalkya," said he, "how many hymns of praise will the udgatri chant today in this sacrifice?"

"Three."

"Which are those three?"

"The introductory hymn, the accompanying hymn, and the benediction hymn as the third."

"Which are those three with reference to the self?"

"The introductory hymn is the in-breath. The accompanying hymn is the out-breath. The benediction hymn is the diffused breath."

"What does one win by these?"

"One wins the earth-world by the introductory hymn, the atmosphere-world by the accompanying hymn, the sky-world by the benediction hymn."

11   Thereupon the hotri-priest Ashvala held his peace.

(*Brihad Aranyaka* 3.1)[22]

The Theoretical Unknowability of the Immanent Brahma

1   Then Ushasta Cakrayana questioned him. "Yajnavalkya," said he, "explain to me him who is the Brahma present and not beyond our ken, him who is the Soul in all things."

"He is your soul [*atman*], which is in all things."

"Which one, O Yajnavalkya, is in all things?"

"He who breathes in with your breathing in is the soul of yours, which is in all things. He who breathes out with your breathing out is the soul of yours, which is in all things. He who breathes about with your breathing about is the soul of yours, which is in all things. He who breathes up with your breathing up is the soul of yours, which is in all things. He is your soul, which is in all things."

2   Ushasta Cakrayana said: "This has been explained to me just as one might say. 'This is a cow. This is a horse.' Explain to me him who is just the Brahma present and not beyond our ken, him who is the soul in all things."

"He is your soul, which is in all things."

"Which one, O Yajnavalkya, is in all things?"

"You could not see the seer of seeing. You could not hear the hearer of hearing. You could not think the thinker of thinking. You could not understand the understander of understanding. He is your soul, which is in all things. Aught else than Him [or, than this] is wretched."

Thereupon Ushasta Cakrayana held his peace.

(*Brihad Aranyaka* 3.4)[23]

The Practical Way of Knowing Brahma—by Renunciation

Now Kahola Kaushitakeya questioned him. "Yajnavalkya," said he, "explain to me him who is just the Brahma present and not beyond our ken, him who is the soul in all things."

"He is your soul, which is in all things."

"He who passes beyond hunger and thirst, beyond sorrow and delusion, beyond old age and death—brahmans who know such a soul overcome desire for sons, desire for wealth, desire for worlds, and live the life of mendicants. For desire for sons is desire for wealth, and desire for wealth is desire for worlds, for both these are merely desires. Therefore let a brahman become disgusted with learning and desire to live as a child. When he has become disgusted both with

the state of childhood and with learning, then he becomes an ascetic. When he
has become disgusted both with the non-ascetic state and with the ascetic state,
then he becomes a brahman."

"By what means would he become a Brahman?"

"By that means by which he does become such a one. Aught else than this
soul (*atman*) is wretched."

Thereupon Kahola Kaushitakeya held his peace.

(*Brihad Aranyaka* 3.5)[24]

The Regressus to Brahma, the Ultimate World-ground

Then Gargi Vacaknavi questioned him. "Yajnavalkya," said she, "since all this
world is woven, warp and woof, on water, on what, pray, is the water woven, warp
and woof?" "On wind, O Gargi."

"On what then, pray, is the wind woven, warp and woof?"

"On the atmosphere-worlds, O Gargi."

"On what then, pray, are the atmosphere-worlds woven, warp and woof?"

"On the worlds of the Gandharvas, O Gargi."

"On what then, pray, are the worlds of the Gandharvas woven, warp and
woof?"

"On the worlds of the sun, O Gargi."

"On what then, pray, are the worlds of the sun woven, warp and woof?"

"On the worlds of the moon, O Gargi."

"On what then, pray, are the worlds of the moon woven, warp and woof?"

"On the worlds of the stars, O Gargi."

"On what then, pray, are the worlds of the stars woven, warp and woof?"

"On the worlds of the gods, O Gargi."

"On what then, pray, are the worlds of the gods woven, warp and woof?"

"On the worlds of Indra, O Gargi."

"On what then, pray, are the worlds of Indra woven, warp and woof?"

"On the worlds of Prajapati, O Gargi."

"On what then, pray, are the worlds of Prajapati woven, warp and woof?"

"On the worlds of Brahma, O Gargi."

"On what then, pray, are the worlds of Brahma woven, warp and woof?"

Vajnavalkya said: "Gargi, do not question too much, lest your head fall off. In
truth, you are questioning too much about a divinity about which further questions cannot be asked. Gargi, do not over-question."

Thereupon Gargi Vacaknavi held her peace.

(*Brihad Aranyaka* 3.6)[25]

Wind, the String Holding the World Together: The Immortal Immanent Soul, the Inner Controller

1   Then Uddalaka Aruni questioned him. "Yajnavalkya," said he, "we were dwelling among the Madras in the house of Patancala Kapya, studying the sacrifice. He had a wife possessed by a spirit. We asked him: "Who are you?" He said: "I am Kabandha Atharvana." He said to Patancala Kapya and to us students of the sacrifice: "Do you know, O Kapya, that thread by which this world and the other world and all things are tied together?" Patancala Kapya said: "I do not know it, sir." He said to Patancala Kapya and to us students of the sacrifice: "Pray do you know, O Kapya, that inner controller who from within controls this world and the other world and all things?" Patancala Kapya said: "I do not know him, sir." He said to Patancala Kapya and to us students of the sacrifice: 'Verily, Kapya, he who knows that thread and the so-called inner controller knows Brahma, he knows the worlds, he knows the gods, he knows the Vedas, he knows created things, he knows the soul, he knows everything.' Thus he [the spirit] explained it to them. And I know it. If you, O Yajnavalkya, drive away the brahma-cows without knowing that thread and the inner controller, your head will fall off."

"Verily, I know that thread and the inner controller, O Gautama."

"Anyone might say 'I know, I know.' Do you tell what you know."

2   He [i.e., Yajnavalkya] said: "Wind, verily, O Gautama, is that thread. By wind, verily, O Gautama, as by a thread, this world and the other world and all things are tied together. Therefore, verily, O Gautama, they say of a deceased person, 'His limbs become unstrung,' for by wind, O Gautama, as by a thread, they are strung together."

"Quite so, O Yajnavalkya. Declare the inner controller."

3   "He who, dwelling in the earth, yet is other than the earth whom the earth does not know, whose body the earth is, who controls the earth from within— He is your soul, the inner controller, the immortal.

4   He who, dwelling in the waters, yet is other than the waters whom the waters do not know, whose body the waters are, who controls the waters from within—He is your soul, the inner controller, the immortal.

5   He who, dwelling in the fire, yet is other than the fire, whom the fire does not know, whose body the fire is, who controls the fire from within—He is your soul, the inner controller, the immortal.

6   He who, dwelling in the atmosphere, yet is other than the atmosphere, whom the atmosphere does not know, whose body the atmosphere is, who controls the atmosphere from within—He is your soul, the inner controller, the immortal.

7   He who, dwelling in the wind, yet is other than the wind, whom the wind does not know, whose body the wind is, who controls the wind from within— He is your soul, the inner controller, the immortal.

8   He who, dwelling in the sky, yet is other than the sky, whom the sky does not know, whose body the sky is, who controls the sky from within—He is your soul, the inner controller, the immortal.

9   He who, dwelling in the sun, yet is other than the sun, whom the sun does not know, whose body the sun is, who controls the sun from within—He is your soul, the Inner controller, the immortal.

10 He who, dwelling in the quarters of heaven, yet is other than the quarters of heaven, whom the quarters of heaven do not know, whose body the quarters of heaven are, who controls the quarters of heaven from within—He is your soul, the inner controller, the immortal.

11 He who, dwelling in the moon and stars, yet is other than the moon and stars, whom the moon and stars do not know, whose body the moon and stars are, who controls the moon and stars from within—He is your soul, the inner controller, the immortal.

12 He who, dwelling in space, yet is other than space, whom space does not know, whose body space is, who controls space from within—He is your soul, the inner controller, the immortal.

13 He who, dwelling in the darkness, yet is other than the darkness, whom the darkness does not know, whose body the darkness is, who controls the darkness from within—He is your soul, the inner controller, the immortal.

14 He who, dwelling in the light, yet is other than the light, whom the light does not know, whose body the light is, who controls the light from within—He is your soul, the inner controller, the immortal.

   —Thus far with reference to the divinities. Now with reference to material existence.

15 He who, dwelling in all things, yet is other than all things, whom all things do not know, whose body all things are, who controls all things from within—He is your soul, the inner controller, the immortal.

   —Thus far with reference to material existence. Now with reference to the self.

16 He who, dwelling in breath, yet is other than breath, whom the breath does not know, whose body the breath is, who controls the breath from within—He is your soul, the inner controller, the immortal.

17 He who, dwelling in speech, yet is other than speech, whom the speech does not know, whose body the speech is, who controls the speech from within—He is your soul, the inner controller, the immortal.

18 He who, dwelling in the eye, yet is other than the eye, whom the eye does not know, whose body the eye is, who controls the eye from within—He is your soul, the inner controller, the immortal.

19 He who, dwelling in the ear, yet is other than the ear, whom the ear does not know, whose body the ear is, who controls the ear from within—He is your soul, the inner controller, the immortal.

20 He who, dwelling in the mind, yet is other than the mind, whom the mind does not know, whose body the mind is, who controls the mind from within — He is your soul, the inner controller, the immortal.

21 He who, dwelling in the skin, yet is other than the skin, whom the skin does not know, whose body the skin is, who controls the skin from within—He is your soul, the inner controller, the immortal.

22 He who, dwelling in the understanding, yet is other than the understanding, whom the understanding does not know, whose body the understanding is, who controls the understanding from within—He is your soul, the inner controller, the immortal.

23 He who, dwelling in the semen, yet is other than the semen, whom the semen does not know, whose body the semen is, who controls the semen from within—He is your soul, the inner controller, the immortal.

He is the unseen seer, the unheard hearer, the unthought thinker, the ununderstood understander. Other than He there is no seer. Other than He there is no hearer. Other than He there is no thinker. Other than He there is no understander. He is your soul, the inner controller, the immortal."

Thereupon Uddalaka Aruni held his peace.

(Brihad Aranyaka 3.7)[26]

The Ultimate Warp of the World—the Unqualified Imperishable

1 Then [Gargi] Vacaknavi said: "Venerable brahmans, lo, I will ask him [Yajnavalkya] two questions. If he will answer me these, not one of you will surpass him in discussions about Brahma."

"Ask, Gargi."

2 She said: "As a noble youth of the Kashis or of the Videhas might rise up against you, having strung his unstrung bow and taken two foe-piercing arrows in his hand, even so, O Yajnavalkya, have I risen up against you with two questions. Answer me these."

Yajnavalkya said: "Ask, Gargi."

3 She said: "That, O Yajnavalkya, which is above the sky, that which is beneath the earth, that which is between these two, sky and earth, that which people call the past and the present and the future—across what is that woven, warp and woof?"

4 He said: "That, O Gargi, which is above the sky, that which is beneath the earth, that which is between these two, sky and earth, that which people call the past and the present and the future—across space is that woven, warp and woof."

5 She said: "Adoration to you, Yajnavalkya, in that you have solved this question for me. Prepare yourself for the other." "Ask, Gargi."

6 She said: "That, O Yajnavalkya, which is above the sky, that which is beneath the earth, that which is between these two, sky and earth, that which

people call the past and the present and the future—across what is that woven, warp and woof?"

7   He said: "That, O Gargi, which is above the sky, that which is beneath the earth, that which is between these two, sky and earth, that which people call the past and the present and the future—across space is that woven, warp and woof."

"Across what then, pray, is space woven, warp and woof?"

8   He said: "That, O Gargi, brahmans call the imperishable. It is not coarse, not fine, not short, not long, not glowing [like fire], not adhesive [like water], without shadow and without darkness, without air and without space, without stickiness, (intangible), odorless, tasteless, without eye, without ear, without voice, without wind, without energy, without breath, without mouth, (without personal or family name, unaging, undying, without fear, immortal, stainless, not uncovered, not covered), without measure, without inside and without outside.

It consumes nothing soever.

No one soever consumes it.

9   Verily, O Gargi, at the command of that Imperishable the sun and the moon stand apart. Verily, O Gargi, at the command of that imperishable the earth and the sky stand apart. Verily, O Gargi, at the command of that imperishable the moments, the hours, the days the nights, the fortnights, the months, the seasons, and the years stand apart. Verily, O Gargi, at the command of that imperishable some rivers flow from the snowy mountains to the east, others to the west, in whatever direction each flows. Verily, O Gargi, at the command of that imperishable men praise those who give, the gods are desirous of a sacrificer, and the fathers [are desirous] of the manes-sacrifice.

10 Verily, O Gargi, if one performs sacrifices and worship and undergoes austerity in this world for many thousands of years, but without knowing that imperishable, limited indeed is that [work] of his. Verily, O Gargi, he who departs from this world without knowing that imperishable is pitiable. But, O Gargi, he who departs from this world knowing that imperishable is a brahman.

11 Verily, O Gargi, that Imperishable is the unseen seer, the unheard hearer, the unthought thinker, the ununderstood understander. Other than It there is naught that sees. Other than It there is naught that hears. Other than It there is naught that thinks. Other than It there is naught that understands. Across this imperishable, O Gargi, is space woven, warp and woof?"

12 She said: "Venerable brahmans, you may think it a great thing if you escape from this man with [merely] making a bow. Not one of you will surpass him in discussions about Brahma."

Thereupon [Gargi] Vacaknavi held her peace.

(*Brihad Aranyaka* 3.7)[27] ▲

▼ **CHANDOGYA UPANISHAD**

The Instruction of Narada by Sanatkumara: Progressive Worship of Brahma up to the Universal Soul

Seventh Khanda

1   "Understanding, assuredly, is more than meditation. Verily, by understanding one understands the Rigveda, the Yajurveda, the Samaveda, the Atharvaveda as the fourth, legend and ancient lore as the fifth, the Veda of the Vedas [grammar], propitiation of the manes, mathematics, augury, chronology, logic, polity, the science of the gods, the science of sacred knowledge, the science of rulership, astrology, the science of snake-charming, and the fine arts, as well as heaven and earth, wind and space, water and heat, gods and men, beasts and birds, grass and trees, animals together with worms, flies and ants, right and wrong, true and false, good and bad, pleasant and unpleasant, food and drink, this world and the yonder—all this one understands just with understanding. Reverence understanding.

2   "He who reverences understanding as Brahma—he, verily, attains the worlds of understanding and of knowledge. As far as understanding goes, so far he has unlimited freedom, he who reverences understanding as Brahma."

    "Is there, sir, more than understanding?"

    "There is, assuredly, more than understanding."

    "Do you, sir, tell me it."

Eighth Khanda

1   "Strength, assuredly, is more than understanding. Indeed, one man of strength causes a hundred men of understanding to tremble. When one is becoming strong, he becomes a rising man. Rising, he becomes an attendant. Attending, he becomes attached as a pupil. Attached as a pupil he becomes a seer, he becomes a hearer, he becomes a thinker, he becomes a perceiver, he becomes a doer, he becomes an understander. By strength, verily, the earth stands; by strength, the atmosphere; by strength, the sky; by strength, the mountains; by strength, gods and men; by strength, beasts and birds, grass and trees, animals together with worms, flies, and ants. By strength the world stands. Reverence strength.

2   "He who reverences strength as Brahma—as far as strength goes, so far he has unlimited freedom, he who reverences strength as Brahma."

    "Is there, sir, more than strength?"

    "There is, assuredly, more than strength."

    "Do you, sir, tell me it."

Ninth Khanda

1   "Food, assuredly, is more than strength. Therefore, if one should not eat for ten days, even though he might live, yet verily he becomes a non-seer, a non-hearer, a non-thinker, a non-perceiver, a non-doer, a non-understander. But on the entrance of food he becomes a seer, he becomes a hearer, he becomes a thinker, he becomes a perceiver, he becomes a doer, he becomes an understander. Reverence food.

2   "He who reverences food as Brahma—he, verily, attains the worlds of food and drink. As far as food goes, so far he has unlimited freedom, he who reverences food as Brahma."

     "Is there, sir, more than food?"

     "There is, assuredly, more than food."

     "Do you, sir, tell me it."

Tenth Khanda

1   "Water, verily, is more than food. Therefore, when there is not a good rain, living creatures sicken with the thought, 'Food will become scarce.' But when there is a good rain, living creatures become happy with the thought, 'Food will become abundant.' It is just water solidified that is the earth, that is the atmosphere, that is the sky, that is gods and men, beasts and birds, grass and trees, animals together with worms, flies, and ants; all these are just water solidified. Reverence water.

2   "He who reverences water as Brahma obtains all his desires and becomes satisfied. As far as water goes, so far he has unlimited freedom, he who reverences water as Brahma."

     "Is there, sir, more than water?"

     "There is, assuredly, more than water."

     "Do you, sir, tell me it."

Eleventh Khanda

1   "Heat, verily, is more than water. That, verily, seizes hold of the wind, and heats the ether. Then people say: 'It is hot! It is burning hot! Surely it will rain!' Heat indeed first indicates this, and then lets out water. So, with lightning darting up and across the sky, thunders roll. Therefore people say: 'It lightens! It thunders! Surely it will rain!' Heat indeed first indicates this, and then lets out water. Reverence heat.

2   "He who reverences heat as Brahma—he, verily, being glowing, attains flowing, shining worlds freed from darkness. As far as heat goes, so far he has unlimited freedom, he who reverences heat as Brahma."

     "Is there, sir, more than heat?"

     "There is, assuredly, more than heat."

     "Do you, sir, tell me it."

Twelfth Khanda

1   "Space, assuredly, is more than heat. In space, verily, are both sun and moon, lightning, stars and fire. Through space one calls out; through space one hears; through space one answers. In space one enjoys himself; in space one does not enjoy himself. In space one is born; unto space one is born. Reverence space.

2   "He who reverences space as Brahma—he, verily, attains spacious, gleaming, unconfined, wide-extending worlds. As far as space goes, so far he has unlimited freedom, he who reverences space as Brahma."

"Is there, sir, more than space?"

"There is, assuredly, more than space."

"Do you, sir, tell me it."

(*Chandogya 7.7–12*)[28] ▲

▼ **THE INSTRUCTION OF SHVETAKETU BY UDDALAKA CONCERNING THE KEY TO ALL KNOWLEDGE**

The Threefold Development of the Elements and of Man from the Primary Unitary Being

First Khanda

1   Om! Now, there was Shvetaketu Aruneya. To him his father said: "Live the life of a student of sacred knowledge. Verily, my dear, from our family there is no one unlearned [in the Vedas], a brahman by connection, as it were."

2   He then, having become a pupil at the age of twelve, having studied all the Vedas, returned at the age of twenty-four, conceited, thinking himself learned, proud.

3   Then his father said to him: "Shvetaketu, my dear, since now you are conceited, think yourself learned, and are proud, did you also ask for that teaching whereby what has not been heard of becomes heard of, what has not been thought of becomes thought of, what has not been understood becomes understood?"

4   "How, pray, sir, is that teaching?"

"Just as, my dear, by one piece of clay everything made of clay may be known—the modification is merely a verbal distinction, a name; the reality is just 'clay'—

5   "Just as, my dear, by one copper ornament everything made of copper may be known—the modification is merely a verbal distinction, a name; the reality is just 'copper'—

6   "Just as, my dear, by one nail-scissors everything made of iron may be known—the modification is merely a verbal distinction, a name; the reality is just 'iron'—so, my dear, is that teaching."

7   "Verily, those honored men did not know this; for, if they had known it,
     why would they not have told me? But do you, sir, tell me it."
        "So be it, my dear," said he.

Second Khanda

1   "In the beginning, my dear, this world was just being, one only, without a sec-
     ond. To be sure, some people say: 'In the beginning this world was just non-
     being, one only, without a second; from that non-being being was produced.'
2   "But verily, my dear, whence could this be?" said he. "How from non-being
     could being be produced? On the contrary, my dear, in the beginning this
     world was just being, one only, without a second.
3   "It bethought itself: 'Would that I were many! Let me procreate myself!' It
     emitted heat. That heat bethought itself: 'Would that I were many! Let me pro-
     create myself.' It emitted water. Therefore whenever a person grieves or per-
     spires from the heat, then water [i.e., either tears or perspiration] is produced.
4   "That water bethought itself: 'Would that I were many! Let me procreate
     myself.' It emitted food. Therefore whenever it rains, then there is abun-
     dant food. So food for eating is produced just from water."

                                                          (Chandogya 6.1–2)[29] ▲

▼   **The Unitary World-Soul, the Immanent Reality of All Things and
     of Man**

Ninth Khanda

1   "As the bees, my dear, prepare honey by collecting the essences of different
     trees and reducing the essence to a unity, as they are not able to discriminate
     I am the essence of this tree, 'I am the essence of that tree'—even so, indeed,
     my dear, all creatures here, though they reach being, know not 'We have
     reached being.'
3   "Whatever they are in this world, whether tiger, or lion, or wolf, or boar, or
     worm, or fly, or gnat, or mosquito, that they become.
4   "That which is the finest essence—this whole world has that as its soul. That
     is reality. That is atman (soul). That art thou, Shvetaketu."
        "Do you, sir, cause me to understand even more."
        "So be it, my dear," said he.

Tenth Khanda

1   "These rivers, my dear, flow, the eastern toward the east, the western toward
     the west. They go just from the ocean to the ocean. They become the ocean
     itself. As there they know not 'I am this one,' 'I am that one' even so indeed,
     my dear, all creatures here, though they have come forth from Being, know
     not 'We have come forth from Being.' Whatever they are in this world,

whether tiger, or lion, or wolf, or boar, or worm, or fly, or gnat, or mosquito, that they become.

2   "That which is the finest essence—this whole world has that as its soul. That is reality. That is *atman* (soul). That art thou, Shvetaketu."

"Do you, sir, cause me to understand even more."

"So be it, my dear," said he.

Twelfth Khanda

1   "Bring hither a fig from there."

"Here it is, sir."

"Divide it."

"It is divided, sir."

"What do you see there?"

"These rather fine seeds, sir."

"Of these, please, divide one."

"It is divided, sir."

"What do you see there?"

"Nothing at all, sir."

2   Then he said to him: "Verily, my dear, that finest essence which you do not perceive—verily, my dear, from that finest essence this great nyagrodha [sacred fig] tree thus arises.

3   "Believe me, my dear," said he, "that which is the finest essence—this whole world has that as its soul. That is reality. That is *atman* [soul]. That art thou, Shvetaketu."

"Do you, sir, cause me to understand even more."

"So be it, my dear," said he.

Thirteenth Khanda

1   "Place this salt in the water. In the morning come unto me."

Then he did so.

Then he said to him: "That salt you placed in the water last evening— please bring it hither."

Then he grasped for it, but did not find it, as it was completely dissolved.

2   "Please take a sip of it from this end," said he. "How is it?"

"Salt."

"Take a sip from the middle," said he. "How is it?"

"Salt."

"Take a sip from that end," said he. "How is it?"

"Salt."

"Set it aside. Then come unto me."

He did so, saying, "It is always the same."

Then he said to him: "Verily, indeed, my dear, you do not perceive being here. Verily, indeed, it is here.

3   "That which is the finest essence—this whole world has that as its soul. That is reality. That is *atman* [soul]. That art thou, Shvetaketu."

   "Do you, sir, cause me to understand even more."

   "So be it, my dear," said he.

Fourteenth Khanda

1   "Just as, my dear, one might lead away from the Gandharvas a person with his eyes bandaged, and then abandon him in an uninhabited place; as there he might be blown forth either to the east, to the north, or to the south, since he had been led off with his eyes bandaged and deserted with his eyes bandaged; as, if one released his bandage and told him, 'In that direction are the Gandharvas; go in that direction!' he would, if he were a sensible man, by asking [his way] from village to village, and being informed, arrive home at the Gandharvas—even so here on earth one who has a teacher knows: 'I shall remain here only so long as I shall not be released [from the bonds of ignorance]. Then I shall arrive home.'

2   "That which is the finest essence—this whole world has that as its soul. That is reality. That is *atman* [soul]. That art thou, Shvetaketu."

   "Do you, sir, cause me to understand even more."

   "So be it, my dear," said he.

Fifteenth Khanda

1   "Also, my dear, around a [deathly] sick person his kinsmen gather, and ask, 'Do you know me?' 'Do you know me?' So long as his voice does not go into his mind, his mind into his breath, his breath into heat, the heat into the highest divinity—so long he knows.

2   "Then when his voice goes into his mind, his mind into his breath, his breath into heat, the heat into highest divinity—then he knows not."

3   "That which is the finest essence—this whole world has that as it should. That is reality. That is *atman* [soul]. That art thou, Shvetaketu."

   "Do you, sir, cause me to understand even more."

   "So be it, my dear," said he.

(*Chandogya* 6.9–15)[30] ▲

▼ **MANDUKYA UPANISHAD**

The Mystic Symbolism of the Word "Om":

(a) Identified with the Fourfold, Monistic Time-Brahma

1   Om!—This syllable is the whole world.
     Its further explanation is:—

The past, the present, the future—everything is just the word "om."

And whatever else that transcends threefold time—that, too, is just the word "om."

2   For truly, everything here is Brahma; this self [atman] is Brahma. This same self has four fourths.

(b) Representing in Its Phonetic Elements the Four States of the Self

3   The waking state, outwardly cognitive, having seven limbs, having nineteen mouths, enjoying the gross, the common-to-all-men, is the first fourth.

4   The dreaming state, inwardly cognitive, having seven limbs, having nineteen mouths, enjoying the exquisite, the brilliant, is the second fourth.

5   If one asleep desires no desire whatsoever, sees no dream whatsoever, that is deep sleep.

    That deep sleep state, unified, just a cognition-mass, consisting of bliss, enjoying bliss, whose mouth is thought, the cognitional, is the third fourth.

6   This is the lord of all. This is the all-knowing. This is the inner controller. This is the source of all, for this is the origin and the end of beings.

7   Not inwardly cognitive, not outwardly cognitive, not both-wise cognitive, not a cognition-mass, not cognitive, not non-cognitive, unseen, with which there can be no dealing, ungraspable, having no distinctive mark, non-thinkable, that cannot be designated, the essence of the assurance of which is the state of being one with the self, the cessation of development, tranquil, benign, without a second [such] they think is the fourth. He is the self [atman]. He should be discerned.

8   This is the self with regard to the word "om," with regard to its elements. The elements are the fourths; the fourths, the elements; the letter *a*, the letter *u*, the letter *m*.

9   The waking state, the common-to-all-men, is the letter *a*, the first element, from *apti* [obtaining] or from *adimalva* [being first].

    He obtains, verily, indeed, all desires, he becomes first—he who knows this.

10 The sleeping state, the brilliant, is the letter *u*, the second element, from *utkarsha* [exaltation] or from *ubhayatva* [intermediateness].

    He exalts, verily, indeed, the continuity of knowledge; and he becomes equal; no one ignorant of Brahma is born in the family of him who knows this.

11 The deep-sleep state, the cognitional, is the letter *m*, the third element, from *miti* [erecting] or from *apiti* [emerging]. He, verily, indeed, erects this whole world, and he becomes its emerging—he who knows this.

12 The fourth is without an element, with which there can be no dealing, the cessation of development, benign, without a second.

Thus *om* is the self [*atman*] indeed.
He who knows this, with his self enters the self—yea, he who knows this!

(Mandukya 1–12)[31] ▲

▼ SVETASVATARA UPANISHAD

The One God, Creator and Lord, In and Over the World

10 The one God who covers himself,
   Like a spider, with threads
   Produced from primary matter, according to his own nature
   May He grant us entrance in Brahma!

11 The one God, hidden in all things,
   All-pervading, the inner soul of all things,
   The overseer of deeds [*karma*], in all things abiding,
   The witness, the sole thinker, devoid of qualities,

12 The one controller of the inactive many,
   Who makes the one seed manifold—
   The wise who perceive Him as standing in one's self—
   They, and no others, have eternal happiness.

13 Him who is the constant among the inconstant, the intelligent among
      intelligences,
   The one among many, who grants desires,
   That cause, attainable by discrimination and abstraction—
   By knowing God, one is released from all fetters!

14 The sun shines not there, nor the moon and stars;
   These lightnings shine not, much less this [earthly] fire!
   After Him, as He shines, doth everything shine.
   This whole world is illumined with His light.

15 The one soul in the midst of this world—
   This indeed is the fire which has entered into the ocean.
   Only by knowing Him does one pass over death.
   There is no other path for going there.

16 He who is the maker of all, the all-knower, self-sourced,
   Intelligent, the author of time, possessor of qualities, omniscient,
   Is the ruler of primary matter and of the spirit, the lord of qualities,
   The cause of reincarnation [*samsara*] and of liberation [*moksa*], of
      continuance and of bondage.

17 Consisting of that, immortal, existing as the Lord,
   Intelligent, omnipresent, the guardian of this world,
   Is He who constantly rules this world.
   There is no other cause found for the ruling.

18 To Him who of old creates Brahma,
    And who, verily, delivers to him the Vedas—
    To that God, who is lighted by his own intellect,
    Do I, being desirous of liberation, resort as a shelter—

19 To Him who is without parts, without activity, tranquil,
    Irreproachable, spotless,
    The highest bridge of immortality,
    Like a fire with fuel burned.

20 When men shall roll up space
    As it were a piece of leather,
    Then will there be an end of evil
    Apart from knowing God!

                              (Svetasvatara 6.10–20)[32] ▲

▼ The One God Identified with Rudra

1 The one spreader of the net, who rules with his ruling powers,
   Who rules all the worlds with his ruling powers,
   The one who alone stands in their arising
         and in their continued existence—
   They who know That, become immortal.

2 For truly, Rudra (the terrible) is the one—they stand not for a second—
   Who rules all the worlds with his ruling powers
   He stands opposite creatures. He, the protector,
   After creating all beings, merges them together at the end of time.

3 Having an eye on every side and a face on every side,
   Having an arm on every side and a foot on every side,
   The one God forges together with hands, with wings,
   Creating the heaven and the earth.

4 He who is the source and origin of the gods,
   The ruler of all, Rudra, the great seer,
   Who of old created the golden germ
   May He endow us with clear intellect!

Prayers from the Scriptures unto Rudra for Favor

5 The form of thine, O Rudra, which is kindly,
   Unterrifying, revealing no evil—
   With that most benign form to us
   Appear, O dweller among the mountains!

6 O dweller among the mountains, the arrow
   Which thou holdest in they hand to throw
   Make kindly, O mountain-protector!
   Injure not man or beast

                              (Svetasvatara 3.1–6)[33] ▲

▼ **ISA UPANISHAD**

Recognition of the Unity Underlying the Diversity of the World

1   By the Lord enveloped must this all be—
    Whatever moving thing there is in the moving world.
    With this renounced, thou mayest enjoy.
    Covet not the wealth of anyone at all.

Non-attachment of Deeds on the Person of a Renouncer

2   Even while doing deeds here,
      One may desire to live a hundred years.
    Thus on thee—not otherwise than this is it—
        The deed [*karma*] adheres not on the man.

The Forbidding Future for Slayers of the Self

3   Devilish are those worlds called,
    With blind darkness covered o'er!
    Unto them, on deceasing, go
    Whatever folk are slayers of the self.

The All-Surpassing Paradoxical World-being

4   Unmoving, the one is swifter than the mind.
    The sense-powers reached not It, speeding on before.
    Past others running, This goes standing.
    In it Matarishvan places action.

5   It moves. It moves not.
    It is far, and It is near.
    It is within all this,
    And It is outside of all this.

6   Now, he who on all beings
    Looks as just in the self [*atman*],
    And on the self as in all beings—
    He does not shrink away from Him.

7   In whom all beings
    Have become just the self of the discerner—
    Then what delusion, what sorrow is there
    Of him who perceives the unity!

                                                    (*Isa* l–7)³⁴ ▲

Legal Literature

Following the canonical, *sruti*, works of Vedic literature, the Indian tradition produced a vast body of semi-canonic texts defined as *smrti*. Translatable as "that which is remembered," *smrti* is classified as being based on (and therefore less authoritative than) the directly revealed, *sruti*, literature.

An important example of *smrti* is the genre of legal literature (*dharma shastra*). Legal literature reflects the continued Hindu concern with order—here primarily defined in terms of *dharma*, or "ordained duties." As such, much consideration is given to matters of caste (*varna*), marriage, the stages of life (*ashrama*), and so on. Of contemporary interest environmental matters such as the pollution of rivers and the cutting of trees are dealt with. Given the importance of custom and law in Hinduism these works rank very high especially those that have acquired authority. The values expounded upon in these texts have been a significant influence within Hindu society from the time of their formulation (circa 500 BCE–CE 500) to the present.[35]

Laws of Manu

The *Laws of Manu* (Manu Smrti), written between 200 and 100 BCE, is the foremost source of legal literature. In addition to the concerns mentioned above, the text deals with defining *dharma*, matters of pollution and purification, funeral rites, royal law, and laws of diet?[36] Thus, the *Laws of Manu* can be viewed as an extensive code of conduct for Indian society. It is important to note, however, that the quest for liberation, often considered incompatible with social relations and stability, is both recognized and incorporated into its legal framework.

▼ CREATION OF CASTES

1   The great sages approached Manu, who was seated with a collected mind, and, having duly worshipped him, spoke as follows:

2   "Deign, divine one, to declare to us precisely and in due order the sacred laws of each of the [four chief] castes [*varna*] and of the intermediate ones.

3   "For thou, O Lord, alone knowest the purport, [i.e.] the rites, and the knowledge of the soul, [taught] in this whole ordinance of the self-existent, which is unknowable and unfathomable."

4   He, whose power is measureless, being thus asked by the high-minded great sages, duly honored them, and answered, "Listen!"

5   This [universe] existed in the shape of darkness, unperceived, destitute of distinctive marks, unattainable by reasoning, unknowable, wholly immersed, as it were, in deep sleep.

6 Then the divine self-existent, indiscernible, [but] making [all] this, the great elements and the rest, discernible, appeared with irresistible [creative] power, dispelling the darkness.

7 He who can be perceived by the internal organ [alone], who is subtle, indiscernible, and eternal, who contains all created beings and is inconceivable, shone forth of his own [will].

8 He, desiring to produce beings of many kinds from his own body, first with a thought created the waters, and placed his seed in them.

9 That [seed] became a golden egg, in brilliancy equal to the sun; in that [egg] he himself was born as Brahman, the progenitor of the whole world.

10 The waters are called narah, [for] the waters are, indeed, the offspring of Nara; as they were his first residence, he thence is named Narayana.

11 From that [first] cause, which is indiscernible, eternal, and both real and unreal, was produced that male [purusha], who is famed in this world [under the appellation of] Brahman.

12 The divine one resided in that egg during a whole year, then he himself by his thought [alone] divided it into two halves;

13 And out of those two halves he formed heaven and earth, between them the middle sphere, the eight points of the horizon, and the eternal abode of the waters.

14 From himself he also drew forth the mind, which is both real and unreal, likewise from the mind egoism, which possesses the function of self-consciousness [and is] lordly;

15 Moreover, the great one, the soul, and all [products] affected by the three qualities, and, in their order, the five organs which perceive the objects of sensation.

16 But, joining minute particles even of those six, which possess measureless power, with particles of himself, he created all beings.

(*Laws of Manu* 1.1–16)[37]

87 But in order to protect this universe He, the most resplendent one, assigned separate [duties and] occupations to those who sprang from his mouth, arms, thighs, and feet.

88 To *brahmanas* he assigned teaching and studying [the Veda], sacrificing for their own benefit and for others, giving and accepting [of alms].

89 The *kshatriya* he commanded to protect the people, to bestow gifts, to offer sacrifices, to study [the Veda], and to abstain from attaching himself to sensual pleasures;

90 The *vaishya* to tend cattle, to bestow gifts, to offer sacrifices, to study [the Veda], to trade, to lend money, and to cultivate land.

91 One occupation only the lord prescribed to the *shudra*, to serve meekly even these [other] three castes.

92 Man is stated to be purer above the navel [than below]; hence the self-existent has declared the purest [part] of him [to be] his mouth.

93 As the *brahmana* sprang from [Brahman's] mouth, as he was the first-born, and as he possesses the Veda, he is by right the lord of this whole creation.

94 For the self-existent, having performed austerities, produced him first from his own mouth, in order that the offerings might be conveyed to the gods and manes and that this universe might be preserved.

95 What created being can surpass him, through whose mouth the gods continually consume the sacrificial viands and the manes the offerings to the dead?

6 Of created beings the most excellent are said to be those which are animated; of the animated, those which subsist by intelligence; of the intelligent, mankind; and, of men, the *brahmanas*;

97 Of *brahmanas*, those learned [in the Veda]; of the learned, those who recognize [the necessity and the manner of performing the prescribed duties]; of those who possess this knowledge, those who perform them; of the performers, those who know the Brahman.

98 The very birth of a *brahmana* is an eternal incarnation of the sacred law; for he is born to [fulfill] the sacred law, and becomes one with Brahman.

(Laws of Manu 1.87–98)[38] ▲

▼ STUDENT AND HOUSEHOLDER

1 The vow [of studying] the three Vedas under a teacher must be kept for thirty-six years, or for half that time, or for a quarter, or until the [student] has perfectly learnt them.

2 [A student] who has studied in due order the three Vedas, or two, or even one only, without breaking the [rules of] studentship, shall enter the order of householders.

(Laws of Manu 4.1–2)[39] ▲

▼ ASCETIC STAGE

1 A twice-born Snataka, who has thus lived according to the law in the order of householders, may, taking a firm resolution and keeping his organs in subjection, dwell in the forest, duly [observing the rules given below].

2 When a householder sees his [skin] wrinkled, and [his hair] white, and the sons of his sons, then he may resort to the forest.

3 Abandoning all food raised by cultivation, and all his belongings, he may depart into the forest, either committing his wife to his sons, or accompanied by her.

4   Taking with him the sacred fire and the implements required for domestic [sacrifices], he may go forth from the village into the forest and reside there, duly controlling his senses.

5   Let him offer those five great sacrifices according to the rule, with various kinds of pure food fit for ascetics, or with herbs, roots, and fruit.

6   Let him wear a skin or a tattered garment; let him bathe in the evening or in the morning; and let him always wear [his hair in] braids, the hair on his body, his beard, and his nails [being unclipped].

7   Let him perform the bali-offering with such food as he eats, and give alms according to his ability; let him honour those who come to his hermitage with alms consisting of water, roots, and fruit.

8   Let him be always industrious in privately reciting the Veda; let him be patient of hardships, friendly [towards all], of collected mind, ever liberal and never a receiver of gifts, and compassionate towards all living creatures.

9   Let him offer, according to the law, the agnihotra with three sacred fires, never omitting the new-moon and full-moon sacrifices at the proper time.

10 Let him also offer the nakshatreshti, the agrayana, and the katurmasya [sacrifices], as well as the turayana and likewise the dakshayana, in due order.

11 With pure grains, fit for ascetics, which grow in spring and in autumn, and which he himself has collected, let him severally prepare the sacrificial cakes and the boiled messes, as the law directs.

12 Having offered those most pure sacrificial viands, consisting of the produce of the forest, he may use the remainder for himself, [mixed with] salt prepared by himself.

13 Let him eat vegetables that grow on dry land or in water, flowers, roots, and fruits, the productions of pure trees, and oils extracted from forest fruits.

14 Let him avoid honey, flesh, and mushrooms growing on the ground [or elsewhere, the vegetables called] bhustrina, and shigruka, and the shleshmantaka fruit.

15 Let him throw away in the month of Ashvina the food of ascetics, which he formerly collected, likewise his worn-out clothes and his vegetables, roots, and fruit.

16 Let him not eat anything [grown on] ploughed [land], though it may have been thrown away by somebody, nor roots and fruit grown in a village, though (he may be) tormented [by hunger].

17 He may eat either what has been cooked with fire, or what has been ripened by time; he either may use a stone for grinding, or his teeth may be his mortar.

18 He may either at once [after his daily meal] cleanse [his vessel for collecting food], or lay up a store sufficient for a month, or gather what suffices for six months or for a year.

19 Having collected food according to his ability, he may either eat at night [only], or in the day-time [only], or at every fourth meal-time, or at every eighth.

20 Or he may live according to the rule of the lunar penance [daily diminishing the quantity of his food] in the bright [half of the month] and [increasing it] in the dark [half]; or he may eat on the last days of each fortnight, once [a day only], boiled barley-gruel.

21 Or he may constantly subsist on flowers, roots, and fruit alone, which have been ripened by time and have fallen spontaneously, following the rule of the [Institutes] of Vikhanas.

22 Let him either roll about on the ground, or stand during the day on tiptoe, [or] let him alternately stand and sit down; going at the savanas [at sunrise, at midday, and at sunset] to water in the forest [in order to bathe].

23 In summer let him expose himself to the heat of five fires, during the rainy season live under the open sky, and in winter be dressed in wet clothes, [thus] gradually increasing [the rigor of] his austerities.

24 When he bathes at the three savanas [sunrise, midday, and sunset], let him offer libations of water to the manes and the gods, and practising harsher and harsher austerities, let him dry up his bodily frame.

25 Having reposited the three sacred fires in himself, according to the prescribed rule, let him live without a fire, without a house, wholly silent, subsisting on roots and fruit.

26 Making no effort [to procure] things that give pleasure, chaste, sleeping on the bare ground, not caring for any shelter, dwelling at the roots of trees.

27 From *brahmanas* [who live as] ascetics, let him receive alms, [barely sufficient] to support life, or from other householders of the twice-born [castes] who reside in the forest.

28 Or [the hermit] who dwells in the forest may bring [food] from a village, receiving it either in a hollow dish [of leaves], in [his naked] hand, or in a broken earthen dish, and may eat eight mouthfuls.

29 These and other observances must a *brahmana* who dwells in the forest diligently practise, and in order to attain complete [union with] the [supreme] soul, [he must study] the various sacred texts contained in the Upanishads.

30 [As well as those rites and texts] which have been practised and studied by the sages [*risis*], and by *brahmana* householders, in order to increase their knowledge [of Brahman], and their austerity, and in order to sanctify their bodies;

31 Or let him walk, fully determined and going straight on, in a north-easterly direction, subsisting on water and air until his body sinks to rest.

32 A *brahmana*, having got rid of his body by one of those modes practised by the great sages, is exalted in the world of Brahman, free from sorrow and fear.

33   But having thus passed the third part of [a man's natural term of] life in the
     forest, he may live as an ascetic during the fourth part of his existence, after
     abandoning all attachment to worldly objects.
34   He who after passing from order to order, after offering sacrifices and subdu-
     ing his senses, becomes, tired with [giving] alms and offerings of food, an asce-
     tic, gains bliss after death.

(Laws of Manu 6.1–34)[40] ▲

Epics

The period from around 400 BCE to CE 300 is known as the epic period. During this time the Aryans, with their Vedic scripture and Sanskrit language,
ceased to be nomadic people by settling into towns and cities across the
plain of the Ganges River in North India and adopting an agricultural lifestyle.
Their religion incorporates influences from the religions of the indigenous
people they had come to dominate. During this period the two great Hindu
epics, the Mahabharata and the Ramayana were composed. Both epics focus
on royal rivalries reflecting the political turmoil of the time. Both also manifest a tension between a religion aimed at supporting kings and maintaining the world order versus a religion aimed at isolating a person from society
in order to realize individual release (*moksa*). Both epics emphasize that the
king has a crucial role in maintaining social order and moral obligation,
and the religious practices that insure it. But both epics also contain persons
who have renounced the world, gone to live in forests and are held to possess special powers. The heroes of the epics almost always treat these world
renouncers with great respect and are often their students or beneficiaries.

The great epics of the Hindu religion, the Mahabharata and the Ra-
Like Hinduism itself, the epics hold together the tension between the
aims of the royal heroes, which have to do with worldly order, and the aims
of the world renouncers, which focus on individual release or liberation. It
is in the isolation of the forests that the royal heroes learn from the world
renouncer teachers the knowledge that allows them to become effective
rulers. The epics also teach that one must first fulfill one's household duties
to family and society before one can go off into the forest to seek individual release (*moksa*). Thus the idea of stages of life serves to resolve the tension between the two aims of life. The ascetic world renouncers, in the last
two stages of life, serve as teachers to society, thus helping to reinvigorate and
sustain the order of the world.

The great epics of the Hindu religion, the Mahabharata and the Ramayana, are virtual storehouses of information, from mythical and religious
to social and political. For the student they reflect a variety of concerns,
including those of ritual performance, the practice of *dharma*, or world order,

and the aspiration for liberation. The events that they relate are thought to have taken place in distant ages; but, told and retold within Indian society, they remain vital, living influences for the tradition.

Bhagavad Gita

The Mahabharata, compiled between 400 BCE and CE 300, is the longest of the Indian epics; with some 100,000 verses, it ranks as the world's largest work of poetry. Contained in this massive text is the famous Bhagavad Gita, the "Lord's Song." The Bhagavad Gita is primarily written in the form of a dialogue between Arjuna, favoured hero of the warring parties in the Mahabharata, and Krishna, his charioteer, advisor and, as we will discover in the next section, God incarnate.

The chapters provided here reflect an important concern in epic literature for the necessity of acting appropriately to one's position in life, that is, with *dharma*. The Gita offers a special solution to the tension between the two aims of Hindu religion in its teaching that by giving up the desire for the fruit of one's actions (e.g., fame or fortune) one may reach release while performing one's social duties (*dharma*).

Although written in formal English pentameter, Sir Edwin Arnold's translation conveys the flavour of the beautiful Sanskrit poetry.

▼ **CHAPTER I**

Dhritirashtra: Ranged thus for battle on the sacred plain—
  On Kurukshetra—say, Sanjaya! say
  What wrought my people, and the Pandavas?

Sanjaya: When he beheld the host of Pandavas,
  Raja Duryodhana to Drona drew,
  And spake these words: "Ah, guru! See this line,
  How vast it is of Pandu fighting-men,
  Embattled by the son of Drupada,
  Thy scholar in the war! Therein stand ranked
  Chiefs like Arjuna, like to Bhima chiefs,
  Benders of bows; Virata, Yuyudhan,
  Drupada, eminent upon his car,
  Dhrishtaket, Chekitan, Kashi's stout lord,
  Purujit, Kuntibhoj, and Shaivya,
  With Yudhamanyu and Uttamauj
  Subhadra's child; and Drupadi's;—all famed!
  All mounted on their shining chariots!
  On our side, too,—thou best of brahmans! see

Excellent chiefs, commanders of my line,
Whose names I joy to count: thyself the first,
Then Bhishma, Karna, Kripa fierce in fight,
Vikarna, Ashvatthaman; next to these
Strong Saumadatti, with full many more
Valiant and tried, ready this day to die
For me their king, each with his weapon grasped;
Each skilful in the field.
Weakest—meseems—
Our battle shows where Bhishma holds command,
And Bhima, fronting him, something too strong!
Have care our captains nigh to Bhishma's ranks
Prepare what help they may! Now, blow my shell!"

Then, at the signal of the aged king,
With blare to wake the blood, rolling around
Like to a lion's roar, the trumpeter
Blew the great conch; and, at the noise of it,
Trumpets and drums, cymbals and gongs and horns
Burst into sudden clamour; as the blasts
Of loosened tempest, such the tumult seemed!
Then might be seen, upon their car of gold
Yoked with white steeds, blowing their battle-shells,
Krishna the God, Arjuna at his side:
Krishna, with knotted locks, blew his great conch
Carved of the "Giant's bone"; Arjuna blew
Indra's loud gift; Bhima the terrible—
Wolf-bellied Bhima—blew a long reed-conch
And Yudhisthira, Kunti's blameless son,
Winded a might shell, "Victory's voice";
And Nakula blew shrill upon his conch
Named the "Sweet-sounding," Sahadev on his
Called "Gem-bedecked," and Kashi's prince on his
Sikhandi on his car, Dhristadyumn,
Virata, Satyaki the unsubdued,
Drupada, with his sons, (O Lord of Earth!)
Long-armed Subhadra's children, all blew loud,
So that the clangour shook their foemen's hearts,
With quaking earth and thundering heav'n.
    Then 'twas—
Beholding Dhritirashtra's battle set,
Weapons unsheathing, bows drawn forth, the war

Instant to break—Arjun, whose ensign-badge
Was Hanuman the monkey, spake this thing
To Krishna the Divine, his charioteer:
"Drive, Dauntless One! to yonder open ground
Betwixt the armies; I would see more nigh
These who will fight with us, those we must slay
To-day, in war's arbitrament; for, sure,
On bloodshed all are bent who throng this plain,
Obeying Dhritirashtra's sinful son."

Thus, by Arjuna prayed, (O Bharata!)
Between the hosts that heavenly charioteer
Drove the bright car, reining its milk-white steeds
Where Bhishma led, and Drona, and their lords,
"See!" spake he to Arjuna, "where they stand,
Thy kindred of the Kurus": and the prince
Marked on each hand the kinsmen of his house,
Grandsires and sires, uncles and brothers and sons,
Cousins and sons-in-law and nephews, mixed
With friends and honoured elders; some this side,
Some that side ranged: and, seeing those opposed,
Such kith grown enemies—Arjuna's heart
Melted with pity, while he uttered this:

Arjuna: Krishna! as I behold, come here to shed
    Their common blood, yon concourse of our kin,
    My members fail, my tongue dries in my mouth,
    A shudder thrills my body, and my hair
    Bristles with horror; from my weak hand slips
    Gandiv, the goodly bow; a fever burns
    My skin to parching; hardly may I stand;
    The life within me seems to swim and faint;
    Nothing do I foresee save woe and wail!
    It is not good, O Keshav! nought of good
    Can spring from mutual slaughter! Lo, I hate
    Triumph and domination, wealth and ease,
    Thus sadly won! aho! what victory
    Can bring delight, Govinda! what rich spoils
    Could profit; what rule recompense; what span
    Of life itself seem sweet, bought with such blood?
    Seeing that these stand here, ready to die,
    For whose sake life was fair, and pleasure pleased,

And power grew precious:—grandsires, sires and sons,
Brothers, and father-in-law, and sons-in-law,
Elders and friends! Shall I deal death on these
Even though they seek to slay us? Not one blow,
O Madhusudan! will I strike to gain
The rule of all three worlds; then, how much less
To seize an earthly kingdom! Killing these
Must breed but anguish, Krishna! If they be
Guilty, we shall grow guilty by their deaths;
Their sins will light on us, if we shall slay
Those sons of Dhritirashtra, and our kin;
What peace could come of that, O Madhava?
For if indeed, blinded by lust and wrath,
These cannot see, or will not see, the sin
Of kingly lines o'erthrown and kinsmen slain,
How should not we, who see, shun such a Crime—
We who perceive the guilt and feel the shame—
O thou delight of men, Janardana?
By overthrow of houses perisheth
Their sweet continuous household piety,
And—rites neglected, piety extinct—
Enters impiety upon that home;
Its women grow unwomaned, whence their spring
Man passions, and the mingling-up of castes,
Sending a hell-ward road that family,
And whoso wrought its doom by wicked wrath.
Nay, and the souls of honoured ancestors
Fall from their place of peace, being bereft
Of funeral-cakes and the wan death-water.
So teach our holy hymns. Thus, if we slay
Kinsfolk and friends for love of earthly power,
Ahovat! what an evil fault it were!
Better I deem it, if my kinsmen strike,
To face them weaponless, and bare my breast
To shaft and spear, than answer blow with blow.
So speaking, in the face of those two hosts,
Arjuna sank upon his chariot-seat,
And let fall bow and arrows, sick at heart.

Here endeth Chapter I of the Bhagavad-Gita, entitled Arjun-Visbad, or "The Book
of the Distress of Arjuna." ▲

▼ **CHAPTER II**

Sanjaya: Him, filled with such compassion and such grief,
      With eyes tear-dimmed, despondent, in stern words
      The driver, Madhusudan, thus addressed:

Krishna: How hath this weakness taken thee? Whence springs
      The inglorious trouble, shameful to the brave,
      Barring the path of virtue? Nay, Arjun!
      Forbid thyself to feebleness! it mars
      Thy warrior-name! cast off the coward-fit!
      Wake! Be thyself! Arise, scourge of thy foes!

Arjuna: How can I, in the battle, shoot with shafts
      On Bhishma, or on Drona—O thou Chief!—
      Both worshipful, both honourable men?

      Better to live on beggar's bread
      With those we love alive,
      Than taste their blood in rich feasts spread,
      And guiltily survive!
      Ah! were it worse—who knows? to be
      Victor or vanquished here,
      When those confront us angrily
      Whose death leaves living drear?

      In pity lost, by doubtings tossed,
      My thoughts—distracted—turn
      To Thee, the guide I reverence most,
      That I may counsel learn:
      I know not what would heal the grief
      Burned into soul and sense,
      If I were earth's unchallenged chief—
      A god—and these gone thence!

Sanjaya: So spake Arjuna to the Lord of hearts,
      And sighing, "I will not fight!" held silence then.
      To whom, with tender smile, (O Bharata!)
      While the prince wept despairing 'twixt those hosts,
      Krishna made answer in divinest verse:

Krishna: Thou grievest where no grief should be! thou speak'st
      Words lacking wisdom! for the wise in heart
      Mourn not for those that live, nor those that die.
      Nor I, nor thou, nor any one of these,

Ever was not, nor ever will not be,
For ever and for ever afterwards.
All, that doth live, lives always! To man's frame
As there come infancy and youth and age,
So come there raisings-up and layings-down
Of other and of other life-abodes,
Which the wise know, and fear not. This that irks—
Thy sense-life, thrilling to the elements—
Bringing thee heat and cold, sorrows and joys,
'Tis brief and mutable! Bear with it, Prince!
As the wise bear. The soul which is not moved,
The soul that with a strong and constant calm
Takes sorrow and takes joy indifferently,
Lives in the life undying! That which is
Can never cease to be; that which is not
Will not exist. To see this truth of both
Is theirs who part essence from accident,
Substance from shadow. Indestructible,
Learn thou! the life is, spreading life through all;
It cannot anywhere, by any means,
Be anywise diminished, stayed, or changed.
But for these fleeting frames which it informs
With spirit deathless, endless, infinite,
They perish. Let them perish, Prince! And fight!
He who shall say, "Lo! I have slain a man!"
He who shall think, "Lo I am slain!" those both
Know naught! Life cannot slay. Life is not slain!
Never the spirit was born; the spirit shall cease to be never;
Never was time it was not; end and beginning are dreams!
Birthless and deathless and changeless remaineth the spirit for ever;
Death hath not touched it at all, dead though the house of it seems!

Who knoweth it exhaustless, self sustained.
Immortal, indestructible,—shall such
Say, "I have killed a man, or caused to kill?"
      Nay, but as when one layeth
      His worn-out robes away,
      And, taking new ones, sayeth,
      "These will I wear to-day!"
      So putteth by the spirit
      Lightly its garb of flesh,
      And passeth to inherit
      A residence afresh.

I say to thee weapons reach not the life;
Flame burns it not, waters cannot o'erwhelm,
Nor dry winds wither it. Impenetrable,
Unentered, unassailed, unharmed, untouched,
Immortal, all-arriving, stable, sure,
Invisible, ineffable, by word
And thought uncompassed, ever all itself,
Thus is the soul declared! How wilt thou, then,—
Knowing it so,—grieve when thou shouldst not grieve?
How, if thou hearest that the man new-dead
Is, like the man new-born, still living man—
One same, existent spirit—wilt thou weep?
The end of birth is death; the end of death
Is birth: this is ordained! and mournest thou,
Chief of the stalwart arm! for what befalls
Which could not otherwise befall? The birth
Of living things comes unperceived; the death
Comes unperceived; between them, beings perceive:
What is there sorrowful herein, dear Prince?
Wonderful, wistful, to contemplate!
Difficult, doubtful, to speak upon!
Strange and great for tongue to relate,
Mystical hearing for every one!
Nor wotteth man this, what a marvel it is,
When seeing, and saying, and hearing are done!

This life within all living things, my Prince!
Hides beyond harm; scorn thou to suffer, then,
For that which cannot suffer. Do thy part!
Be mindful of thy name, and tremble not!
Nought better can betide a martial soul
Than lawful war; happy the warrior
To whom comes joy of battle—comes, as now,
Glorious and fair, unsought; opening for him
A gateway unto heav'n. But, if thou shunn'st
This honourable field—a kshatriya—
If, knowing thy duty and thy task, thou bidd'st
Duty and task go by—that shall be sin!
And those to come shall speak thee infamy
From age to age; but infamy is worse
For men of noble blood to bear than death!
The chiefs upon their battle-chariots

Will deem't was fear that drove thee from the fray.
Of those who held thee mighty-souled the scorn
Thou must abide, while all thine enemies
Will scatter bitter speech of thee, to mock
The valour which thou hadst; what fate could fall
More grievously than this? Either—being killed—
Thou wilt win Svarga's safety, or—alive
And victor—thou wilt reign an earthly king.
Therefore, arise, thou son of Kunti! brace
Thine arm for conflict, nerve thy heart to meet—
As things alike to thee—pleasure or pain,
Profit or ruin, victory or defeat:
So minded, gird thee to the fight, for so
Thou shalt not sin!

Thus far I speak to thee
As from the "Samkhya"—unspiritually—
Hear now the deeper teaching of the yoga,
Which holding, understanding, thou shalt burst
Thy *karmabandh*, the bondage of wrought deeds.
Here shall no end be hindered, no hope marred,
No loss be feared: faith—yea, a little faith—
Shall save thee from the anguish of thy dread.
Here, glory of the Kurus! shines one rule—
One steadfast rule—while shifting souls have laws
Many and hard. Specious, but wrongful deem
Thy speech of those ill-taught ones who extol
The letter of their Vedas, saying, "This
Is all we have, or need"; being weak at heart
With wants, seekers of heaven: which comes—they say—
As "fruit of good deeds done"; promising men
Much profit in new births for works of faith;
In various rites abounding; following whereon
Large merit shall accrue towards wealth and power;
Albeit, who wealth and power do most desire
Least fixity of soul have such, least hold
On heavenly meditation. Much these teach,
From Vedas, concerning the "three qualities";
But thou, be free of the "three qualities,"
Free of the "pairs of opposites," and free
From that sad righteousness which calculates;
Self-ruled, Arjuna! simple satisfied!

Look! like as when a tank pours water forth
To suit all needs, so do these brahmans draw
Text for all wants from tank of holy writ.
But thou, want not! ask not! Find full reward
Of doing right in right! Let right deeds be
Thy motive, not the fruit which comes from them.
And live in action! Labour! Make thine acts
Thy piety, casting all self aside,
Condemning gain, and merit; equable
In good or evil: equability
Is yoga, is piety!

Yet, the right act
Is less, far less, than the right-thinking mind.
Seek refuge in thy soul; have there thy heaven!
Scorn them that follow virtue for her gifts!
The mind of pure devotion—even here—
Casts equally aside good deeds and bad,
Passing above them. Unto pure devotion
Devote thyself: with perfect meditation
Comes perfect act, and the right-hearted rise—
More certainly because they seek no gain—
Forth from the bands of body, step by step,
To highest seats of bliss. When thy firm soul
Hath shaken off those tangled oracles
Which ignorantly guide, then shall it soar
To high neglect of what's denied or said,
This way or that way, in doctrinal writ,
Troubled no longer by the priestly lore,
Safe shall it live, and sure; steadfastly bent
On meditation. This is yoga—and peace!

Arjuna: What is his mark who hath that steadfast heart,
          Confirmed in holy meditation? How
          Know we his speech, Keshava? Sits he, moves he
          Like other men?

Krishna: When one, O Pritha's son!—
          Abandoning desires which shake the mind—
          Finds in his soul full comfort for his soul,
          He hath attained the yoga—that man is such!
          In sorrows not dejected, and in joys
          Not overjoyed; dwelling outside the stress

Of passion, fear, and anger; fixed in calms
Of lofty contemplation;—such an one
Is muni, is the sage, the true recluse!
He who to none and nowhere overbound
By ties of flesh, takes evil things and good
Neither desponding nor exulting, such
Bears wisdom's plainest mark! He who shall draw
As the wise tortoise draws its four feet safe
Under its shield, his five frail senses back
Under the spirit's buckler from the world
Which else assails them, such an one, my Prince!
Hath wisdom's mark! Things that solicit sense
Hold off from the self-governed; nay, it comes,
The appetites of him who lives beyond
Depart,—aroused no more. Yet may it chance,
O son of Kunti! that a governed mind
Shall some time feel the sense-storms sweep, and wrest
Strong self-control by the roots. Let him regain
His kingdom! let him conquer this, and sit
On Me intent. That man alone is wise
Who keeps the mastery of himself! If one
Ponders on objects of the sense, there springs
Attraction; from attraction grows desire,
Desire flames to fierce passion, passion breeds
Recklessness; then the memory—all betrayed—
Lets noble purpose go, and saps the mind,
Till purpose, mind, and man are all undone.
But, if one deals with objects of the sense
Not loving and not hating, making them
Serve his free soul, which rests serenely lord,
Lo! such a man comes to tranquility;
And out of that tranquility shall rise
The end and healing of his earthly pains,
Since the will governed sets the soul at peace.
The soul of the ungoverned is not his,
Nor hath he knowledge of himself; which lacked,
How grows serenity? and, wanting that,
Whence shall he hope for happiness?

The mind
That gives itself to follow shows of sense seeth its helm of
Wisdom rent away,

And, like a ship in waves of whirlwind, drives
To wreck and death. Only with him, great Prince!
Whose senses are not swayed by things of sense—
Only with him who holds his mastery,
Shows wisdom perfect. What is midnight-gloom
To unenlightened souls shines wakeful day
To his clear gaze; what seems as wakeful day
Is known for night, thick night of ignorance,
To his true-seeing eyes. Such is the saint!
And like the ocean, day by day receiving
Floods from all lands, which never overflows;
Its boundary-line not leaping, and not leaving,
Fed by the rivers, but unswelled by those;
So is the perfect one! to his soul's ocean
The world of sense pours streams of witchery,
They leave him as they find, without commotion,
Taking their tribute, but remaining sea.
Yea, whoso, shaking off the yoke of flesh
Lives Lord, not servant, of his lusts; set free
From pride, from passion, from the sin of "self,"
Toucheth tranquility! O Pritha's son!
That is the state of Brahma! There rests no dread
When that last step is reached! Live where we will,
Die when he may, such passeth from all 'plaining,
To blest nirvana, with the gods, attaining.

Here endeth Chapter II of the Bhagavad-Gita, entitled SamkhyaYoga, or "The Book of Doctrines."

(Sir Edwin Arnold, trans., *The Song Celestial*, chaps. I–II)[41] ▲

Ramayana

Although the Ramayana (200 BCE–CE 200) is dated at approximately the same time as the Mahabharata, tradition states that its events took place during an earlier age. The poet Valmiki is credited with composing the epic, but it is thought that in doing so he was elaborating on an already existing oral tradition.[42] The central character of the Ramayana is the dharmic king Rama, an embodiment (*avatar*) of the God Vishnu.

As in the preceding selection, the following chapter indicates the essential quality of *dharma* (order) as a determinant of moral activity.

▼ **CHAPTER XLI**

The Persuasions

Bharata then addressing Rama, said before all:

"My Lord, the kingdom by bestowing which on me, father wanted to pacify my mother, I do now make over to your hands. Enjoy the kingdom free from all thorns. Who, excepting you can now protect the kingdom torn asunder like a dam breached by strong currents of water during the rain? As the mule cannot imitate a horse, or a common fowl, the king of birds, so you should know me [to be the same] in comparison with you. Happy is the man upon whom depend others for their sustenance, but unhappy is he who depends on others for his own support. Let all people witness you duly established on the throne."

Every one praised Bharata for his noble words.

Then gentle Rama replied, "My boy, a created being does not enjoy any independent existence, he has no freedom of will, he can't act as he likes, he is subject to death. Everything is perishable, every rise has its fall, where there is composition, there is decomposition, there is life as well as death. As a ripe fruit has on other course but to fall, as an edifice standing on massive pillars grows weak when dilapidated with age, so a man grows feeble and the night that hath passed away will not return back, as the stream of the Jamuna flowing towards the ocean does not recede in its course. As summer's heat continually dries up the water of a tank, so ever-fleeting days and nights rob people of their longevity. Whether you be stationary in one place or roam about hither and thither, your life must run to its end. So think about yourself and don't bother about others. Death accompanies you in your walk, sits down when you sit, he travels long distance with you, and returns with thee. With age a man grows weak, his skin is wrinkled and his hair turns gray. Now tell me how can you prevent these? Man rejoices at the rise of the sun and he feels delighted at the approach of night, but he does not understand that his life by this time has been shortened. People are delighted at the advent of a new season, but they do not understand that with the revolution of seasons their longevity has been shortened. As in the vast ocean one piece of wood comes in contact with another (by the force of the current, i.e., by mere accident) but in time becomes separated, so you should understand a man's association with wealth, wife and children. It is impossible to get rid of this eternal chain of birth and death. He who laments for another's death cannot, however, prevent his own.

"As a traveller follows another seeing him going ahead of him, so we shall have to follow our predecessors. Why should then a man mourn for another when he cannot alter his own inevitable end? Seeing life ebbing fast like the flow of a stream which cannot be called back, man should engage himself in search of happiness since happiness is the end of all. Our virtuous father after performing many meritorious sacrifices has repaired to heaven. It is not proper to mourn for him. He has attained heavenly bliss by casting off his infirm body, so we must no more weep for him. In all circumstances, intelligent people subdue grief, lamentations and tears, so be not overwhelmed with grief, go back to Ayodhya and reside in the capital. This was the wish of our father and let me pursue my own duties here. He was our father and it is not proper to disobey his commands. You ought to honour him. It is our duty to obey our superiors who wish for our ultimate good. Father has attained heaven by his own merits, you may rest assured. Now attend to your own duties."

Thus saying Rama lapsed into silence.

Then Bharata returned, "My noble Lord, who is like you in this world? Sorrow cannot afflict you, nor pleasure can buoy you up. You are an ideal to the aged people, though you consult them in times of doubt. To you, life and death, good and evil are all equal. You have nothing to grieve for. In fact, one who has acquired self-knowledge like you is not moved by any calamity or sorrow. You are truthful, wise and divine in nature, the mysteries of life and death are not unknown to you, so even intense sorrow cannot overpower you.

"What my mean-minded mother has done in my absence in a distant land had not the least approval of mine so be with me. It is for religious consideration that I have not as yet taken the life of this sinful woman. How would I commit such a nefarious act being born of illustrious Dasaratha? King Dasaratha was our father, king and preceptor, so I should not speak anything ill of him, but was this right [being cognizant of what is right and what is wrong] to act in this manner at the instigation of his wife? It is said that "when one's end is near, his sense becomes perverted." From the conduct of the king this adage seems to be true. However, now rectify the wrong that has been committed either through anger, ignorance or wrecklessness. The son is called "Apatya" because he saves his father from fall, so be thou a true son.

"It is not becoming of you to perpetuate the wrong done by father. What he has done is most unjust and highly reprehensible. So be gracious to comply with my request. How ill-matched is kshatriya valour with forest-life, and matted locks with sovereignty? How monstrous, it is not at all becoming of you to pursue such a perverse line of action. Governing the people is the duty of a kshatriya, but which kshatriya by putting aside this kshatriya morality will adopt a dubious and an arduous course resorted to by old people? But if you are inclined to arduous duties, then adopt the onerous duty of governing the four orders of people according to custom and morality. Virtuous people say that of the four orders the life of a house-holder is the best, then why do you intend to abandon that? My Lord, in attainments and in age I am a boy to you. Who can govern in your presence? I even lack in common sense. I cannot live without your help, so you rule over the earth. Vasishtha and other Ritvigas versed in Mantras with the subjects will present you the crown even here. After the coronation ceremony, go back to

Ayodhya like Indra, the ruler of heaven. Absolve yourself from the threefold debts, viz., to the gods, to the ancestors and to the risis; heighten the miseries of your enemies and increase the pleasure of your friends, and rule over me. Rescue our revered father Dasaratha from sin by removing the disgrace of my mother Kaikeyi. I throw myself at thy feet and entreat you again and again and do me this favour. If you retire to another forest without granting my prayers. I tell you that I shall go along with you."

Bharata bowed down and thus entreated, but Rama did not acquiesce in his words; he was determined to carry out the mandate of his father. So he was both pleased and pained by Bharata's entreaties. Then all praised Bharata for his noble speech, and they all entreated Rama again and again.

Rama then returned, "Bharata, you are born of king Dasaratha, and what you have proposed is worthy of you. But father at the time of marrying your mother promised to the king of Kekaya that he would bestow the kingdom upon the son born of that marriage. Then he promised your mother two boons being pleased with her nursing at the time of the war between the gods and the Asuras; therefore, your mother asked for the two boons, my exile and your installation to the throne. I have come to the forest with Janaki and Lakshmana to redeem father from his pledge, so you should also without further delay accept the kingdom for observance of truth. Even for my satisfaction you should redeem father from his obligation and should greet your mother. Hear me, my boy, in Gaya high-souled Gaya at the time of sacrifice to please his departed ancestors, this Vedic hymn is recited: "He who saves his father from the hell named Put is called putra, and he who saves his father from all sorts of difficulties is also a Putra (or a true son). The wise people pray for many sons because at least one of them may go to Gaya (to offer pindas). Bharata, such was the belief of the former kings. So go back to Ayodhya and get yourself installed and rule over the people for their welfare with the help of Satrughna and the brahmanas. I shall shortly repair with Janaki to the Dandaka forest. You rule over men, let me rule over the animals here. Go back with a contented mind and I shall too set forth to the Dandaka with delight. Let white umbrella shade your head, I shall take refuge under the cooler shadow of these forest trees. As Lakshmana is of great help to me, Satrughna will be of great help to you. Thus let us fulfil the vow of our father."

(Makhan Lal Sen, *The Ramayana*, vol. 1, from chap. XLI)[43] ▲

Devotional Literature

The Hindu epics nurtured a popular religious culture—beginning in South India—which by the sixth century CE began to dominate Hindu religious expression.[44] The literature of this culture characteristically expresses devotion, or *bhakti*, for a particular deity (Vishnu, Shiva, the Goddess, etc.) who is depicted in a personal form. Textual examples of divine power, grace, and conduct provide devotees with concrete objects for their adoration.

Bhagavad Gita

In addition to its concern with social activity, moral order, and with the means to attain individual liberation, the Bhagavad Gita provides the Hindu tradition with a powerful description of God made visible upon which devotion may be focused.

▼ **CHAPTER XI**

Arjuna: This, for my soul's peace, have I heard from Thee,
    The unfolding of the mystery supreme
    Named Adhyatman; comprehending which,
    My darkness is dispelled; for now I know—
    O Lotus-eyed!—whence is the birth of men,
    And whence their death, and what the majesties
    Of Thine immortal rule. Fain would I see,
    As though Thyself declar'st it, sovereign Lord!
    The likeness of that glory of Thy form
    Wholly revealed. O Thou divinest one!
    If this can be, if I may bear the sight,
    Make Thyself visible, Lord of all prayers!
    Show me Thy very self, the eternal God!

Krishna: Gaze, then, thou son of Pritha! I manifest for thee
    Those hundred thousand thousand shapes that clothe my mystery:
    I show thee all my semblances, infinite, rich, divine,
    My changeful hues, my countless forms.
    See! in this face of mine,
    Adityas, Vasus, Rudras, Ashvins, and Maruts; see
    Wonders unnumbered, Indian Prince! Revealed to none save thee.
    Behold! this is the universe!—Look! what is live and dead
    I gather all in one—in Me! Gaze, as thy lips have said.
    On God eternal, very God! See Me! see what thou prayest!

    Thou canst not!—not, with human eyes, Arjuna! ever mayest!
    Therefore I give thee sense divine. Have other eyes, new light!
    And, look! This is My glory, unveiled to mortal sight!

Sanjaya: Then, O King! the God, so saying,
    Stood, to Pritha's son displaying
    All the splendour, wonder, dread

Of His vast almighty-head.
Out of countless eyes beholding,
Out of countless mouths commanding,
Countless mystic forms enfolding
In one form: supremely standing
Countless radiant glories wearing,
Countless heavenly weapons bearing,
Crowned with garlands of star-clusters,
Robed in garb of woven lustres,
Breathing from His perfect presence
Breaths of every subtle essence
Of all heavenly odours; shedding
Blinding brilliance; overspreading—
Boundless, beautiful—all spaces
With His all-regarding faces;
So He showed! If there should rise
Suddenly within the skies
Sunburst of a thousand suns
Flooding earth with beams undeemed-of,
Then might be that holy one's
Majesty and radiance dreamed of!

So did Pandu's son behold
All this universe enfold
All its huge diversity
Into one vast shape, and be
Visible, and viewed, and blended
In one body—subtle, splendid,
Nameless—the all-comprehending
God of gods, the never-ending
Deity!

But, sore amazed,
Thrilled, o'erfilled, dazzled, and dazed,
Arjuna knelt; and bowed his head,
And clasped his palms; and cried, and said:

Arjuna: Yea! I have seen! I see!
Lord! all is wrapped in Thee!
The gods are in Thy glorious frame! The creatures
Of earth, and heaven, and hell
In Thy divine form dwell,
And in Thy countenance shine all the features

Of Brahma, sitting lone
 Upon His lotus-throne;
Of saints and sages, and the serpent races
 Ananta, Vasuki;
 Yea! mightiest Lord! I see
Thy thousand thousand arms, and breasts
 And eyes,—on every side
 Perfect, diversified;
And nowhere end of Thee, nowhere beginning,
 Nowhere a centre! Shifts—
 Wherever soul's gaze lifts—
Thy central self, all-wielding, and all-winning!

 Infinite King! I see
 The anadem on Thee,
The club, the shell, the discus; see Thee burning
 In beams insufferable,
 Lighting earth, heaven, and hell
With brilliance blazing, glowing, flashing; turning

 Darkness to dazzling day
 Look I whichever way;
Ah, Lord! I worship Thee, the undivided,
 The uttermost of thought
 The treasure-palace wrought
To hold the wealth of the worlds; the shield provided

 To shelter virtue's laws;
 The fount whence life's stream draws
All waters of all rivers of all being;
 The one unborn, unending:
 Unchanging and unblending!
With might and majesty, past thought, past seeing!

 Silver of moon and gold
 Of sun are glories rolled
From Thy great eyes; Thy visage, beaming tender

 Throughout the stars and skies,
 Doth to warm life surprise
Thy universe. The worlds are filled with wonder

 Of Thy perfections! Space
 Star-sprinkled, and void place

From pole to pole of the blue, from bound to bound,
　　Hath Thee in every spot,
　　Thee, Thee!—Where Thou are not,
O holy, marvellous form! is nowhere found!
　　O mystic, awful one!
　　At sight of Thee, made known,
The three worlds quake; the lower gods draw nigh Thee;
　　Thy fold their palms, and bow
　　Body, and breast, and brow,
And, whispering worship, laud and magnify Thee!

　　Rishis and Siddhas cry
　　"Hail! highest majesty!"
From sage and singer breaks the hymn of glory
　　In dulcet harmony,
　　Sounding the praise of Thee;
While countless companies take up the story,

　　Rudras, who ride the storms,
　　The 'Adityas' shining forms,
Vasus and Sadhyas, Vishvas, Ushmapas;
　　Maruts, and those great Twins
　　The heavenly, fair Ashvins,
Gandharvas, Rakshasas, Siddhas, and Asuras,—

　　These see Thee, and revere
　　In sudden-stricken fear;
Yea! the worlds,—seeing Thee with form stupendous,
　　With faces manifold,
　　With eyes which all behold,
Unnumbered eyes, vast arms, members tremendous,

　　Flanks, lit with sun and star,
　　Feet planted near and far,
Rushes of terror, mouths wrathful and tender;—
　　The three wide worlds before Thee
　　Adore, as I adore Thee,
Quake, as I quake, to witness so much splendour!

　　I mark Thee strike the skies
　　With front, in wondrous wise
Huge, rainbow-painted, glittering; and thy mouth
　　Opened, and orbs which see

All things, whatever be
In all Thy worlds, east, west, and north and south

    O eyes of God! O head!
    My strength of soul is fled,
Gone is heart's force, rebuked is mind's desire!
    When I behold Thee so.
    With awful brows a-glow,
With burning glance, and lips lighted by fire

    Fierce as those flames which shall
    Consume, at close of all,
Earth! heaven! Ah me! I see no earth and heaven!
    Thee, Lord of lords! I see,
    Thee only—only Thee!
Now let Thy mercy unto me be given.

    Thou refuge of the world!
    Lo! to the cavern hurled
Of Thy wide-opened throat, and lips white-tushed,
    I see our noblest ones,
    Great Dhritarashtra's sons,
Bhishma, Drona, and Karna, caught and crushed!

    The kings and chiefs drawn in,
    That gaping gorge within;
The best of both these armies torn and riven!
    Between Thy jaws they lie
    Mangled full bloodily,
Ground into dust and death! Like streams down-driven
    With helpless haste, which go
    In headlong furious flow
Straight to the gulfing deeps of th' unfilled ocean,
    So to that flaming cave
    Those heroes great and brave
Pour, in unending streams, with helpless motion!

    Like moths which in the night
    Flutter towards a light,
Drawn to their fiery doom, flying and dying,
    So to their death still throng,
    Blind, dazzled, borne along
Ceaselessly, all those multitudes, wild flying!

Thou, that hast fashioned men,
Devourest them again,
One with another, great and small, alike!
The creatures whom Thou mak'st,
With flaming jaws Thou tak'st,
Lapping them up! Lord God! They terrors strike

From end to end of earth,
Filling life full, from birth
To death, with deadly, burning, lurid dread!
Ah, Vishnu! make me know
Why is Thy visage so?
Who art Thou, feasting thus upon Thy dead?

Who? awful Deity!
I bow myself to Thee,
O mightiest Lord! rehearse
Why hast Thou face so fierce?
Whence doth this aspect horrible proceed?

Krishna: Thou seest Me as time who kills, time who brings all to doom,
The slayer time, ancient of days, come hither to consume;
Excepting thee, of all these hosts of hostile chiefs arrayed,
There stands not one shall leave alive the battle-field!
Dismayed
No longer be! Arise! obtain renown! destroy they foes!
Fight for the kingdom waiting thee when thou hast vanquished those.
By Me they fall—not thee! the stroke of death is dealt them now,
Even as they show thus gallantly; My instrument art thou!
Strike, strong-armed Prince, at Drona! at Bhishma strike! deal death
On Karna, Jyadratha; stay all their warlike breath!
'Tis I who bid them perish! Thou wilt but slay the slain;
Fight! they must fall, and thou must live, victor upon this plain!

Sanjaya: Hearing mighty Keshav's word,
Tremblingly that helmed Lord
Clasped his lifted palms, and—praying
Grace of Krishna—stood there, saying,
With bowed brow and accents broken,
These words, timorously spoken:

Arjuna: Worthily, Lord of might!
The whole world hath delight
In Thy surpassing power, obeying Thee;

The Rakshasas, in dread
At sight of Thee, are sped
To all four quarters; and the company

Of Siddhas sound Thy name,
How should they not proclaim
Thy majesties, divinest, mightiest?
Thou Brahma, than Brahma greater!
Thou infinite creator!
Thou God of gods, life's dwelling-place and rest.

Thou, of all souls the soul!
The comprehending whole!
Of being formed, and formless being the framer;
O utmost one! O Lord!
Older than eld, Who stored
The worlds with wealth of life! O treasure-claimer,

Who wottest all, and art
Wisdom Thyself! O part
In all, and all; for all from Thee have risen
Numberless now I see
The aspects are of Thee!
Vayu Thou art, and He who keeps the prison
Of Narak, Yama dark;
Varuna's waves are Thy waves. Moon and starlight
Are thine! Prajapati
Art Thou, and 'Tis to Thee
They knelt in worshipping the old world's farlight,

The first of mortal men
Again, Thou God! again
A thousand thousand times be magnified!
Honour and worship be—
Glory and praise,—to Thee
Namo Namaste, cried on every side;

Cried here, above, below,
Uttered when Thou dost go,
Uttered where Thou dost come! Namo! We call;
Namostu! God adored!
Namostu! Nameless Lord!
Hail to Thee! Praise to Thee! Thou one in all;

For Thou art all! Yea, Thou!
　　Ah! if in anger now
Thou shouldst remember I did think Thee friend,
　　Speaking with easy speech,
　　As men use each to each;
Did call Thee "Krishna," "Prince," nor comprehend

　　Thy hidden majesty,
　　The might, the awe of Thee;
Did, in my heedlessness, or in my love,
　　On journey, or in jest,
　　Or when we lay at rest,
Sitting at council, straying in the grove,

　　Alone, or in the throng,
　　Do Thee, most holy! wrong,
Be Thy grace granted for that witless sin
　　For Thou art, now I know,
　　Father of all below,
Of all above, of all the worlds within

　　Guru of gurus; more
　　To reverence and adore
Than all which is adorable and high!
　　How, in the wide worlds three
　　Should any equal be?
Should any other share Thy majesty!

　　Therefore, with body bent
　　And reverent intent,
I praise, and serve, and see Thee, asking grace.
　　As father to a son,
　　As friend to friend, as one
Who loveth to his lover, turn Thy face

　　In gentleness on me!
　　Good is it I did see
This unknown marvel of Thy form! But fear
　　Mingles with joy! Retake,
　　Dear Lord! for pity's sake
Thine earthly shape, which earthly eyes may bear

　　Be merciful, and show
　　The visage that I know;
Let me regard Thee, as of yore, arrayed

With disc and forehead-gem,
With mace and anadem,
Thou that sustainest all things!
Undismayed

Let me once more behold
The form I loved of old,
Thou of the thousand arms and countless eyes!
This frightened heart is fain
To see restored again
My charioteer, in Krishna's kind disguise.

Krishna: Yea! thou has seen, Arjuna! because I loved thee well,
The secret countenance of me, revealed by mystic spell.
Shining, and wonderful, and vast, majestic, manifold,
Which none save thou in all the years had favour to behold;
For not by Vedas cometh this, nor sacrifice, nor alms,
Nor works well-done, nor penance long, nor prayers,
nor chaunted psalms,
That mortal eyes should bear to view the immortal soul unclad,
Prince of the Kurus! This was kept for thee alone!
Be glad!
Let no more trouble shake thy heart, because thine eyes have seen
My terror with My glory. As I before have been
So will I be again for thee; with lightened heart behold!
Once more I am thy Krishna, the form thou knew'st of old!

Sanjaya: These words to Arjuna spake
Vasudev, and straight did take
Back again the semblance dear
Of the well-loved charioteer;
Peace and joy it did restore
When the prince beheld once more
Mighty Brahma's form and face
Clothed in Krishna's gentle grace

Arjuna: Now that I see come back, Janardana!
This friendly human frame, my mind can think
Calm thoughts once more; my heart beats still again!

Krishna: Yea! it was wonderful and terrible
To view me as thou didst, dear Prince! The gods
Dread and desire continually to view!
Yet not by Vedas, nor from sacrifice,
Nor penance, nor gift-giving, nor with prayer

Shall any so behold, as thou has seen!
Only by fullest service, perfect faith,
And uttermost surrender am I known
And seen, and entered into, Indian Prince!
Who doeth all for Me; who findeth Me
In all; adoreth always; loveth all
Which I have made, and Me, for Love's sole end,
Than man, Arjuna! unto Me doth wend.

Here endeth Chapter XI of the Bhagavad-Gita, entitled Vishvarupadarshanam, or "The Book of the Manifesting of the One and Manifold."

(Arnold, *The Song Celestial*, chap. XI)[45] ▲

Ramayana

While Rama's more rigid perception of *dharma* may render him somewhat less appealing than Krishna, he too is revered as an *avatara*. In the selection below, his position as God descended to restore earthly order is clear. The response of Sita (also called Janaki) to Rama, like Arjuna's response to Krishna in the previous selection, is often considered an ideal example of devotional surrender.

▼   **CHAPTER LXXIX**

Rama's Accusation

Then, Rama asking Janaki, standing humbly before him, said, "Gentle lady! I have brought you hither after conquering the enemies in war. I have done all that could possibly be done by valour. My anger has been satisfied, and I have avenged my insult. Everybody, this day has witnessed my prowess. I have fulfilled my promise and I am now clear to my own self. That the fickle-minded Rakshasa stole you in my absence is due to your fate, but I have absolved you from that calumny. He who does not avenge by his own valour the insult offered to him by his enemies, is a mean-minded fellow. This day, the crossing of the sea by heroic Hanuman has been crowned with success; the burning of Lanka and other glorious achievements have been fruitful. This day the prowess and counsels of Sugriva have been consummated with success, so also the efforts of him who forsaking his worthless brother took up my cause under my shelter."

At these words, Janaki opened wide her eyes bathed in tears. At that time, seeing that lotus-faced beauty with waving dark curls before him, Rama's heart was smitten with grief, but in fear of public scandal, addressing her before others, Rama said, "In order to take revenge for insult, I have done what a man ought to do, and I have destroyed Ravana under such circumstances. As the great sage Agastya of austere penance freed the southern countries from the terror of Ilval and Vatapi, so I have freed the world from the fear of Ravana. Know it for certain, that it is not for you that I have come to the termination of war with the help of my friends. I have done this for my dignity, for removing the stain of a scandal, and for the prestige and honour of my renowned family. I have done the deed, just to prove that I do not belong to a mean family. I do now, doubt your character for your stay in a stranger's house. You are standing before me, but your sight is unbearable to me, as light to a man suffering from eye-disease, so I tell you to go wherever you like, I do not want you. Who being born of a noble family, can take back his wife who lived in another's house, simply because she is an object of love? You were molested on Ravana's lap, his sinful eyes floated over your person, now how can I receive you back, thinking of the noble family from which I come?

"The object for which I have rescued you has been fulfilled, now I no longer need you. Go where you please. O noble lady! I say unto you without any hesitation whatsoever, that you can pay your attentions upon Lakshmana, Bharata, Satrughna and Sugriva, or if you like, you may follow Vibhishana.

"Finding you charming and beautiful and having got you in his house Ravana did not refrain long."

Janaki having heard those angry words of Rama, was smothered with grief, as a creeper is torn off by an elephant's trunk. Having heard all these unheard-of accusations in the presence of such a large number of persons, Janaki became mortally ashamed of her own existence, and she wanted to bury herself within her flesh. Rama's words pierced her heart like a dart. She began to shed a torrent of tears. Then she wiped her tears by the end of her cloth and told Rama in a gentle voice, broken with sobs, "As a low person abuses a low woman, why do you use all such unutterable rude expressions against me? I am not what you take me to be.

"I can swear about my character, have faith in my honour. Having seen the conduct of low women, you suspect all woman as a class, but that is not proper. If you have any experience of me then give up that unfounded suspicion.

"You see, Ravana touched my body when I was not in my senses. How could I help it? My fate is to be blamed for that, but what was within my control, i.e., my heart, belonged to you. What could I do about my body, that could be subjected by another person, for then I was thoroughly under another's power? I am undone, if you could not as yet know me from my love and from the contact of my soul. When you sent Hanuman for my information, why did you not send me the word that you had renounced me? Then, I could have put an end to my existence even before that Vanara. If it were so, then there would not have been any need for taking such risks to your own self, and your friends could have been spared from all these troubles and sufferings. O King! being overwhelmed with anger, like a low person, you are thinking me like an ordinary woman. My name is Janaki, because I am connected with Janaka's sacrifice but not because of my birth there, the Earth alone is my mother.

"Being unable to judge correctly, you have failed to comprehend my nature. You do not take into consideration why you married me in youth. My love and devotion now seems to be quite ineffectual."

With these words Janaki broke into tears and then addressing Lakshmana, sad and brooding, said, "Lakshmana! just prepare a funeral pyre for me. This is my only remedy in the present trouble. I do not want to live after these false accusations. My husband is not pleased with me, he has renounced me before everybody. I shall now give myself up to the flames."

Then, Lakshmana with a suppressed rage, looked at Rama and having divined the latter's motives from his looks and gestures, prepared a funeral pyre for Sita.

At that time, none amongst the friends dared to talk to Rama, or to look at him; he then looked formidable like death.

Rama was seated, fixing his gaze on earth. Sita circumambulated him and came near the fire, and after bowing to the gods and Brahma she said addressing Agni, the god of fire, "If I am thoroughly devoted to Rama, then let fire protect me in every possible way. Rama takes a chaste woman for a false one, but if I be pure, let Agni protect me."

With these words, Janaki circumambulated the pyre and then fearlessly entered the flame. Everybody—the old and the young alike—witnessed in pain that Janaki was in fire. That paragon of beauty fell into flame in the presence of all. The sages, gods and saints saw Janaki leaped into the flames, like an oblation offered in sacrifice.

Women raised a piteous cry seeing her thus fallen into fire, like an angel dislodged from heaven on account of a curse. Both the Rakshasas and the Vanaras raised a hue and cry at that sight. ▲

▼ **CHAPTER LXXX**

The Ordeal

The virtuous Rama hearing different persons speaking different things brooded in silent tears.

In the meantime, Yama with the manes of the departed ancestors, Indra with the gods, Kuvera with the Yakshas, Varuna, the god of the sea, three-eyed Mahadeva riding a bull, and Brahma, the creator of all things and the foremost of those versed in the Vedas, appeared on the scene and said to Rama by raising their hands:

"Rama! you are Lord of all and foremost of the wise. Why do you slight Janaki's entrance into the flames? You are Prajapati himself. You are the Lord of the universe and in the former cycle of creation, you were Vasu bearing the name of Krutadhana. There is no ruler above you. You art the eighth Mahadeva amongst the objects of a adoration.

"The twin Ashvinikumaras are your ears, and the sun and the moon eyes. You are present through the beginning, end and the middle. Then why do you forsake Sita so unjustly?"

Hearing these words Rama said, "I am the son of king Dasaratha and consider myself a human being; now tell me what I really am!"

Brahma replied, "Rama! just listen to me, I am narrating to you the true state of things.

"You are self-revealing Gadadhara holding conch-shell, disc and mace in hands; You are one-tusked boar. You are truth and death-less Brahma; You are ever-existing. You are virtue to the virtuous; Your law is observed everywhere. You are four-handed and hold Sanga bow like death itself. There is no limit to your powers. You are intellect, forgiveness and patience. You are creation and destruction. Saints assign you to be the refuge of all creatures. You are the Vedas with their thousand branches. You are sacrifice, vashatkara, omkara; there is none above you. You are omnipresent and omniscient. You have a thousand feet, a thousand eyes and hundreds of heads. You hold the universe in you. You lie on the waters of the universal dissolution on the bed of the ananta snake. O Rama! I am your heart, goddess Sarasvati is your tongue, spiritual gods are your hairs, night is the closing of your eyes, day is the opening of your eyes, the Vedas are your convictions; there is nothing else besides you. The universe is your body, your forgiveness is earth, fire is your anger, and pleasure is the moon. You have bound down Vali and made Indra the king of heaven. Janaki is Lakshmi personified and you are Vishnu himself. You have assumed this human form for the destruction of Ravana. Ravana has been destroyed; now come back to the sphere of the gods. Unlimited are your glory and prowess, and your devotees get everything that is desirable in this life and in the next."

After Brahma had finished, Agni appeared carrying Janaki on his lap. Janaki looked like the glittering moon; she was adorned in red, her dark curls were streaming behind. Fire could not scorch her garlands, ornaments or dress.

The god Agni, the witness of everything, handing over Janaki to Rama, said, "Rama! this is your Janaki. She is stainless. She has not committed any sin by word, action, or thought. Since her forcible abduction by Ravana, she passed her days alone in silent sorrow for your separation. So long she was confined in a harem, so long she was under another's power, but her mind was ever fixed upon you. You are her only prop. Grim Rakshasis frightened her in various ways, oppressed her in different manners, but in her heart there was not even the slightest thought of Ravana. Her heart is pure and she is absolutely sinless. Accept her now: I ask you to do so. Don't suspect her even for a moment."

Then virtuous Rama, hearing these words of worshipful Agni, was exceedingly pleased and after thinking for a moment said with a cheerful look, "O god! Janaki's purification was necessary. She was long confined in Ravana's harem.

Had I accepted her without her purification, then people would have accused me, saying that the son of king Dasaratha is foolish and lustful. However, I do now find that Janaki's heart is pure and full of devotion, and there could not be any stain on her character. She is protected by her own chastity. As the shore cannot be over-stepped by the sea, so she could not be overcome by Ravana. That any villain could not insult her even in his thoughts. She was untouchable to him like pure flame of fire. As light is inseparable from the sun, so she is inseparable from me. Now, I cannot renounce her on account of her residing in a stranger's house. She is the purest in the three worlds. O gods! you are adorable beings, and you speak just for my good. Now, I shall protect her for ever."

With these words, heroic Rama received Janaki with delight, and everybody praised him for that.

(The Ramayana, vol. III, chaps. LXXIX–LXXX, 340–48)[46] ▲

The Goddess

Another important element in the genre of devotional literature is that which is devoted to one of the several forms of the Goddess, or Devi. Although evidence from prehistoric times indicates the presence of a prominent female god, or gods, it was not until the medieval period that the Goddess acquired the attributes of a supreme deity.[47] Worship of the Goddess is extremely prevalent in modern India—in any of her forms, from the creative and protective to the horrific and destructive.

Some of Devi's many, sometimes paradoxical, qualities are related in the passage provided, which is from a work known as the Devi—Mahatmyam.

▼   The King said:

1.45   "Venerable Sir, who is that Goddess whom you call Mahamaya? How was She born? What is Her activity? O Sage!

1.46   What is Her nature? What is Her form? Whence was Her origin? All that I wish to hear from you, O, foremost amongst those who know Brahman!"

The rishi said:

1.47   "She is eternal having the universe as Her form. All these worlds are Her man-ifestation. Even so She is incarnating in manifold ways. Hear it from me.

1.48   When She becomes incarnate for fulfilling the divine purpose then She is said to be born in the world, though She is eternal.

1.49   When the universe was converted into an infinite ocean and Lord Vishnu having entered Yoganidra became asleep on the couch of the cosmic ser-pent Shesha then at the end of the kalpa.

1.50   Two terrible Asuras, the well known Madhu and Kaitabha sprang from the impurity of the two ears of Vishnu, attacked Brahma to slay him.

1.51 Prajapati Brahma, seated on the lotus rising from the navel of Vishnu, saw those violent Asuras, and also noticing Narayana in dream-state.

1.52 Began to invoke with a concentrated mind the Goddess Yoganidra dwelling in the eyes of Hari with a view to bring the Lord in a conscious state.

1.53 The resplendent Lord Brahma praised the Goddess of sleep, the incomparable power of Vishnu, the queen of the cosmos, the supporter of the world and the cause of its maintenance and dissolution."

Brahma said:

1.54 "You are Svaha. You are Svadha. You are Vashatkara.
Speech is yourself. Oh, the indestructible and the eternal one! you are immortality. You are the embodiment of the threefold matras A-U-M in the eternal akshara, Brahma.

1.55 The eternal half-matra is also thyself, which being of universal connotation is difficult to be expressed through utterance.

1.56 This universe is upheld by you. The world is created by you and the creation is protected by you. Oh, Goddess! at the end of time you also consume it.

1.57 In creation you are the creative force. In its maintenance you are the protective power. In its dissolution you are the destructive power—thus, the totality of the world form is thyself.

1.58 You are the supreme knowledge, the supreme power, the supreme mind, the supreme memory and the great delusion. Oh, Great Goddess! you are the great Asuri.

1.59 You are the primordial Prakriti which brings into force the triple gunas. You are Kalaratri, Maharatri and the terrible Moharatri.

1.60 You are Shri, you are Ishvari, you are modesty, you are intelligence whose sign is consciousness. You are bashfulness, nourishment and contentment as well as peace and forgiveness.

1.61 Terrible is your form armed with sword, spear, club, discus, conch, bow, arrows, sling and mace.

1.62 Oh, of pleasing form! You are the most beautiful of all beauties. You are exceedingly good-looking. You are the highest of all the high and the low, you are the supreme Goddess.

1.63 Oh, you, the soul of everything! whatever or wherever anything exists the power of all that is yourself. How can I fully praise you?

1.64 By you even the creator of the world, the preserver of the world and the destroyer of the world, is put to sleep. Who is here capable of praising you adequately?

1.65 It is you who has made Vishnu, myself and Shiva manifest forms. Hence who can have the power to praise you properly?"

(Vasudeva S. Agarwala, *The Glorification of the Great Goddess* 1.45–65)[48] ▲

Indian Devotional Poet-Saints

By about the sixth century CE in the south of India, and somewhat later in the north, popular religious figures were providing a vibrant focus for Indian devotional movements. The earliest of these, the Tamil poet-saints, flourished between the seventh and ninth centuries,[49] but others gradually spread into various regions of the sub-continent. Rather than the orthodox Sanskrit, regional languages like Tamil, Bengali, and Hindi were often used by these figures. In addition to devotional poems, translations, and elaborations of the epics (or portions thereof), like those of the Hindi author Tulsidas (circa 1550), were produced.

This digression from Sanskrit as the normative literary language indicates a general, and noteworthy, tendency of devotional movements to reject certain formal Hindu values. For instance, devotees—at least in the early stages of these movements—were considered equals, regardless of caste or sex.

Manikkavachakar

Manikkavachakar was an eighth-century devotee of Shiva and wrote in Tamil.

▼

25.1   My flawless Gem, in Love, I pine, I yearn
       That Thou may chase the gathering darkness around me
       And command me to come to Thee.

25.2   That I may see Thee, Oh Honey distilled,
       Incomprehensible to many, my father!

25.3   That Thou may look at me, my face awhile,
       And be moved to pity and love.

25.4   That I may see Thy radiance and hold on for ever
       To thy blessed feet of compassion.

25.5   That my nectar sweet be moved to listen
       To my magnificat of praise to Thee.

25.6   That the light of Thy face, Thy sweet benignant smile,
       I may see and relish, My Father.

25.7   That I may magnify Thee as my Lord,
       And praise thy name a thousand times.

25.8   I shall raise my hands in prayer to thee;
       I shall clasp Thy holy feet; and call on Thy name
       I shall melt like wax before the flame,
       Incessantly calling out, "my beloved Father."

25.9   I shall cast off this body, and enter the
       Celestial city of Sivapura. I shall behold Thy

Effulgent glory. In joyful bliss shall I join
The society of Thy true devotees.
25.10 Then I shall look up, to hear Thee say
With thy beauteous lips, "Fear not"—
The assurance of Thy all-embracing love
Alone can set my soul at ease and peace.

(*Ratna Navaratnam, Tiruvachakam* 25.1–10) [50] ▲

Appar

The seventh-century saint Appar, like Manikkavachakar, wrote in Tamil and was a devotee of Shiva. (Note: the final four poems selected were written later than the first two and reflect the end of a stomach ailment which had afflicted him.)

1   Death, it has become; thou hast not banished it.
     I committed wrongs, many they were—I'm ignorant
     [O noble one,] thou didst shelter me at thy feet
     All the time, day and night, never apart, I pray to thee.
     Unseen, within my stomach, it holds and folds, my intestine too.
     I cannot bear it, I thy servant,
     O the presiding Lord of Tiruvatikai Viirattaanam.

2   I kept my heart for thee, thee alone.
     Never was I without thinking of thee.
     I know no deception matching this—
     Poison it has become, my stomach knots and twists;
     This thou didst neither destroy nor abort
     So it may not approach me.
     Thou didst not say, "Be not afraid,"
     O the presiding Lord of Tiruvatikai Viirattaanam.

3   I will come dancing in delight, with the beats now ringing, now pausing,
     I will come singing the praise of him—he who wears the
            crescent moon and flower grommet—and of her, the bejewelled wife.
     As I reached Ayyaaru, where flows the milky river,
            I witnessed the pretty koels, he with her, come in peace.
     [Now] I have been his holy feet; I have seen
            them, those that could not been seen.

4   I will sing the praise of him and her,
     He with the crescent moon and flower grommet, she in bangles rich.
     I pray fervently, my shoulders in tremors, showering fresh flowers of many
            a kind that the banks of the waters yield.

As I reached Ayyaaru, where koels hop and sing,
I witnessed the swans coming, he and she dancing along.
[Now] I have seen his holy feet; I have seen them, those that could
    not been seen.

5   I will sing the praise of him—he who wears the crescent moon
        and flower grommet—and of her, the bejewelled wife,
And I will dance and pray with folded hands to the woods, the country,
    and the hills.
And I reached Ayyaaru where he ever dances in delight,
    I witnessed the peacock coming joined to her.
[Now] I have seen his holy feet; I have seen them, those that could
    not been seen.

8   I will sing the praise of him and her—
    He with the coveted crescent and the flower grommet,
    She in all her tenderness.
I will rise before the dawn and come to thee with flowers in offering.
As I reached Ayyaaru, which carries along the precious stones and gold,
I witnessed the spotted buck and his doe in unison dancing along.
[Now] I have seen his holy feet; I have seen them, those that could
    not be seen.

(from Studies in Religion 8 [1979], 177–79)⁵¹ ▲

Kabir

Kabir (1440–1518) is an important devotional figure of North India. This work, written in Hindi, reflects Muslim as well as Hindu influences.

▼   O servant, where dost thou seek Me?
    Lo! I am beside thee
    I am neither in temple nor in mosque: I am neither in Kaaba nor in Kailash:
    Neither am I in rites and ceremonies, nor in yoga and renunciation.
    If thou art a true seeker, thou shalt at once see Me: thou shalt meet
        Me in a moment of time.
    Kabir says, "O Sadhu! God is the breath of all breath."

    It is needless to ask of a saint the caste to which he belongs;
    For the priest, the warrior, the tradesman, and all the thirty-six castes,
        alike are seeking for God.
    It is but folly to ask what the caste of a saint may be;
    The barber has sought God, the washerwoman, and the carpenter—
    Even Raidas was a seeker after God.
    The rishi Swapacha was a tanner by caste.

Hindus and Moslems alike have achieved that end, where remains
   no mark of distinction.

Tell me, O Swan, your ancient tale.
From what land do you come, O Swan? to what shore will you fly?
Where would you take your rest, O Swan, and what do you seek?
Even this morning, O Swan, awake, arise, follow me!
There is a land where no doubt nor sorrow have rule:
   where the terror of death is no more.
There the woods of spring are a bloom, and the fragrant scent "He is I"
   is borne or, the wind:
There the bee of the heart is deeply immersed, and desires no other joy.

O Lord Increate, who will serve Thee?
Every votary offers his worship to the God of his own creation:
   each day he receives service—
None seek Him, the perfect: Brahma, the indivisible Lord.
They believe in ten avatars; but no avatar can be the Infinite spirit,
   for he suffers the results of his deeds:
The supreme one must be other than this.
The yogi, the sannyasi, the ascetics, are disputing one with another:
Kabir says, "O brother! he who has seen the radiance of love, he is saved."

O brother! when I was forgetful, my true guru showed me the way.
Then I left off all rites and ceremonies, I bathed no more in the holy water:
Then I learned that it was I alone who was mad, and the whole world
   beside me was sane; and I had disturbed these wise people.
From that time forth I knew no more how to roll in the dust in obeisance:
I do not ring the temple bell:
I do not set the idol on its throne:
I do not worship the image with flowers.
It is not the austerities that mortify the flesh which are pleasing
   to the Lord,
When you leave off your clothes and kill your senses, you do not
   please the Lord:
The man who is kind and who practices righteousness, who remains
   passive amidst the affairs of the world, who considers all creatures
   on earth as his own self,
He attains the immortal being, the true God is ever with him.
Kabir says: "He attains the true name whose words are pure, and
   who is free from pride and conceit."

If God be within the mosque, then to whom does this world belong?
If Ram be within the image which you find upon your pilgrimage,

then who is there to know what happens without?
Han is in the East: Allah is in the West. Look within your heart,
    for there you will find both Karim and Ram;
All the men and women of the world are His living forms.
Kabir is the child of Allah and of Ram: He is my guru, He is my Pir.

                         (de Bary, *Sources*, 355–57)[52] ▲

Mirabai

Also writing in Hindi and from the north of India, the Rajput princess Mirabai (1503–1573) was a devotee of Krishna. She is one of several influential
female poet-saints.

4   O Hari! Thou art the support of my life!
    I have no other refuge but Thee
    In all the three worlds.
    Thou I have searched the whole universe,
    Nothing pleases me but Thou.
    Says Mira, "O Lord, I am Thy slave.
    Do not forget me."

5   Deign to favour me, O Hari,
    With the gift of a single glance.
    My gaze is ever fixed on Thee,
    But Thine is withdrawn.
    Hard indeed must be Thy heart.
    All my hopes are fixed
    On receiving a single glance;
    I have no other refuge whatever.
    I am standing before Thee in supplication,
    And behold! The dawn has come.
    Mira's Lord is Han, the indestructible.
    To Him would she sacrifice her life.

7   Sister, Shyam smiles
    And gazes at my body with His lustrous eyes.
    His eyebrows are the bow,
    And His side-long glances the arrows
    Which strike against my heart.
    Come, says my companion, heal thyself.
    See, I will draw a *yantra*
    And affix it to thy body;

I will crush herbs and bring them for Thee.
But if thou art smitten with the disease of love
Such remedies will not avail.
How can I heal myself, O my companion?
I may crush cool sandalpaste and apply it,
I may resort to the magic of *yantra* and mantra,
But that sweet image has entered my heart
And the damage is done.
Bring that dark-faced one before me,
I stand smiling in His expectation.
Pierce my body, look within
And see the broken fragments of my heart.
Without vision of her Lord Giridhara,
How can Mira continue to inhabit this house?

63   Without Hari, behold my wretched condition.
They say that Thou art my protector
And I Thy servant.
I have practised remembrance of Thy name
In my heart, day and night.
Again and again I call upon Thee,
In grievous affliction.
This world is a threatening sea,
Surrounding me on every side.
My boat has broken,
Hoist the sail quickly
Before it sinks.
This forlorn one waits anxiously for her Lord,
Grant her Thy proximity
Servant Mira repeats "Ram Ram!"
I take refuge in Thee alone.

66   Sister, Han will not speak to me,
Why does not my wretched breath
Abandon my body?
The night passed
And I neither removed my veil nor spoke,
An age has passed without converse,
How can I prosper in conditions like this?
I heard that Han would come in the rainy season.
The nights were thick with darkness,
Lightning flashed

And I would count the hours till dawn.
Servant Mira is dyed in the love of Shyam:
Her whole life passes in longing.

67   I am invaded by memories
Of the conduct of the supremely affectionate Krishna.
Krishna belongs to me
And I belong to Him:
Without Him, nothing pleases me.
He said He would come but has not appeared,
My heart is deeply distraught,
My only desire, O Krishna,
Is to enjoy vision of Thee.
When will Han grant me His holy sight?
Deep is my love for those lotus feet,
And without His sight I suffer greatly.
When Mira's Lord grants her His sight
Her joy will be beyond description.

68   My darling Beloved has gone abroad.
My lost one has not returned
Or even sent me a message.
I have put off my jewellery
And shaved my hair.
For Thy sake have I donned the orange robe
And gone forth searching the four quarters.
Say Mira: O my Lord Shyam,
Unless I can be with Thee,
My birth and life are but an affliction.

69   O my companion,
Without Shyam I cannot survive.
Charmed by Thy beauty, O my Beloved,
I offer Thee my body, mind and life.
I have lost all appetite for food and drink
And my eyes have gone dim.
O Murari, day and night
I dream of meeting Thee,
When shall I have Thy sight?
Days and nights pass
As I call upon Thee.
Says Mira: O Hari,
Without Thee my life flickers feebly on.

70 I am mad with love
  And no one understands my plight.
  Only the wounded
  Understand the agonies of the wounded,
  When a fire rages in the heart
  Only the jeweller knows the value of the jewel,
  Not the one who lets it go.
  In pain I wandered from door to door
  But could not find a doctor.
  Says Mira: Harken, my Master,
  Mira's pain will subside
  When Shyam comes as the doctor.

(A.J. Alston, *The Devotional Poems of Mirabai*,
Nos. 4, 5, 7, 63, 66–70)[53] ▲

Hindu Ethics and Dharma

Having concluded our reading of the devotional poet-saints with the female voice of Mirabai, it is fitting that when we move to a consideration of ethics and *dharma* (the way Hindus live), it is to a leading Hindu scholar of today that we turn. Professor Narayanan is not only a leading scholar, she is also a mother, wife, and one who, in her own life, remains traditional while at the same time being fully modern. This she accomplishes through her sensitive reading of the ethics, or *dharma*, texts and her living of them in daily life as a North American Hindu woman of the twenty-first century.

Hindu Ethics and Dharma—Vasudha Narayanan[54]

Although scholars have, in general, assumed that the word "religion" is a suitable term to describe the Hindu tradition,[55] it is commonly agreed that there is no category in Hindu thought and literature which is an exact fit for "ethics." The general perception is that there is no formal discipline in Hinduism which has "an internally consistent rational system in which patterns of human conduct are justified with reference to ultimate norms and values."[56] This does not mean that Hindus did not know about ethics or that they were immoral; it is simply that there is no discipline in Indian thought directly congruent with "ethics," just as there is no Western area of inquiry which matches the Hindu category of *dharma*. Many articles and books have been written on Hindu ethics, but by and large they deal with selected aspects of what Hindus call *dharma*.[57]

Hindus today use the word *dharma* (from the root *dhr*, "to sustain, to uphold") to refer to religion, ethics, and moral behaviour in general and to their religion in particular. The term *Santana dharma* (the eternal or perennial *dharma*) has been used to designate the Hindu tradition as a whole in the last two centuries. Indeed Buddhists, Jains, and Hindus all use the term *dharma* to indicate a wide variety of concepts and issues, and the word has some recognition in the Western world as well. In the last two centuries, the texts on *dharma* also formed the basis for formulating the administration of law in India.

As is true with most concepts and words, the meaning of *dharma* depends on the context; further, there have been changes in emphasis over the centuries. The Monier–Williams Sanskrit–English dictionary gives about seventeen meanings: *dharma* means religion; the customary observances of a caste, sect, etc.; law usage; practice; religious or moral merit; virtue; righteousness; duty; justice; piety; morality; sacrifice; and more. When used as a name, Dharma may refer to Yudhishthira, one of the Pandava brothers in the epic story of *Mahabharata*, or to Yama, his father. Yama, the god associated most commonly with death today, was known as the presiding deity of *dharma*.

This preliminary set of meanings gives us some indication of the parameters of the concept and practice of *dharma*. The word *dharma* appears in the early vedic texts several times. In many later contexts, it means "religious ordinances and rites," and in others it refers to "fixed principles or rules of conduct." In conjunction with other words, *dharma* also means "merit acquired by the performance of religious rites" and "the whole body of religious duties." Eventually, the predominant meaning of *dharma* came to be "the privileges, duties and obligations of a man [or woman], his [or her] standard of conduct as a member of the Aryan community, as a member of one of the castes, as a person in a particular stage of life."[58] Texts on *dharma* both described and prescribed these duties and responsibilities and divided up the subject matter into various categories.

Dharma is said to deal with behaviour, justice, and repentance/atonement rites. Other classifications are more elaborate. Pandurang Kane, the pre-eminent writer of the history of *dharma* in the twentieth century, starts his second volume on the subject with "The Topics of *Dharmashastra*." He cites dozens of traditional books on *dharma* and proceeds to list the domains of this concept. His list covers about twenty-four topics and includes the duties of the classes/castes of society; the sacraments from conception to death; the days when one should not study the *Vedas*; marriage; the duties of women; the relationship between husband and wife; ritual purity and impurity; rituals for ancestors; gifts and donations; crime and punishment; contacts; inheritance; activities done only at times of crises; mixed castes; and more. If one goes through the texts carefully, one will also find discussions on the geographic areas of the world most fit for a human being to lead a righteous and meritorious life (i.e., northern India), and on charity and humanitarian and ecological concerns. Although this list is extensive, it does not exhaust the other areas that the term *dharma* covers. It is obvious that the areas and concerns of what is deemed to be righteous behaviour in the Hindu tradition do not fit closely with Western notions of ethics. With abundant caution, then, we begin our discussion of *dharma*, with full cognizance that it intersects with ethics but does not purport to parallel that discipline.

Further caveats are in order. This survey is not in any way exhaustive. Ideally, a study of *dharma* and righteousness that pays attention to some Western academic concerns as well as to Indian categories would look at *dharma* in connection with human accountability and responsibility, free will, *karma*, individual and social justice, cycles of time, divine grace, and liberation from the cycle of life and death—but a brief survey cannot do justice to these categories. Second, although several Sanskrit texts are examined here—texts that are the *locus classicus* of *dharma*—one must be aware that these were aimed only at high-caste brahmanic males. In many parts and communities of India, these texts were not held as normative, and vernacular texts and local customs vied with dharmic texts for attention. Finally, with regard to areas in which correct behaviour is important, Hindus have been particularly concerned with ritual purity and impurity and with auspiciousness and inauspiciousness. In philosophy and in the ordering of Hindus' lives, the two categories that have had overriding importance are *dharma* and liberation (*moksha*).

Sources of Dharma

The earliest texts on *dharma* are the *Dharma Sutras*. These are part of the *Kalpa Sutras,* which are considered to be an ancillary to the *Vedas*. Thus, the earliest and pre-eminent source for *dharma*, at least in theory if not in practice, is considered to be the vedic corpus. In addition to these texts, many treatises on the nature of righteousness, moral duty, and law had been written by the first centuries CE. This corpus of texts, known as *dharma shastras*, contains the most famous works on *dharma,* and they form the basis for later Hindu laws. Among these the *Manava Dharmasastra*, or the *Laws of Manu*, is the most well known and was probably codified around the first century CE, reflecting the social norms of that time.

The *Laws of Manu*, along with some other texts, lists the foundations for our understanding of *dharma*. *Manu* 2:6 lists these as the *Vedas* (*shruti*); the epics, *puranas,* and other *smriti* literature; the behaviour and practices of the good people (*sadachara*); and the promptings of one's mind or conscience. Variations of this list are found in the earliest texts on *dharma* as well.[59] Although these texts deal with common topics, they vary in their opinions and provide plenty of room for interpretation. Since these rule books were written by *brahman* men for other *brahman* men (a very small but influential percentage of society that considered itself the elite), they were by no means followed widely. Norms differed all over India according to caste, area, region, gender, and age.

Far better known than the treatises on *dharma* is the narrative literature of the epics and the *puranas* ("ancient lore"). Hindus in India and the diaspora know the epics (the *Ramayana* and the *Mahabharata*) and *puranas*, and they understand stories from these texts as exemplifying values of *dharma* and as situations presenting dharmic dilemmas. Rama, the hero of the *Ramayana*, followed his filial path and went into exile; Sita is the paradigm of *stri* (womanly) *dharma*, and so on. The people of these epics are exemplary paradigms to be imitated or avoided. Also influential are the collections of folk tales both in Sanskrit and in the vernacular. Many times the vernacular tales challenge and even subvert the value system found in the Sanskrit works. However, there is a consensus in all these texts that this span of time during which we are living—this span of 432,000 years known as the *kali yuga*—is the worst possible time for *dharma*.

Ages of Time

The *puranas* composed through the first millennium CE speak about cycles of creation and destruction of the cosmos. These cycles are known as the days and nights of Brahma, the creator god. During each of his days, the creator god brings out the universe periodically and withdraws it into himself. These days of Brahma are divided into many cycles of great eons, which are in turn divided into four *yugas*, or eons. A single one of these eons is the basic cycle. The *krita*, or golden age, lasts 4,800 divine years (1,728,000 human or earthly years). During this time, *dharma* is on a firm footing. To use traditional animal imagery, *dharma*, or righteousness, stands on all four legs. The *treat* age is shorter, lasting 3,600 god years, that is, 1,296,000 earthly years; at this time *dharma* is on three legs. The *dvapara* age lasts half as long as the golden age; it is 2,400 god years long (864,000 earthly years), and *dharma* is now hopping on two legs. During the *kali yuga*, the worst of all possible ages, *dharma* is on one leg, and things get progressively worse. This age lasts for 1,200 god years (432,000 earthly years). We live in this degenerate *kali yuga*, which, according to traditional Hindu reckoning, began around 3102 BCE.

There is a steady decline through the *yugas* in morality, righteousness, life span, and human satisfaction. At the end of the *kali yuga*—still a long time away—there will be no righteousness, no virtue, no trace of justice. When the world ends, seven scorching suns will dry up the oceans. There will be wondrously shaped clouds, torrential rains will fall, and eventually the cosmos will be absorbed into Vishnu. We must keep in mind, however, that although, according to many Hindu systems of thought, it is entirely possible for a human being to end his or her cycle of birth and death through transforming wisdom and/or through devotion, the cycles of creation and destruction of the universe are independent of the human being's attainment of liberation from the cycle of life and death. Regardless of individual morality and *dharma*, we should keep in mind this big picture of the general atrophy of righteousness and moral behaviour in this worst age as we discuss the topic.

Specific *Dharma* and "Universal" or Common *Dharma*

"satyam vada, dharmam chara"
("Speak the Truth; be on the path of righteousness")
—*Taittriya Upanishad*

Dharma is not homogeneous. Some virtues and behaviour patterns are recommended for all human beings, whereas others are incumbent according to one's caste in society, stage of life, and gender. Many Hindus in the nineteenth and twentieth centuries have emphasized what has been called the common (*samanya*, or *sadharana*) *dharma* for all human beings—what some call the "universal" *dharma*. The epics speak of this universal *dharma* as the *sanatana*, or eternal *dharma*. The following are typical examples of virtues that all human beings should have:

> Remembering a good deed and returning it with another; this is *sanatana dharma*.[60]

> Lack of enmity to all beings in thought word and deed; compassion and charity are the eternal *dharma* of the good.[61]

The ultimate importance of eight virtues is extolled in Gautama's *Dharma Sutra*, one of the earliest texts on *dharma*. These are compassion to all creatures, patience, lack of envy, purification, tranquility, having an auspicious disposition, generosity, and lack of greed. A person with these qualities may not have performed all sacraments but will still reach the ultimate goal of being with Brahman, the supreme being.[62] There are many such lists in the texts on *dharma*, and the individual virtues are also illustrated in the epic narratives.

Although these virtues and recommendations for behaviour are considered to be common to all human beings, the texts on *dharma* emphasize the specific behaviour enjoined upon people of the four major castes and upon males who are in the various stages of life. There is also considerable discussion of women's duties (*stridharma*). The longest discussions focus on marriages, death rituals, food laws, and caste regulations.

Food Regulations [63]

Right eating is not just a matter of what one can eat or should avoid; in the texts on *dharma* as well as in orthoprax houses, it involves issues like the caste and gender of the cook (preferably male and high caste, or the lady of the house, except when she is menstruating); the times one may eat (twice a day, not during twilight times, eclipses, or a wide variety of other occasions); not eating food cooked the day before; and so on. In earlier times, other directives were also in vogue. In attention to detail, some of these regulations equal or even surpass those given in many legal texts of other traditions. The order of food courses in a meal; the direction in which the diner must sit (preferably facing east or north); how much one may eat (the number of morsels depends on the stage of life); the materials out of which the eating vessels should be made; what is to be done with leftover food—are all topics for discussion, and many of these directives and more have been followed for centuries.

There were several strict rules regarding with whom one may dine (best to dine alone!). Silence was recommended for the time of dining except to inquire about a guest's needs. Most texts said—and this was followed until probably the mid-twentieth century—that one may dine only with people of the same caste and with people one knew. It was believed in many circles that one shares the sins of the people with whom one dines—especially if one sits in a single row with them. Through the centuries, we see Hindus from many communities visiting shrines of other religious traditions; but many seldom ate with anyone other than their own caste and community. Even until the time of India's independence (when there was a general effort to introduce more "socialistic" and "democratic" practices such as inter-dining), college food services in the hostels (dormitories) in South India were divided along simplified caste lines; most commonly seen were the dining halls for *brahmans*, with separate ones for non-*brahman* (vegetarian) and non-*brahman* (non-vegetarian).

The greatest amount of space in *dharma shastra* discussions of right eating is spend on forbidden foods, which varied between different time periods and between authors. It is generally agreed that most people ate meat, even beef, possibly up to the beginning of the Common Era. It is a matter of some controversy whether Indians ate beef during the time of the *Vedas* and whether the cow was a protected animal; however, it seems to be fairly well accepted that most Indians ate other kinds of meat and fowl then. It is remarkable that a whole culture seems to have slowly given up eating meat—

or at least that it ceased to be the norm after the first centuries of the Common Era. During these centuries, *ahimsa*, or nonviolence, became normative in the many texts on *dharma*.

Varna-Ashrama Dharma

Although there are common virtues that all human beings should have, the texts on *dharma* speak of context-specific *dharma* that is incumbent on the different classes or castes of society (*varna*). The texts say that male members of the upper three castes—the priestly *brahmans*, the rulers, and the merchants—should ideally go through four stages (*ashrama*) of life. The behaviour recommended for each caste and each stage of life is called *varna-ashrama dharma*. The responsibility to behave thus is called *sva* (self) *dharma*. Whenever books describe the decline of the social order in the world, they refer to the abandoning of the duties that are incumbent on one by virtue of one's station in life.

The word "caste" (derived from a Portuguese word to mean a division in society) is used as a shorthand term to refer to thousands of stratified and boundaried social communities that have multiplied through the centuries. The beginnings of the caste system is seen in the "Hymn to the Supreme Person" in the *Rig Veda*, with its enumeration of priestly, ruling, mercantile, and servant classes. From this simple fourfold structure eventually arose a plethora of endogamous social and occupational divisions. The texts on *dharma* specify the names of various subcastes that come from marriages between the various classes. There are more than one thousand *jatis* ("birth groups") in India. Ritual practices, dietary rules, and sometimes dialects differ among the castes.

Deviation from caste practices in past centuries sometimes resulted in one's being excluded from the caste. *Brahmans* were supposed to learn and teach the *Vedas*. The monopoly that they exercised in teaching the *Vedas* orally was jealously guarded, and for centuries these hymns were not written down. The *kshatriya* ("royal") class was the one from which kings and rulers emerged. The men from this community were allowed to learn but not teach the *Vedas*, and their *dharma* was to protect the people and the country. Arjuna, the hero of the *Bhagavad Gita*, is from this class. One famous text is a conversation between the warrior Arjuna and his cousin Krishna, an incarnation of Vishnu who is considered here to be the supreme being).[64] When Krishna urges Arjuna to do his *dharma*, he is reminding him of the duties incumbent on him by virtue of his birth. The mercantile class (*vaishyas*) was in charge of most commercial transactions. According to the codes of law, they, like the ruling class, had the authority to study but not teach the *Vedas*. They were to rear cattle, trade, and deal with agricultural work. The last class mentioned formally in the *dharma shastra* is the *shudras*, a term that has generally been translated as servants." The *dharma shastras* say that the duty of a *shudra* is to serve the other classes, especially the *brahmans*. The *Laws of Manu* and the *Bhagavad Gita* tell us that it is better to do one's own *dharma* imperfectly than to do another's well. However, the law books acknowledge that in times of adversity, one may do other tasks, and they list these in order of preference for each class.

Despite these textual injunctions, Manu's advice was apparently not followed in many parts of India. The caste system is far more complex and flexible than the *dharma shastra* descriptions. The Vellalas of South India, for instance, were technically considered a *shudra* caste, but they wielded considerable economic and political power as a wealthy caste of landowners, and the *dharma shastra* prohibitions against *shudras* owning land do not seem to have had any effect on their fortunes. We will see soon that custom and tradition seem to override the literature of the *dharma* texts.

Although these codes of law emphasize the importance of marrying within one's own caste, they recognize that mixed marriages take place quite often, and so go on to list the kinds of subcastes that emerge from various permutations. A marriage is generally acceptable if the male partner is of a higher caste. However, if a woman is higher, the offspring is considered to be of a lower caste than either parent. The Indian caste system is not a feature of the Hindu tradition alone. It is such a strong social force that non-Hindu communities such as the Christians, Jains, and Sikhs have absorbed parts of it. Nadar Christians from the south, for instance, will marry only people of the same heritage, and one may draw similar parallels all over India.

The code of Manu also contains prescriptions of criminal law, in which the punishment frequently varied with the castes of both the offender and the victim. The gravity of the crime and how heinous the sin was considered to be were dependent on the castes of the perpetrator and the victim. The lower castes faced harsher punishments for the same crime than the higher castes, according to this text. But one is not sure whether these prescriptions were followed and enforced. Scholars have shown that the *Laws of Manu* had limited import, that in fact the law was mitigated by learned people, and each case was decided with reference to the immediate circumstances. It was only in the nineteenth century, after the establishment of British rule, that the *Laws of Manu* and other texts received more attention than they had commanded in the previous centuries. The British assumed that these laws were binding, when in fact they had been only one factor among many considerations in the judicial process.

In addition to caste, the texts of law recognized four stages of life, called the four *ashramas*, for males of the upper three castes of society, each with different dharmic responsibilities. First, a young boy was initiated into the stage of a student, and during his student years he was to remain celibate and to concentrate on learning. Although in the earlier vedic literature there is some evidence that girls could also become students, it is probable that by the time of Manu in the first century CE this right had been withdrawn. After being a student, a young man was to get married and to repay his debt to society and his ancestors and his spiritual debt to the gods. He earned a living to support his family and other students. Whereas it was a student's *dharma* not to work for a living and to remain celibate, a householder's *dharma* was to be employed and to lead a conjugal life with his partner in *dharma* (*saha-dharmacharini*). Probably most men never went beyond these two stages, and even the first may have been of a cursory nature for some. The *Laws of Manu*, however, gives details of two more stages—those of a forest dweller and an ascetic. When a man sees his skin wrinkled and his hair gray, says Manu, when he sees his grandchildren (that is, when his children have reached the householder stage and become the economic pillars of society), he may retire to the forest with his wife, lead a simple life, and spend his time in reciting the *Vedas* and in quietude.

The final stage, *sannyasa*, was entered by very few. A man apparently staged his own social death and became an ascetic. His old personality was now dead. The ascetic owned nothing, living off the food given as alms and eating but once a day. He was to spend his time pursuing salvific knowledge and cultivating detachment from life. However, with the increasing popularity of the *Bhagavad Gita*, which stresses detached action even while a person lives in the thick of society, the need to enter formally into the life of a reclusive renunciant was diminished considerably in the Hindu tradition. Still, Sanskrit and vernacular texts on *dharma* extol the importance of becoming an ascetic (*sannyasi*). Indeed, in India one does see such ascetics in ochre or saffron clothes. And though the texts on *dharma* specify that only male members of the upper three classes of society have the right to become ascetics, we shall see that this was sometimes challenged. When a man enters this stage of life, he is considered to be socially dead and is formally disassociated from all his relationships. He is now religiously (and legally, today) a new person without connections.

Text and Practice

It is important to note that the texts on *dharma* were frequently superseded by local practices. Let us consider just one question: can a member of the fourth class, i.e., a *shudra*, become a renunciant? This question was debated by the Supreme Court of India. According to the classical texts of *dharma*, only men of the upper three classes could go through all the four stages of life. *Shudras* and women are usually lumped together in one low category, even for apparently trivial issues. For instance, according to Manu, men of the upper classes will sip water three times to purify themselves, but women and *shudras* should sip water only once (Manu 5:139). Despite these statements, *shudra* ascetics are seen in the tradition of the theologian Ramanuja (eleventh century) and in many Shaiva orders in South India.

When one *shudra*, traditionally barred from becoming an ascetic, became one, the validity of his action was legally challenged in the case of *Krishna Singh v. Mathura Ahir* (AIR 1980 SC 707; 1980 ALL LJ 299) over a question of the inheritance of some property. It was alleged that a *shudra* cannot become an ascetic, and so the property of the *shudra sannyasi* in question should devolve to the natural relatives and not to the spiritual community. This issue was debated in the High Court of Allahabad and then went all the way up to the Supreme Court of India. In a landmark decision in this case, the Supreme Court of India made it clear that though the orthodox view does not allow *shudras* to become *sannyasis*, the existing practice in India is contrary to such a view and that at the present time a Hindu of any caste can adopt the life of a *sannyasi*. It was further declared that where according to custom or usage a *shudra* can enter a religious order, such usage will be recognized and the ban on *shudras* becoming *sannyasis* stands abrogated by virtue of the mandates embodied in Part III of the Constitution of India.[65]

Because such issues as becoming a renunciant are, for Hindus, governed by personal law, which is derived from Hindu texts, one can reflect on the formal authority of the *dharma* literature and legal commentaries. In *Krishna Singh v. Mathura Ahir*, the Supreme Court observed, "In applying Personal Laws of the parties [the judge] could not introduce his concept of modern times, but should have enforced the law as derived from recognized authority sources of Hindu Law, i.e., *smritis* [texts on *dharma*] and commentaries referred to and interpreted in various judgements of the High Courts except where such law is altered by usage or custom as modified or abrogated by statue."[66]

What the Supreme Court of India declared here is very important. The Court articulated an understanding that has been applied all over the country for centuries: although the *dharma* and legal texts are important, local custom and tradition are even more important. When dispensing justice, kings and other rulers traditionally favoured custom over texts. What it is necessary to prove is that the usage has been acted upon in practice for such a long period and with such invariability as to show that it has by common consent been submitted to as the established governing rule of the district concerned. The diversity of the Hindu traditions, rather than the uniform straitjacket of a dharmic text, is showcased in this context. The Supreme Court asserted that indeed a *shudra* could become a *sannyasi*, and therefore the natural relatives could not be his heirs.

We see the importance of custom over text in other areas as well. Although the texts on *dharma* state several times that a woman is dependent on male relatives, we see that women in many areas of India, especially if they were from the so-called "lower castes," exercised considerable independence. Many women have donated money to charitable institutions and to temples in their own name, as the many hundreds of temple inscriptions attest.[67] Although *Brahman* widows seldom remarried in most areas of India, the custom was quite prevalent in parts of Gujarat.[68] The notion of what was right and wrong, therefore, was not just incumbent on scriptural injunctions but also on local practice and custom.

Moral Paradigms

Many stories in the *puranas* do not make a direct correlation between goodness of character and piety. The *puranas* are filled with stories of demon men and women who show intense devotion to a deity and practice severe austerities to receive certain divine favours. Such favours may include being invulnerable to death at the hands of human beings or beasts, long life, etc. Having received these favours, the characters then terrorize human beings. A typical story is that of Mahisha, a buffalo demon, who had practised austerities and received a divine boon that he would not be killed by a man or a god. He proceeded to ravage the earth and was eventually destroyed by a *woman* deity—one of the categories of people he did not seek to be protected from when he got his original boon from the gods. Although stories such as these do not relate ethical behaviour with devotion to a deity, we will soon see the connection between devotion and liberation.

Epic narratives and *puranas* in the Hindu tradition do portray other characters who have served as moral exemplars for centuries. As in any other culture, characters are selectively chosen and held as moral ideals. Rama, the great hero of the *Ramayana* and an incarnation of the deity Vishnu, is considered to be one such person. He is hailed as the paragon of virtue and as one who struggles to lead a dharmic life. Many of Rama's actions are taken at face value—thus, he is an ideal son who obeys his father and goes into exile, an ideal husband who loves his wife Sita, and an ideal monarch. The other characters in the *Ramayana* are also said to embody behaviour that is to be followed or shunned; thus one is to emulate the fraternal affection seen between Rama and his brothers and not the wrath that Vali shows to his brother Sugriva. Ravana, the demon king of Lanka, has many virtues; yet his lust for Sita causes his downfall. Similarly, in the *Mahabharata*, Yudhishthira, who is the embodiment of *dharma* itself, has one weakness—a penchant for gambling.

On the other hand, Krishna, another incarnation of Vishnu, is understood to be one whose actions were right for him but not for others. Although there is a popular saying, *krishnam dharman sanatanam* (Krishna's *dharma* is eternal), he is not held as one whose behaviour is to be followed. It is Krishna's advice, especially that given in the *Bhagavad Gita*, which is to be followed, not his actions. One way of interpreting stories of Krishna is to understand them as having a symbolic, spiritual value; thus his dancing the moonlit night away with the many cowherd girls is said to portray the relationship between the human being and the deity. The Hindu use of multiple interpretive strategies like these was frequently missed by outside scholars in earlier centuries, leading to misperceptions of Hindu ethics and allegations of apparent lack of morality in the Hindu tradition.

Hindus have wrestled with many ethical issues over the centuries. The caste system is one issue that has frequently been questioned and which is subverted in folk tales and in hagiographic narratives. Whereas early and popular understanding of caste connect it to being born in a particular family, some conversations in the *Mahabharata* link caste to human character and propensity and not to biological birth. Interpretations given by A.C. Prabhupada, the founder of the International Society for Krishna Consciousness (the "Hara Krishna" movement) in the West, follow this line of reasoning.

Stories like Rama's treatment of his wife Sita in the *Ramayana* have also troubled some Hindus. Rama's behaviour is paradigmatic, as we saw earlier, yet there are one or two instances that have been grist for multiple interpretations in the last two millennia. Although Rama shows his love for Sita in most of the narrative, toward the end a question is raised about her chastity. Sita has been held captive by Ravana, and after an epic battle Rama has rescued her. He now feigns disinterest toward her, and Sita, saddened by his behaviour, steps into fire. The god of fire returns her unharmed as proof of her chastity, but women have seen this as a paradigmatic instance of the victim being blamed. There have been many interpretations of this story, with questions about and rationalizations of Rama's behaviour. Not all of them are orthodox; nevertheless, this dynamic continuous tradition of interpretation has kept these questions alive and the epic ethics flourishing for centuries.

Dharma and Liberation

Dharma is one of the main categories of Hindu life and thought; *moksha* (or liberation) is another. However, though *dharma* in many contexts focuses on order in this world, *moksha* leads one away from existence in this world. *Dharma* frequently refers to actions that promote righteousness, order, and well-being in this world; the realms of monetary success and power encompassed by the term *artha*, as well as the sensual love denoted by *kama*, are also of this world. *Moksha*, on the other hand, generally refers to liberation from the cycle of life and death and is otherworldly in character.

Many texts and theologies have, however, seen *moksha* and *dharma* as part of the same continuum. The *Bhagavad Gita* makes it clear that if one does one's *dharma*, that is, perform one's daily work without any attachment to the reward, it will lead to liberation. Is there a connection between *dharma* and *moksha*, or are they fundamentally opposed to each other, pointing in different directions and having different aims? Books on *dharma* say that one is to be married at a certain age, beget children (especially sons), perform acts of righteousness and ritual actions, and so on. However, to obtain liberation, one is advised to be detached from all of these worldly actions. Scholars such as Daniel Ingalls and J.A.B. van Buitenen have offered different opinions on whether *dharma* and *moksha* are part of a continuum or are like parallel lines that never meet.[69]

The word *dharma*, as we saw at the beginning of this essay, has many meanings; in some contexts *dharma* is, indeed, considered a path to liberation. Although some injunctions of *dharma* are directed to worldly order, others seem to lead away from it, toward liberation. In a famous liturgical work called the *Thousand Names of Vishnu* (*Vishnu Sahasranama*), the protagonist, Yudhishthira asks, "What is that *dharma* that you consider to be highest of all?" Bhishma, the elderly statesman to whom this question has been addressed, answers, "The best among all *dharmas* is to have devotion to the Lord whose eyes are like lotus flowers [Vishnu] and praise his qualities." Devotion to the deity has been seen as a way to liberation, and the classical text that speaks extensively about this is the *Bhagavad Gita*. This text also deals with unselfish action as the ideal action. In the course of the *Bhagavad Gita*, Krishna describes three ways to liberation (or, as some Hindus believe, three aspects of one way to liberation) from the cycle of births and death: (1) the way of action; (2) the way of knowledge; and (3) the way of devotion. Each way (*marga*) is spoken of also as a discipline (*yoga*).

The way of action (*karma yoga*) entails the path of unselfish action; one must do one's duty, but it should not be done either for fear of punishment or in the hope of reward. The right action should be done without expectation of praise or blame. For example, one is to study or do good acts because it is correct to do so—because it is one's duty (*dharma*) to do so, not because other people will reward and praise one for it.

Acting with expectation of future reward leads to bondage and unhappiness. On one level, such actions instigate further action and thus further *karma* is incurred, for one is never satisfied when one reaches a goal. One may long for a promotion, for more money, or to be loved by a particular person, and when one acts with these goals in mind, one may meet with disappointment and react with anger or grief. Even if one is temporarily successful, the goal that has been reached is replaced with another. Thus the thirst for material success is never quenched. Instead, one succeeds only in accumulating more *karma*, which leads to further rebirth.

Indeed, on one level (according to other books of the Gita's time), even the *karma* one gets from performing good deeds is ultimately bad and causes bondage because to enjoy the good *karma* one has to be reborn. A later Hindu philosopher calls good *karma* "golden handcuffs." Therefore, one is to act according to one's *dharma*, but Krishna urges Arjuna to act without any attachment to the consequences. Evil will not touch such a person, just as water does not stick to a lotus leaf. All actions are to be offered to Krishna. By discarding the fruits of one's action, one attains abiding peace.

The third way is the most emphasized throughout the *Bhagavad Gita*: the way of devotion (*bhakti yoga*). If there is a general amnesty program offered to those who sin, those who have a karmic overload, it is through the way of devotion:

> Even if a sinful person adores me with exclusive devotion
> He must be regarded as righteous...
> Quickly his soul becomes righteous and
> He gets eternal peace...
> My devotee is never lost.
>
> (*Bhagavad Gita* 9:30–1)

In verses like these, it is implied that by divine grace a sinful person becomes virtuous.

Ultimately, Krishna makes his promise to Arjuna: if one surrenders to the Lord, he will forgive the human being all sins:

> Letting go all *dharma*, take refuge in me alone;
> I shall deliver you from all sins; do not grieve.
>
> (*Bhagavad Gita* 18:66)

In this context, *dharma* is interpreted as ritual actions or as actions of atonement. Others interpret it as the fruit of one's action; giving them up is said to lead one to the highest good. These are held to be almost the last words of the *Bhagavad Gita*, and thus the ultimate teaching of this work.

New Reproductive Technology and the Hindu Tradition

How do we move from such understandings of *dharma* and *moksha* to the ethical dilemmas of new reproductive technology? Not only are the ethical issues surrounding reproductive technology still being debated, but some of their basic logic may at first seem to run contrary to the *smriti* literature dealing with *dharma*. Books on *dharma* written about two thousand years ago by Manu and others emphasized the importance of married couples having children. Many Hindus today accept advances in reproductive technology, such as artificial insemination, as a means toward this goal. Since considerable importance is placed on biological descent, the husband is generally the only acceptable donor. Sperm banks as a source are sometimes rejected by "higher" castes, who value the perceived purity of their lineage. For similar reasons, adoption of an unknown child may be unacceptable for caste-conscious Hindus.

The Hindu epics and *puranas* offer stories about supernatural means of conception and giving birth. In the *Mahabharata*, a hundred embryos are grown in separate containers by a queen called Gandhari. In other texts, an embryo is transplanted from one woman to another; Krishna's brother Balarama is transplanted into another womb when still in an embryonic stage. Divine potions are consumed, and children are born miraculously. Deities are invoked to fertilize the woman if the husband cannot procreate. Even though these tales that could legitimate the new reproductive technologies are generally not invoked, the technologies seem to have been accepted easily.

What about abortion? In ancient India, society was patrilineal and patriarchal. By having male children, one was fulfilling one's obligations to one's forefathers. In time, wedding gifts to a daughter became a significant financial burden. Because of both these factors, male children were more welcome in many Hindu families. Though abortions are done for a number of reasons, a growing recent trend has appeared related to sex selection. Sonograms and amniocentesis are performed to ascertain the sex of the unborn, and female fetuses are aborted. Statistics available from many parts of India, for instance, show that in recent years there has been a dramatic drop in the number of live births of girls.

According to the texts on *dharma*, the unborn fetus has life. According to popular belief and stories from the *puranas*, the fetus is even capable of hearing conversations that take place around it and learning from them. Thus, according to popular belief and the texts on *dharma*, the fetus is an entity. One would logically think, then, that terminating its life would be ethically reprehensible according to the texts on *dharma*; yet abortions are conducted legally in India. Laws permitting abortion were enacted and accepted without any strong dissent from religious leaders or prolonged editorial, legislative, or judicial debate. Thus, despite the *dharma* texts' vehemence in condemning abortion, and despite notions of embryonic life, *karma*, and so on, decisions about abortions are less likely to be made according to scriptural injunctions than according to how much a child, particularly a female child, is wanted by the couple.

The religio-legal texts that condemn the willful killing of a fetus have very limited bearing on daily life. Many Hindus are not even aware of the *dharmasastras'* pronouncements, and many who are so aware apparently find it easy to ignore them. In order words, the *dharma* texts simply have not had the compelling authority that religious law has had in some other religious traditions. Just as there were selective ways in which the caste system played out in Hindu societies through the centuries, despite the rigid pronouncements of the texts on the duties of each caste, birth technologies have been used selectively by Hindus.

Hindu *dharma*, thus, has been and continues to be a dynamic tradition, reinventing itself constantly, but within certain parameters. As in any other tradition, incongruous practices may exist side by side. The same rocket scientist who works with NASA may also be doing ancestral rituals on new moon days; the woman who utilizes new reproductive technology may also have ritually purifying baths after every menstruation. In transmitting and adapting the old and in assimilating the new, the tradition lives up to its name of the eternal or *sanatana dharma*.

Vasudha Narayanan teaches Hinduism at the University of Florida, Gainesville, where she lives with her husband and children. She recently served as president of the American Academy of Religion.

Notes

1 J.A.B. van Buitenen, "Hindu Sacred Literature," in *Encyclopedia Britannica*, 15th ed., 932–33.
2 Ibid., 936.
3 Wendy Donigen O'Flaherty, trans., *The Rig Veda: An Anthology* (1981; rpt. Middlesex, UK: Penguin, 1983), 25–26.
4 Ibid., 30–31.
5 Ibid., 35–36.
6 Ibid., 43–45.
7 Ibid., 49–50.
8 Ibid., 57–58.
9 Ibid., 66–67.
10 Ibid., 89–92.
11 Ibid., 99.
12 Ibid., 149–51.
13 Ibid., 213–14.

14 van Buitenen, "Hindu Sacred Literature," 936.

15 Wm. Theodore de Bary, ed., *Sources of Indian Tradition*, 1 (New York: Columbia University Press, 1958), 16.

16 Ibid., 17.

17 van Buitenen, "Hindu Sacred Literature," 936.

18 de Bary, *Sources*, 19–20.

19 Julius Eggeling, trans., The Satapatha-Brahmana, part 1, *Sacred Books of the East*, 12 (1882; rpt., Delhi: Motilal Banarsidass, 1972), 322–27.

20 David R. Kinsley, *Hinduism: A Cultural Perspective* (Englewood Cliffs, NJ: Prentice-Hall, 1982), 14–15.

21 de Bary, *Sources*, 24–25.

22 Robert Ernest Hume, trans., *The Thirteen Principal Upanishads* (2nd rev. ed.; 1877; rpt., Madras: Oxford University Press, 1968), 107–109.

23 Ibid., 111–12.

24 Ibid., 112–13.

25 Ibid., 113–14.

26 Ibid., 114–17.

27 Ibid., 117–19.

28 Ibid., 254–57. The progression continues through memory, hope, life-breath, truth, thought, faith, activity, pleasure, and plenum until the soul, or self (*atman*), is reached in the Twenty-sixth Khanda.

29 Ibid., 240–41.

30 Ibid., 246–49.

31 Ibid., 391–93.

32 Ibid., 409–11.

33 Ibid., 399–400.

34 Ibid., 362–63.

35 de Bary, *Sources*, 212–13.

36 van Buitenen, "Hindu Sacred Literature," 938–39.

37 G. Ehler, trans., The *Laws of Manu*, Sacred Books of the East, 25 (1886; rpt., Delhi: Motilal Banarsidass, 1967), 1–8.

38 Ibid., 24–25.

39 Ibid., 74–75.

40 Ibid., 198–205.

41 Sir Edwin Arnold, trans., *The Song Celestial* or Bhagavad Gita (Allahabad: Kitabistan, 1939), 1–16.

42 Kinsley, *Hinduism*, 25–26.

43 Makhan Lal Sen, trans., *The Ramayana of Valmiki* (2nd rev. ed.; New Delhi: Munshiram Manoharlal, 1978), 146–49.

44 Kinsley, *Hinduism*, 17.

45 Arnold, *Song Celestial*, 60–73.

46 Sen, *Ramayana*, 340–48.

47 Wendy Donigen O'Flaherty, *Hindu Myths: A Sourcebook Translated from the Sanskrit* (1975; rpt., Middlesex, UK: Penguin, 1982), 238.

48 Vasudeva S. Agrawala, trans., *The Glorification of the Great Goddess* (Varanasi: All-India Kashiraj Trust, 1963), 37–41.

49 de Bary, *Sources*, 348.

50 Ratna Navaratnam, trans., *Tiruvachakam: The Hindu Testament of Love*, 2nd ed., (Bombay: Bharatiya Vidya Bhavan, 1975), 179–80.

51 Harold Coward, "Can Jungian Psychology Be Used to Interpret Tamil Devotional Poetry?" *Studies in Religion* 8 (1979): 177–79. Trans. R. Radhakrishnan.

52 de Bary, *Sources*, 355–57.

53 A.J. Alston, trans., *The Devotional Poems of Mirabai* (Delhi: Motilal Banarsidass, 1980), 34–35, 60–63.

54 Reprinted from *Ethics in the World Religions*, ed. Joseph Runzo and Nancy M. Martin (Oxford: Oneworld, 2001), 177–95.

55 Notable exceptions are J.F. Staal, *Rules without Meaning: Ritual, Mantras and the Human Sciences* (New York: Peter Lang, 1989), and S.N. Balagangadhara, *The "Heathen in His Blindness": Asia, the West and the Dynamic of Religion* (Leiden: E.J. Brill, 1994).

56 Barbara A. Holdrege in her survey article "Hindu Ethics," in *A Bibliographic Guide to the Comparative Study of Ethics*, ed. John Carman and Mark Juergensmeyer (Cambridge: Cambridge University Press, 1991), 12–69. For the importance of moral behaviour in Hindu thought, see Pandurang Vaman Kane, *History of Dharmasastra*, vol. 2, part 1 (Poona: Bhandarkar Oriental Research Institute, 1974), 3–11.

57 See, for example, S.K. Saksena, "Oral Philosophy of India," in *Studies in the Cultural History of India*, ed. Guy S. Metraux and Francois Crouzet (Agra: Shiva Lal Agarwala, 1965); Sanat Kumar Sen, "Indian Philosophy and Social Ethics," *Journal of the Indian Academy of Philosophy*, 6 (1–2), 1967: 63–74; Balbir Singh, *Hindu Ethics: An Exposition of the Concept of Good* (New Delhi: Arnold Heinemann, 1984); and Purusotamma Bilimoria, "Indian Ethics," in *A Companion to Ethics*, ed. Peter Singer (Oxford: Basil Blackwell, 1991), 43–57.

58 Descriptions and definitions of *dharma* in this paragraph have been taken from Pandurang Vaman Kane, *History of Dharmasastra*, vol. 2, part 1 (Poona: Bhandarkar Oriental Research Institute, 1974), 1–3.

59 *Baudhayana Dharma Sutra* 1.1.1–6; *Gautama's Dharma Sutra* 1.1.1–6; see translation in Patrick Olivelle, *Dharmasutras: The Law Codes of Ancient India* (New York: Oxford University Press, 1999).

60 *Ramayana*, Sundarakanda 1.

61 *Mahabharata*, Santi Parva 160.21. For more examples, see also Pandurang Vaman Kane, *History of Dharmasastra*, vol. 2, part 1, 5–9.

62 *Dharma Sutra of Gautama* 8.22–24; in Olivelle, *Dharmasutras*, 90–91.

63 The discussion on food is based on the extensive writings of Kane, *History of Dharmasastra*, vol. 2, part 2, 757–99.

64 The Bhagavad Gita is eighteen chapters long and was probably composed just before the Common Era. It is a part of the *Mahabharata*.

65 Vasudha Narayanan, "Renunciation and the Law in India," in *Religion and Law in Independent India*, ed. Robert Baird (New Delhi: Manohar, 1993), pp. 279–92.

66 Ibid.

67 See Leslie C. Orr, *Donors, Devotees, and Daughters of God: Temple Women in Tamilnadu* (New York: Oxford University Press, 2000).

68 Vatsala Mehta, "The Hindu Widow with Special Reference to Gujarat" (MA thesis, Department of Sociology, University of Bombay, 1956).

69 Daniel H.H. Ingalls, *"Dharma* and *Moksha,"* *Philosophy East and West* 7, 1 (1957), 41–48; and J.A.B. van Buitenen, *"Dharma* and *Moksha,"* *Philosophy East and West* 7, 1 (1957), 33–40.

Jainism

TWO

Jainism

Jain Sutras

JAINISM, ALONG WITH BUDDHISM, is an important religious system regarded as "heretical" (i.e., a teaching that denies the authority of Vedic literature) by the Hindu tradition. Famous for its strict code of non-harming (*ahimsa*), this religion continues as a small but significant part of the religious life in India.[1] The religious literature of the Jains is known by several names, including simply the "doctrine," or siddhanta, and is not claimed to be the exact utterances of the principal teacher, Mahavira (599–527 BCE).[2]

The following reading illustrates several Jaina religious concerns and is part of a larger work meant as a guide to those bent on entering the monastic life.[3]

▼ **NINETEENTH LECTURE**

The Son of Mriga

1   In the pleasant town of Sugriva, which is adorned with parks and gardens, there was the king Balabhadra and Mriga, the principal queen.

2   Their son Balashri, also known as Mrigaputra [son of Mriga], the darling of his father and mother, was crown-prince, a (future) lord of ascetics.

3   In his palace Nandana he dallied with his wives, like the god Dogundaga, always happy in his mind.

4   Standing at a window of his palace, the floor of which was inlaid with precious stones and jewels, he looked down on the squares, places, and roads of the town.

5   Once he saw pass there a restrained shramana, who practised penance, self-restraint, and self-control, who was full of virtues, and a very mine of good qualities.

6   Mrigaputra regarded him with fixed eyes, trying to remember where he had seen the same man before.

7   While he looked at the saint, and his mind became pure, the remembrance of his former birth came upon him as he was plunged in doubt.

8   When the remembrance of his former birth came upon the illustrious Mrigaputra, he remembered his previous birth and his having been then a shramana.

9   Being not delighted with pleasures but devoted to self-control, he went to his father and mother, and spoke as follows:

10 "I have learned the five great vows; [I know] the suffering [that awaits the sinner] in hell or in an existence as a brute; I have ceased to take delight in the large ocean [of the samsara]; therefore, O mother, allow me to enter the order.

11 "O mother, O father, I have enjoyed pleasures which are like poisonous fruit: their consequences are painful, as they entail continuous suffering.

12 "This body is not permanent, it is impure and of impure origin; it is but a transitory residence [of the soul] and a miserable vessel of suffering.

13 "I take no delight in this transitory body which one must leave sooner or later, and which is like foam or a bubble.

14 "And this vain human life, an abode of illness and disease, which is swallowed up by old age and death, does not please me even for a moment.

15 "Birth is misery, old age is misery, and so are disease and death, and ah, nothing but misery is the samsara, in which men suffer distress.

16 "Leaving behind my fields, house, and gold, my son and wife, and my relations, leaving my body I needs must, one day, depart.

17 "As the effect of kimpaka-fruit is anything but good, so the effect of pleasures enjoyed is anything but good.

18 "He who starts on a long journey with no provisions, will come to grief on his way there, suffering from hunger and thirst.

19 "Thus he who without having followed the Law, starts for the next world, will come to grief on his way there, suffering from illness and disease.

20 "He who starts on a long journey with provisions, will be happy on his way there, not suffering from hunger and thirst.

21 "Thus he who after having followed the Law, starts for the next world, will be happy on his journey there, being exempt from karma and suffering.

22, 23 "As when a house is on fire, the landlord carries away valuable things and leaves behind those of no value; so when the whole world is on fire, as it were, by old age and death, I shall save my self, if you will permit me."

24 To him his parents said: "Son, difficult to perform are the duties of a shramana; a monk must possess thousands of virtues.

25 "Impartiality towards all beings in the world, whether friends or enemies, and abstention from injury to living beings throughout the whole life: this is a difficult duty.

26 "To be never careless in abstaining from falsehood, and to be always careful to speak wholesome truth: this is difficult duty.

27 "To abstain from taking of what is not given, even of a toothpick etc., and to accept only alms free from faults: this is a difficult duty.

28 "To abstain from unchastity after one has tasted sensual pleasures, and to keep the severe vow of chastity: this is a very difficult duty.

29 "To give up all claims on wealth, corn, and servants, to abstain from all undertakings, and not to own anything; this is a very difficult duty.

30 "Not to eat at night any food of the four kinds, not to put away for later use or to keep a store (of things one wants): this is a very difficult duty.

31, 32 "Hunger and thirst, heat and cold, molestation by flies and gnats, insults, miserable lodgings, pricking grass, and uncleanliness, blows and threats, corporal punishment and imprisonment, the mendicant's life and fruitless begging: all this is misery.

33 "Such a life is like that of pigeons (always afraid of dangers); painful is the plucking out of one's hair; difficult is the vow of chastity and hard to keep (even) for a noble man.

34 "My son, you are accustomed to comfort, you are tender and cleanly; you are not able, my son, to live as a shramana.

35 "No repose as long as life lasts; the great burden of duty is heavy like a load of iron, which is difficult to be carried, O son.

36 "As it is difficult to cross the heavenly Ganges, or to swim against the current, or to swim with one's arms over the sea, so it is difficult to get over the ocean of duties.

37 "Self-control is untasteful like a mouthful of sand, and to practise penance is as difficult as to walk on the edge of a sword.

38 "It is difficult [always to observe the rules of] right conduct with one's eyes for ever open like [those of] a snake, O son; it is difficult to eat iron grains, as it were.

39 "As it is very difficult to swallow burning fire, so it is difficult for a young man to live as a shramana.

40 "As it is difficult to fill a bag with wind, so is it difficult for a weak man to live as a shramana.

41 "As it is difficult to weigh Mount Mandara in a balance, so it is difficult to live as a shramana with a steady fearless mind.

42 "As it is difficult to swim over the sea with one's arms, so it is difficult for one whose mind is not pacified, [to cross] the ocean of restraint.

43 "Enjoy the fivefold human pleasures. After you have done enjoying pleasures, O son, you may adopt the Law."

44 He answered: "O father and mother, it is even thus as you have plainly told; but in this world nothing is difficult for one who is free from desire.

45 "An infinite number of times have I suffered dreadful pains of body and mind, repeatedly misery and danger.

46 "In the samsara, which is a mine of dangers and a wilderness of old age and death, I have undergone dreadful births and deaths.

47 "Though fire be hot here, it is infinitely more so there [viz., in hell]; in hell I have undergone suffering from heat.

48 "Though there may be cold here, it is of infinitely greater intensity there; in hell I have undergone suffering from cold.

49 "An infinite number of times have I been roasted over a blazing fire in an oven, screaming loud, head down and feet aloft.

50 "In the desert which is like a forest on fire, on the Vagravaluka and the Kadambavaluka rivers, I have been roasted an infinite number of times.

51 "Being suspended upside down over a boiler, shrieking, with no relation to help me, I was cut to pieces with various saws, an infinite number of times.

52 "I have suffered agonies when I was fastened with fetters on the huge Shalmali tree, bristling with very sharp thorns, and then pushed up and down.

53 "An infinite number of times have I been crushed like sugar-cane in presses, shrieking horribly, to atone for my sins, great sinner that I was.

54 "By black and spotted wild dogs I have, ever so many times, been thrown down, torn to pieces, and lacerated, screaming and writhing.

55 "When I was born in hell for my sins, I was cut, pierced, and hacked to pieces with swords and daggers, with darts and javelins.

56 "I have been forcibly yoked to a car of red-hot iron full of fuel, I have been driven on with a goad and thongs, and have been knocked down like an antelope.

57 "On piles, in a blazing fire, I have forcibly been burnt and roasted like a buffalo, in atonement for my sins.

58 "An infinite number of times have I violently been lacerated by birds whose bills were of iron and shaped like tongs, by devilish vultures.

59 "Suffering from thirst I ran towards the river Vaitaranti to drink its water, but in it I was killed [as it were] by blades of razors.

60 "When suffering from the heat, I went into the forest in which the trees have a foliage of daggers; I have, ever so many times, been cut to pieces by the dropping dagger-leaves.

61 "An infinite number of times have I suffered hopelessly from mallets and knives, forks and maces, which broke my limbs.

62 "Ever so many times have I been slit, cut, mangled, and skinned with keen-edged razors, knives, and shears.

63 "As an antelope I have, against my will, been caught, bound, and fastened in snares and traps, and frequently I have been killed.

64 "As a fish I have, against my will, been caught with hooks and in bow-nets; I have therein been scraped, slit, and killed, an infinite number of times.

65 "As a bird I have been caught by hawks, trapped in nets, and bound with bird-lime, and I have been killed, an infinite number of times.

66 "As a tree I have been felled, slit, sawn into planks, and stripped of the bark by carpenters with axes, hatchets, etc., an infinite number of times.

67 "As iron I have been malleated, cut, torn, and filed by blacksmiths, an infinite number of times.

68 "I have been made to drink hissing molten copper, iron, tin, and lead under horrid shrieks, an infinite number of times.

69 "You like meat minced or roasted; I have been made to eat, every so many times, poisoned meat, and red-hot to boot.

70 "You like wine, liquor, spirits, and honey; I have been made to drink burning fat and blood.

71　"Always frightened, trembling, distressed, and suffering, I have experienced the most exquisite pain and misery.

72　"I have experienced in hell sharp, acute and severe, horrible, intolerable, dreadful, and formidable pain.

73　"O father, infinitely more painful is the suffering in hell than any suffering in the world of men.

74　"In every kind of existence I have undergone suffering which was not interrupted by a moment's reprieve."

75　To him his parents said: "Son, a man is free to enter the order, but it causes misery to a shramana that he may not remedy any ailings."

76　He answered: "O father and mother, it is even thus as you have plainly told; but who takes care of beasts and birds in the woods?

77　"As a wild animal by itself roams about in the woods, thus I shall practise the Law by controlling myself and doing penance.

78　"When in a large forest a wild animal falls very sick at the foot of a tree, who is there to cure it?

79　"Or who will give it medicine? or who will inquire after its health? or who will get food and drink for it, and feed it?

80　"When it is in perfect health, it will roam about in woods and on [the shores of] lakes in search of food and drink.

81　"When it has eaten and drunk in woods and lakes, it will walk about and go to rest according to the habits of wild animals.

82　"In the same way a pious monk goes to many places and walks about just as the animals, but afterwards he goes to the upper regions.

83　"As a wild animal goes by itself to many places, lives in many places, and always gets its food; thus a monk on his begging-tour should not despise nor blame [the food he gets].

84　"I shall imitate this life of animals." "Well, my son, as you please." With his parents' permission he gave up all his property.

85　"I shall imitate this life of animals, which makes one free from all misery, if you will permit me." "Go, my son, as you please."

86　When he had thus made his parents repeat their permission, he gave up for ever his claims in any property, just as the snake casts off its slough.

87　His power and wealth, his friends, wives, sons, and relations he gave up as if he shook off the dust from his feet, and then he went forth.

88 He observed the five great vows, practised the five samitis, and was protected by the three guptis; he exerted himself to do mental as well as bodily penance.

89 He was without property, without egoism, without attachment, without conceit, impartial towards all beings, whether they move or not.

90 He was indifferent to success or failure [in begging], to happiness and misery, to life and death, to blame and praise, to honour and insult.

91 He turned away from conceit and passions, from injurious, hurtful, and dangerous actions, from gaiety and sadness; he was free from sins and fetters.

92 He had no interest in this world and no interest in the next world; he was indifferent to unpleasant and pleasant things, to eating and fasting.

93 He prevented the influx of karma through all bad channels; by meditating upon himself he obtained praiseworthy self-purification and sacred knowledge.

94, 95 Thus he thoroughly purified himself by knowledge, right conduct, faith, penance, and pure meditation, and after having lived many years as a shramana, he reached perfection after breaking his fast once only every month.

96 Thus act the enlightened one, the learned, the clever, like Mrigaputra they turn away from pleasures.

97, 98 When you have heard the words of the illustrious and famous son of Mriga, his perfect practice of austerities, and his liberation, famous in the three worlds, you will despise wealth, the cause of misery, and the fetter of egoism, the cause of many dangers, and you will bear the excellent and pleasant yoke of the Law that leads to the great happiness of Nirvana.

  Thus I say.

(Jaina Sutras, Uttaradhayayana 19:1–98)[4] ▲

Notes

1 Wm. Theodore de Bary, ed., *Sources of Indian Tradition*, I (New York: Columbia University Press, 1958), 16.

2 J.A.B. v[an] B[uitenen], "Hindu Sacred Literature," *Encyclopedia Britiannica*, Macropedia, 1974 ed., 936.

3 van Buitenen, ibid.

4 Hermann Jacobi, trans., Jaina Sutras, part 2, *Sacred Books of the East*, XLV (1895; rpt. Delhi: Motilal Banarsidass, 1973), 88–89.

Buddhism

THREE

Buddhism

BUDDHISM ORIGINATED IN INDIA about 2,500 years ago, at a time when Hinduism was still in its infancy, a stage known as Late Vedic Religion, a time when hundreds of thinkers, priests, women, philosophers, householders, warriors, and kings wrestled with the eternal questions of humankind: Who am I? What is the reason for the pervasive feeling of discontent with the state of this world? or, as the ancient texts say: What is the cause of suffering? Is there a state of never-ending peace, stillness of mind? And if so, how can it be obtained? What is the true nature of this world?

The founder of Buddhism asked these questions, as did so many of his contemporaries. Hundreds of truth-seekers discovered hundreds of answers; some of these wise men attracted disciples (no woman is known to have attracted a lasting following) and started a school of thought, which perpetuated their main philosophical concepts and religious practice. But only a few of these groups had a lasting impact on the formation of Indian thought in general. One of these came to be called Buddhism after the honorary title "Buddha" (Awakened or Enlightened One) given to its founder, Prince Siddhartha, also known as Gautama (according to his mother's family) or "the sage of the Shakya clan" (according to his father's ancestry).

Despite its antiquity, Buddhism has preserved a remarkable cultural plasticity. That is, the capability to adapt to different cultures and societies spread not only over most of Asia but increasingly over the Western world. For instance, the Buddhism of China has traits and characteristics that are not present in Indian Buddhism and vice versa. Contemporary Western Buddhism adopts traits and ideas typical of the modern West but alien to pre-modern India. Contemporary social activism inspired several Buddhist movements in India, Southeast and East Asia, as well as in the Western world. Women as teachers of the Buddhist doctrine, a very rare phenomenon in pre-modern Buddhism, are increasingly common among the various branches of modern Buddhism. Despite these significant cultural diversities, Buddhism maintains a cohesive system of thought and ethics. Once the cultural idiosyncrasies are put aside, Buddhists around the world can easily recognize one another as members of the same belief system.

In pre-modern times Buddhism owed its spread throughout Asia largely to the patronage of kings and emperors, as well as that of wealthy merchants. In the West, however, the spread of Buddhism was more of a "bottom up" movement. While at first scholars of Asian languages, artists, and writers promoted in the West a mainly textual knowledge of Buddhism, by the early twentieth century Buddhism gained a limited popularity as a religion. In the late twentieth century we can observe a fusion between American pop culture and some strands of Buddhism; the beat poets are one example of this. While in the 1920s learned people in Europe and North America studied the Buddhist texts in order to understand this religion, by the late twentieth century most Western people who embraced Buddhism did so due to personal contacts that often happened while travelling in Buddhist countries. Thus, the intellectual quest for what was genuine Buddhist teaching was displaced by a search for spiritual enrichment and personal growth. Rather than studying the philosophy of Buddhism, today's Western Buddhist is often more interested in meditation and rituals—in a word, practice.

Contemporary Buddhism consists, roughly speaking, of three constituencies: the Buddhists living in countries that embraced Buddhism as a major religion in pre-modern times (Sri Lanka, Myanmar [Burma], Thailand, Cambodia, Laos, Vietnam, Japan, China, Tibet, and Mongolia; in India Buddhism disappeared by the beginning of the second millennium with the exception of some pockets in remote areas); Buddhists with roots in these countries who now live in the West (they are often referred to as "ethnic Buddhists"); and, finally, the converts, people who were not born into Buddhism but who chose it as their own religion. All these communities face challenges of different natures. The Buddhist communities of Asia face their greatest challenge in the post-colonial situation where the old privileges bestowed by monarchs and the political and economic elite have vanished. This situation often resulted in de-emphasizing the monastic structure of Buddhism and the emergence of a Buddhism that is engaged in socio-political issues. Indigenous Buddhist communities that view Buddhism more as a way of living than as a spiritual and moral doctrine face the challenges of a secular and science-driven modernity. The various diaspora communities often want to preserve their native tradition without recognizing that being surrounded by another culture inevitably affects their own native form of Buddhism. Often the sheer force of demographics (small groups living among an overwhelming majority of people who have adopted modern and secular views or embrace another religion, such as Christianity) results in cultural adaptations. For instance, different Buddhist traditions are often forced to share one place of worship, which entails negotiating which icons and statues can be on display. The diverse groups of Buddhist converts are still rooted in their indigenous world view and cultural identities while embracing Buddhism either as a form of moral humanism or as a spiritual practice that enriches them personally.

Buddhism in the West has been exposed to all the social and intellectual movements of the twentieth century, including secular humanism, individualism, liberalism, pop and drug culture, feminism, and the gay rights movement. The response of the various Buddhist traditions that took root in the West varied a great deal. In general, the Theravada tradition was inclined to adopt a science-based world view based on nineteenth-century positivism, but has so far been hesitant to respond to the movements characteristic of the late twentieth century. The Tibetan and Zen traditions have been most responsive to the challenges put forward by the modern Western world. Tibetan traditions decreased their emphasis on rituals but eagerly addressed issues central to Europeans and North Americans. The Dalai Lama became a widely respected spokesperson, translating ancient Buddhist and Tibetan beliefs into a vocabulary appealing to a Western audience. Chögyam Trungpa, Lama Yeshe, and Tartang Tulku pioneered the reinterpretation of Tibetan Buddhism for Westerners. Chinese Buddhism had not only to free itself from the age-old customs and dependencies but had to find a synthesis between a modern, science-based world view and a Chinese ethos. The Chinese monk T'ai Hsu devoted his life to reform Chinese Buddhism, which lead to a strong revival of the faith. Cheng Yen, a Buddhist nun from Taiwan, applied the Buddhist concept of compassion by working among the poor and sick. Thich Nhat Hanh from Vietnam and many Zen masters from Japan reinterpreted Zen tradition and practice for a modern and mainly Western audience. The Beat poets, in their search for meaning in human existence, became influenced by Zen teachings. Jack Kerouac, Gary Snyder, Philip Whalen, and other poets of the Beat generation became important messengers of Buddhism, targeting a young generation affected by the trauma of the Vietnam War. These intersections of traditional Buddhist belief and modern secular concepts resulted in numerous religious centres, each with its own following and idiosyncratic culture. Magazines, the modern vehicle for creating a virtual community, catered to the need of Western Buddhists to stay in touch with the larger community of Buddhists. *Shambhala Sun* as well as *Tricycle* have their own followings.

Although Buddhist doctrine emphasizes the spiritual equality of men and women and the emptiness of gender distinction, Buddhist cultures adopted androcentric structures. Western feminism attempts to construct a feminine identity and a feminine self-appreciation that seems to be diametrically opposed to the Buddhist idea of no-self. Western Buddhist women often take issue with the low status of women in Buddhist countries, the androcentric interpretation of Buddhist texts, the dominant position of men in Buddhist institutions, and the authoritarian role of male teachers. The organization *Sakyadhita International* (http://www.sakyadhita.org/) provides a forum for exchanging ideas and reflections on these controversial topics. In response to the androcentric structures of most Buddhist institutions, Western women tried to enter the ranks of Buddhist teachers, but only in some traditions were these attempts successful. How feminism will transform traditional Buddhist cultures and institutions in the future is yet to be seen.

The following selection of Buddhist texts attempts to introduce the reader to the core concepts of Buddhism—that is, to ideas that are shared by the vast majority of Buddhists regardless of their country or the era they live in. But beyond that, the readings also illustrate the doctrinal differences that have arisen over time in the various traditions. Furthermore, large segments of text that record Buddha's last weeks and his own death due to food poisoning will expose the reader to the way Buddhists approach such fundamental human issues as illness and death. Thus, it is hoped that these selections convey more than just doctrinal views. The texts that are the product of pre-modern Asia provide the reader with a solid foundation in Buddhist thought from which he or she can expand their studies. Specimens from the writings of some of the foremost voices of modern Buddhism will complement the main selection of canonical texts. Due to limitations of space, however, only a few excerpts from the writings of modern Buddhist masters and women teachers could be incorporated.

The sacred texts of Buddhism are by tradition defined as words spoken by Buddha himself or by disciples whose elaborations were inspired and authorized by Buddha. Modern philology (the science of language and textual transmission) has modified this claim by documenting that the texts were the product of socio-historical circumstances while preserving some of Buddha's key phrases and core ideas. Scholars assume that Buddha spoke a Middle Indian dialect native to the area of Magadha (the eastern part of the Ganges valley). No extant text is preserved in this language. Recent manuscript discoveries from Afghanistan suggest that Buddhist texts were put into writing about one hundred years before the Common Era (CE), and that they were composed not only in Pali, a language not identical with but related to Buddha's own tongue, but also in other middle-Indian vernaculars. As Buddhism spread along trade routes over most of South and East Asia, Buddhist texts were translated and composed in a number of Asian languages; beside Pali, the most important ones are Sanskrit, Chinese, and Tibetan. The translating of thousands of texts and their circulation either as handwritten manuscripts or as wood-carved block prints required large assets usually provided by monarchs. Over time, significant numbers of Indian Buddhist texts were lost due to climate and historical circumstances. This situation makes their Tibetan and Chinese translations as well as the discoveries of text fragments in the sand of Inner Asia all the more important for our understanding of Buddhism.

All Buddhist traditions agree that Buddha's word is preserved as scripture, but they disagree on which texts constitute the canon (*tripitaka*), which convey the meaning in an unmediated language and which require explanation through commentaries. Two complete sets of scripture are extant. First, the canon preserved in Pali, which renders the doctrinal stand of non-Mahayana Buddhism.[1] Around CE 500 Theravada monk-scholars added voluminous commentaries to the Pali Canon, thus interpreting the Pali texts from a Theravada viewpoint. Since then the Pali Canon has been considered to represent the Theravada tradition. Second, the Mahayana Canon is mainly preserved in Chinese and Tibetan translations. While the Mahayana Canon includes a few texts also found in the Pali Canon, it contains large numbers of texts absent from the Pali Canon. They represent the Mahayana viewpoint, emphasizing the career of the Bodhisattva (a being poised to enter nirvana who delays doing so out of compassion for suffering souls) rather than that of the arhat, who is convinced that every person has to work out his or her own enlightenment. The Tibetan Canon also contains numerous works of ritual, apotropaic, and magical content that were obviously meant to address peoples' everyday concerns. The development of the various canons and their textual interdependency is still debated among scholars. Recent finds of manuscripts buried in the deserts of Inner Asia contribute new insights into the development of Buddhist literature.

The following selection contains specimens from both canons. Passages from major Buddhist texts are thematically arranged and so should make the doctrinal development apparent. To permit a historical placing of an individual text, its affiliation with a particular tradition (Mahayana or Hinayana, Pali, Chinese, or Tibetan) is given. The organization follows the pattern chosen by Buddhist traditions in their beginner's handbooks—that is, Buddha as the source of the teaching, the *Dharma* as the collective teaching, and the *Sangha*, or community, of Buddha's followers.

Buddha, the Awakened

Our knowledge of the life of the Buddha is based upon various written sources. The first group of sources contains first-person reports given by Gautama himself (see Autobiographical Records, below). These reports are part of the oldest extant complete collection of Buddhist scripture, the Pali Canon (*Pali tripitaka*). On several occasions, the Buddha recounted events of his life that occurred before he became enlightened. He sometimes referred to himself then as bodhisattva, which in this context means "a person on his/her way to enlightenment (bodhi)." Although these records were embedded in sermons given by Buddha to his disciples, and were not written down until centuries later, they proved to be reliable. Some of the phrases may even be Gautama's own words.

These reports portray Gautama not only as a truth-seeker with an extraordinary dedication to his aims but also as a human being not substantially different from us. Nowhere is there a statement saying he was sent by a superhuman force or a god, or that his fate was predestined. But in some instances he is recorded as saying that he only rediscovered a timeless truth, which is unveiled by each Buddha who appears in every cosmic eon. This idea is expressed in the term *tathagata*, which means "who has come like those before," and which is used by Buddha when referring to himself after he became enlightened. In a sense, these first-person reports picture Gautama as human (subject to sickness, thirst, emotions), but in another sense they have him transcend the human realm of suffering and ignorance. This tendency intensifies over time and results in a different perception of Buddha, then seen as the embodiment of the absolute. This perception we find mainly in Mahayana texts.

A second group of sources, transmitted by the same tradition (i.e., Theravada), and contained in the same body of scripture or in its appendix, speaks a different language: Gautama, the human being, becomes insignificant, while Buddha, the Awakened One, stands out as the embodiment of truth. Buddha becomes, then, a timeless cipher of the reality of the universe. The story of his life is turned into an exemplification of the Buddhist belief. Siddhartha's birth became a cosmic event, hailed by gods and men; his renunciation of home and family became filled with legendary events deemed suitable to glorify this decisive occurrence (excerpts will be found below, under The Buddha Biography Told by a Narrator).

At the beginning of Buddhist studies, modern scholarship tended to consider only the austere references as authentic, while the more flowery reports were seen as later additions of legendary material that lacked historical relevance. This opinion is diametrically opposed to the view held by Buddhists, who see no inconsistency between portraying the Buddha as a human being and as a transcendent being—a perception now accepted by more Western scholars. The various Buddhist traditions deal with these different perceptions of the Buddha in different ways: some emphasize his human, yet extraordinary nature (like the Theravada), while others stress his ultimate nature by considering his earthly activity as a mere "sign" to guide the disciples (like the Mahayana). This "Buddhology" culminates in a Mahayana text, which rejects any attempt to capture the idea of Buddha in a comprehensible form. Passages pertaining to the question of who the Buddha is appear below, under Buddha's Intrinsic Nature.

Autobiographical Records

The following selection contains passages wherein Gautama speaks of his life before his enlightenment. They do not offer a continuous story of his life, but recall only various episodes, which are retold for propaedeutic purposes. These texts are part of the Pali Canon and represent the Theravada perception of the Buddha. In a way, these records may be called autobiographical because Buddha speaks there in the first person. One must, however, acknowledge that modern scholarship is critical in attributing any utterance verbatim to Buddha.

The following excerpt is taken from the *Majjhima-nikaya*, a collection of 152 discourses or *suttas*. Some of the first fifty *suttas* contain autobiographical information about Buddha's life. Our excerpt is taken from the thirty-sixth *sutta*, the *Mahasaccakasutta*. This text tells us about how Buddha tried to achieve enlightenment by observing traditional methods, such as asceticism and meditation.

The excerpt leads us to the following scene: While his father was carrying out ceremonial obligations in connection with the spring festival, the boy experiences a state of altered consciousness. As an adult truth seeker, the future Buddha remembers this serene experience:

> Once, seated in the cool shade of a rose-apple tree on the lands of my father the Shakyan, I, divested of pleasures of sense and of wrong states of mind, entered upon, and abode in, the first stage of deep meditation, with all its zest and satisfaction,—a state bred of inward aloofness but not divorced from observation and reflection.
>
> (*Majjhima-nikaya* 36)[2]

As a member of the political elite, the future Buddha lived a life of affluence and luxury. Later he recalls this experience with the following words:

> Now, I myself, Magandiya, in those days when I had a home, was lapped in the pleasures of the five senses and revelled in sights, sounds, odours, tastes and touch,—which are desirable, agreeable, pleasant and

attractive, bound up with pleasures of sense, and exciting. Three palaces were mine, one for the rainy season, another for the winter, and another for the summer, in the palace for the rainy season I lived during the four months of the rains, ministered to by bands of women musicians, never coming down to the lower floors.

(*Mafihima-nikaya* 75)[3]

In the following excerpt, which is taken from the twenty-sixth sutta, the *Ariyapariyesanasutta*, Buddha recalls his renunciation, studies and enlightenment, and subsequent ministry. While later accounts of Buddha's life claim that he had secretly left the palace of his father, this account tells us that his parents were aware of his intent to become a migrant ascetic. They reacted with grief and despair to his resolve. Furthermore, the text tells us that his parents did not agree with his decision, which is in contrast to a rule that a person who wants to join the Buddhist Order has to obtain the parents' permission. We see here how certain concepts and ideas developed over time, despite later traditions that claim that these concepts and rules had been in place since the beginning of Buddhism.

We learn first of the future Buddha's yearning for a state beyond the cycle of rebirth and its endless sufferings, which leads him to practise different forms of meditation under the instruction of several teachers of yoga. These exercises, however, resulted not in what he had hoped for. He decided to seek his own way. This leads us to the second event, Buddha's enlightenment and his reluctance to share his experience with others. Only after the god Brahma convinced Buddha that some individuals would be capable of understanding his teaching did he agree to teach. This is the beginning of the third event, Buddha's ministry. For more than forty years Buddha traveled across the eastern part of the Ganges valley, engaging all kinds of people in conversations and responding to their queries. The main concept of his teachings we shall explore the section entitled *Dharma*.

▼   "Yes, I myself too, in the days before my full enlightenment, when I was but a Bodhisatta, and not yet fully enlightened,—I too, being subject in myself to rebirth, decay and the rest of it, pursued what was no less subject thereto. But the thought came to me: Why do I pursue what, like myself, is subject to rebirth and the rest? Why, being myself subject thereto, should I not, with my eyes open to the perils which these things entail, pursue instead the consummate peace of nirvana,—which knows neither rebirth nor decay, neither disease nor death, neither sorrow nor impurity?

"There came a time when I, being quite young, with a wealth of coal-black hair untouched by grey and in all the beauty of my early prime—despite the wishes of my parents, who wept and lamented—cut off my hair and beard, donned the yellow robes and went forth from home to homelessness on pilgrimage. A pilgrim now, in search of the right, and in quest of the excellent road to peace beyond compare, I came to Alara Kalama and said:—It is my wish, reverend Kalama, to lead the higher life in this your doctrine and rule. Stay with us, venerable sir, was his answer; my doctrine is such that ere long an intelligent man can for himself discern, realize, enter on, and abide in, the full scope of his master's teaching. Before long, indeed very soon, I had his doctrine by heart. So far as regards mere lip-recital and oral repetition, I could say off the [founder's] original message and the elders' exposition of it, and could profess, with others, that I knew and saw it to the full. Then it struck me that it was no doctrine merely accepted by him on trust that Alara Kalama, preached, but one which he professed to have entered on and to abide in after having discerned and realized it for himself; and assuredly he had real knowledge and vision thereof. So I went to him and asked him up to what point he had for himself discerned and realized the doctrine he had entered on and now abode in.

"'Up to the plane of naught,' answered he.

"Hereupon, I reflected that Alara Kalama was not alone in possessing faith, perseverance, mindfulness, rapt concentration, and intellectual insight; for, all these were mine too. Why, I asked myself, should not I strive to realize the doctrine which he claims to have entered on and to abide in after discerning and realizing it for himself? Before long, indeed very soon, I had discerned and realized his doctrine for myself and had entered on it and abode therein. Then I went to him and asked him whether this was the point up to which he had discerned and realized for himself the doctrine which he professed. He said yes; and I said that I had reached the same point for myself. It is a great thing, said he, a very great thing for us, that in you, reverend sir, we find such a fellow in the higher life. That same doctrine which I for myself have discerned, realized, entered on, and profess—that have you for yourself discerned, realized, entered on and abide in; and that same doctrine which you have for yourself discerned, realized, entered on, and profess. The doctrine which I know, you too know; and the doctrine which you know, I too know. As I am, so are you; and as you are, so am I. Pray, sir, let us be joint wardens of this company! In such wise did Alara Kalama, being my master, set me, his pupil, on precisely the same footing as himself and show me great worship. But, as I bethought me that his doctrine merely led to attaining the plane of naught and not to renunciation, passionlessness, cessation, peace, discernment, enlightenment and nirvana,—I was not taken with his doctrine but turned away from it to go my way.

"Still in search of the right, and in quest of the excellent road to peace beyond compare, I came to Uddaka Ramaputta and said:—It is my wish, reverend sir, to lead the higher life in this your doctrine and rule. Stay with us, (same passage as in the second last one) ... vision thereof. So I went to Uddaka Ramaputta and asked him up to what point he had for himself discerned and realized the doctrine he had entered on and now abode in.

"'Up to the plane of neither perception nor nonperception,' answered he.

"Hereupon, I reflected that Uddaka Ramaputta was not alone in possessing faith (see second last passage)... show me great worship. But, as I bethought me that his doctrine merely led to attaining the plane of neither perception nor non-perception, and not to renunciation, passionlessness, cessation, peace, discernment, enlightenment and nirvana,—I was not taken with his doctrine but turned away from it to go my way.

"Still in search of the right, and in quest of the excellent road to peace beyond compare, I came, in the course of an alms-pilgrimage through Magadha, to the Camp township at Uruvela and there took up my abode. Said I to myself on surveying the place:—Truly a delightful spot, with its goodly groves and clear flowing river with ghats and amenities, hard by a village for sustenance. What more for his striving can a young man need whose heart is set on striving? So there I sat me down, needing nothing further for my striving.

"Subject in myself to rebirth—decay—disease—death—sorrow—and impurity, and seeing peril in what is subject thereto, I sought after the consummate peace of nirvana, which knows neither rebirth nor decay, neither disease nor death, neither sorrow nor impurity—this I pursued, and this I won; and there arose within me the conviction, the insight, that now my deliverance was assured, that this was my last birth, nor should I ever be reborn again.

"I have attained, thought I, to this doctrine profound, recondite, hard to comprehend, serene, excellent, beyond dialectic, abstruse, and only to be perceived by the learned. But mankind delights, takes delight, and is happy in what it clings on to, so that for it, being thus minded, it is hard to understand causal relations and the chain of causation,—hard to understand the stilling of all plastic forces, or the renunciation of all worldly ties, the extirpation of craving, passionlessness, peace, and nirvana. Were I to preach the doctrine, and were others not to understand it, that would be labour and annoyance to me! Yes, and on the instant there flashed across my mind these verses, which no man had heard before:

Must I now preach what I so hardly won?"

Men sunk in sin and lusts would find it hard to plumb this doctrine,—up stream all the way, abstruse, profound, most subtle, hard to grasp.

Dear lusts will blind them that they shall not see,—in densest mists of ignorance befogged.

"As thus I pondered, my heart inclined to rest quiet and not to preach my doctrine. But, Brahma Sahampati's mind came to know what thoughts were passing within my mind, and he thought to himself:—The world is undone, quite undone, inasmuch as the heart of the truth-finder inclines to rest quiet and not to preach his doctrine! Hereupon, as swiftly as a strong man not to preach his doctrine! Hereupon, as swiftly as a strong man might stretch out his arm or might draw back his outstretched arm, Brahma Sahampati vanished from the Brahma-world and appeared before me. Towards me he came with his right shoulder bared, and with his clasped hands stretched out to me in reverence, saying:—May it please the Lord, may it please the Blessed One, to preach his doctrine! Beings there are whose vision is but little dimmed, who are perishing because they do not hear the doctrine;—these will understand it! And Brahma Sahampati went on to say:

> An unclean doctrine reigns in Magadha,
> by impure man devised. Open thou the door
> of deathless truth. Let all the doctrine hear
> from his pure lips who first conceived its thought.
> As from a mountain's rocky pinnacle
> the folk around are clear to view, so, sage,
> from thy truth's palace, from its topmost height,
> survey with eye all-seeing folk beneath,—
> poor thralls of birth and swift decay, whose
> doom is that same sorrow thou no more will know.
> So up, great hero, victor in the fight!
> Thy debt is paid. Lead on thy pilgrim train
> through all the world. They doctrine preach;—
> among thy hearers some will understand.

"Thereupon, almsmen, heeding Brahma's entreaties and moved by compassion for all beings, I surveyed the world with the eye of enlightenment and therewith saw beings with vision dimmed little or much, beings with acute or dull faculties, beings of dispositions good or bad, beings docile or indocile, with some among them alive to the terrors hereafter, of present wrongdoing. As in a pond of lotuses, blue or red or white, some lotuses of each kind are born and grow in the water, never rising above the surface but flourishing underneath; while others, born and growing in the water, either rise level with the surface or stand right out of the water and are not wetted by it;—even so with the eye of enlightenment did I see beings with vision dimmed … wrongdoing now. Thereon, I made answer to Brahma Sahampati in these verses:

> Nirvana's doors stand open wide to all with ears to hear.
>   Discard your outworn creeds!
> The weary task ahead made me forbear to preach to men
>   my doctrine's virtues rare.

"Mine has it been to secure from the Lord the preaching of the doctrine! said Brahma Sahampati, and, so saying, with due obeisance and reverently keeping his right side towards me as he passed, he vanished there and then.

"I now asked myself to whom first I should preach the doctrine, and who would understand it quickly. The thought came to me that there was Alara Kalama, who was learned, able, and intelligent, whose vision had long been but little dimmed; suppose I chose him to be my first hearer, for he would be quick to understand? Word, however, was brought to me by deities that he had died seven days before, and insight assured me this was so. Great nobility, thought I, was his! Had he heard my doctrine, he would have understood it quickly.

"Again I asked myself to whom first I should preach the doctrine, and who would understand it quickly. The thought came to me that there was Uddaka Ramaputta, who was learned.... Word, however, was brought me by deities that he had died yesterday at midnight, and insight, understood it quickly.

"Again I asked myself to whom first I should preach the doctrine and who would understand it quickly. The thought came to me that there were the five almsmen who had served me so well in my struggles to purge myself of self; suppose I chose them to be my first hearers? Wondering where they were dwelling now, I saw with the eye celestial—which is pure and far surpasses the human eye—those five almsmen dwelling at Benares in the Isipatana deerpark. So, when I had stayed as long as pleased me at Uruvela, I set out on an alms-pilgrimage for Benares.

"On the highway from the Bo-tree to Gaya, Upaka the mendicant saw me and said:—'Reverend sir, your faculties are under control, and your complexion is clear and bright. To follow whom have you gone forth on pilgrimage? Or who is your teacher? Or whose doctrine do you profess?' Him I answered in these verses:—

> All-vanquishing, all-knowing, lo! am I, from
>   all wrong thinking wholly purged and free.
> All things discarded, cravings rooted out,—
>   whom should I follow? I have found out all.
> No teacher's mine, no equal. Counterpart to me
>   there's none throughout the whole wide world.
> The arahat am I, teacher supreme, utter enlightenment
>   is mine alone; unfever'd calm is mine, nirvana's peace.
> I seek the Kaasis' city, there to start my doctrine's wheel,
>   a world purblind to save, sounding the tocsin's
>   call to deathlessness.

> 'According to your claim, sir,' said Upaka,
>   'you should be the universal conqueror.'

> Like me, those conquer who the cankers quell;—
>   by conquering bad thoughts, I'm conqueror.

"When I had thus answered, Upaka the mendicant said: Mebbe, sir, and, shaking his head, took a different road and went his way.

"In the course of my alms-pilgrimage, I came at last to Bernares and the deerpark of Isipatana, in which were the five almsmen. From afar the five saw me coming and agreed among themselves as follows:—Here come the recluse

Gotama, the man of surfeits, who has abandoned the struggle and reverted to surfeiting. We must not welcome him, nor rise to receive him, nor relieve him of bowl and robes. Yet let us put out a seat; he can sit on it if he wants to. But, as I drew nearer and nearer, those five almsmen proved less and less able to abide by their compact;—some came forward to relieve me of my bowl and robes; other indicated my seat; while others brought water for me to wash my feet. But they addressed me by my name and by the style of reverend. So I said to the five almsmen; almsmen, do not address the truth-finder by his name or by the style of reverend. Arahat all enlightened is the truth-finder. Hearken to me, almsmen. The deathless has been won; I teach it; I preach the doctrine. Live up to what I enjoin, and in no long time you will come—of yourselves, here and now—to discern and realize, to enter on and to abide in, that supreme goal of the higher life, for the sake of which young men to forth from home to homelessness on Pilgrimage."

(Majihima-nikaya 26)[4] ▲

The Great Passing Away or Parinirvana

Having criss-crossed the eastern parts of the Ganges valley for four decades, Buddha returned as an old man to the hills and mountains of his birthplace—the Himalayan foothills of Nepal. There he passed away in the small town of Kushinagara. The events surrounding his entering into final nirvana (*parinirvana*) tell how Buddhists ought to see the world, how Buddha saw himself and the religious movement he had started. In the following, excerpts are collected from a lengthy report called *The Book of the Great Decease*. The text contains an account of Buddha's wanderings during the months prior to his death and tells about the distribution of his remains. It is extant in various versions preserved in different languages and by different traditions. The story presented in this text fits well together with events related in another text, the *Cullavagga*. Scholars assume that the two accounts were once one coherent narrative. Although there are clear indications that this text had been enlarged by means of insertions and expansions, its main account seems to date back to the time of Buddha's last days.

It was customary that lay people would invite Buddha and his following of monks to a meal in their homes. Chunda, a blacksmith, offered such a meal to Buddha and his monks, but the food served proved to be a health hazard leading to Buddha's death. In ancient India as well as in present Ladakh and Tibet, blacksmiths are considered ritually polluted. Thus, their vicinity is shunned. It is telling that Buddha disregarded such social taboos, as he was critical of the caste system.

13   Now when the Exalted One had remained as long as he desired at Bhoga-gama, he addressed the venerable Ananda, and said:—"Come, Ananda, let us go on to Pava."

"Even so, lord!" said the venerable Ananda, in assent to the Exalted One. And the Exalted One proceeded with a great company of the brethren to Pava.

And there at Pava the Exalted One stayed at the Mango Grove of Chunda, who was by family a smith.

14   Now Chunda, the worker in metals, heard that the Exalted One had come to Pava, and was staying there in his Mango Grove.

And Chunda, the worker in metals, went to the place where the Exalted One was, and saluting him took his seat respectfully on one side. And when he was thus seated, the Exalted One instructed, aroused, incited, and glad-dened him with religious discourse.

15   Then he, instructed, aroused, incited, and gladdened by the religious dis-course, addressed the Exalted One, and said:—"May the Exalted One do me the honour of taking his meal together with the brethren, at my house to-morrow?"

And the Exalted One signified, by silence, his consent.

16   Then seeing that the Exalted One had consented, Chunda, the worker in met-als, rose from his seat and bowed down before the Exalted One, and keep-ing him on his right hand as he passed him, departed thence.

17   Now at the end of the night, Chunda, the worker in metals, made ready in his dwelling-place sweet rice and cakes, and a quantity of truffles. And he announced the hour to the Exalted One, saying:—"The hour, lord, has come, and the meal is ready."

18   And the Exalted One robed himself early in the morning, and taking his bowl, went with the brethren to the dwelling-place of Chunda, the worker in metals. When he had come thither he seated himself on the seat pre-pared for him. And when he was seated he addressed Chunda, the worker in metals, and said: "As to the truffles you have made ready, serve me with them, Chunda: and as to the other food, the sweet rice and cakes, serve the brethren with it."

"Even so, Lord!" said Chunda, the worker in metals, in assent, to the Blessed One. And the truffles he had made ready he served to the Exalted One; whilst the other food, the sweet rice and cakes, he served to the members of the Order.

19   Now the Exalted One addressed Chunda, the worker in metals, and said:— "Whatever truffles, Chunda, are left over to thee, those bury in a hole. I see no one, Chunda, on earth nor in Mara's heaven, nor in Brahma's heaven, no one among Samanas and Brahmanas, among gods, and men, by whom,

when he has eaten it, that food can be properly assimilated, save by a tatha-gata."

"Even so, lord!" said Chunda, the worker in metals, in assent, to the Exalted One. And whatever truffles remained over those he buried in a hole. And he went to the place where the Exalted One was; and when he had come there, took his seat respectfully on one side, and when he was seated, the Exalted One instructed and aroused and incited and gladdened Chunda, the worker in metals, with religious discourse. And the Exalted One then rose from his seat and departed thence.

20 Now when the Exalted One had eaten the rice prepared by Chunda, the worker in metals, there fell upon him a dire sickness, the disease of dysentery, and sharp pain came upon him, even unto death. But the Exalted One, mindful and self-possessed, bore it without complaint.

And the Exalted One addressed the venerable Ananda, and said:— "Come, Ananda, let us go on to Kusinara."

"Even so, Lord!," said the venerable Ananda, in assent, to the Exalted One.

(Mahaparinibbana Sutta)[5] ▲

For the first time Buddha hints at his imminent death when a golden robe appears dulled by the golden shine of Buddha's skin.

▼ Now Pukkusa, the young Mallian, addressed a certain man and said:—"Fetch me, I pray you, my good man, a pair of robes of cloth of gold, burnished and ready for wear."

"So be it, sir!" said that man, in assent, to Pukkusa, the young Mallian; and he brought a pair of robes of cloth of gold, burnished and ready for wear.

And the Mallian Pukkusa presented the pair of robes of cloth of gold, bur-nished and ready for wear, to the Exalted One, saying:—"Lord, this pair of robes of burnished cloth of gold is ready for wear. May the Exalted One show me favour and accept it at my hands!"

"In that case, Pukkusa, robe me in one, and Ananda in one."

"Even so, lord!" said Pukkusa, in assent, to the Exalted One; and in one he robed the Exalted One, and in one, Ananda.

Then the Exalted One instructed and aroused and incited and gladdened Pukkusa, the young Mallian, with religious discourse. And Pukkusa, the young Mallian, when he had been instructed and aroused and incited and gladdened by the Exalted One with religious discourse, arose from his seat, and bowed down before the Exalted One; and keeping him on his right hand as he passed him, departed thence.

Now not long after the Mallian Pukkusa had gone, the venerable Ananda placed that pair of robes of cloth of gold, burnished and ready for wear, on the body of the Exalted One; and when it was so placed on the body of the Exalted One it appeared to have lost its splendour!

And the venerable Ananda said to the Exalted One:—"How wonderful a thing is it, Lord, and how marvellous, that the colour of the skin of the Exalted One should be so clear, so exceeding bright! For when I placed even this pair of robes of burnished cloth of gold and ready for wear on the body of the Exalted One, lo! it seemed as if it had lost its splendour!"

"It is even so, Ananda. There are two occasions, Ananda, on which the colour of the skin of a tathagata becomes clear and exceeding bright. What are the two?

"On the night, Ananda, on which a tathagata attains to the supreme and perfect insight, and on the night in which he passes finally away in that utter passing away which leaves nothing whatever to remain—on these two occasions the colour of the skin of the tathagata becomes clear and exceeding bright.

"And now this day, Ananda, at the third watch of the night, in the Upavattana of Kusinara, in the Sala Grove of the Mallians, between the twin Sala trees, the utter passing away of the tathagata will take place. Come, Ananda! Let us go on to the river Kakuttha."

"Even so, Lord!" said the venerable Ananda, in assent, to the Exalted One.

(*Mahaparinibbana Sutta*)[6] ▲

Chunda's meal caused physical discomfort to the Buddha. The Buddhist commentators had to wrestled with the fact that the text describes Buddha's physical weakness and his pain while maintaining that Buddha, the Enlightened One, cannot be subject to suffering. They explained that the pain caused by the spoiled dish was only a physical pain, while Buddha's mind remained untainted.

▼

39   Now the Exalted One with a great company of the brethren went on to the river Kakuttha; and when he had come there, he went down into the water, and bathed, and drank. And coming up out again on the other side he went on to the Mango Grove.

And when he was come there he addressed the venerable Chundaka, and said:—"Fold, I pray you, Chundaka, a robe in four and spread it out. I am weary, Chundaka, and would lie down."

"Even so, Lord!" said the venerable Chundaka, in assent, to the Exalted One. And he folded a robe in four, and spread it out.

40   And the Exalted One laid himself down on his right side, with one foot resting on the other; and calm and self-possessed he meditated, intending to rise up again in due time. And the venerable Chundaka seated himself there in front of the Exalted One.

42   And the Exalted One addressed the venerable Ananda, and said:—"Now it
     may happen, Ananda, that some one should stir up remorse in Chunda, the
     smith, by saying:—'This is evil to thee, Chunda, and loss to thee in that
     when the tathagata had eaten his last meal from thy provision, then he
     died.' Any such remorse, Ananda, in Chunda, the smith, should be checked
     by saying:—'This is good to thee, Chunda, and gain to thee in that when the
     tathagata had eaten his last meal from thy provision,' then he died. From the
     very mouth of the exalted One, Chunda, have I heard, from his own mouth
     have I received this saying:—'These two offerings of food are of equal fruit,
     and of equal profit, and of much greater fruit and much greater profit than
     any other—and which are the two? The offering of food which, when a
     tathagata has eaten, he attains to supreme and perfect insight; and the
     offering of food which, when a tathagata has eaten, he passes away by that
     utter passing away in which nothing whatever remains behind—these two
     offerings of food are of equal fruit and of equal profit, and of much greater
     fruit and much greater profit than any others. There has been laid up by
     Chunda, the smith, a karma redounding to length of life, redounding to
     good birth, redounding to good fortune, redounding to good fame, redound-
     ing to the inheritance of heaven, and of sovereign power.' In this way,
     Ananda, should be checked any remorse in Chunda the smith."

43   Then the Exalted One, perceiving how the matter stood, uttered on that
     occasion this hymn of exultation:

> "To him who gives shall virtue be increased;
> In him who curbs himself, no anger can arise;
> The righteous man casts off all evil ways,
> And by the rooting out of lust, and bitterness,
> And all infatuation, is at peace!"

(*Mahaparinibbana Sutta*)[7] ▲

The subsequent passages describe the events preceding Buddha's parinirvana:

▼

1   Now the Exalted One addressed the venerable Ananda, and said:—"Come,
    Ananda, let us go on to the Sala Grove of the Mallas, the Upavattana of
    Kusinara, on the further side of the river Hiranyavati."
        "Even so, lord!" said the venerable Ananda, in assent, to the Exalted One.
        And the Exalted One proceeded with a great company of the brethren
    to the Sala Grove of the Mallas, the Upavattana of Kusinara, on the further side
    of the river Hiranyavati: and when he had come there he addressed the ven-
    erable Ananda, and said:—

"Spread over for me, I pray you, Ananda, the couch with its head to the north, between the two Sala trees. I am weary, Ananda, and would lie down."

"Even so, lord!" said the venerable Ananda, in assent, to the Exalted One. And he spread a covering over the couch with its head to the north, between the twin Sala trees. And the Exalted One laid himself down on his right side, with one leg resting on the other; and he was mindful and self-possessed.

(Mahaparinibbana Sutta) [8] ▲

With some reluctance the Buddha recommends that his bodily remains should be treated like a king's.

▼

10   "What are we to do, Lord, with the remains of the tathagata?"

"Hinder not yourselves, Ananda, by honouring the remains of the tathagata. Be zealous, I beseech you, Ananda, in your own behalf! Devote yourselves to your own good! Be earnest, be zealous, be intent on your own good! There are wise men, Ananda, among the nobles, among the brahmins, among the heads of houses who are firm believers in the tathagata; and they will do due honour to the remains of the tathagata."

11   "But what should be done, Lord, with the remains of the tathagata?"

"As men treat the remains of a king of kings, so, Ananda, should they treat the remains of a tathagata."

"And how, Lord, do they treat the remains of a king of kings?"

"They wrap the body of a king of kings, Ananda, in a new cloth. When that is done they wrap it in carded cotton wool. When that is done they wrap it in a new cloth, and so on till they have wrapped the body in five hundred successive layers of both kinds. Then they place the body in an oil vessel of iron, and cover that close up with another oil vessel of iron. They then build a funeral pyre of all kinds of perfume, and burn the body of the king of kings. And then at the four cross roads they erect a cairn to the king of kings. This, Ananda, is the way in which they treat the remains of a king of kings.

"And as they treat the remains of a king of kings, so, Ananda, should they treat the remains of the tathagata. At the four cross roads a cairn should be erected to the tathagata. And whosoever shall there place garlands or perfumes of paint, or make salutation there, or become in its presence calm in heart—that shall long be to them for a profit and a joy."

12   "The men, Ananda, worthy of a cairn, are four in number. Which are the four?

"A tathagata, an Able Awakened One, is worthy of a cairn. One awakened for himself alone is worthy of a cairn. A true hearer of the tathagata is worthy of a cairn. A king of kings is worthy of a cairn.

"And on account of what circumstance, Ananda, is a tathagata, an Able Awakened One, worthy of a cairn?

"At the thought, Ananda:—'This is the cairn of that Exalted One, of that Able Awakened One,' the hearts of many shall be made calm and happy; and since they there had calmed and satisfied their hearts they will be reborn after death, when the body has dissolved, in the happy realms of heaven. It is on account of this circumstance, Ananda, that a tathagata, an Able Awakened One, is worthy of a cairn.

"And on account of what circumstance, Ananda, is one awakened for himself alone worthy of a cairn?

"At the thought, Ananda:—'This is the cairn of that Exalted One awakened for himself alone,' the hearts of many shall be made calm and happy; and since they there had calmed and satisfied their hearts they will be reborn after death, when the body has dissolved, in the happy realms of heaven. It is on account of this circumstance, Ananda, that one awakened for himself alone is worthy of a cairn.

"And on account of what circumstance, Ananda, is a true hearer of the Exalted One, the Able Awakened One, worthy of a cairn?

"At the thought, Ananda: 'This is the cairn of that true hearer of the Exalted Able Awakened One,' the hearts of many shall be made calm and happy; and since they there had calmed and satisfied their hearts they will be reborn after death, when the body has dissolved, in the happy realms of heaven. It is on account of this circumstance, Ananda, that a true hearer of the Exalted One, the Able Awakened One, is worthy of a cairn.

"And on account of what circumstances, Ananda, is a king of kings worthy of a cairn?

"At the thought, Ananda: 'This is the cairn of that righteous king who ruled in righteousness,' the hearts of many shall be made calm and happy; and since they there had calmed and satisfied their hearts they will be reborn after death, when the body has dissolved, in the happy realms of heaven. It is on account of this circumstance, Ananda, that a king of kings is worthy of a cairn.

"These four, Ananda, are the persons worthy of a cairn."

13 Now the venerable Ananda went into the vihara, and stood leaning against the lintel of the door and weeping at the thought:—"Alas! I remain still but a learner, one who has yet to work out his own perfection. And the Master is about to pass away from me—he who is so kind!"

Now the Exalted One called the brethren, and said:—"Where then, brethren, is Ananda?"

"The venerable Ananda, Lord, has gone into the vihara, and stands leaning against the lintel of the door, and weeping at the thought:—'Alas! I remain still but a learner, one who has yet to work out his own perfection. And the Master is about to pass away from me—he who is so kind!'"

And the Exalted One called a certain brother, and said:—"Go now, brother, and call Ananda in my name, and say:—'Brother Ananda, the Master calls for thee.'"

"Even so, Lord!" said that brother, in assent, to the Exalted One. And he went up to the place where the Exalted One was: and when he had come there, he said to the venerable Ananda:—"Brother Ananda, the master calls for thee."

"Very well, brother," said the venerable Ananda, in assent, to that brother. And he went up to the place where the Exalted One was, and when he had come there, he bowed down before the Exalted One, and took his seat respectfully on one side.

14 Then the Exalted One said to the venerable Ananda, as he sat there by his side:—"Enough, Ananda! Do not let yourself be troubled; do not weep! Have I not already, on former occasions, told you that it is in the very nature of all things most near and dear unto us that we must divide ourselves from them, leave them, sever ourselves from them? How, then, Ananda, can this be possible—whereas anything whatever born, brought into being, and organized, contains within itself the inherent necessity of dissolution—how, then, can this be possible, that such a being should not be dissolved? No such condition can exist! For a long time, Ananda, have you been very near to me by acts of love, kind and good, that never varies, and is beyond all measure. For a long time, Ananda, have you been very near to me by words of love, kind and good, that never varies, and is beyond all measure. For a long time, Ananda, have you been very near to me by thoughts of love, kind and good, that never varies, and is beyond all measure. You have done well, Ananda! Be earnest in effort, and you too shall soon be free from the Intoxications—[of sensuality, and individuality, and delusion, and ignorance]!"

(*Mahaparinibbana Sutta*)[9] ▲

Later the Buddha announces the entering into nirvana to the Malla family:

▼

19 "Go now, Ananda, and enter into Kusinara, and inform the Mallas of Kusinara, saying:—'This day, O Vasetthas, in the last watch of the night, the final passing away of the tathagata will take place. Be favourable herein, O Vasetthas, be favourable. Give no occasion to reproach yourselves hereafter, saying:— In our own village did the death of our tathagata take place, and we took not the opportunity of visiting the tathagata in his last hours.'"

"Even so, Lord," said the venerable Ananda, in assent, to the Exalted One; and he robed himself and taking his bowl, entered into Kusinara attended by another member of the order.

20 Now at that time the Mallas of Kusinara were assembled in the council hail on some [public] affair.

And the venerable Ananda went to the council hail of the Mallas of Kusinara; and when he had arrived there, he informed them, saying:—"This day, O Vasetthas, in the last watch of the night, the final passing away of the tathagata will take place. Be favourable herein, O Vasetthas, be favourable. Give no occasion to reproach yourselves hereafter, saying:—'In our own village did the death of our tathagata take place, and we took not the opportunity of visiting the tathagata in his last hours.'"

21 And when they had heard this saying of the venerable Ananda, the Mallas with their young men and maidens and their wives were grieved, and sad, and afflicted at heart. And some of them wept, dishevelling their hair, and stretched forth their arms and wept, fell prostrate on the ground, and rolled to and fro in anguish at the thought:—"Too soon will the Exalted One die! Too soon will the Happy One pass away! Full soon will the light of the world vanish away!"

Then the Mallas, with their young men and maidens and their wives, being grieved, and sad, and afflicted at heart, went to the Sala Grove of the Mallas, to the Upavattana, and to the place where the venerable Ananda was.

22 Then the venerable Ananda thought:—"If I allow the Mallas of Kusinara, one by one, to pay their respects to the Exalted One, the whole of the Mallas of Kusinara will not have been presented to the Exalted One until this night brightens up into the dawn. Let me now, cause the Mallas of Kusinara to stand in groups, each family in a group, and so present them to the Exalted One, saying:—'Lord! a Malla of such and such a name, with his children, his wives, his retinue and his friends, humbly bows down at the feet of the Exalted One.'"

And the venerable Ananda caused the Mallas of Kusinara to stand in groups, each family in a group, and so presented them to the Exalted One, and said: "Lord! a Malla of such and such a name, with his children, his wives, his retinue, and his friends, humbly bows down at the feet of the Exalted One."

And after this manner the venerable Ananda presented all the Mallas of Kusinara to the Exalted One in the first watch of the night.

(*Mahaparinibbana Sutta*)[10] ▲

Buddha's last advice for his disciples and his entering into nirvana:

▼

1 Now the Exalted One addressed the venerable Ananda, and said: "It may be, Ananda, that in some of you the thought may arise, 'The word of the master is ended, we have no teacher more!': But it is not thus, Ananda, that

you should regard it. The truths, and the rules of the order, which I have set forth and laid down for you all, let them, after I am gone, be the Teacher to you."

2   "Ananda! when I am gone address not one another in the way in which the brethren have heretofore addressed each other—with the epithet that is, of *avuso* (friend). A younger brother may be addressed by an elder with his name, or his family name, or the title 'Friend.' But an elder should be addressed by a younger brother as 'Sir' or as 'Venerable Sir.'"

3   "When I am gone, Ananda, let the order, if it should so wish, abolish all the lesser and minor precepts."...

5   Then the Exalted One addressed the brethren, and said: "It may be, brethren, that there may be doubt or misgiving in the mind of some brother as to the Buddha, or the doctrine, or the path, or the method. Inquire, brethren, freely. Do not have to reproach yourselves afterwards with the thought: 'Our teacher was face to face with us, and we could not bring ourselves to inquite of the Exalted One when we were face to face with him.'"

And when he had thus spoken the brethren were silent.

And again the second and the third time the Exalted One addressed the brethren.

And when he had thus spoken the brethren were silent....

6   And the venerable Ananda said to the Exalted One: "How wonderful a thing is it, Lord, and how marvellous! Verily, I believe that in this whole assembly of the brethren there is not one brother who has any doubt or misgiving as to the Buddha, or the doctrine, or the path, or the method!"

"It is out of the fullness of faith that thou hast spoken, Ananda! But, Ananda, the tathagata knows for certain that in this whole assembly of the brethren there is not one brother who has any doubt or misgiving as to the Buddha, or the doctrine, or the path, or the method! For even the most backward, Ananda, of all these five hundred brethren has become converted, is no longer liable to be born in a state of suffering, and is assured of hereafter attaining to the Enlightenment [of arahantship]."

7   Then the Exalted One addressed the brethren, and said: "Behold now, brethren, I exhort you, saying: 'Decay is inherent in all component things! Work out your salvation with diligence!'"

This was the last word of the tathagata!

8   Then the Exalted One entered into the first stage of deep meditation. And rising out of the first stage he passed into the second. And rising out of the second he passed into the third. And rising out of the third stage he passed into the fourth. And rising out of the fourth stage of deep meditation, he entered into the state of mind to which the infinity of space is alone present. And passing out of the mere consciousness of the infinity of space he entered into the state of mind to which the infinity of thought is alone present. And passing

out of the mere consciousness of the infinity of thought he entered into a state of mind to which nothing at all was specially present. And passing out of the consciousness of no special object he fell into a state between consciousness and unconsciousness. And passing out of the state between consciousness and unconsciousness he fell into a state in which the consciousness both of sensations and of ideas had wholly passed away.

Then the venerable Ananda said to the venerable Anuruddha: "O my Lord, O Anuruddha, the Exalted One is dead!"

"Nay! brother Ananda, the Exalted One is not dead. He has entered into that state in which both sensations and ideas have ceased to be!"

9 Then the Exalted One passing out of the state in which both sensations and ideas have ceased to be, entered into the state between consciousness and unconsciousness. And passing out of the state between consciousness and unconsciousness he entered into the state of mind to which nothing at all is specially present. And passing out of the consciousness of no special object he entered into the state of mind to which the infinity of thought is alone present. And passing out of the mere consciousness of the infinity of thought he entered into the state of mind to which the infinity of space is alone present. And passing out of the mere consciousness of the infinity of space he entered into the fourth stage of deep meditation. And passing out of the fourth stage he entered into the third. And passing out of the third stage he entered into the second. And passing out of the second he entered into the first. And passing out of the first stage of deep meditation he entered into the second. And passing out of the second stage he entered into the third. And passing out of the third stage he entered into the fourth stage of deep meditation. And passing out of the last stage of deep meditation he immediately expired.

10 When the Exalted One died there arose, at the moment of his passing out of existence, a mighty earthquake, terrible and awe-inspiring: and the thunders of heaven burst forth.

When the Exalted One died, the venerable Anuruddlia, at the moment of his passing away from existence, uttered these stanzas:

"When he who from all craving want was free,
Who to nirvana's tranquil state had reached,
When the great sage finished his span of life,
No gasping struggle vexed that steadfast heart!

All resolute, and with unshaken mind,
He calmly triumphed o'er the pain of death.
E'en as a bright flame dies away, so was
The last emancipation of his heart."

When the Exalted One died, the venerable Ananda, at the moment of his passing away from existence, uttered this stanza:

"Then was there terror!
Then stood the hair on end!
When he endowed with every grace—
The supreme Buddha—died!"

When the Exalted One died, of those of the brethren who were not yet
free from the passions, some stretched out their arms and wept, and some
fell headlong on the ground, rolling to and fro in anguish at the thought: "Too
soon has the Exalted One died! Too soon has the Happy One passed away!
Too soon has the Light gone out in the world!"

But those of the brethren who were free from the passions [the Arahants]
bore their grief collected and composed at the thought: "Impermanent are
all component things! How is it possible that [they should not be dissolved]?"

11   Then the venerable Anuruddha exhorted the brethren, and said: "Enough, my
brethren! Weep not, neither lament! Has not the Exalted One formerly
declared this to us, that it is in the very nature of all things near and dear unto
us, that we must divide ourselves from them, leave them, sever ourselves from
them? How then, brethren, can this be possible—that whereas anything
whatever born, brought into being, and organized, contains within itself
the inherent necessity of dissolution—how then can this be possible that
such a being should not be dissolved? No such condition can exist! Even the
spirits, brethren, will reproach us."

(Mahaparinibbana Sutta)[11] ▲

Buddha's body is treated like that of a ruler in order to please his disciples
while he himself suggested a more modest treatment. Once the cremation
is completed, the remains are divided among several noble families. They and
their successors build funeral mounds (*stupas*) over them, which in some
cases can be still visited.

▼

12   Now the venerable Anuruddha and the venerable Ananda spent the rest of
that night in religious discourse. Then the venerable Anuruddha, said to the
venerable Ananda: "Go now, brother Ananda, into Kusinara and inform the
Mallas of Kusinara, saying: 'The Exalted One, O Vasetthas, is dead; do, then,
whatever seemeth to you fit!'"

"Even so, Lord!" said the venerable Ananda, in assent, to the venerable
Anuruddha. And having robed himself early in the morning, he took his
bowl, and went into Kusinara with one of the brethren as an attendant.

Now at that time the Mallas of Kusinara were assembled in the council
hail concerning that very matter.

And the venerable Ananda went to the council hail of the Mallas of Kusinara; and when he had arrived there, he informed them, saying: "The Blessed One, O Vasetthas, is dead; do, then, whatever seemeth to you fit!"

13 Then the Mallas of Kusinara gave orders to their attendants, saying:—"Gather together perfumes and garlands, and all the music in Kusinara!"

And the Mallas of Kusinara took the perfumes and garlands, and all the musical instruments, and five hundred suits of apparel, and went to the Upavattana, to the Sala Grove of the Mallas, where the body of the Exalted One lay. There they passed the day in paying honour, reverence, respect, and homage to the remains of the Exalted One with dancing, and hymns, and music, and with garlands and perfumes; and in making canopies of their garments, and preparing decoration wreaths to hang thereon.

14 Then on the seventh day the Mallas of Kusinara thought:—"Let us carry the body of the Exalted One, by the south and outside, to a spot on the south, and outside of the city,—paying it honour, and reverence, and respect, and homage, with dance, and song, and music, with garlands and perfumes,—and there, to the south of the city, let us perform the cremation ceremony."

17 Then the Mallas of Kusinara said to the venerable Ananda:—"What should be done, Lord, with the remains of the tathagata?"

"As men treat the remains of a king of kings, so, Vasetthas, should they treat the remains of a tathagata."

"And how, Lord, do they treat the remains of a king of kings?"

"They wrap the body of a king of kings, Vasetthas, in a new cloth. When that is done they wrap it in carded cotton wool. When that is done they wrap it in a new cloth,—and so on till they have wrapped the body in five hundred successive layers of both kinds. Then they place the body in an oil vessel of iron, and cover that close up with another oil vessel of iron. They then build a funeral pyre of all kinds of perfumes, and burn the body of the king of kings. And then at the four cross roads they erect a cairn to the king of kings. This, Vasetthas, is the way in which they treat the remains of a king of kings.

"And as they treat the remains of a king of kings, so Vasettlias, should they treat the remains of the tathagata. At the four cross roads a cairn should be erected to the tathagata. And whosoever shall there place garlands or perfumes or paint, or make salutation there, or become in its presence calm in heart—that shall long be to them for a profit and a joy."

18 Therefore the Mallas gave orders to their attendants, saying:—"Gather together all the carded cotton wool of the Mallas!"

Then the Mallas of Kusinara wrapped the body of the Exalted One in a new cloth. And when that was done, they wrapped it in carded cotton wool. And when that was done, they wrapped it in a new cloth,—and so on till they had wrapped the body of the Exalted One in five hundred layers of both kinds.

And then they placed the body in an oil vessel of iron, and covered that close up with another oil vessel of iron. And then they built a funeral pyre of all kinds of perfumes and upon it they placed the body of the Exalted One....

And when the homage of the venerable Maha Kassapa and of those five hundred brethren was ended, the funeral pyre of the Exalted One caught fire of itself.

23   Now as the body of the Exalted One burned itself away, from the skin and the integument, and the flesh, and the nerves, and the fluid of the joints, neither soot nor ash was seen. Only the bones remained behind. Just as one sees no soot or ash when ghee or oil is burned; so, as the body of the Exalted One burned itself away, from the skin and the integument, and the flesh, and the nerves, and the fluid of the joints, neither soot nor ash was seen. Only the bones remained behind. And of those five hundred pieces of raiment the very innermost and outermost were both consumed.

And when the body of the Exalted One had been burnt up, there came down streams of water from the sky and extinguished the funeral pyre of the Exalted One; and there burst forth streams of water from the storehouse of the waters [beneath the earth], and extinguished the funeral pyre of the Exalted One. The Mallas of Kusinara also brought water scented with all kinds of perfumes, and extinguished the funeral pyre of the Exalted One.

Then the Mallas of Kusinara surrounded the bones of the Exalted One in their council hail with a lattice work of spears, and with a rampart of bows; and there for seven days they paid honour, and reverence, and respect, and homage to them with dance, and song, and music, and with garlands and perfumes.

24   Now the king of Magadha, Ajatasattu, the son of the queen of the Videha clan, heard the news that the Exalted One had died at Kusinara.

Then the king of Magadha, Ajatasattu, the son of the queen of the Videha clan, sent a messenger to the Mallas, saying:—"The Exalted One was a Kshatriya and so am I. I am worthy to receive a portion of the relics of the Exalted One. Over the remains of the Exalted One will I put up a sacred cairn, and in their honour will I celebrate a feast!"

And the Licehavis of Vesali heard this news and demanded their share of the relics.

And so did the Sakiyas of Kapila-vatthu, the Bulis of Allakappa and the Koliyas of Ramagama as well the brahmin of Vethadipa and the Mallas of Pava.

25   When they heard these things the Mallas of Kusinara spoke to the assembled crowds, saying:—"The Exalted One died in our village domain. We will not give away any part of the remains of the Exalted One!"

When they had thus spoken, Dona the brahmin addressed the assembled crowds, and said:—

"Hear, gracious sirs, one single word from me.
Forbearance was our Buddha wont to teach.
Unseemly is it that over the division
Of the remains of him who was the best of beings
Strife should arise, and wounds, and war!
Let us all, sirs, with one accord unite
In friendly harmony to make eight portions.
Wide spread let cairns spring up in every land
That in the Light of the world mankind may trust!"

"Do thou then, O brahmin, thyself divide the remains of the Exalted One equally into eight parts, with fair division."

"Be it so, sirs!" said Dona the brahmin, in assent, to the assembled brethren. And he divided the remains of the Exalted One equally into eight parts, with fair division. And he said to them:—"Give me, sirs, this vessel, and I will set up over it a sacred cairn, and in its honour will I establish a feast."

And they gave the vessel to Dona the brahmin.

26 And the Moriyas of Pipphalivana heard the news that the Exalted One had died at Kusinara.

Then the Moriyas of Pipphalivana sent a messenger to the Mallas, saying:—"The Exalted One was a Kshatriya and so are we. We are worthy to receive a portion of the relics of the Exalted One. Over the remains of the Exalted One will we put up a sacred cairn, and in their honour will we celebrate a feast!"

And when they heard the answer, saying:—"There is no portion of the remains of the Exalted One left over. The remains of the Exalted One are all distributed," then they took away the embers.

(*Mahaparinibbana Sutta*)[12] ▲

The Buddha Biography Told by a Narrator

The number of elaborate reports about Buddha's life, told by a third person, a narrator, and containing elements labelled "legendary" by nineteenth-century positivism, run into the hundreds. The core elements of Buddha's life story, which we have already encountered, are now embellished to reflect the image pious Buddhists had created of their faith's founder. While these later accounts of Buddha's life lack historical validity, they tell us about how Buddhists of a past era envisioned their teacher. Among the most famous poetical biographies of Buddha is the one composed by the Indian poet Ashvaghosha, who lived during the beginning of the Christian era, although his exact dates are unknown. As one of the foremost hagiographies of Buddhism, the Life of the Buddha became a template of one's path toward

enlightenment. Thousands of Buddhist sacred biographies (i.e., the life stories of exemplary Buddhists) emulated the stages given in the Life of the
Buddha. From the fourteen songs of the *Buddhacarita* (Life of Buddha), we
shall read some excerpts shedding light on how faithful Buddhists of India
felt about Buddha's life.

Soon after Siddhartha is born, his father Shuddhodana, who is now ele-
vated from a nobleman to a king, asks the sage Asita to foretell the future of
the young prince:

▼

54   When the sage was invited in this befitting fashion by the king with all cor-
diality, his large eyes opened wide in admiration and he spoke these profound
and solemn words:—

55   "It indeed accords with your great soul, your hospitality, your generosity, your
piety, that you should thus show to me a kindly disposition, so worthy of your
nature, family, wisdom and age.

56   And this is the course by which those royal seers, acquiring wealth by the subtle Law, ever continued giving it away according to rule, thus being rich in austerities and poor in worldly goods.

57   But hear the reason for my visit and be rejoiced. In the path of the sun I heard
a divine voice saying, 'To thee is born a son for Enlightenment.'

58   As soon as I heard the voice, I put my mind into trance and understood the
matter through the signs. Then I came here to see the lofty banner of the
Shakya race uplifted like the banner of Indra."

59   When the king heard him speak thus, his bearing was disordered with delight,
and he took the prince, as he lay on his nurse's lap, and showed him to the
ascetic.

60   Then the great seer wonderingly beheld the prince, the soles of his feet
marked with a wheel, the fingers and toes joined by a web, the circle of
hair growing between his eyebrows and the testicles withdrawn like an elephant's.

61   And when he saw him resting on the nurse's lap, like the son of Agni on Devi's
lap, the tears flickered on his eyelashes and, sighing, he looked up to heaven.

62   But when the king saw Asita's eyes swimming with tears, he trembled from
affection for his son, and sobbing with his throat choked with weeping, he
clasped his hands and bowed his body, asking him:—

63   "Why are you, who are so steadfast, tearful on seeing him who differs little
in form from the gods, whose brilliant birth has been attended by many
miracles and whose future lot you say is to be the highest?

64   Will the prince be long-lived, Holy One? Surely he is not born for my sorrow?
Shall the two handfuls of water have been obtained by me with such difficulty,
only for Death to come and drink them up?

65 Is the treasure of my fame inexhaustible? Is the dominion to last for ever in the hands of my family? Shall I win bliss in the next world, even in the sleep of death having one eye open in the shape of my son?

66 Is this young shoot of my family, just sprung up, fated to wither without flowering? Tell me quickly, Lord, I am all uneasy; for you know the love of fathers for their sons."

67 The seer understood how the king was troubled by the thought of misfortune and said: "Let not your mind, O king, be disturbed; what I have said is not open to doubt.

68 My agitation is not over aught untoward for him, but I am distressed for my own disappointment. For my time to depart has come, just when he is born who shall understand the means, so hard to find, of destroying birth.

69 For he will give up the kingdom in his indifference to worldly pleasures, and, through bitter struggles grasping the final truth, he will shine forth as a sun of knowledge in the world to dispel the darkness of delusion.

70 With the mighty boat of knowledge he will bring the world, which is being carried away in affliction, up from the ocean of suffering, which is over-spread with the foam of disease and which has old age for its waves and death for its fearsome flood.

71 The world of the living, oppressed with the thirst of desires, will drink the flow-ing stream of his most excellent Law, which is cooled by concentration of thought and has mystic wisdom for the current of its water, firm discipline for its banks and vows for its Braliminy ducks.

72 For to those who, finding themselves on the desert-tracks of the cycle of existence, are harassed by suffering and obstructed by the objects of sense, he will proclaim the way of salvation, as to travellers who have lost their road.

73 Like a mighty cloud with its rain at the close of the summer heat, he will give relief with the rain of the Law to men burnt up in the world with the fire of the passions, whose fuel is the objects of sense.

74 With the most excellent irresistible key of the good Law he will throw open for the escape of living beings the door whose bolt is the thirst of desire and whose leaves are delusion and the darkness of ignorance.

75 And, as king of the Law, he will reach Enlightenment and release from prison the world which is entangled in its own snares of delusion and which is overwhelmed by suffering and destitute of refuge.

76 Therefore be not grieved for him; in this living world that man is to be deplored who through delusion by reason of the sensual pleasures or through intoxication of mind refuses to hear his, the final, Law." ▲

The narrator has the young prince experience a life of wealth and luxury whereby the court women are more a decoration than autonomous human beings:

▼

31 There the women delighted him with their soft voices, charming blandish-
ments, playful intoxications, sweet laughter, curvings of eyebrows and side-
long glances.

32 Then, a captive to the women, who were skilled in the accessories of love and
indefatigable in sexual pleasure, he did not descend from the palace to the
ground, just as one who has won Paradise by his merit does not descend to
earth from the heavenly mansion.

33 But the king, for the sake of his son's prosperity and spurred on by the goal
predicted for him, abode in holy peace, desisted from sin, practised self-
restraint and rewarded the good.

34 He did not, like one wanting in self-control, indulge in the pleasures of the
senses, he cherished no improper passion for women, with firmness he overcame the rebellious horses of the senses, and conquered his kinsmen and subjects by his virtues.

35 He did not learn science to cause suffering to others, but studied only the
knowledge that was beneficient; for he wished well to all people as much as
to his own subjects.

(*Buddhacarita* II)[13] ▲

In the first-person accounts, the presence of women as court entertainers and
courtesans is acknowledged as a matter of fact. The later biographies create
a tension between the future Buddha in full control of his passion and desire
and the women who are "given free rein." We see here the beginning of a
trend in Buddhist literature that often resulted in outright misogynist statements that depict women as caught in the fangs of lust and passion while
men are in control of their senses.

In the following verses, the future Buddha is presented as if he had
already the composure and self-control of later:

▼

53 Thus these young women, to whose minds love had given free rein, assailed
the prince with wiles of every kind.

54 But despite such allurements the prince firmly guarded his senses, and in his
perturbation over the inevitability of death, was neither rejoiced nor distressed.

55 He, the supreme man, saw that they had no firm footing in the real truth, and
with mind that was at the same time both perturbed and steadfast he thus
meditated:

56 "Do these women then not understand the transitoriness of youth,
that they are so inebriated with their own beauty, which old age will
destroy?..."

(*Buddhacarita* II)[14] ▲

All accounts of Buddha's life affirm a youth of comfort and luxury, but assert that the young prince saw behind the sensory pleasures only dissatisfaction and pain. Our narrator constructs an outing into the world beyond the palace walls as a seminal experience that brought the young prince to a more philosophical appreciation of life. In the jungle the prince encounters the ever-present state of pain in this world and its possible defeat:

2   Then longing for spiritual peace, he set forth outside with the king's permission in order to see the forest, and for companions he had a retinue of ministers' sons, chosen for their reliability and skill in converse.

(*Buddhacarita* II)[15]

4   Desire for the forest as well as the excellence of the land led him on to the more distant jungle-land, and he saw the soil being ploughed, with its surface broken with the tracks of the furrows like waves of water.

5   When he saw the ground in this state, with the young grass torn up and scattered by the ploughs and littered with dead worms, insects and other creatures, he mourned deeply as at the slaughter of his own kindred.

6   And as he observed the ploughmen with their bodies discoloured by wind, dust and the sun's rays, and the oxen in distress with the labour of drawing, the most noble one felt extreme compassion.

7   Then alighting from his horse, he walked slowly over the ground, overcome with grief. And as he considered the coming into being and the passing away of creation, he cried in his afflication, "How wretched this is."

8   And desiring to reach perfect clearness with his mind, he stopped his friends who were following him, and proceeded himself to a solitary spot at the root of a jambu-tree, whose beautiful leaves were waving in all directions.

9   And there he sat down on the clean ground, with grass bright like beryl; and reflecting on the origin and destruction of creation he took the path of mental stillness.

10 And his mind at once came to a stand and at the same time he was freed from mental troubles such as desire for the objects of sense, etc. And he entered into the first trance of calmness which is accompanied by gross and subtle cogitation and which is supermundane in quality.

(*Buddhacarita* II)[16]

Siddhartha left his home and subjected himself to studies and ascetic practices. Determined to achieve a breakthrough, which will give stillness and peace to his mind, he is attacked by Mara, the Buddhist symbol of impermanence and illusion of this world, before he is defeated. Mara's attack became a famous subject of Buddhist art. Many temple walls illustrate the attack pitching demon-like creatures against Buddha absorbed in serenity:

▼

18 Then as soon as Mara thought of his army in his desire to obstruct the tran-
    quillity of the Shakya sage, his followers stood round him, in various forms and
    carrying lances, trees, javelins, clubs and swords in their hands;

19 Having the faces of boars, fishes, horses, asses and camels, or the counte-
    nances of tigers, bears, lions and elephants, one-eyed, many-mouthed, three-
    headed, with pendulous bellies and speckled bellies;

20 Without knees or thighs, or with knees vast as pots, or armed with tusks or
    talons, or with skulls for faces, or with many bodies, or with half their faces
    broken off or with huge visages;

21 Ashy-grey in colour, tricked out with red spots, carrying ascetics' staves,
    with hair smoke-coloured like a monkey's, hung round with garlands, with
    pendent ears like elephants, clad in skins or entirely naked;

22 With half their countenances white or half their bodies green; some also
    copper-coloured, smoke-coloured, tawny or black; some too with arms
    having an overgarment of snakes, or with rows of jangling bells at their
    girdles; ...

(Buddhacarita II)[17]

25 Some, as they ran, leapt wildly about, some jumped on each other; while
    some gambolled in the sky, others sped along among the treetops.

26 One danced about, brandishing a trident; another snorted, as he trailed a club;
    one roared like a bull in his excitement, another blazed fire from every hair.

27 Such were the hordes of fiends who stood encompassing the root of the bodhi
    tree on all sides, anxious to seize and to kill, and awaiting the command of
    their master.

28 Beholding in the beginning of the night the hour of conflict between Mara
    and the bull of the Shakyas, the sky lost its brightness, the earth shook and
    the quarters blazed and crashed.

29 The wind raged wildly in every direction, the stars did not shine, the moon
    was not seen, and night spread forth still thicker darkness and all the oceans
    were troubled.

30 And the earth-bearing Nagas, devoted to dharma, did not brook obstruction
    to the great sage and, turning their eyes wrathfully on Mara, they hissed and
    unwound their coils.

31 But the divine sages of the Pure Abodes, absorbed in the fulfilment of the good
    Law, developed compassion for Mara in their minds, but were untouched by
    anger, because they were freed from all passion.

(Buddhacarita II)[18]

70 And when Mara heard that speech of his and observed the great sage's
    unshakenness, then, his efforts frustrated, he went away dejectedly with the
    arrows by which the world is smitten in the heart.

71 Then his host fled away in all directions, its elation gone, its toil rendered fruitless, its rocks, logs and trees scattered everywhere, like a hostile army whose chief has been slain by the foe.

72 As he of the flower-banner fled away defeated with his following, and the great seer, the passion-free conqueror of the darkness of ignorance, remained victorious, the heavens shone with the moon like a maiden with a smile, and there fell a rain of sweet-smelling flowers filled with water.

(*Buddhacarita* II) [19] ▲

During the night the awakening Buddha, as Siddhartha is now called, gains insight into the true nature of things. He articulates the core of Buddhist belief:

▼

49 Then as the third watch of that night drew on, the best of those who understand trance meditated on the real nature of this world:—

50 "Alas! Living creatures obtain but toil; over and over again they are born, grow old, die, pass on and are reborn.

51 Further man's sight is veiled by passion and by the darkness of delusion, and from the excess of his blindness he does not know the way out of this great suffering."

52 After thus considering, he reflected in his mind, "What is it verily, whose existence causes the approach of old age and death?"

53 Penetrating the truth to its core, he understood that old age and death are produced, when there is birth.

54 He saw that head-ache is only possible when the head is already in existence; for when the birth of a tree has come to pass, then only can the felling of it take place.

55 Then the thought again arose in him, "What does this birth proceed from?" Then he saw rightly that birth is produced from existence due to the power of the act.

56 With his divine eyesight he saw that active being proceeds from the act, not from a creator or from nature or from a self or without a cause.

57 Just as, if the first know in a bamboo is wisely cut, everything quickly comes into order, so his knowledge advanced in proper order.

58 Thereon the sage applied his mind to determining the origin of existence. Then he saw that the origin of existence was to be found in appropriation.

59 This act arises from appropriating the various vows and rules of life, sensual pleasure, views of self and false views, as fire arises by appropriating fuel.

60 Then the thought occurred to him, "From what cause does appropriation come?" Thereon he recognised the causal condition of appropriation to lie in thirst.

61 Just as the forest is set ablaze by a little fire, when the wind fans it, so thirst
    gives birth to the vast sins of sensual passion and the rest.

62 Then he reflected, "From what does thirst arise?" Thereon he concluded
    that the cause of thirst is sensation.

63 Mankind, overwhelmed by their sensations, thirst for the means of satisfying
    them; for no one in the absence of thirst takes pleasure in water.

64 Then he again meditated, "What is the source of sensation?" He, who had put
    an end to sensation, saw also the cause of sensation to be in contact.

65 Contact is to be explained as the uniting of the object, the sense and the mind,
    whence sensation is produced, just as fire is produced from the uniting of the
    two rubbing sticks and fuel.

66 Next he considered that contact has a cause. Thereon he recognised the
    cause to lie in the six organs of sense.

67 The blind man does not perceive objects, since his eye does not bring them
    into junction with his mind; if sight exists, the junction takes place. Therefore
    there is contact, when the sense-organ exists.

68 Further he made up his mind to understand the origin of the six organs of
    sense. Thereon the knower of causes knew the cause to be name-and-form.

69 Just as the leaf and the stalk are only said to exist when there is a shoot in exis-
    tence, so the six organs of sense only arise when name-and-form is in exis-
    tence.

70 Then the thought occurred to him, "What is the cause of name-and-form?"
    Thereon he, who had passed to the further side of knowledge, saw its origin
    to lie in consciousness.

71 When consciousness arises, name-and-form is produced. When the develop-
    ment of the seed is completed, the sprout assumes a bodily form.

72 Next he considered, "From what does consciousness come into being?"
    Then he knew that it is produced by supporting itself on name-and-form.

73 Then after he had understood the order of causality, he thought over it; his
    mind travelled over the views that he had formed and did not turn aside to
    other thoughts.

74 Consciousness is the causal condition from which name-and-form is pro-
    duced. Name-and-form again is the support on which consciousness is based.

75 Just as a boat conveys a man … so consciousness and name-and-form are
    causes of each other.

76 Just as redhot iron causes grass to blaze and as blazing grass makes iron
    redhot, of such a kind is their mutual causality.

                                                    (*Buddhacarita* II)[20]

86 At that moment of the fourth watch when the dawn came up and all that
    moves or moves not was stilled, the great seer reached the stage which
    knows no alteration, the sovereign leader the state of omniscience.

87   When, as the Buddha, he knew this truth, the earth swayed like a woman
     drunken with wine, the quarters shone bright with crowds of Siddhas, and
     mighty drums resounded in the sky.

                                                      (*Buddhacarita* II)[21] ▲

Buddha's Intrinsic Nature

After Gautama became enlightened and was therefore known as Buddha, disciples and other ascetics and mendicants continued to ask him: Who are you?
Buddha answered according to the questioner's mental set. Thus, when a
Brahmin asked him, Buddha would employ brahmanical terminology, and
when asked by a warrior, he would use warrior expressions and images. Consequently, we find a broad spectrum of answers to this question.

▼ WHO IS BUDDHA?

At one time the Lord (i.e., Buddha) was journeying along the road between
Ukkattha and Setabhya; so also was the Brahmin Dona. He saw on the Lord's footprints the wheels[22] with their thousand spokes, their rims and hubs and all their
attributes complete, and he thought: "Indeed, how wonderful and marvellous—
it cannot be that these are the footprints of a human being." Then Dona, following the Lord's footprints, saw that there was [a monk] sitting under a tree, comely,
faith-inspiring, his senses and mind peaceful, attained to the calm of uttermost control, restrained, tamed and guarded as to his senses. Seeing this well disciplined
monk, Dona approached the Lord and said:
    "Is your reverend a god?"
    "No indeed, brahmin, I am not a god."
    "Then a spirit of the air?"
    "No indeed, brahmin."
    "A ghost of fertility then?"[23]
    "No indeed, brahmin, I am not a fertility ghost."
    "Then is your reverend a human being?"
    "No indeed, brahmin, I am not a human being."
    "You answer No to all my questions. Who then is your reverend?"
    "Brahmin, if these mental obstructions had not been extinguished, I might
have been a god, ghost of the air or of fertility, or a human being. But these
obstructions are extinguished in me, cut off at the root, made like a palm-tree
stump that can come to no further existence in the future. Just as a blue, red or
white lotus, although born in the water, grown in the water, when it reaches
the surface stands there unsoiled by the water—just so, brahmin, although born
in the world, grown up in the world, having overcome the world, I abide unsoiled
by the world. Take it that I am Buddha, brahmin."

                                              (*Anguttara Nikaya* II, 37 ff.)[24] ▲

The Buddha Claims to Be the Supreme Teacher

▼ All-vanquishing, all-knowing, lo! am I, from all
       wrong thinking wholly purged and free.
   All things discarded, cravings rooted out,—whom
       should I follow?—I have found out all.
   No teacher's mine, no equal. Counterpart to me
       there's none throughout the whole wide world.
   The arahat am I, teacher supreme, utter
       enlightenment is mine alone; unfever'd calm is mine,
       nirvana's peace.
   I seek the Kasis' city, there to start my
       Doctrine's wheel, a world purblind to save,
       sounding the tocsin's call to Deathlessness.

                                        (*Majihima-nikaya* 26)[25] ▲

The Human Teacher

In the following excerpt Buddha presents himself as a teacher, fully human.
He would adapt himself to whatever level the other was on. The reference
to using different languages is important, as Buddhism from its beginning
never endorsed the idea of one sacred or authoritative language. Unlike the
teachings of early Hinduism, which ought to be transmitted in Sanskrit only,
Buddhist teachings could be given in whatever language the people would
speak:

▼ Now I know well that when I approached various large assemblies, even
before I had sat down there or had spoken or begun to talk to them, whatever
might have been their sort I made myself of like sort, whatever their language so
was my language. And I rejoiced them with a talk on dhamma, made it acceptable to them, set them on fire, gladdened them.

                                        (*Digha-nikaya* II, 109)[26] ▲

The Tathagata—Unfathomable

In the following excerpt Buddha, while affirming his human nature, points
at the unfathomable nature of the transcendent Buddha, the *tathagata*:

▼ "If a fire were blazing in front of you, Vaccha, would you know what is was?"
   "Yes, good Gotama."
   "And would you know the reason for its blazing?"
   "Yes, because it had a supply of grass and sticks."
   "And would you know if it were to be put out?"

"Yes, good Gotama."

"And on its being put out, would you know the direction the fire had gone to from here—east, west, north, south?"

"This question does not apply, good Gotama. For the fire blazed because it had a supply of grass and sticks; but when it had consumed this and had no other fuel, then, being without fuel, it is reckoned as gone out."

"Even so, Vaccha, that material shape, that feeling, perception, those impulses, that consciousness by which one, in defining the tathagata, might define him—all have been got rid of by the tathagata, cut off at the root, made like a palm-tree stump that can come to no further existence in the future. Freed from reckoning by material shape, feeling, perception, the impulses, consciousness is the tathagata; he is deep, immeasurable, unfathomable, as is the great ocean. 'Arises' does not apply, nor does 'does not arise,' nor 'both arises and does not arise,' nor 'neither arises nor does not arise.'"

(*Majihima-nikaya* 1, 487–88)[27] ▲

The Body of Dharma

Buddha himself, as well as the Buddhist traditions, never made any claim that Buddha was anything but human, although extraordinary. This extraordinary quality was seen as Buddha's different "bodies" or modes of being. Above we have learned that Buddha's true nature is ineffable; in the following excerpt we learn that his true being is *dhamma*, a term that is not to be rendered with one English expression. *Dhamma* incorporates such meanings as the totality of the perceivable world (everything with the exception of *nirvana*), the components of this totality, and Buddha's entire teaching. This excerpt also introduces the term *brahma* as a synonym for *dhamma*. Why is this Hindu term introduced here? In this passage Buddha is talking to Vasettha, a Brahmin. In order to make his concept understandable to the Brahmin, Buddha uses the other's terminology to explain what he means by *dhamma*:

▼   He, Vasettha, whose faith in the tathagata is settled, rooted, established, firm, a faith not to be shaken by a recluse or brahmin or deva or by Mara or Brahma or by anyone in the world—he may say: "I am the Lord's own son, born of his mouth, born of dhamma, formed by dhamma, heir to dhamma." What is the reason for this? This, Vasettha, is a synonym for the tathagata: dhamma-body and again brahma-body, and again Dhamma-become and again Brahma-become.

(*Dighanikaya* III, 84)[28] ▲

Dharma, Buddha's Intrinsic Nature

▼ The king said: "Did you, revered Nagasena, see the Buddha?"

"No, sire."

"Then did your teachers see the Buddha?"

"No, sire."

"Well then, revered Nagasena, there is not a Buddha."

"But have you, sire, seen the Himalayan river Uha?"

"No, revered sir."

"Then did your father ever see it?"

"No, revered sire.

"Well then, sire, there is not a river Uha."

"There is, revered sir. Even if neither my father nor I have seen it, there is the river Uha all the same."

"Even so, sire, even if neither my teachers nor I have seen the Lord, there is the Lord all the same."

"Very good, revered Nagasena. But is the Buddha preeminent?"

"Yes, sire."

"But how do you know, revered Nagasena, when you have not seen in the past, that the Buddha is pre-eminent?"

"What do you think about this, sire? Could those who have not already seen the great ocean know that it is so mighty, deep, immeasurable, unfathomable, that although these five great rivers—the Ganges, Jumna, Aciravati, Sarabhu and the Mahi—flow into it constantly and continually, yet is neither its emptiness nor its fullness affected thereby?"

"Yes, they could know that, revered sir."

"Even so, sire, having seen great disciples who have attained nirvana, I know that the Lord is pre-eminent."

"Very good, revered Nagasena. Is it then possible to know this?"

"Once upon a time, sire, the Elder named Tissa was a teacher of writing. Many years have passed since he died. How is it that he is known?"

"By his writing, revered sir.

"Even so, sire, he who sees dhamma sees the Lord; for dhamma, sire, was taught by the Lord."

"Very good, revered Nagasena. Have you seen dhamma?"

"Sire, disciples are to conduct themselves for as long as life lasts with the Buddha as conduit, with the Buddha as designation."

"Very good, revered Nagasena. But is there a Buddha?"

"Yes, sire, there is a Buddha."

"But is it possible, revered Nagasena, to point to the Buddha as being either here or there?"

"Sire, the Lord has attained nirvana in the nirvana-element that has no groups of existence still remaining. It is not possible to point to the Lord as being either here or there."

"Make a simile."

"What do you think about this, sire? When some flame in a great burning mass of fire goes out, is it possible to point to the flame as being either here or there?"

"No, revered sir. That flame has ceased to be, it has disappeared."

"Even so, sire, the Lord has attained nirvana in the nirvana-element that has no groups of existence still remaining. The Lord has gone home. It is not possible to point to him as being here or there. But it is possible, sire, to point to the Lord by means of the dhamma-body; for dhamma, sire, was taught by the Lord."

"Very good, revered Nagasena."

(*Millindapanha* 70–73)[29] ▲

▼ What is there, Vakkali, in seeing this vile body? Whoso sees the doctrine, sees me; whoso sees me sees the doctrine. Seeing the doctrine, Vakkali, he sees me; seeing me, he sees the doctrine.

(*Samyutta-nikaya* III, 120)[30] ▲

▼ Since a tathagata, even when actually present, is incomprehensible, it is inept to say of him—of the uttermost person, the supernal person, the attainer of the supernal—that after dying the tathagata is, or is not, or both is and is not, or neither is nor is not.

(*Samyutta-nikaya* III, 118)[31] ▲

Excerpts from Mahayana Sutras

In the following three passages, taken from important Mahayana sutras, Buddha is presented as transcendental reality that manifests itself as the various Buddhas who have appeared over time in the different worlds of the universe. Buddha declares in this section from the *Lotus sutra* that the teachings of the various Buddhas who follow each other in strict succession is nothing but a pedagogical means to guide the disciples to enlightenment. The true Buddha is unfathomable and inconceivable. On the one hand, the passage affirms the existence of many Buddhas, while on the other hand, it denies their true existence. Thus, the historical reality of Buddha is subsumed in the ahistorical and eternal reality of his transcendence. The *Vajracchedika* passage emphasizes the identity of Buddha and *dharma*. The last passage, taken from the *Saptashatika*, reflects on how Buddha as *tathagata*, that is, in his synchronic transcendental existence, relates to *tathata*, that is, suchness or reality-as-is. All three texts from which the excerpts are taken are foundational to Mahayana Buddhism.

▼   The Lord said: As a result of my sustaining power this world, with its Gods, men and Asuras, forms the notion that recently the Lord Shakyamuni, after going forth from his home among the Shakyas, has awoken to full enlightenment, on the terrace of enlightenment, by the town of Gaya.

But one should not see it thus, sons of good family. In fact it is many hundreds of thousands of myriads of *kotis* of aeons ago that I have awoken to full enlightenment.... Ever since, during all that time I have demonstrated dharma to beings in this *saha* world system, and also in hundreds of thousands of myriades of *kotis* of other world systems. But when I have spoken of other tathagatas, beginning with the tathagata Dipankara, and of the nirvana of these tathagatas, then that has just been conjured up by me as an emission of the skill in means by which I demonstrate dharma.

Moreover, the tathagata surveys the diversity in the faculties and vigour of successive generations of beings. To each generation he announces his name, declares that he has entered nirvana, and brings peace to beings by various discourses on dharma. To beings who are of low disposition, whose store of merit is small, and whose depravities are many, he says in that case: "I am young in years, monks, I have left the homes of my family, and but lately have I won full enlightenment." But when the tathagata, although fully enlightened for so long, declares that he has been fully enlightened but recently, then such discourses on dharma have been spoken for no other reason than to bring beings to maturity and to save them. All these discourses on dharma have been taught by the tathagata in order to discipline beings.

(Saddharmapundarika XV, 268 ff) [32] ▲

▼   The Lord: Those who by my form did see me,
       And those who followed me by my voice,
       Wrong are the efforts they engaged in,
       Me those people will not see.
       From the dharma one should see the Buddha,
       For the dharma-bodies are the guides.
       Yet dharmahood is not something one
       should become aware of,
       Nor can one be made aware of it.

(Vajracchedika 26 a, b) [33] ▲

▼   The Lord: How, Manjushri, should the tathagata be seen and honoured?

Manjushri: Through the mode of suchness (tathata) do I see the tathagata, through the mode of non-discrimination, in the manner of non-observation. I see him through the mode of non-production and non-existence. But suchness does not attain full knowledge,—thus do I see the tathagata. Suchness does not stand at any point or spot,—thus do I see the tathagata. Suchness is not past, future, or present,—thus do I see the tathagata. Suchness is neither brought about by duality nor by non-duality,—thus do I see the tathagata. Suchness is neither defined nor purified,—thus do I see the tathagata. Suchness is neither produced nor stopped,—thus do I see the tathagata. In this way the tathagata is seen and honoured.

(*Saptashatika* 195)[34] ▲

Excerpts from the Tantras

The Diamond Vehicle, or *Vajrayana*, was the third major doctrinal and ritual movement that swept over the Buddhist world from around the fifth century on. It affected mainly the Indian subcontinent, Southeast Asia, and Tibet, while its affect on East Asia was less pronounced. The *Vajrayana* system of thought and practice was build on *Mahayana* philosophy, that is, it ascribed to the idea of the *bodhisattva*, the concept of emptiness (*shunyata*), and the idea, borrowed from the *Tathagata-garbha* tradition, that Buddha nature permeates the entire universe. The latter concept spawned a fruitful development within the *Vajrayana* tradition as it permitted the assumption that every creature is already a Buddha, that there is no path to be pursued and no enlightenment to be obtained. The here and now is *nirvana*—one must only be able to recognize it. The *Vajrayana*, however, added some novel ideas to the inherited system of Buddhist thought: an elaborate system of visualization of numerous deities symbolizing different Buddhist concepts and virtues (such as Perfection of Wisdom); diverse and rich rituals designed to alleviate everyday anxieties as well as paving the way to enlightenment, and, most prominently, the view that sexuality may be used as a vehicle to actualize enlightenment rather than seeing it as an obstacle. Over time, the *Vajrayana* tradition produced a large literature, which is available to us mainly in Tibetan translations but also as a few ancient Sanskrit manuscripts and as fragments found in Inner Asia. While many tantric texts claim to be translations of Indian originals, only in a few cases could this claim be verified. The origin and transmission of most tantric texts is still shrouded in mystery. One thing, however, is clear: the transmission of the sacred texts was not static. This implies that the body of the texts has undergone significant changes and modifications over the centuries.

The text from which the following excerpt is taken is preserved in Tibetan only, despite its claim to be a translation of an Indian text. This text is one of the seminal texts of the *Atiyoga* or *Dzogchen* tradition, which flourished in Tibet during the eighth century and experienced a revival during the fourteenth century. The ultimate, here addressed as *bodhicitta*, is seen as a king who is the origin or ground of the entire universe. This language has certain similarities with theistic texts of Hinduism, and is unusual in the Buddhist material as it refers to *bodhicitta* in its primordial being as creator (*byed pa po*), a term usually shunned in Buddhism. It documents, however, the broad range of how Buddha's intrinsic nature was envisaged by the Buddhists.

▼ The Bodhicitta, the All-Creating King, proclaimed:

"I am the Creator of all phenomena in the past, Mahasattva, pay attention to your ear, reflect on what you will hear now: I am the All-Creating King. I am the Mind of Pure Perfection (*byung chub sems*). If I would not be pre-existent, the phenomena would not have a point from where their existence could start. If I would not be pre-existent there would be no King who creates all phenomena. If I would not be pre-existent, no Buddha would ever be. If I would not be pre-existent, no doctrine would every be. If I would not be pre-existent, no entourage would ever be."

(*Kun byed rgyal po'i mdo*)[35] ▲

Dharma: The Teaching of the Buddha

Ethics (Shila)

Refuge in Buddha, Dharma, and Sangha

"To go for refuge" is the Buddhist equivalent of the Christian sacrament of baptism. Through the rite of taking refuge a Buddhist expresses a firm faith in Buddha, his teaching, and the community (*sangha*); it is the formal expression of becoming a Buddhist. It is called "to go for refuge" because one takes refuge in Buddha as the right teacher, in the doctrine as the right teaching, and in the community or *Sangha* as the right group of friends. Buddhists repeat this act whenever they enter a temple and bow in front of the statues and at the start of most prayers or meditation sessions. It is believed that going for refuge will plant a seed in one's mind that will come to fruition in later lives.

In the following, we shall first read an excerpt from an early *Theravada* text that emphasizes that taking refuge is not a magical ablution of all misdeeds but rather a personal commitment. The second excerpt, taken from the writings of Gampopa, a Tibetan master (1079–1153), teaches us that depending on nature, gods, or even parents and friends is futile as they all are prone to fear and misery, which does not apply to Buddha, the teaching, and the *Sangha*.

▼ Quite so, Ananda; quite so. For, if a man has been led by a teacher to find refuge in the Buddha and his doctrine and his confraternity, the service rendered him cannot be requited by salutations or civilities or by presents of robes and other requisites; not again are such things a recompense for being led either to abstain from taking life, stealing, lechery, lying and strong drink, or to have absolute faith in the Buddha and his doctrine and his confraternity, or to have become an embodiment of all noble and lovely virtue, or to have an unclouded belief in the four truths.

(*Majjhima-nikaya* 142)[36] ▲

▼ The world takes refuge in mountains,
Forests and shrines,
Groves and stones,
And deities of trees:
But these are no proper asylum.

Should we then take refuge in father or mother, in friends and other persons who are dear to us and who rejoice at our well-being? The answer again is that they are unable to protect us. You may now ask why they all are unable to protect us. The reply is that a protector must himself be free from fear and not suffer from misery. But all those who have been mentioned are frightened and subject to misery. Therefore, since only the Buddha is perfectly free from misery, while the dharma provides the only attainment of buddhahood and the sangha alone can help with the dharma, we must take refuge in them. So also it has been said:

Take now your refuge in the Buddha,
The dharma and the sangha,
Who eradicate fear in the frightened
And who protect the unprotected.

(*The Jewel Ornament of Liberation*)[37] ▲

The Five Precepts

The Five Precepts are the fundamental rules of Buddhist ethics, observed by laity and clerics of all traditions. The abstention from taking any life should result in all Buddhists being vegetarians, which, however, is not the case. In several Buddhist traditions the eating of meat is accepted as long as the Buddhist had no part in the killing. The fifth precept, i.e., to abstain from intoxicants, is often disregarded by laity while monks and nuns in all regularity are expected to observe this rule.

▼ "I undertake to observe the rule
to abstain from taking life;
to abstain from taking what is not given;
to abstain from sensuous misconduct;
to abstain from false speech;
to abstain from intoxicants as tending to cloud the mind." ▲

The first four precepts are explained by Buddhaghosa as follows:

▼

1   "Taking life" means to murder anything that lives. It refers to the striking and
     killing of living being. "Anything that lives"—ordinary people speak here of
     a "living being," but more philosophically we speak of "anything that has the
     life force." "Taking life" is then the will to kill anything that one perceives as
     having life, to act so as to terminate the life-force in it, insofar as the will finds
     expression in bodily action or in speech. With regard to animals it is worse to
     kill large ones than small. Because a more extensive effort is involved. Even
     where the effort is the same, the difference in substance must be considered.
     In the case of humans the killing is the more blameworthy the more virtuous
     they are. Apart from that, the extent of the offence is proportionate to the
     intensity of the wish to kill. Five factors are involved; a living being, the per-
     ception of a living being, a thought of murder, the action of carrying it out,
     and death as a result of it. And six are the ways in which the offence may be
     carried out; with one's own hand, by instigation, my missiles, by slow poison-
     ing, by sorcery, by psychic power.

2   "To take what is not given" means the appropriation of what is not given. It
     refers to the removing of someone else's property, to the stealing of it, to theft.
     "What is not given" means that which belongs to someone else. "Taking what
     is not given" is then the will to steal anything that one perceives as belong-
     ing to someone else, and to act so as to appropriate it. Its blameworthiness
     depends partly on the value of the property stolen, partly on the worth of its
     owner. Five factors are involved: someone else's belongings, the awareness
     that they are someone else's, the thought of theft, the action of carrying it out,
     the taking away as a result of it. This sin, too, may be carried out in six ways.
     One may also distinguish unlawful acquisition by way of theft, robbery,
     underhand dealings, stratagems, and the casting of lots.

3   "Sensuous misconduct"—here "sensuous" means "sexual" and "miscon-
     duct" is extremely blameworthy bad behaviour. "Sensuous misconduct" is the
     will to transgress against those whom one should not go into, and the car-
     rying out of this intention by unlawful physical action. By "those one should
     not go into," first of all men are meant. And then also twenty kinds of
     women. Ten of them are under some form of protection, by their mother,
     father, parents, brother, sister, family, clan, co-religionists, by having been
     claimed from birth onwards, or by the king's law. The other ten kinds are:
     women bought with money, concubines for the fun of it, kept women,
     women bought by the gift of a garment, concubines who have been acquired
     by the ceremony which consists of dipping their hands in water, concubines
     who once carried burdens on their heads, slave girls who are also concubines,
     servants who are also concubines, girls captured in war, temporary wives. The

offence is the more serious, the more moral and virtuous the person transgressed against. Four factors are involved: someone who should not be gone into, the thought of cohabiting with that one, the actions which lead to such cohabitation, and its actual performance. There is only one way of carrying it out: with one's own body.

4 "False"—this refers to actions of the voice, or actions of the body, which aim at deceiving others by obscuring the actual facts. "False speech" is the will to deceive others by words or deeds. One can also explain: "False," means something which is not real, not true. "Speech" is the intimation that is real or true. "False speech" is then the volition which leads to the deliberate intimation to someone else that something is so when it is not so. The seriousness of the offence depends on the circumstances. If a householder, unwilling to give something, says that he has not got it, that is a small offence; but to represent something one has seen with one's own eyes as other than one has seen it, that is a serious offence. If a mendicant has on his rounds got very little oil or ghee, and if the then exclaims, "What a magnificent river flows along here, my friends!," that is only a rather stale joke, and the offence is small; but to say that one has seen what one has not seen, that is a serious offence. Four factors are involved: something which is not so, the thought of deception, an effort to carry it out, the communication of the falsehood to someone else. There is only one way of doing it: with one's own body.

"To abstain from"—one crushes or forsakes sin. It means an abstention which is associated with wholesome thoughts. And it is threefold: (i) one feels obliged to abstain; (ii) one formally undertakes to do so; (iii) one has lost all temptation not to do so.

(i) Even those who have not formally undertaken to observe the precepts may have the conviction that it is not right to offend against them. So it was with Cakkana, a Ceylonese boy. His mother was ill, and the doctor prescribed fresh rabbit meat for her. His brother sent him into the field to catch a rabbit, and he went as he was bidden. Now a rabbit had run into a field to eat of the corn, but in its eagerness to get there had got entangled in a snare, and gave forth cries of distress. Cakkana followed the sound, and thought: "This rabbit has got caught there, and it will make a fine medicine for my mother!" But then he thought again: "It is not suitable for me that, in order to preserve my mother's life, I should deprive someone else of his life." And so he released the rabbit, and said to it: "Run off, play with the other rabbits in the wood, eat grass and drink water!" On his return he told the story to his brother, who scolded him. He then went to his mother, and said to her: "Even without having been told, I know quite clearly that I should not deliberately deprive any living being of life." He then fervently resolved that these truthful words of his might make his mother well again, and so it actually happened.

(ii)   The second kind of abstention refers to those who not only have formally undertaken not to offend against the precepts, but who in addition are willing to sacrifice their lives for that. This can be illustrated by a layman who lived near Uttaravarddhamana. He had received the precepts from Buddharakkhita, the Elder. He then went to plough his field, but found that his ox had got lost. In his search for the ox he climbed up the mountain, where a huge snake took hold of him. He thought of cutting off the snake's head with his sharp knife, but on further reflection he thought to himself: "It is not suitable that I, who have received the precepts from the venerable guru, should break them again." Three times he thought, "My life I will give up, but not the precepts!" and then he threw his knife away. Thereafter the huge viper let him go, and went somewhere else.

(iii) The last kind of abstention is association with the holy Path. It does not even occur to the Holy persons to kill any living being.

(Buddhaghosa's *Pancasudani-sutta*)[38] ▲

Code of Ethics for Monks and Nuns

The life of nuns and monks is subject to hundreds of rules, which regulate important issues, such as how to relate to the political powers, right to property, and interactions and contacts between the sexes, but also trivial rules such as how much salt one is allowed to store, how to close doors, and how to eat. Each rule has a story attached that details the circumstances under which it came into existence. It is obvious from this context that many rules were imposed in response to concerns from laity. The *Vinaya Pitaka* contains all the rules and regulations governing the life of monks and nuns. As a collection of case law it has grown over time and is the oldest legal document of India. The set of rules for nuns and monks is contained in the *Pratimoksha sutra* and its commentaries. Every two weeks the monastic community of a monastery has to assemble in order to listen to the reading of the rules and to confess violations. Penalties for violations vary from expulsion from the Order for the most serious crimes (e.g., murder) to a mere confession of the violation for the least serious offences. Several versions of these texts exist. Over the course of centuries, many of the rules became practically obsolete, for instance the rule not to handle money or to avoid eating after noon.

▼   Here, venerable gentlemen, are the four rules about the offences which deserve expulsion. They should be recited every fortnight in the *Pratimoksha-sutra*:

1   If a monk should have sexual intercourse with anyone, down to an animal, this monk has fallen into an offence which deserves expulsion, and he should no longer live in the community. This holds good for any monk who has entered on a life based on a monk's training, unless he has thereafter repudiated the training, and declared his weakness.

2   If a monk, whether he dwells in a village or in solitude, should take anything not given, he should no longer live in the community. This, however, only applies to thefts for which a king or his police would seize a thief and kill, imprison, banish, fine, or reprove him.

3   If a monk should intentionally take the life of a human being or of one like a human being, with his own hand, or with a knife, or by having him assassinated, then he has fallen into an offence which deserves expulsion. And this applies also to a monk who incites others to self-destruction, and who speaks to them in praise of death, with such words as, "O man, what is the use to you of this miserable life? It is better for you to die than be alive!"

4   Unless a monk be actuated by excessive self-conceit, he commits an offence which deserves expulsion if, vainly and without basis in fact, he falsely claims to have realized and perceived superhuman states or the fullness of the insight of the saints; and if later on, whether questioned or not, in his desire to get rid of his fault and regain his purity, he admits that he had claimed to have realized, without having done so, that he had claimed to have perceived, without having done so, and that he had told a falsehood and lie.

Venerable gentlemen, the four offences leading to expulsion have been recited. A monk who has committed any of them should no longer live in the community. Now, I ask you, venerable ones! "Are you quite pure in this matter?" A second and a third time I ask, "Are you quite pure in this matter?" The venerable ones keep silence. They are therefore quite pure in this matter. So I do take it to be.

Here, venerable gentlemen, are the thirteen offences which deserve suspension, and which should every fortnight be recited in the Pratimokshasutra. These forbid a monk:

1   Intentionally to emit his semen, except in a dream.

2   With a mind excited and perverted by passion to come into bodily contact with a woman; he must not hold her hand or arm, touch her hair or any other part of her body, above or below, or rub or caress it.

3   With a mind excited and perverted by passion to persuade a woman to sexual intercourse, speaking wicked, evil, and vulgar words, as young men use to their girls.

4   With a mind excited and perverted by passion, in the presence of a woman to speak highly of the merit of the gift of her own body, saying: "That is the supreme service or gift, dear sister, to offer intercourse to monks like us,

who have been observing strict morality, have abstained from intercourse and lived lovely lives!"

5　To act as a go-between between women and men, arranging marriage, adultery, or even a brief meeting.

6　To build for himself without the help of a layman, a temporary hut on a site which involves the destruction of living beings and has no open space round it, and that without showing the site to other monks, and without limiting its size to the prescribed measurements.

7　To build for himself with the help of a layman, a more permanent living place on a dangerous and inaccessible site, which involves the destruction of living beings and has no open space round it, and that without showing the site to other monks.

8　From anger, malice, and dislike to accuse falsely a pure and faultless monk of an offence which deserves expulsion, intent on driving him out of the religious life. That becomes an offence which deserves suspension if on a later occasion he withdraws his accusation, and admits to having spoken from hatred; and likewise if...

9　He tries to base his false accusation on some trifling matter or other which is really quite irrelevant.

10　To persist, in spite of repeated admonitions, in trying to cause divisions in a community which lives in harmony, and in emphasizing those points which are calculated to cause division.

11　To side with a monk who strives to split the community.

12　To refuse to move into another district when reproved by the other monks for habitually doing evil deeds in a city or village where he resides, deeds which are seen, heard, and known, and which harm the families of the faithful. This becomes an offence deserving suspension when the erring monk persistently answers back, and says: "You, venerable monks, are capricious, spiteful, deluded, and over-anxious. For you now want to send me away, though you did not send away other monks who have committed exactly the same offence."

13　To refuse to be admonished by others about the nonobservance of the Pratimoksha rules.

These, venerable gentlemen, are the thirteen offences which deserve suspension. The first nine become offences at once, the remaining four only after the third admonition. The offending monk will first be put on probation, then for six days and nights he must do penance, and thereafter he must undergo a special ceremony before he can be rehabilitated. But he can be reinstated only by a community which numbers at least twenty monks not one less.

"Now, three times I ask the venerable ones, 'Are you quite pure in this matter?' The venerable ones keep silent. They are therefore quite pure in this matter. And so I take it to be."

The recitation then continues to enumerate two sexual offences which are "punishable according to the circumstances," and then thirty offences which "involve forfeiture" of the right to share in garments belonging to the order, and which expose one to an unfavourable rebirth. I am content to give four of these:

"It is an offence of this kind for a monk: (18) to accept gold or silver with his own hand, or get someone else to accept or hold it in deposit for him; (19) to buy various articles with gold and silver; (20) to engage in any kind of buying or selling; (29) to divert to himself good which he knows that the donor had intended for the community."

Next we come to the ninety offences which, unless repented of and expiated, will be punished by an unfavourable rebirth. I give eighteen of these:

"It is an offence of this kind for a monk: (1) knowingly to tell a lie; (2) to belittle other monks; (3) to slander them; (4) to reopen a dispute which he knows has already been settled by the community in accordance with the monastic rules; (5) to preach dharma in more than five or six words to a woman, except in the presence of an intelligent man; (6) to teach dharma word by word to an unordained person; (7) to announce his superhuman qualities to an unordained person, even though he may actually possess them; (8) to inform, except by permission of the community, an unordained person of a fellow-man's grave offence; (11) to destroy any kind of vegetation; (29) to sit alone with a woman in the open; (4) to ask, when in good health, householders for delicacies like milk, curds, butter, ghee, oil, fish, cooked or dried meat; (45) to go to look at an army drawn up in battle-array, except for a valid reason; (54) to lie down with an unordained person for more than two nights in the same room; (59) to omit discolouring his new robe with either dark-blue, dirt-coloured, or black paint; (61) deliberately to deprive an animal of life; (73) to dig the earth with his own hands, or have it dug, or hint at the desirability of it being dug; (79) to drink alcoholic beverages; (85) to have a chair or bed made with legs higher than eight inches."

(*Sarvastivada, Pratimoksha-sutra*)[39] ▲

The Bodhisattva's Code of Ethics

Many traditions of Mahayana Buddhism adopted the above-mentioned rules but expanded them with the rules specifically pertinent to the *bodhisattva*. The bodhisattva practises the six perfections (generosity, morality, patience, vigour, meditation, and wisdom) in order to guide all living beings to enlightenment, i.e., nirvana.

The following excerpt is taken from the oldest *Perfection of Wisdom* sutra of *Eight Thousand Lines*. It outlines the Mahayana ethics as follows:

▼   Subhuti: How should a bodhisattva who is only just beginning stand in perfect wisdom, how train himself?

The Lord: Such a bodhisattva should tend, love and honour the good friends. His good friends are those who will instruct and admonish him in perfect wisdom, and who will expound to him its meaning. They will expound it as follows: "Come here, son of good family, make endeavours in the six perfections. Whatever you may have achieved by way of giving a gift, guarding morality, perfecting yourself in patience, exertion of vigour, entering into concentration, or mastery in wisdom,—all that turn over into full enlightenment. But do not misconstrue full enlightenment as form, or any other *skandha*. For intangible is all-knowledge. And do not long for the level of disciple or pratyedkabuddha. It is thus that a bodhisattva who is just beginning should gradually, through the good friends, enter into perfect wisdom."

(*The Perfection of Wisdom in Eight Thousand Lines*)[40] ▲

The sense of a bodhisattva's ethics is well captured by the Indian poet Shantideva:

12　As I have given up this body
　　For the pleasure of all living beings,
　　By constant killing, abusing and beating it
　　May they do as they please

13　Whether they will play with my body
　　Or make it a source of jest and blame,
　　How could it affect me, As I have given my body?

14　Therefore I shall let them do anything to it
　　That does not cause them any harm,
　　And when anyone encounters me
　　May it never be meaningless for him.

15　If in those who encounter me
　　A thought of anger or disbelief arises,
　　May that eternally become the source
　　For fulfilling all their wishes.

16　May all who say bad things to me
　　Or cause me any other harm,
　　And those who mock and insult me
　　Have the fortune to fully awaken.

17　May I be a protector for those without one,
　　A guide for all travellers on the way;
　　May I be a bridge, a boat and a ship
　　For all who wish to cross (the water).

18 May I be an island for those who seek one
    And a lamp for those desiring light,
    May I be a bed for all who wish to rest
    And a servant for all who want a servant.

19 May I be a wishing jewel, a magic vase,
    Powerful mantras and great medicine,
    May I become a wish-fulfilling tree
    And a cow of plenty for all living beings.

20 Like the earth and the other elements
    Variously nourish
    The numberless creatures
    Inhabiting the space

21 May I nourish the beings of all realms
    That reach unto the ends of space
    Until they pass beyond suffering.

22 Just as the previous Buddhas
    Gave birth to an Awakening Mind,
    And just as they successively dwelt
    In the bodhisattva practices;

23 Likewise for the sake of all that lives
    Do I give birth to an Awakening Mind,
    And likewise shall I too
    Successively follow the practices.

(*Bodhicatyavatara* III, 12–24)[41] ▲

Cultivation of a Spiritual Life (bhavana)

The Buddhist teaching has as its goal to assist in actualizing enlightenment. To this end, the teaching is divided into three sections: ethics, mental cultivation, and wisdom, the three themes of the Noble Eightfold Path ([1] right view; [2] right resolve; [3] right speech; [4] right action; [5] right livelihood; [6] right effort; [7] right mindfulness; and [8] right concentration). The previous section introduced the main concepts of Buddhist ethics; this section contains important texts of how to cultivate the mind through meditation and analytical reflection. Over time, a rich literature evolved with numerous different and often mutually exclusive methods as to how to cultivate the mind. The excerpts presented here try to give a glimpse of some of the most important practices.

The first excerpt, taken from a Pali *sutta*, details how one obtains mindfulness by means of observing one's breathing. This is a foundational text that inspired many traditions from Sri Lanka to Japan. The practice of mindfulness is certainly very ancient within the Buddhist traditions and may go back to Buddha Gautama himself.

The second excerpt is taken from a much later text composed by the Tibetan master Gampopa (11th century CE). Gampopa argues here that in order to break down the misguided idea of a static and autonomous self, one ought to identify with all sentient creatures of the universe. The best way to achieve this is to understand and feel that—due to the endless cycle of rebirth—all creatures had been once one's mother. For Gampopa and many more Buddhist thinkers and masters the greatest benefactor in our life is our mother, as she gives us an embodied life, is willing to endure all kinds of hardship in order to protect and nurture us, and guides us into the world. The phrase "the innumerable sentient beings, my mothers" has become an integral part of many Tibetan prayer and meditation rituals.

The third excerpt explains what one must do to generate the mind of enlightenment (bodhicitta); it is taken from the Compendium of Learning (Siksasamuccaya), an Indian work on how to successfully pursue the Buddhist path. The generation of love and compassion is a prerequisite for acquiring the "mind of enlightenment" (bodhicitta), which is the main task of those wishing to become bodhisattvas. When they are about to enter the bodhisattva path they will pledge not to enter nirvana until all sentient beings are capable of joining them; all virtuous acts will be executed to these ends; they will not spare their life in fulfilling this vow. To take the bodhisattva's pledge asks for a genuine religious commitment with dire consequences if violated. Usually the pledge is taken in presence of a spiritual teacher (guru) and is embedded in a ritual.

The fourth excerpt is a part of the Treatise on the Two Entrances and Four Practices by Bodhidharma, the first patriarch of Ch'an Buddhism (in Japan known as Zen). In the selected portion, Bodhidharma initially affirms the statements found in the third excerpt but then concludes that by not letting one become affected by suffering one experiences one's own mind as identical with the absolute principle (Buddha nature).

The fifth excerpt is taken from The Recorded Conversations of Shen-hui (684–758), a Ch'an master of the Southern School. Shen-hui explains how the view of a gradual ascend toward enlightenment is untenable and that enlightenment is a sudden event like a sword cutting through many strands of silk.

The sixth excerpt takes us into the world of tantric yogis in Tibet. Naropa and Milarepa are among the most prominent Tibetan yogis and mystics. Both talk about the mystic transformation.

The seventh excerpt by Ashvaghosha introduces us to the concept of guru and guru worship as a distinct trait of tantric Buddhism developed in ancient India.

▼ MINDFULNESS

Thus have I heard. Once the Lord was staying at Savatthi in the Old Pleasaunce in the palace of Migara's mother, with numbers of well-known elders and disciples,—the revered Sariputta, Maha-Moggallana, Maha-Kassapa, Maha-Kaccayana, Maha-Kotthita, Maha-Kappina, Maha-Cunda, Anuruddha, Revata and Ananda, together with other well-known elders and disciples. At the time the almsmen who were elders were instructing and teaching the novices,—some taking ten, others twenty or thirty or forty; and under this instruction and teaching the novices grew to higher and higher specific attainments.

On the day of the full-moon at the end of the rains the Lord was sitting in the open in the moonlight, with the confraternity gathered around him, when, observing silence to reign among them all, he addressed the almsmen in these words:—I find content in this vocation; in it I find contentment of heart. Wherefore, almsmen, strive ever more and more zealously to attain the yet unattained, to gain the yet ungained and to realize the yet unrealized. I look to be back here again in Savatthi by Komudi, the full-moon day of the fourth month.

When it reached the ears of the almsmen belonging to that country that the Lord was expected back in Savatthi at this date, they came into the city to see the Lord; the Elders grew keener and keener in instructing and teaching each of their novices,—ten, twenty, thirty or forty of them as the case might be; and under this instruction and teaching the novices grew to higher and higher specific attainments. On the day of Komudi, on the fifteenth, the full-moon day of the fourth month, the Lord was sitting in the open in the moonlight, with the confraternity gathered around him, when, observing silence to reign among them all, he addressed the almsmen in these words:—There is no talking, all talk is stilled in this assembly which is set (as it were) in a shining mere. Such is this confraternity of almsmen—or a company like this,—that it is worthy of oblations, offerings, gifts and homage and is the richest field in which to sow the seed of merit. Such is this confraternity and such this company that a little thing given to it thereby becomes great and a great thing becomes greater still. Such a confraternity or company as this would be hard to find in the whole world. To see such a confraternity and company as this it is worth journeying many a league carrying the burden of provisions for the journey. Such is this confraternity and such is this company. Within this confraternity there are Arahats,—almsmen in whom the cankers are dead, who have lived the highest life, whose task is done, who have cast off their burden, who have won their weal, who have destroyed all bonds that bound them to their ceaseless round of existence, who have found the deliverance of utter knowledge. Within this confraternity there are almsmen who, by destroying the five bonds which bind men to the sensuous world, will pass hence to appear spontaneously elsewhere, never to return thence to earth. Within this confraternity are almsmen who, by destroying the three bonds and also by diminishing passion malice and delusion, have become once-returners and, on their last return to this world, will make an end of ill. Within this confraternity there are almsmen who, by destroying the three bonds, are launched on the stream of salvation, safe from any evil doom hereafter, assured of their future, destined to find enlightenment. Within this confraternity there are almsmen who live in the practice of the four mindful meditations,—of the four exertions—of the four bases of psychic power—of the five faculties of sense—of the five forces—of the seven factors of enlightenment—of the noble eightfold path—of friendliness to all—of compassion for all—of rejoicing with all—of poised equanimity—of pondering on foulness—and on the perception of transiency.

Within this confraternity there are almsmen who live in the practice of cultivating mindfulness by breathing exercises. If cultivated and developed, mindfulness by breathing is very fruitful and profitable;—it perfects the four bases of mindfulness, which, being perfected, perfect the seven factors of enlightenment, which, being perfected, perfect in turn deliverance by comprehension.

How, almsmen, is mindfulness by breathing cultivated and developed so as to approve very fruitful and profitable?—Take the case of an almsman who, in the forest or at the foot of a tree or in an abode of solitude, sits cross-legged with body erect, with mindfulness as the objective he sets before himself. In mindfulness he takes in breath and in mindfulness he exhales it; he knows precisely what he is doing when he is inhaling either a long breath or a short breath; he schools himself, as he draws his breath in and out, to be alive to his body as a whole—or to still bodily factors—or to experience contentment—or to experience well-being; he schools himself, in drawing his breath in and out, to experience the heart's several factors—or to still them—or to experience the heart as a whole—or to satisfy the heart—or to keep the heart steadfast—or to set the heart free. He schools himself in drawing his breath in and out, to dwell on the impermanence of things—or on passionlessness—or on the cessation of things—or on eschewing them.—This is how mindfulness in breathing is cultivated and developed so as to prove very fruitful and profitable.

How is mindfulness by breathing cultivated and developed so as to perfect the four bases of mindfulness?—While he is engaged in inhaling or exhaling, with a precise knowledge of what he is doing, either when inhaling or when exhaling either a long breath or a short breath, when schooling himself either to experience the body as a whole or to still the several bodily factors,—all this time, in his contemplation of the body as an aggregation, the almsman dwells ardent, alive to all he is doing, and mindful,—quit of all wordly wants and discontents. Among the corporeal elements (earth, water, fire, and air) I classify breath inhaled or exhaled. Therefore the almsman who contemplates the body as an aggregation, dwells the while ardent, alive to what he is doing, and mindful,—quit of all wordly wants and discontent. While he is engaged in schooling himself in his breathing to experience contentment or well-being or to experience the heart's several factors or to still them—all this time, in his contemplation of feelings as an aggregation, the almsman dwells ardent, alive to all he is doing, and mindful—quit of all worldly wants and discontent. Among feelings I classify thorough attention to breath inhaled or exhaled. Therefore the almsman who contemplates feeling as an aggregation, dwells the while ardent, alive to all he is doing, and mindful—quit of all worldly wants and discontent. While he is engaged in schooling himself, as he inhales or exhales, to experience the heart as a whole, or to satisfy the heart, or to keep the heart steadfast, or to set the heart free,—all this time, in his contemplation of the heart as an aggregation, the almsman dwells ardent, alive to all he is doing, and mindful,—quit of all worldly wants and discontent; the man of distracted mind, say I, cannot develop mindfulness in breathing. While he is engaged in schooling himself, as he inhales or exhales, to dwell either on the impermanence of things or on passionlessness or on the cessation of things or on eschewing them—all this time in his contemplation of mental objects as an aggregation, the almsman dwells ardent, alive to everything, mindful, quit of all worldly wants and discontent. Discerning by understanding the abandonment of all wants and discontent, he surveys this theme exhaustively. Therefore, in his contemplation of mental objects as an aggregation, the almsman dwells ardent, alive to all he is doing, mindful, quite of all worldly wants and discontent.— This is how mindfulness in breathing is cultivated and developed so as to perfect the four bases of mindfulness.

How are the four bases of mindfulness cultivated and developed so as to perfect the seven factors of enlightenment?—While, in his contemplation of the body as an aggregation, the almsman dwells ardent, alive to all he is doing, mindful, quit of all wordly wants and discontent, all this time his mindfulness is growing fixed and undistracted, with the result meanwhile that the factor of enlightenment which consists of mindfulness is implanted, that the almsman develops it, and that it moves on to perfect development. Living thus mindful, he examines and scrutinizes, and analyzes the mental object with his understanding; and as he is doing so, the analytical factor of enlightenment is meantime being implanted, is being developed by the almsman, and is moving on to its perfect development with the concomitant result that indomitable zeal is implanted, and that this further factor of enlightenment is implanted, is developed by the almsman and moves on to its perfect development. To the man with zeal implanted in him comes satisfaction without alloy, and concomitantly the factor of enlightenment which consists in satisfaction is implanted, is developed by the almsman, and moves on to its perfect development. The man with his mind satisfied comes to enjoy tranquillity alike of body and of heart, and concomitantly the factor of tranquillity is implanted, is developed by the almsman, and moves on to its perfect development. The man with tranquillity and well-being of body finds concentration of heart, and concomitantly the concentration factor of enlightenment is implanted, is developed by the almsman, and moves on to its perfect development. He surveys exhaustively as his theme his heart thus steadfast, and concomitantly the factor of poised equanimity is implanted, is developed by the almsman, and moves on to its perfect development.

(And as it is with his contemplation of the body, so it is with his contemplation of feelings—of the heart—and of mental objects, each resulting in the perfect development of the several factors of enlightenment).—This is how the four bases of mindfulness are cultivated and developed so as to perfect the seven factors of enlightenment.

How are the seven factors of enlightenment cultivated and developed so as to perfect deliverance by comprehension?—Take an almsman who develops in turn each of the aforesaid seven factors of enlightenment,—each dependent on aloofness, passionlessness and stilling, each maturing by renunciation.—This is how the seven factors of enlightenment are cultivated and developed so as to perfect deliverance by comprehension.

Thus spoke the Lord. Glad at heart, those almsman rejoiced in what the Lord had said.

(*Anapana-sati-sutta, Majjhima-nikaya* 118)[42] ▲

▼ LOVE FOR ALL SENTIENT BEINGS

In this book, I shall discuss only the first type of benevolence because of its practical importance, and you have to bear in mind that its frame of reference is the totality of sentient being.

The causal characteristic, is the desire that all beings find happiness.

The method of practice, is pondering over the benefits that stem from sentient beings, because the root of benevolence lies in the memory of benefits received. In this life here on earth the greatest benefactor is our mother, because she (i) provides us with a body; (ii) suffers for our sake; (iii) gives us life; and (iv) shows us the world. As is recorded in the *Ashtasahasrika-prajnaparamita*:

Why is this so? Our mother raises us;
undergoes hardships for our sake; gives
us life; and shows us the world.

(i)   This is the benefit of providing us with a body. It did not start fully grown, complete with muscles and of a pleasant complexion. In our mother's womb from its stages of an oval spot and oblong lump it has been built up in a special and gradual way by the nutritive essences of her flesh and blood. It has grown bigger by the nourishing properties of her food; and it has been produced by the endurance of all kinds of acts we feel shy about, of indispositions, and of pain. Even after birth, by nursing us from a tiny little infant to a big, strong person she contributes to the forming of our body.

(ii) The benefit of going through hardships for our sake means that she not only dressed and adorned us, but gave us her inheritance, keeping nothing of her own, not even a crumb, giving us all her food and drink, so that when we set out for foreign parts we should not suffer from hunger and thirst, giving us clothes to keep out the cold and money to prevent our pining in poverty. Unlike people who, because they do not want a thing, give it to a child, she allows herself a minimum of food, drink and clothing. A mother does not do things for the sake of happiness in this life, nor refrains from action for the sake of enjoyment in the hereafter, she just nurses and protects her baby. When for instance she has done evil and unwholesome things, such as fishing and butchering, she brings him up on what she earns in that way: or, when her circumstances are unpleasant, after going to market or to work in the fields, day and night with the coarse soil as her shoes, wearing the stars as her cap, riding her legs as a horse, using the woollen threads of her torn frock as a whip, offering her legs to the dogs [to bite and bark at] and her face to men [to gaze at], she gives whatever she has gained by her efforts to her child.

She loves the helpless unknown baby more than her own benefactors, than her father, mother and teacher; she looks on her baby with eyes of love, wraps him in gentle warmth, dangles him on her ten fingers, calls him with words of kindness: "Oh my joy, my lovely one, lu, lu, how you delight Mummy."

(iii) The benefit of giving us life, means that we have not come into the world knowing how to use our hands and our mouth and how to perform difficult tasks with all out strength. While we were feeble like a worm, of no importance and silly, our mother did not throw us away but served us, took us on her lap, protected us from fire and water, held us back from precipices, removed what might harm us, and made religious offerings for our wellbeing. Out of fear that we might die or fall ill, she did things nobody else would think of or could be enumerated, such as casting dice, consulting astrologers, observing omens, reading the lines in our hands, and so on, thus giving life to her child.

(iv) The benefit of showing us the world, means that we did not come here, knowing and understanding everything merely by seeing it and having keen senses. When we cried for friendly company, when we could not use our hands and feet and knew nothing, she taught us how to eat, dress, walk and speak. Having taught us all sorts of crafts by saying Yes or No, she made the uneven even for us and the unusual usual.

But this does not exhaust what a mother is always doing and has always done since beginningless samsara. As is said in the *Khorbathogmamedpa 'imdo*:

> If one individual were to transform all
> the earth, stones, trees and groves in
> this world into single juniper kernels,
> another might well be able to finish
> counting them. But no one can count what
> his mother has done for him.

And in the *Suhrllekha*:

> If a man were to count the times a mother
> has come to him by grains of soil not
> larger than juniper kernels, the earth
> would not be able to produce a like quantity.

In this way the benefit of a mother's every single action is to be counted.

Thus, since a mother's kindness is immeasureable, we should ponder about what makes her heart full of happiness and bliss, and this is not all. Since all beings have been our mother (from time out of mind), they have all benefitted by what a mother has done. Should you ask what is the limit of sentient beings, the answer is that they encompass the bounds of heaven. As is stated in the *Bhadra-carapranidhanamaharajaparibandha*:

> What is the end of the sky
> Is also that of all beings.

Therefore we should develop concentrated attention to the growth of a worthy mind, desiring all sentient beings to profit and to feel happy.

Such an attitude leads to real benevolence. In the *Mahayana-sutralankar* (XIII, 20) also is declared:

> A bodhisattva is towards all beings
> As to a child
> With great benevolence out of his innermost heart
> He always desires to procure their happiness.

When through the power of benevolence out of our eyes tears spring forth or when on our body the hair rises in delight, then there is great benevolence. When the latter is enjoyed by all sentient beings, then it is immeasurable.

The measure of perfection, means that when we only desire the happiness of all sentient beings instead of ourselves, then there is perfection of benevolence.

The merits accruing from having practised it cannot be measured. As is stated in the *Candrapradipasutra*:

Whatever immeasurable offerings there may be and however varied,
Filling millions and millions of universes—
Offering them to the most sublime being (the Buddha)
Does not equal the merits of Benevolence.

The merits occurring from having practised benevolence only for a little while also cannot be measured. As is written in the *Ratnavali*:

Even if one were to give our food
Cooked in three hundred pots, daily thrice a day,
This would not equal the merits
Of one moment of benevolence.

When we practise benevolence and until we reach enlightenment, we possess eight qualities. This is stated in the *Ratnavali*:

Beloved by gods and men,
And also protected by them,
Peace of mind and many other blessings of this kind,
Not being harmed by poison or by weapons,
Attaining our aim without exertion,
And being reborn in the Brahma world—
Even if we should not attain final liberation.
At least we obtain these eight qualities through benevolence.

However, the practice of benevolence is good for preserving ourselves and for protecting others as may be seen respectively from the stories of the Great Bram.ze sbyin.pa (Brahmadatta) and of King Byams.pa'i stobs (Maitribala).

When benevolence has been perfected then there is no difficulty in practising compassion.

Compassion is our next theme.

Boundless compassion is dealt with
Under the six heads of
Classification, frame of reference, casual characteristic,
Method of practice, measure of perfection and merits.

Classification is threefold: (i) compassion with reference to sentient beings; (ii) the nature of the whole of reality; and (iii) without reference to any particular object.

The first means that compassion arises by seeing the misery of sentient beings in evil lives; the second that when we have practised the four truths and thereby understood the relation between cause and effect our mind turns away from the concepts of permanence and solidity. Here compassion arises by thinking that other beings live in bewilderment, ignorant of the relation between cause and effect and clinging thereby to permanence and solidity. The third means that by having understood thoroughly the shunyata of all entities through immediate experience compassion arises in particular for sentient beings who cling to the idea of material reality. As has been said:

A bodhisattva who has become perfected
Through the power of practising compassion
Is particularly merciful
To sentient beings who are obsessed by the
    demon of material reality.

Of the three types of compassion mentioned in this book the first is recommended for practical purposes.

The frame of reference is the totality of sentient beings.

The casual characteristic is the desire to liberate beings from misery and its cause.

The method of its practice is our capacity for feeling deep compassion for our mother (the root of our being) if she is beaten, burnt or boiled alive, or if in very cold weather blisters appear on her body, break and begin to ooze. So also, since all sentient beings who are now in hell have in fact been our mother, how should we not feel compassion for them when they are struck to the core by such misery? Compassion should be practised in the desire to free them both from it and its cause.

Again we feel deep compassion when our mother is pained by thirst or hunger, suffers from disease and fever and is disheartened by fear and anxiety. So also, since all sentient beings who are now born as spirits have been our mother, how should we not feel compassion for them, when they are struck by such misery? Compassion should be practised in the desire to liberate them from it.

Similarly we feel deep compassion when our mother has become old and feeble, is enslaved by others since she is powerless, or when she is beaten, perhaps to death. So also, since all sentient beings who have been born as animals have been our mother, why should we not feel compassion for them, when they suffer such misery? Compassion should be practised in the desire to free them from it.

Again we feel the same way if our mother suffers great distress through finding herself on the brink of a precipice and about to fall into a very deep abyss out of which she could never climb. So also why should we not feel compassion over this great abyss of the bad existences of gods, men and demons, from which it is difficult for us to escape once we have fell in, and in which we suffer through not having a spiritual friend at hand and so not knowing how to abjure evil. Compassion should be practised in the desire to liberate beings from this misery.

Measure of perfection means that when we have broken the fetters that hold us to deem ourselves better than others and when the wordless desire to liberate all sentient beings from misery has risen, perfection of compassion is present.

(Gam-po-pa, *The Jewel Ornament of Liberation*)[43] ▲

▼ **GENERATING THE MIND OF ENLIGHTENMENT**

A bodhisattva resolves: I take upon myself the burden of all suffering, I am resolved to do so, I will endure it. I do not turn or run away, do not tremble, am not terrified, not afraid, do not turn back or despond.

And why? At all costs I must bear the burdens of all beings. In that I do not follow my own inclinations. I have made the vow to save all beings. All beings I must set free. The whole world of living beings I must rescue, from the terrors of birth, of old age, of sickness, of death and rebirth, of all kinds of moral offence, of all states of woe, of the whole cycle of birth-and-death, of the jungle of false views, of the loss of wholesome dharmas, of the concomitants of ignorance,—from all these terrors I must rescue all beings I walk so that the kingdom of unsurpassed cognition is built up for all beings. My endeavours do not merely aim at my own deliverance. For with the help of the boat of the thought of all-knowledge, I must rescue all these beings from the stream of samsara, which is so difficult to cross, I must pull them back from the great precipice, I must free them from all calamities, I must ferry them across the stream of samsara. I myself must grapple with the whole mass of suffering of all beings. To the limit of my endurance I will experience in all the states of woe, found in any world system, all the abodes of suffering. And I must not cheat all beings out of my store of merit. I am resolved to abide in each single state of woe for numberless aeons; and so I will help all beings to freedom, in all the states of woe that may be found in any world system whatsoever.

And why? Because it is surely better than I alone should be in pain than that all these beings should fall into the states of woe. There I must give myself away as a pawn through which the whole world is redeemed from the terrors of the hells, of animal birth, of the world of Yama, and with this my own body I must experience, for the sake of all beings, the whole mass of all painful feelings. And on behalf of all beings I give surety for all beings, and in doing so I speak truthfully, am trustworthy, and do not go back on my word. I must not abandon all beings.

And why? There has arisen in me the will to win all knowledge, with all beings for its object, that is to say, for the purpose of setting free the entire world of beings.

(*Siksasamuccaya* 280–81)[44] ▲

▼ **Treatise on the Two Entrances and Four Practices**

What is the practice of the retribution of enmity? When the practitioner of Buddhist spiritual training experiences suffering, he should think to himself: "for

innumerable eons I have wandered through the various states of existence, forsaking the fundamental for the derivative, generating [in myself] a great deal of
enmity and distaste and [bringing] an unlimited amount of injury and discord
[upon others]. Although I have not committed any offence in this [lifetime, my
present suffering constitutes] the fruition of my past crimes and bad karma, rather
than anything bequeathed to me by any heavenly or nonhuman being. I shall
accept it patiently and contentedly, completely without enmity or complaint." The
sutra says: "Do not be saddened by the experience of suffering. Why? Because your
mind penetrates the fundamental [nature of things]." When you react to events
in this fashion (literally, "generate this [state of] mind"), you can be in accord with
the [Absolute] Principle as you progress upon the path [toward enlightenment]
through the experience of [the results of your past] enmity. Therefore, this is
called the practice of the retribution of enmity.[45] ▲

▼   **The Recorded Conversations of Shen-hui**

Teacher of the Law Chih-te asked, "Zen Master, you teach living beings to seek only
sudden enlightenment. Why not follow the gradual cultivation of Hinayana? One
can never ascend a nine-storey tower without going up the steps gradually."

Answer: "I am afraid the tower you talk about ascending is not a nine-storey
tower but a square tomb consisting of a pile of earth. If it is really a nine-storey
tower, it would mean the principle of sudden enlightenment. If one directs one's
thought to sudden enlightenment as if one ascend a nine-storey tower with the
necessity of going through the steps gradually, one is not aiming right but sets up
the principle of gradual enlightenment instead. Sudden enlightenment means satisfying both principle (li) and wisdom. The principle of sudden enlightenment
means to understand without going through gradual steps, for understanding is
natural. Sudden enlightenment means that one's own mind is empty and void from
the very beginning. It means that the mind has no attachment. It means to
enlighten one's mind while leaving dharmas as they are and to be absolutely
empty in mind. It means to understand all dharmas. It means not to be attached
to Emptiness when one hears about it and at the same time not to be attached to
the absence of Emptiness. It means not to be attached to the self when one
hears about it and at the same time not to be attached to the absence of the self.
It means entering Nirvana without renouncing life and death. Therefore the
scripture says, "[Living being] have spontaneous wisdom and wisdom without
teacher.' He who issues from principle approaches the Way rapidly, whereas he who
cultivates externally approaches slowly. People are surprised and skeptical when
they hear that there is supramundane mystery. There are sudden mysteries in the
world. Do you believe it?"[46] ▲

The Tantric Transformation

The transformation of an ego-centred person to a being pivoting around universal compassion and the awareness of voidness is painful, as it requires the dismantling of age-old and much cherished conceptions about one's own person. Tilopa, a Buddhist tantric of tenth-century India, is engaged in the following dialogue with his disciple Naropa:

▼   Like deer without a shelter
     I suffer with no refuge and my pleasure flies

     Tilopa said:
     This deer of your body believing in an I
     Deserves to be killed, Naropa.

     Look into the mirror of your mind which is resurrection
     The mysterious home of the Dakini.

                              (*Life and Teachings of Naropa*)[45] ▲

In mystical rapture, Milarepa (1040–1123), the greatest of all Buddhist Yogis, sings this song:

▼   I am the Yogi Milarepa—a lion among men.
     Proficient and victorious, I am skilled in meditation.
     On the snow mountain I practise in solitude.
     I am the yogi who obtains the fruits of merit,
     I am the Yogi Milarepa, a tiger among men.

     I have thrice animated the bodhi-Mind,
     I smile with joy at the non-distinction of means and wisdom,
     I dwell in the woods of the Radiant Valley of Remedy,
     And produce the fruits of the welfare of sentient beings.

     I am the Yogi Milarepa—an eagle among men
     I have a pair of mighty wings of the clear-sighted arising yoga;
     I possess two flying wings of the stable perfecting yoga.
     I soar to the sky of two-in-one suchness;
     I attain the fruits of self and others' benefit.
     I am the Yogi Milarepa—a man among men.
     I am the one who sees the face of form,
     I am he who gives good counsel.
     I am a yogi without attributes.

     I am a man who cares not what may happen.
     I am an almsbeggar who has no food,

A nude hermit without clothes,
A beggar without jewels.
I have no place to lay my head;
I am the one who never thinks of external objects—
The master of all yogic action.

Like a madman, I am happy if death comes;
I have nothing and want nought.

(Milarepa, *Hundred Thousand Songs*)[48] ▲

The Guru

In tantric Buddhism, the guru is to be venerated like Buddha, because he opens the door of the dharma. Without the guru, the teaching that leads towards liberation would never be heard of. Guru-worship became in India, and later in Tibet, a powerful tool in forging the disciple's mind till it radiated like pure gold. To bring about the disciple's mystical transformation from an ego-centred person to an enlightened one, the guru seems to create scenes of severe pain and trauma that, considered from the aspect of ultimate reality, are only tools of his compassion. The disciple willingly submits to these trials. The Indian Buddhist thinker Ashvaghosha (probably first or second century CE) is credited with the composition of fifty verses of guru worship:

1 Bowing in the proper way to the lotus feet of my guru who is the cause for me to attain the state of a glorious Diamond-being, I shall condense and explain in brief what has been said in many stainless tantric texts about guru-devotion. (Therefore) listen with respect.

2 All the Buddhas of the past, present and future, residing in every land in the ten directions, have paid homage to the tantric masters from whom they have received the highest initiations. (Is there need to mention that you should too?)

3 Three times each day with supreme faith you must show the respect you have for your guru who teaches you (the tantric path), by pressing your palms together, offering a mandala as well as flowers and prostrating your head to his feet.

4 Those who hold ordination vows, if [your guru] is a layman or your junior, prostrate [in public] while facing such things as his scriptural texts in order to avoid wordly scorn. But in your mind [prostrate to your guru].

5 As for serving [your guru] and showing him respect such as obeying what he says, standing up [when he comes] and showing him to his seat—these should be done even by those with ordination vows [whose gurus are laymen

or their juniors]. But [in public] avoid prostrating and unorthodox actions [such as washing his feet].

6   In order for the words of honour of neither the guru nor the disciple to degenerate, there must be a mutual examination beforehand [to determine if each can] brave a guru-disciple relationship.

7   A disciple with sense should not accept as his guru someone who lacks compassion or who is angersome, vicious or arrogant, possessive, undisciplined or boasts of his knowledge.

8   [A guru should be] stable [in his actions], cultivated [in his speech], wise, patient and honest. He should neither conceal his shortcomings nor pretend to possess qualities he lacks. He should be an expert in the meanings [of the tantra] and in its ritual procedures [of medicine and turning back obstacles]. Also he should have loving compassion and a complete knowledge of the scriptures.

17 It has been taught that for the guru to whom you have pledged your word of honour [to visualise as one with your meditational deity], you should willingly sacrifice your wife, children and even your life, although these are not [easy] to give away. Is there need to mention your fleeting wealth?

18 [Such practice of offering] can confer even Buddhahood on a zealous [disciple] in his very lifetime, which otherwise might be difficult to attain even in countless millions of eons.

(Ashvaghosha, *Gurupancashika*)[49] ▲

Spiritual Guidance for Common People

The spiritual practices covered in the previous passages ask for total commitment and dedication, which is difficult to develop for ordinary people, both lay and monastic. In a sense the practices discussed above constitute the exception rather than the norm, despite the fact that everybody praises these practices as the fulfillment of spiritual life.

To guide common followers of Buddha through a less rigorous curriculum of spiritual practices to higher levels of religious realization, several religious practices were developed. It is a very common practice among Buddhist lay people to take the ten precepts for a short period during which they stay in a temple, spending their days in meditation, and reciting sutras. A popular theme for these retreat days is the contemplation of Amitabha's Pure Land. Amitabha is one of five allegoric Buddhas symbolizing the innate structure of the universe. Amitabha represents in this system love, compassion, emotion, etc. His sacred realm, the Pure Land (Sukhavati), is beyond this world and offers a supreme milieu for studying the Buddhist doctrine. Only those who firmly believe in Amitabha's commitment to guide every creature to buddhahood will be reborn in this Pure Land.

Amitabha devotion had much to offer to lay people and less spiritually advanced monastics. The practice became popular in Japan and to a lesser degree in Tibet, although the basic sutras were most likely written in India. Western scholarship has sometimes seen Amitabha devotion as a departure from an earlier and "purer" form of Buddhism and likened it to certain trends in Christianity. Followers of Amitabha devotion reject this as simplification of a complex process of mystical transformation, which, admittedly, operates outside the realm of Buddhist philosophy and epistemology, but which leads, nevertheless, to enlightenment.

The first excerpt is taken from the smaller *Sukhavati sutra*,[50] wherein Amitabha is addressed as Amitayus, a name which emphasizes his limitless life.

The second excerpt focuses also on the worship of Amitabha but this time it is Honen (1133–1212), a Japanese master who sees the recitation of Amitabha's name (*nembutsu*) as the only means to practise Buddhism at his time. Honen is one of several distinguished reformers of Japanese Buddhism. Though he admits that Buddha's teaching comprises many ways, he insists that present lack of acumen of human beings constitutes a serious impediment for their progress on the path to enlightenment, thus to put their faith into the efficacy of the *nembutsu* (i.e., the reciting of the name of Buddha Amitabha) is their only choice.

The third excerpt, taken from *The Tibetan Book of Dead* or, more appropriately, the *Listen and Be Liberated from the Intermediary State (Bar-do thos-grol)*, is a precise instruction of what the dying person will perceive during and after the moment of death. The book gained enormous popularity in the West after it was rendered into English by W.Y. Evans-Wentz, an American psychologist who had no access to its original language, Tibetan. C.G. Jung wrote a commentary on this first English translation, which accelerated its distribution. Since then, various other, more correct, translations have appeared in the West. Today its content is largely corroborated by reports of people who were clinically dead but recovered due to advanced medical treatment. Within the Tibetan Buddhist tradition, the book is looked upon as a guide through the most difficult moment of person's entire life. Its instructions should be practised before the moment of death approaches and its text should be known by heart. But when death draws close, a Buddhist monk, nun, a good friend, or anybody who is familiar with the book and has the dying person's confidence, should sit beside the person's bed and read the text so that he or she will remember the content more easily. In general, the text is used among certain traditions of Tibetan Buddhism and for this reason it does not constitute the equivalent of funeral prayers. In parts, the book uses powerful images of archaic character, but its philosophy is Buddhist. This has led some scholars to believe that the text predates the existence of the Buddhist religion in Tibet, but this is mere speculation.

According to this text, the dying person will first perceive a vision of "clear light," a metaphor for the ultimate, the Buddha nature. If properly trained, the dying person may obtain enlightenment at this moment; more likely, however, he or she will turn to less pristine visions which eventually end in a nightmarish experience: the mind becomes increasingly aware of its fragile character, there is no place to rest, nothing to give shelter. Haunted by demonic visions and attracted to sexual imagery, the mind will seek asylum in a dark place, which is the womb of the being who will later give birth to the dead person's reincarnation.

▼ THE SMALLER SUKHAVATI SUTRA

"And again, O Shariputra, of those beings also who are born in the Buddha country of the tathagata Amitayus as purified bodhisattvas, never to return again and bound by one birth only, of those bodhisattvas also, O Shariputra, the number is not easy to count, except they are reckoned as infinite in number.

"Then again all beings, O Shariputra, ought to make fervent prayer for that Buddha country. And why? Because they come together there with such excellent men. Beings are not born in that Buddha country of the tathagata Amitayus as a reward and result of good works performed in this present life.

"No, whatever son or daughter of a family shall hear the name of the blessed Amitayus, the tathagata, and having heard it, shall keep it in mind, and with thoughts undisturbed shall keep it in mind for one, two, three, four, five, six or seven nights,—when that son or daughter of a family comes to die, then that Amitayus, the tathagata, surrounded by an assembly of disciples and followed by a host of bodhisattvas, will stand before them at their hour of death, and they will depart this life with tranquil minds. After their death they will be born in the world Sukhavati, in the Buddha country of the same Amitayus, the tathagata. Therefore, then, O Shariputra, having perceived this cause and effect, I with reverence say thus, Every son and every daughter of a family ought with their whole mind to make fervent prayer for that Buddha country."

(*The Smaller Sukhavati Sutra*)[50] ▲

▼ HONEN (1133–1212) ON THE PURE LAND

I wonder at what corner of the three worlds I was wandering and thus failed to encounter Buddha Shakyamuni during his life-time. Which phase of the chain of transmigration I was going through and thus failed to hear him preaching the law? Could it be that I was like those who lived at the town of Shravasti where the Buddha lived and yet had no knowledge of him? Or, I might have been dwelling at the bottom of the scorching hell! Wherever I was, and however I think, I am struck by a sense of shame and sorrow.

But now, after many births I was born as a human being, and had the good fortune of encountering the teaching of the Buddha. While I still lament the fact that I failed to live at the time when the Buddha lived, I rejoice that I was born in the age when the Buddha's law is spreading, whereby we are all able to learn about the path of deliverance. Wouldn't it be regrettable, then, if we wasted our days and nights instead of taking advantage of our good fortune and pursue the spiritual life? There are some who become slaves to the affection of their families and relatives, while others become slaves to hatred which keeps the torch of anger burning in their hearts. In so doing, they simply pile up karma day and night as they walk, as they stand, as they sit, and as they sleep. Indeed, as the scripture reminds us, a man's action in every second of the day produces karma to lead him to hell. In this manner, our yesterdays were wasted, and our todays too are passing away. How long do we keep on living this way? Is it not the truth that the glory of the morning flower vanishes by the evening breeze, and the life of the dew which develops at night is melted by the morning sunshine? But the people, not realizing this truth, think of the temporary glory and life in this world as permanent realities. And yet, the dew of our life is bound to disappear by the onslaught of the wind of transitoriness, and our corpses are thrown into the wildness or sent to distant mountains. Our corpses, then, remain under the moss, and our souls are destined to wander alone in the journey of after-life. No one, not even the members of the family, can accompany our lonely souls, and no amount of wealth can help us; only the sense of regret follow us. Eventually, we come to the seat of the ruler of hell who evaluates the weight of our sins and karma. And, when the ruler of hell asks why we, living in the age when Buddha's law was widely spread, failed to follow its teaching and return to hell, what kind of answer can we present to him? In order to avoid such an eventuality, you should seek the path of deliverance while you are here on earth.

It is to be noted in this connection that the doctrines preached by the Buddha included both the exoteric and esoteric teachings as well as the Great Vehicle and the Small Vehicle. Subsequently different schools of interpretation developed, so that some of them teach the emptiness of all phenomena, while others teach the existence of reality in the heart. Also, according to some schools there are five distinct natures, whereas according to others all existences share the same buddhahood. All these teachings, different though they may appear to be, were based on the scriptures or their commentaries, and as such they can be traced to the golden words of the Buddha himself who gave different teachings to different people depending on the circumstances. If we follow any one of these doctrines and endeavor to practise it, we will be able to attain the same enlightenment. Take, for example, the difference between the two gates of the Holy Path and of the Pure Land, as taught by Doshaku (Tao-ch'o in Chinese, 562–645). The former is the path for a person to seek enlightenment by eliminating wordly passions while he is on this earth, whereas the latter is the path for a person to be born in the Pure Land where he eliminates passions and attains enlightenment....

I am told that there are some learned monks of various sects who argue that the spread of the practice of reciting Amida's name might cause the decline of Buddhism, and that some people have given up the practice of nembutsu for that reason. This I find difficult to comprehend....

It must be stated emphatically that those who practise nembutsu should not slander other Buddhist practices. Conversely, those who follow other practices should not speak disparagingly of nembutsu. Such behavior is against the spirit of Amida's vow.

It is clear that for ordinary mortals in this contaminated world there is no way to reach the Pure Land except by depending on the saving power of Amida. To be sure, all the Buddhas of the ten regions teach on the one hand the enlightenment of this world for those who live here, and on the other, the enlightenment of the Pure Land for those who live there. Only Amida, unlike other Buddhas, pledged simultaneously to teach the enlightenment of the Pure Land and to save those who live in this world. Understandably, ordinary mortals who have not eliminated their illusions cannot be expected to be born in the Pure Land which is a realm set aside for superior bodhisattvas as the reward for their good deeds in this world. However, Amida's Pure Land was created by his compassion to save those who have committed evil deeds, those who have failed to keep the precepts, and those who, otherwise, because of their lack of saving knowledge, are destined to be caught endlessly in the illusory chain of transmigration. With great compassion, Amida reflected on the principle of cause and effect for as long as the five aeons, and devised a means to bring the unworthy creatures, who could not possibly attain salvation by their own meritorious deeds, to this Pure Land. He resolved, therefore, that he himself would undergo many years of disciplines, engage in numerous good deeds, and practice bodhisattvahood, whereby all his accumulated merit would be represented by his name which can be recited by all creatures. It is the power of this vow which enables those who recite his name in faith to attain salvation. Indeed, according to the eighteenth article of Amida's vows [vows to save all beings, made by Amida when he was still a bodhisattva called Dharmakara], if any one should fail to attain salvation after reciting his name at least ten times, Amida himself would not accept the gift of enlightenment.

(*Tozanjo*)[52] ▲

▼   **The Tibetan Book of Dead**

The method of instruction: The best time for transferring the consciousness is when the breath is about to cease. If this is not done then one should instruct the dying as follows:

"Noble person, (his/her name), now the time has come for you to seek a path. After your breath has almost ceased that which is called the Clear Light of the first phase of the Intermediary State will dawn upon you. Its meaning was explained to you by your lama.[53] It is existence as such, empty and bare like the sky and it will appear to you as the stainless and bare mind, clear and empty, without limitations or a centre. At this moment you should recognize this and remain therein. I shall guide you to this insight." Before the physical breath has totally ceased one should repeat this close to the dying person's ear many times so that it is imprinted on his mind....

"Noble son, N.N., listen! The intrinsic light of true being will now become apparent to you. This you must recognize! Noble son, the innate being of your present cognition is this very naked voidness, which does not exist as a thing, phenomenon, or colour, it is mere voidness. This is the absolute reality of the female Buddha Samantabhadra.[54] As your cognition consists in voidness, don't let this opportunity become meaningless.... The nature of your own mind is void of an inherent being and of any substance, but your intelligence is crystal clear. This nature of your mind is inseparable from your intelligence; together they are the true being, the Buddha. The nature of your mind, equally clear and void, consists in a mass of light, and because of being free of becoming and decaying it is the Buddha of boundless light. This you must recognize!...

"Noble son, for three and a half days you will be unconscious. When you awake from the coma you will think: 'What happened to me?' For this reason you have to recognize that you are now in the intermediary state. At this time, when you depart from the world, all things will appear to you as light, and as celestial beings. The entire sky will shine with bright blue....

"You should yearn for the light blue light, which is so brilliant and clear; and full of devotion you should address Vairocana with this prayer which you should repeat after me: 'Alas! At this time as I am wandering through the world because of my great ignorance, I beg you, Vairocana, to guide me on the bright path of the primordial wisdom of the sphere "being-as-such," the right path. May the divine mother, Akashesvari (Protector of the heavens) protect me from behind. I beg you, rescue me from the abyss of the intermediary state and guide me to to perfect buddhahood.'

"Noble son, N.N., hear me! You have not understood me even though I have directed you toward the right insight according to the instructions of this text. Now when you can't close the womb, then the time has truly come when you have to acquire a new body. There is more than only one profound and authentic instruction for closing the door of the womb. Remember them, be not distracted, imprint them on your mind.

"Noble son, although you are reluctant to go, torturers—which are your evil deeds—chase you. Powerless, you have to go where you don't want to. Torturers and executioners pull you and you feel as if you are running away from darkness, tornadoes, cries of war, snowrain, hail, and blizzards. In your anxiety you are looking for a refuge, and you escape and hide—as I have said before—in mansions, rock crevasses, caves, thick undergrowth, or in lotus flowers which close over you. You ask yourself whether they will get you there. 'If they detect me here, then everything is lost,' and while questioning whether you have escaped you cling to this spot. If they take you from there you are afraid of being overcome by the anxieties and terrors of the intermediary state. Thus you feel fear and anxiety and you hide in the middle of these burrows. Therein you seize a bad body which did not exist before, and you will suffer from various ills. This is a sign that the devils and demons have prevented your escape.

"Listen and memorize this instruction suitable for such an occasion! When the torturers chase you into a state of helplessness, or when fear and anxiety threaten you then you should visualize a wrathful deity who destroys all these forms of threat. Quickly perfect your vision of the deity with all his limbs,—may he be the Great Heruka, Hayagriva, Vajrapani, or your own protector. Through their blessing and compassion you will rid yourself from the torturers and will have the strength to close the door of the womb. This profound and accurate instruction you should keep in mind!"

(Bar-do thos-grol)[55] ▲

The Development of Wisdom (prajna)

The development of the correct understanding of reality—wisdom—is the third pillar upon which the actualization of enlightenment rests. Morality, cultivation of the mind, and the generation of wisdom are not issues that should be pursued sequentially; they are, rather, three interrelated aspects of actualizing enlightenment. The development of an accurate understanding of reality is for the Buddhist a long and arduous enterprise. A voluminous literature evolved out of this endeavour. Indian masters condensed the *sutras* as the professed word of the Buddha into manuals of Buddhist thought and contemplation, which received numerous commentaries and sub-commentaries, some written by Indian Buddhists and many more written by Chinese, Japanese, and Tibetan monks. In this section, we learn about how some foundational principles of Buddhism, such as, the Four Noble Truths, the doctrines of Dependent Co-arising, and of No-Self are understood by pre-Mahayana thinkers as well as by later Mahayana masters. These excerpts are followed by two others that explore the ineffable concept of voidness as the only true and lasting nature of reality. The next excerpt introduces us to the concept of *tathagata-garbha*, i.e., the germ of Buddha-nature, a concept that became very fertile within East Asian Buddhism and in the *Atiyoga* tradition of Tibet.

The goal of Buddhism, "to see things as they are," requires scrutiny to be a life-long commitment. Buddhists are asked to examine the world around and within them as thoroughly as possible. This is done through meditation, during which the mind is emptied of all contents, and through discursive investigation, which relentlessly analyzes all mental and physical processes.

In the everyday life of monks and serious lay practitioners, periods of meditation interchange with periods reserved for analytically penetrating what happened while the mind was focussed on no object. Both exercises appeal to different types of people. This resulted in two streams of Buddhist spirituality: one advocating a life of meditation as a recluse and another emphasizing the study of Buddhist philosophy to equip the mind with all the tools necessary for a critical and unbiased analysis of the world. Each tradition attempted to integrate these two trends according to its own cultural structure. Certain eras favoured one method over the other, while different nations responded to the challenge of these two streams in different ways. But at all times Buddhists agreed that the integration of both methods must be achieved, otherwise nirvana will never be attained.

At first glance Buddhism may seem to be a religion of intellectuals, because of its enormous amount of philosophical and logical literature and its emphasis on "wisdom," insight, and critical penetration of the world and our mind. But Buddhism offers a simplified version of its philosophy to the novice and an elaborate one to the master of philosophy. The novice is asked to have faith in the truth of the doctrine as a person setting out for a journey has faith in the accuracy of the maps he or she will use. Like the traveller, the novice will eventually realize in person the accuracy of the doctrine. Thus, things may seem complex and even bewildering at the beginning, but in the course of spiritual progress they present themselves in an ever-simpler manner. This experience is well captured in the saying: "Before I got interested in the doctrine, a cup was a cup and tea was tea. But when I started to study the doctrine, a cup was not any more a cup and tea not tea. After being awoken to the truth a cup is a cup and tea is tea." Buddhism does not promise a transcendental world but a true vision of the world in which we live. The final goal of Buddhism, nirvana, is not beyond this world, but right here—we have only to see it.

The Four Noble Truths

The four noble truths are considered to be the hallmark of Buddhist thought taught by Buddha Gautama at his first sermon at Benares. Every Buddhist tradition accepts them as the basis of the doctrine, but comments upon them in different ways.

▼   Reverence to the Blessed One, the Holy One, the Fully Enlightened One.

1   Thus have I heard. The Blessed One was once staying at Benares, at the hermitage called Migadaya. And there the Blessed One addressed the company of the five bhikkhus and said:

6   "Now this, O bhikkhus, is the noble truth concerning the origin of suffering.

"Verily, it is that thirst (or craving), causing the renewal of existence, accompanied by sensual delight, seeking satisfaction now here, now there— that is to say, the craving for the gratification of the passions, or the craving for (a future) life, or the craving for success (in this present life).

"This then, O bhikkhus, is the noble truth concerning the origin of suffering.

7   "Now this, O bhikkhus, is the noble truth concerning the destruction of suffering.

"Verily, it is the destruction, in which no passion remains, of this very thirst; the laying aside of, the getting rid of, the being free from, the harbouring no longer of this thirst.

"This then, O bhikkhus, is the noble truth concerning the destruction of suffering.

8   "Now this, O bhikkhus, is the noble truth concerning the way which leads to the destruction of sorrow. Verily! it is this noble eightfold path; that is to say:

Right views;
Right aspirations;
Right speech;
Right conduct;
Right livelihood;
Right effort;
Right mindfulness; and
Right contemplation.

"This then, O bhikkhus, is the noble truth concerning the destruction of sorrow.

9   "That this was the noble truth concerning sorrow, was not, O bhikkhus, among the doctrines handed down, but there arose within me the eye [to perceive it], there arose the knowledge [of its nature], there arose the understanding [of its cause], there arose the wisdom [to guide in the path of tranquility], there arose the light [to dispel darkness from it].

10 "And again, O bhikkhus, that I should comprehend that this was the noble truth concerning sorrow, thought it was not among the doctrines handed down, there arose within me the eye, there arose the knowledge, there arose the understanding, there arose the wisdom, there arose the light.

11 "And again, O bhikkhus, that I had comprehended that this was the noble truth concerning sorrow, though it was not among the doctrines handed down, there arose within me the eye, there arose the knowledge, there arose the understanding, there arose the wisdom, there arose the light.

12 "That this was the noble truth concerning the origin of sorrow, though it was not among the doctrines handed down, there arose within me the eye; but there arose, within me the knowledge, there arose the understanding, there arose the wisdom, there arose the light.

13 "And again, O bhikkhus, that I should put away the origin of sorrow, though the noble truth concerning it was not among the doctrines handed down, there arose within me the eye, there arose the knowledge, there arose the understanding, there arose the wisdom, there arose the light.

14 "And again, O bhikkhus, that I had fully put away the origin of sorrow, though the noble truth concerning it was not among the doctrines handed down, there arose within me the eye, there arose the knowledge, there arose the understanding, there arose the wisdom, there arose the light.

15 "That this, O bhikkhus, was the noble truth concerning the destruction of sorrow, though it was not among the doctrines handed down; but there arose within me the eye, there arose the knowledge, there arose the understanding, there arose the wisdom, there arose the light.

16 "And again, O bhikkhus, that I should fully realise the destruction of sorrow, though the noble truth concerning it was not among the doctrines handed down, there arose within me the eye, there arose the knowledge, there arose the understanding, there arose the wisdom, there arose the light.

17 "And again, O bhikkhus, that I had fully realised the destruction of sorrow, though the noble truth concerning it was not among the doctrines handed down, there arose within me the eye, there arose the knowledge, there arose the understanding, there arose the wisdom, there arose the light.

18 "That this was the noble truth concerning the way which leads to the destruction of sorrow, was not, O bhikkhus, among the doctrines handed down; but there arose within me the eye, there arose the knowledge, there arose the understanding, there arose the wisdom, there arose the light.

19 "And again, O bhikkhus, that I should become versed in the way which leads to the destruction of sorrow, though the noble truth concerning it was not among the doctrines handed down, there arose within me the eye, there arose the knowledge, there arose the understanding, there arose the wisdom, there arose the light.

20 "And again, O bhikkhus, that I had become versed in the way which leads to the destruction of sorrow, though the noble truth concerning it was not among the doctrines handed down, there arose within me the eye, there arose

the knowledge, there arose the understanding, there arose the wisdom, there arose the light.

21   "So long, O bhikkhus, as my knowledge and insight were not quite clear, regarding each of these four noble truths in this triple order, in this twelvefold manner—so long was I uncertain whether I had attained to the full insight of that wisdom which is unsurpassed in the heavens or on earth, among the whole race of Samanas and Brahmans or of gods or men.

22   "But as soon, O bhikkhus, as my knowledge and insight were quite clear regarding each of these four noble truths, in this triple order, in this twelvefold manner—then did I become certain that I had attained to the full insight of that wisdom which is unsurpassed in the heavens or on earth, among the whole race of Samanas and Brahmans, or of gods or men.

23   "And now this knowledge and this insight has arisen within me. Immovable is the emancipation of my heart. This is my last existence. There will now be no rebirth for me!"

24   Thus spake the Blessed One. The company of the five bhikkhus, glad at heart, exalted the worlds of the Blessed One.

(*Dhamma-cakka-ppavattana-sutra*)[56] ▲

About six centuries after Gautama had proclaimed the four noble truths, Nagarjuna, the greatest of all Buddhist thinkers, wrote *Fundamentals of the Middle Way* (*Mulamadhyamka-karika*), in which he scrutinized fundamental concepts of the Buddhist doctrine with the result that none is true in an absolute sense, but all are valid as provisional tools for spiritual progress. In Nagarjuna's view reality is beyond the reach of conceptual thinking, therefore all doctrines and concepts belong to the realm of conventional truth. The true nature of things is voidness, which means they do not contain an inherently existing substance as their "being," but exist solely because of their interrelatedness.

Nagarjuna's philosophy became known as *Madhyamaka*, the philosophy of the Middle Way, because it avoids both affirming and negating the existence of things. In the course of history hundreds of commentaries were written on the "Fundamentals," which embody the essence of Mahayana thought. With regard to the first noble truth, the arising of suffering, Nagarjuna points out that it is absurd to think that suffering could be caused by either self or other. He added tremendous depth to words of the Pali Canon that at first sight may seem unpretentious. This text became seminal for many Buddhist traditions throughout East and Central Asia.

▼ AN ANALYSIS OF SORROW (DUHKHA)*

1 Some say: Sorrow is produced by oneself, or by another, or by both [itself and another], or from no cause at all; But [to consider] that [sorrow] as what is produced is not possible.

2 If it were produced by itself, it would not exist dependent on something else. Certainly those "groups of universal elements" exist presupposing these "groups."

3 If these were different from those, or if those were different from these, Sorrow would be produced by something other than itself, because those would be made by these others.

4 If sorrow is made through one's own personality then one's own personality would be without sorrow; Who is that "own personality" by which sorrow is self-produced?

5 If sorrow were produced by a different personality, How would he, to whom is given that sorrow by another after he had produced it, be without sorrow?

6 If sorrow is produced by a different personality, who is that different personality. Who, while being without sorrow, yet makes and transmits that [sorrow] to the other?

7 It is not established that sorrow is self-produced, [but] how is [sorrow] produced by another? Certainly the sorrow, which would be produced by another, in this case would be self-produced.

8 Sorrow is not self-produced, for that which is produced is certainly not produced by that [personality]. If the "other" is not produced by the individual self, how would sorrow be that produced by another?

9 Sorrow could be made by both [self and the "other"] if it could be produced by either one. [But] not produced by another, and not self-produced—how can sorrow exist without a cause?

10 Not only are the four [casual] interpretations not possible in respect to sorrow, [but also] none of the four [casual] interpretations is possible even in respect to external things.

(Mulamadhyamaka-karika)[57] ▲

In the following excerpt the third Noble Truth, i.e., the cessation of suffering or nirvana, is the subject of a discussion between King Milinda (an heir to Alexander the Great's campaign to India) and Nagasena, a Buddhist monk, who presents the Buddhist doctrine "in a nutshell." While the previous excerpt introduced us to the typical style of Madhyamaka argumentation, the subsequent one represents pre-Mahayana argumentation. It puts to rest the often-read view that nirvana is a nihilistic concept.

---

* Copyright: Frederick J. Streng, from *Emptiness: A Study in Religious Meaning* (New York: Abingdon Press, 1967), 197, 215–217; chap. 25, verses 9, 24 (revised by the author).

58 "Venerable Nagasena, how is it? Is nirvana all bliss, or is it partly pain?"
   "Nirvana is all bliss, O king. There is no intermingling of pain in it."
   "That, Sir, is a saying we cannot believe—that nirvana is all bliss. On this
   point, Nagasena, we maintain that nirvana must be alloyed with pain. And
   there is a reason for our adopting that view. What is that reason? Those,
   Nagasena, who seek after nirvana are seen to practise exertion and application both of body and of mind, restraint in standing, walking, sitting, lying,
   and eating, suppression of sleep subjugation of the organs of sense, renunciation of wealth and corn, of dear relatives and friends. But all those who are
   joyful and happy in the world take delight in, are devoted to, the five pleasures of sense—they practise and delight their eyes in many kinds of pleasurable forms, such as at any time they like the best—they practise and delight
   their ears in many kinds of pleasurable sounds of revelry and song, such as at
   any time they like the best—they practise and delight their sense of smell with
   many kinds of perfumes of flowers, and fruits, and leaves, and bark, and
   roots, and sap, such as at any time they like the best—they practise and
   delight their tongue with many kinds of pleasurable tastes of hard foods
   and soft, of syrups, drinks, and beverages, such as at any time they like the
   best—they practise and delight their sense of touch with many kinds of
   pleasurable feelings, tender and delicate, exquisite and soft, such as at any
   time they like the best—they practise and delight their minds with many sorts
   of conceptions and ideas, pure and impure, good and bad, such as at any time
   they like the best. You, on the other hand, put a stop to and destroy, maim
   and mangle, put a drag on and restrain the development of your eye, and ear,
   and nose, and tongue, and body, and mind. Therefore is your body afflicted
   and your mind afflicted too, and your body being afflicted you feel bodily discomfort and pain, and your minds being afflicted you feel mental discomfort
   too and pain. Did not even Magandiya, the ascetic, find fault with the Blessed
   One, and say: 'The Samana Gotama is a destroyer of increase?'"
59 "Nirvana, O king, has no pain in It. It is bliss unalloyed. When you, O king,
   maintain that nirvana is painful, that which you call 'painful' is not nirvana.
   It is the preliminary stage to the realisation of nirvana, it is the process of seeking after nirvana. Nirvana itself is bliss pure and simply there is no pain
   mixed with it...."

                                        (The Questions of King Milinda) [58] ▲

   Nagarjuna devoted a whole chapter to the same topic of nirvana. In his
view, nirvana is not a state that can be achieved; it is the accurate insight into
the nature of this world. In other words, the transcendental goal and humanity's immanent existence coincide. Nirvana and samsara are not different—

this is Nagarjuna's famous statement, which became a landmark in the development of Buddhist thought.

▼ **AN ANALYSIS OF NIRVANA**

1   [An opponent says:] If all existence is empty, here is no origination nor destruction.

Then whose nirvana through elimination [of suffering] and destruction [of illusion] would be postulated?

2   [Nagarjuna replies:] If all existence is non-empty, there is no origination nor destruction.

Then whose nirvana through elimination [of suffering] and destruction [of illusion] would be postulated?

3   Nirvana has been said to be neither eliminated nor attained, neither annihilated nor eternal,

Neither disappeared nor originated.

4   Nirvana is certainly not an existing thing, for then it would be characterized by old age and death.

In consequence it would involve the error that an existing thing would not become old and be without death.

5   And if nirvana is an existing thing, nirvana would be a constructed product,

Since never ever has an existing thing been found to be a non-constructed product.

6   But if nirvana is an existing thing, how could [nirvana] exist without dependence [on something else]?

Certainly nirvana does not exist as something without dependence.

7   If nirvana is not an existing thing, will nirvana become a non-existing thing?

Wherever there is no existing thing, neither is there a non-existing thing.

8   But if nirvana is a non-existing thing, how could [nirvana] exist without dependence [on something else]?

Certainly nirvana is not a non-existing thing which exists without dependence.

9   That state which is the rushing in and out [of existence] when dependent and acquired—

This [state], when not dependent and not acquired, is seen to be nirvana.

10 The teacher [Gautama] has taught that a "becoming" and a "non-becoming" are destroyed;

Therefore it obtains that: nirvana is neither an existence thing nor a non-existent thing.

11 If nirvana were both an existent and a nonexistent thing,

Final release would be [both] an existent and a nonexistent thing; but that is not possible.

12 If nirvana were both an existent and a nonexistent thing,
    There would be no nirvana without conditions, for these both [operate with] conditions.
13 How can nirvana exist as both an existent thing and a non-existent thing;
    For nirvana is a non-composite-product, while both an existent thing and a non-existent thing are composite products.
14 How can nirvana exist as both an existent and a non-existent thing?
    There is no existence of both at one and the same place, as in the case of both darkness and light.
15 The assertion: "Nirvana is neither an existent thing nor a non-existent thing."
    Is proved if [the assertion]: "It is an existent thing and a non-existent thing" were proved.
16 If nirvana is neither an existent thing nor a nonexistent thing,
    Who can really arrive at [the assertion]: "neither an existent thing nor a non-existent thing"?
17 It is not expressed if the Glorious One [the Buddha] exists after his death,
    Or does not exist, or both or neither.
18 Also, it is not expressed if the Glorious One exists while remaining [in the world],
    Or does not exist, or both or neither.
19 There is nothing whatever which differentiates the existence-in-flux from nirvana;
    And there is nothing whatever which differentiates nirvana from existence-in-flux.
20 The extreme limit of nirvana is also the extreme limit of existence-in-flux;
    There is not the slightest bit of difference between these two.
21 The views [regarding] whether that which is beyond death is limited by a beginning or an end or some other alternative
    Depend on a nirvana limited by a beginning and an end.
22 Since all dharmas are empty, what is finite? What is infinite?
    What is both finite and infinite? What is neither finite nor infinite?
23 Is there anything which is this or something else, which is permanent or impermanent,
    Which is both permanent and impermanent, or which is neither?
24 The quieting and acquisition is a salutary quieting of image-production;
    No dharma of anything anywhere has been taught by the Buddha.

                    (*Mulamadhyamaka-karika*, chap. 25)[59] ▲

Dependent Co-arising

The four noble truths explicate how and why suffering arises and how it can be ended, but they did not explain how this is played out within a personal life. The concept of dependent co-arising does just that. It explains the interrelatedness of things as a chain of twelve limbs called "the twelve limbs of dependent co-arising." The Theravada commentators understood this as a doctrine of lineal causality where one limb is the cause for the next following one.

▼   At that time the Buddha, the Blessed One, recently having become fully enlightened, was dwelling at Uruvilva on the bank of the Nairanjana River at the foot of the Bodhi Tree. Then the Blessed One sat in meditative posture for seven days at the foot of the Bodhi Tree, enjoying the bliss of release.

Then the Blessed One, during the first watch of the night, meditated on dependent origination [*pratitya-samutpada*] in direct and reverse order: because of ignorance there are the predispositions; because of the predispositions, there is consciousness; because of consciousness there is name and form; because of name and form there are the six sense spheres; because of the six sense spheres there is contact, because of contact there is feeling; because of feeling there is craving; because of craving there is grasping; because of grasping there is becoming; because of becoming there is birth; because of birth old age and death, grief, lamentation, suffering, dejection, and despair come into being. Such is the origination of the whole mass of suffering. But from the cessation and complete fading away of ignorance, the predispositions cease; from the cessation of the predispositions, consciousness ceases; from the cessation of consciousness, name and form ceases; from the cessation of name and form the six sense spheres cease; from the cessation of the six sense spheres, contact ceases; from the cessation of contact, feeling ceases; from the cessation of feeling, craving ceases; from the cessation of craving, grasping ceases; from the cessation of grasping, becoming ceases; from the cessation of becoming, birth ceases; from the cessation of birth, old age and death, grief, lamentation, suffering, dejection, and despair cease. Such is the cessation of the whole mass of suffering.

Then the Blessed One, having understood this matter, uttered this solemn verse at that time:

"When the real nature of things grows clear to the ardently meditating Brahmana,

Then all his doubts fade away, as he understands [each] thing together with its cause."

(*Maahavagga*)[60] ▲

The Mahayana tradition, however, understood the twelve limbs of dependent co-arising as situational causality, where all twelve limbs are interrelated and create a fabric of different karmic forces where each element requires the existence of the entirety. In this case, causality is a situation which can be appreciated only in its totality but not in its detail. Thus, to adhere to the doctrine of causality became a characteristic of a narrow mind that was unable to grasp the inexplicable interrelatedness of things, called voidness. This is explained in the *Perfection of Wisdom* sutras in the following words:

▼ Subhuti: Deep is this conditioned coproduction!

The Lord: Subhuti, will that [first] thought which has stopped [after its momentary appearance] be gain produced [at the time of the second thought]?

Subhuti: No, Lord.

The Lord: That thought which has [in the past] been produced, is that by its very nature doomed to stop?

Subhuti: Yes it is, O Lord,

The Lord: If something is by its very nature doomed to stop, will that be destroyed?

Subhuti: No, Lord.

The Lord: That thought which has [not yet] been produced, is that by its very nature doomed to stop?

Subhuti: No, Lord [because something which has not been produced cannot be stopped].

The Lord: But when it comes to the point when by its own nature it is doomed to stop, will it then be destroyed?

Subhuti: No, Lord.

The Lord: If the essential nature of that thought involves neither production nor stopping, will that then be stopped?

Subhuti: No, Lord.

The Lord: If a dharma is, by its essential original nature, stopped already in its own-being, will that dharma be stopped?

Subhuti: No, Lord.

The Lord: Will the true nature of dharmas be stopped?

Subhuti: No, Lord.

The Lord: Will be Bodhisattva stand firm in the same way in which Suchness stands firm?

Subhuti: Yes, he will.

The Lord: Will then that Suchness not be in danger of being changed away from its overtowering immobility?

Subhuti: No, Lord.

The Lord: Deep is Suchness.

Subhuti: It is deep, O Lord.

(Ashta-sahasrika Prajnapaamita-sutra)[61] ▲

No-Self and the Five Aggregates

The concept of no-self (*anatman*) is the hallmark of Buddhist thought; it sets Buddhism apart from all other religions. The concept has often been misunderstood in pre-modern India, where the sect of *Pudgala-vadins* that asserted a kind of independent self existed for about a millennium, and in the contemporary West where some groups attempted to defend the concept of self. The concept of no-self is a result of the concept of the five aggregates (*skandhas*), which accommodate any existing thing in any world: name and form (which stand for matter), emotions, perceptions, predispositions, and consciousness. Sentient beings consist of elements of momentary existence, which belong to one of these five categories, and there is no substance within or behind these five aggregates which would exist independently or permanently. In other words, the concept of *atman* as an autonomous and static core of the individual is a fallacy; if the definition of atman were correct, then it could not be an object of our perception; if it is an object of our perception, its definition has to be false.

The first excerpt is taken from the *Questions of King Milinda*, an early work of the pre-Mahayana tradition, while the second one represents the Mahayana view on the same topic. In the *Questions of King Milinda*, Nagasena, the Buddhist monk, explains that the human subject is nothing but a function of different constituents, i.e., the five aggregates. The excerpt form the *Large Sutra of the Perfection of Wisdom* affirms that even these constituting components lack inherent reality; they are only an illusion.

▼ **THE DISTINGUISHING CHARACTERISTICS OF ETHICAL QUALITIES**

Chapter 1

1   Now Milinda the king went up to where the venerable Nagasena was, and addressed him with the greetings and compliments of friendship and courtesy, and took his seat respectfully apart. And Nagasena reciprocated his courtesy, so that the heart of the king was propitiated.

And Milinda began by asking, "How is your Reverence known, and what, Sir, is your name?"

"I am known as Nagasena, O king, and it is by that name that my brethren in the faith address me. But although parents, O king, give such a name as Nagasena, or Surasena, or Virasena, or Sihasena, yet this, Sire,— Nagasena and so on—is only a generally understood term, a designation in common use. For there is no permanent individuality (no soul) involved in this matter."

Then Milinda called upon the Yonakas and the brethren to witness: "This Nagasena says there is no permanent individuality (no soul) implied in his name. Is it now even possible to approve him in that?" And turning to Nagasena, he said: "If, most reverend Nagasena, there be no permanent individuality (no soul) involved in the matter, who is it, pray, who gives to you members of the Order your robes and food and lodging and necessaries for the sick? Who is it who enjoys such things when given? Who is it who devotes himself to meditation? Who is it who attains to the goal of the excellent way, to the nirvana of arahatship? And who is it who destroys living creatures? Who is it who takes what is not his own? Who is it who lives an evil life of wordly lusts, who speaks lies, who drinks strong drink, who [in a word] commits any one of the five sins which work out their bitter fruit even in this life? If that be so there is neither merit nor demerit; there is neither doer nor causer of good or evil deeds; there is neither fruit nor result of good or evil karma. If, most reverend Nagasena, we are to think that were a man to kill you there would be no murder, then it follows that there are no real masters or teachers in your order, and that your ordinations are void.—You tell me that your brethren in the order are in the habit of addressing you as Nagasena. Now what is that Nagasena? Do you mean to say that the hair is Nagasena?"

"I don't say that, great king."

"Or the hairs on the body, perhaps?"

"Certainly not."

"Or is it the nails, the teeth, the skin, the flesh, the nerves, the bones, the marrow, the kidneys, the heart, the liver, the abdomen, the spleen, the lungs, the larger intestines, the lower intestines, the stomach, the faeces, the bile, the phlegm, the pus, the blood, the sweat, the fat, the tears, the serum, the saliva, the mucus, the oil that lubricates the joints, the urine, or the brain, or any or all of these, that is Nagasena?"

And to each of these he answered no.

"Is it the outward form then (*rupa*) that is Nagasena, or the sensations (vedana), or the ideas, or the confections (the constituent elements of character), or the consciousness, that is Nagasena?"

And to each of these also he answered no.

"Then is all these *skandhas* combined that are Nagasena?"

"No! great king."

"But is there anything outside the five *skandhas* that is Nagasena?"

And still he answered no.

"Then thus, ask as I may, I can discover no Nagasena. Nagasena is a mere empty sound. Who then is the Nagasena that we see before us? It is a falsehood that your reverence has spoken, an untruth!"

And the venerable Nagasena said to Milinda the king: "You, Sire, have been brought up in great luxury, as beseems your noble birth. If you were to walk this dry weather on the hot and sandy ground, trampling under foot the gritty, gravelly grains of the hard sand, your feet would hurt you. And as your

body would be in pain, your mind would be disturbed, and you would experience a sense of bodily suffering. How then did you come, on foot, or in a
chariot?"

"I did not come, Sir, on foot. I came in a carriage."

"Then if you came, Sire, in a carriage, explain to me what that is. Is it the
pole that is the chariot?"

"I did not say that."

"Is it the axle that is the chariot?"

"Certainly not."

"Is it the wheels, or the framework, or the ropes, or the yoke, or the
spokes of the wheels, or the goad, that are the chariot?"

And to all these he still answered no.

"Then is it all these parts of it that are the chariot?"

"No, Sir."

"But is there anything outside them that is the chariot?"

And still he answered no.

"Then thus, ask as I may, I can discover no chariot. Chariot is a mere
empty sound. What then is the chariot you say you came in? It is a falsehood
that your Majesty has spoken, an untruth! There is no such thing as a chariot! You are king over all India, a mighty monarch. Of whom then are you
afraid that you speak untruth?" And he called upon the Yonakas and the
brethren to witness, saying: "Milinda the king here has said that he came by
carriage. But when asked in that case to explain what the carriage was, he is
unable to establish what he averred. Is it, forsooth, possible to approve him
in that?"

When he had thus spoken the five hundred Yonakas shouted their
applause, and said to the king: "Now let your Majesty get out of that if you
can?"

And Milinda the king replied to Nagasena, and said: "I have spoken no
untruth, reverend Sir. It is on account of its having all these things—the
poke, and the axle, the wheels, and the framework, the ropes, the yoke, the
spokes, and the goad—that it comes under the generally understood term,
the designation in common use, of 'chariot.'"

"Very good! Your Majesty has rightly grasped the meaning of 'chariot.'
And just even so it is on account of all those things you questioned me
about—the thirty-two kinds of organic matter in a human body, and the five
constituent elements of being—that I come under the generally understood
term, the designation in common use, of 'Nagasena.'"

For it was said, Sire, by your Sister Vagira in the presence of the Blessed
One: "Just as it is by the condition precedent of the co-existence of its various parts that the word 'chariot' is used, just so is it that when the Skandhas
are there we talk of a 'being.'"

"Most wonderful, Nagasena, and most strange. Well has the puzzle put to you, most difficult though it was, been solved. Were the Buddha himself here he would approve your answer. Well done, well done, Nagasena!"

(*Milinda pannha*)[62] ▲

▼ **THE CONCEPT OF THE SKANDHAS AND THAT OF ILLUSION**

Chapter 10

Subhuti: If, O Lord, someone should ask—will this illusory man go forth to the knowledge of all modes, will he reach the knowledge of all modes after he has trained in perfect wisdom and in the other wholesome practices, up to the knowledge of all modes—how should one explain it?

The Lord: I will ask you a counterquestion which you may answer as best you can. What do you think, Subhuti, is form, etc., one thing and illusion another?

Subhuti: No, O Lord.

The Lord: And does that hold good not only for the *skandhas*, but also for the sense fields, to elements, the six kinds of contact, the eighteen kinds of feeling, the six physical elements to links of conditioned coproduction, to thirty-seven wings of enlightenment, to concentrations on Emptiness, the Signless, and the Wishless, to trances and the formless attainments, to eighteen kinds of emptiness, to ten powers, the eighteen special dharmas of a Buddha, and enlightenment itself?

Subhuti: Yes, it does, O Lord. Illusion is not one thing and form another. But the very form is illusion, the very illusion is form. And so for all other dharmas.

The Lord: What do you think, Subhuti, is there a production or stopping of illusion?

Subhuti: No, Lord.

The Lord: Is there a defilement of purification of illusion?

Subhuti: No, Lord.

The Lord: What do you think, Subhuti, that which is without production or stopping, without defilement or purification, can that train itself in perfect wisdom or in the other perfections, and can that go forth to all-knowledge, can that reach the knowledge of all modes?

Subhuti: No, Lord.

The Lord: What do you think, Subhuti, is that notion "Bodhisattva," that denomination, that concept, that conventional expression—in the five grasping *skandhas*?

Subhuti: No, Lord.

The Lord: What do you think, Subhuti, can one through what is merely a notion, denomination, concept, conventional expression, apprehend the production or stopping, the defilement or purification of the five grasping *skandhas*?

Subhuti: No, Lord.

The Lord: What do you think, Subhuti, could someone, after he has trained in perfect wisdom, go forth to the knowledge of all modes, if he had no notion, denomination, concept, conventional expression, name or verbal concept; no body, speech, or mind, and no deeds of body, speech or mind; no production or stopping, no defilement or purification?

Subhuti: No, Lord.

The Lord: It is thus that a Bodhisattva, after he has trained in perfect wisdom, goes forth to the knowledge of all modes in consequence of the fact that there is nothing that could be apprehended.

Subhuti: Therefore a Bodhisattva, who trains in perfect wisdom, should train himself for full enlightenment just like an illusory man. And why? Because he, or rather the five grasping skandhas, should be known as just like an illusory man.

The Lord: What do you think, Subhuti, do the five grasping skandhas after they have trained in perfect wisdom, go forth to the knowledge of all modes?

Subhuti: No, Lord. And why? Because the own-being of the five grasping skandhas is nonexistent. The five skandhas are similar to a dream. A dream cannot be apprehended, because its own-being does not exist, and in the same way the five skandhas cannot be apprehended, because of the nonexistence of their own-being.

The Lord: What do you think, Subhuti, could the five skandhas, after they have trained in perfect wisdom, go forth to the knowledge of all modes, if they were similar to an echo, to an apparition, to a magical creation, to an image of the moon reflected in the water?

Subhuti: No, Lord. And why? For the own-being of an echo, of an apparition, of a magical creation, of a reflected image, is nonexistent, and just so the five skandhas can, because of the nonexistence of their own-being, not be apprehended. And form is like an illusion, and so the other skandhas, and likewise all dharmas. If, when this is being taught, a Bodhisattva does not become cowed or stolid, has no regrets, does not tremble, is not frightened or terrified, then one should know that he will go forth to all-knowledge, and will reach the knowledge of all modes.

(The Large Sutra of Perfect Wisdom)[63] ▲

Voidness—The True Nature of Things

The concept of voidness (shunyata) is central to Mahayana philosophy. In short, it says that due to the impermanent nature of all phenomena that make up the world, none of these phenomena nor their compounds are of an independent and static nature. On the contrary, they are void or empty (shunya) of inherent being. Nagarjuna, an original thinker of the early Mahayana, was the first Buddhist thinker to articulate this concept in detail. He is seen as the founder of the Madhyamaka system. Later thinkers composed commentaries on Nagarjuna's works to elucidate the meaning of his works. But there are also other Madhyamaka texts, some of them claiming the authoritative status of a *sutra*. The following excerpt is taken from such a text, the *Teachings of Vimalakirti*. The second excerpt is taken from the *Large Sutra of Perfect Wisdom*, one of the foundational scriptures of the Mahayana.

▼ **THE DHARMA-DOOR OF NONDUALITY***

Then, the Licchavi Vimalakirti asked those bodhisattvas, "Good sirs, please explain how the bodhisattvas enter the dharma-door of nonduality!"

The Bodhisattva Dharmavikurvana declared, "Noble sir, production and destruction are two, but what is not produced and does not occur cannot be destroyed. Thus the attainment of the tolerance of the birthlessness of things is the entrance into nonduality."

The Bodhisattva Shrigandha declared, "'I' and 'mine' are two. If there is no presumption of a self, there will be no possessiveness. Thus, the absence of presumption is the entrance into nonduality."

The bodhisattva Shrikuta declared, "'Defilement' and 'purification' are two. When there is thorough knowledge of defilement, there will be no conceit about purification. The path leading to the complete conquest of all conceit is the entrance into nonduality."

The bodhisattva Bhadrajyotis declared, "'Distraction' and 'attention' are two. When there is no distraction, there will be no attention, no mentation, and no mental intensity. Thus, the absence of mental intensity is the entrance into nonduality."

The bodhisattva Subahu declared, "'Bodhisattva-spirit' and 'disciple-spirit' are two. When both are seen to resemble an illusory spirit, there is no dobhisattva-spirit, nor any disciple-spirit. Thus, the sameness of natures of spirits is the entrance into nonduality."

The bodhisattva Animisha declared, "'Grasping' and 'nongrasping' are two. What is not grasped is not perceived, and what is not perceived is neither presumed no repudiated. Thus, the inaction and noninvolvement of all things is the entrance into nonduality."

The bodhisattva Sunetra declared, "'Uniqueness' and 'characterlessness' are two. Not to presume or construct something is neither to establish its uniqueness nor to establish its characterlessness. To penetrate the equality of these two is to enter nonduality."

The bodhisattva Tishya declared, "'Good' and 'evil' are two. Seeking neither good nor evil, the understanding of the nonduality of the significant and the meaningless is the entrance into nonduality."

---

* From *The Holy Teaching of Vimalakirti*, translated by Robert A.F. Thurman (University Park: Pennsylvania State University Press, 1976). Reprinted with the permission of the publisher.

The bodhisattva Simha declared, "'Sinfulness' and 'sinlessness' are two. By means of the diamond-like wisdom that pierces to the quick, not to be bound or liberated is the entrance into nonduality."

The bodhisattva Simhamati declared, "To say, 'This is impure' and 'This is immaculate' makes for duality. One who, attaining equanimity, forms no conception of impurity or immaculateness, yet is not utterly without conception, has equanimity without any attainment of equanimity—he enters the absence of conceptual knots. Thus, he enters into nonduality."

The bodhisattva Shuddhadhimukti declared, "To say, 'This is happiness' and 'That is misery' is dualism. One who is free of all calculations, through the extreme purity of gnosis—his mind is aloof, like empty space; and thus he enters into nonduality."

The bodhisattva Narayana declared, "To say, 'This is mundane' and 'That is transcendental' is dualism. This world has the nature of voidness, so there is neither transcendence nor involvement, neither progress nor standstill. Thus, neither to transcend nor to be involved, neither to go nor to stop—this is the entrance into nonduality."

The bodhisattva Dantamati declared, "'Life' and 'liberation' are dualistic. Having seen the nature of life, one neither belongs to it nor is one utterly liberated from it. Such understanding is the entrance into nonduality."

The bodhisattva Pratyakshadarshana declared, "'Destructible' and 'indestructible' are dualistic. What is destroyed is ultimately destroyed. What is ultimately destroyed does not become destroyed; hence it is called 'indestructible.' What is indestructible is instantaneous, and what is instantaneous is indestructible. The experience of such is called 'the entrance into the principle of nonduality.'"

The bodhisattva Parigudha declared, "'Self' and 'selflessness' are dualistic. Since the existence of self cannot be perceived, what is there to be made 'selfless'? Thus, the nondualism of the vision of their nature is the entrance into nonduality."

The bodhisattva Vidyuddeva declared, "'Knowledge' and 'ignorance' are dualistic. The natures of ignorance and knowledge are the same, for ignorance is undefined, incalculable, and beyond the sphere of thought. The realization of this is the entrance into nonduality."

The bodhisattva Priyadarshana declared, "Matter itself is void. Voidness does not result from the destruction of matter, but the nature of matter is itself voidness. Therefore, to speak of voidness on the one hand, and of matter, or of sensation, or of intellect, or of motivation, or of consciousness on the other—is entirely dualistic. Consciousness itself is voidness. Voidness does not result from the destruction of consciousness, but the nature of consciousness is itself voidness. Such understanding of the five compulsive aggregates and the knowledge of them as such by means of gnosis is the entrance into nonduality."

The bodhisattva Prabhaketu declared, "To say that the four main elements are one thing and the etheric space-element another is dualistic. The four main elements are themselves the nature of space. The past itself is also the nature of space. The future itself is also the nature of space. Likewise, the present itself is also the nature of space. The gnosis that penetrates the elements in such a way is the entrance into nonduality."

The bodhisattva Pramati declared, "'Eye' and 'form' are dualistic. To understand the eye correctly, and not to have attachment, aversion, or confusion with regard to form—that is called 'peace.' Similarly, 'ear' and 'sound,' 'nose' and 'smell,' 'tongue' and 'taste,' 'body' and 'touch,' and 'mind' and 'phenomena'— all are dualistic. But to know the mind, and to be neither attached, averse, nor confused with regard to phenomena—that is called 'peace.' To live in such peace is to enter into nonduality."

The bodhisattva Akshayamati declared, "The dedication of generosity for the sake of attaining omniscience is dualistic. The nature of generosity is itself omniscience, and the nature of omniscience itself is total dedication. Likewise, it is dualistic to dedicate morality, tolerance, effort, meditation, and wisdom for the sake of omniscience. Omniscience is the nature of wisdom, and total dedication is the nature of omniscience. Thus, the entrance into this principle of uniqueness is the entrance into nonduality."

The bodhisattva Gambhiramati declared, "It is dualistic to say that voidness is one thing, signlessness another, and wishlessness still another. What is void has no sign. What has no sign has no wish. Where there is no wish there is no process of thought, mind, or consciousness. To see the doors of all liberations in the door of one liberation is the entrance into nonduality."

The bodhisattva Shantendriya declared, "It is dualistic to say 'Buddha,' 'Dharma,' and 'Sangham.' The dharma is itself the nature of the Buddha, the Sangha is itself the nature of the dharma, and all of them are uncompounded. The uncompounded is infinite space, and the processes of all things are equivalent to infinite space. Adjustment to this is the entrance into nonduality."

The bodhisattva Apratihatanetra declared, "It is dualistic to refer to 'aggregates' and to the 'cessation of aggregates.' Aggregates themselves are cessation. Why? The egoistic views of aggregates, being unproduced themselves, do not exist ultimately. Hence such views do not really conceptualize 'These are aggregates' or 'These aggregates cease.' Ultimately, they have no such discriminative constructions and no such conceptualizations. Therefore, such views have themselves the nature of cessation. Nonoccurrence and nondestruction are the entrance into nonduality."

The bodhisattva Suvinita declared, "Physical, verbal, and mental vows do not exist dualistically. Why? these things have the nature of inactivity. The nature of inactivity of the body is the same as the nature of inactivity of speech, whose nature of inactivity is the same as the nature of inactivity of the mind. It is necessary to know and to understand this fact of the ultimate inactivity of all things, for this knowledge is the entrance into nonduality."

The bodhisattva Punyakshetra declared, "It is dualistic to consider actions meritorious, sinful, or neutral. The non-undertaking of meritorious, sinful, and neutral actions is not dualistic. The intrinsic nature of all such actions is voidness, wherein ultimately there is neither merit, nor sin, nor neutrality, nor action itself. The nonaccomplishment of such actions is the entrance into nonduality."

The bodhisattva Padmavyuha declared, "Dualism is produced from obsession with self but true understanding of self does not result in dualism. Who thus abides in nonduality is without ideation, and that absence of ideation is the entrance into nonduality."

The bodhisattva Shrigarbha declared, "Duality is constituted by perceptual manifestation. Nonduality is objectlessness. Therefore, nongrasping and nonrejection is the entrance into nonduality."

The bodhisattva Candrottara declared, "'Darkness' and 'light' are dualistic, but the absence of both darkness and light is nonduality. Why? At the time of absorption in cessation, there is neither darkness nor light, and likewise with the nature of all things. The entrance into this equanimity is the entrance into nonduality."

The bodhisattva Ratnamudrahasta declared, "It is dualistic to detest the world and to rejoice in liberation, and neither detesting the world nor rejoicing in liberation is nonduality. Why? Liberation can be found where there is bondage, but where there is ultimately no bondage where is there need for liberation? The mendicant who is neither bound nor liberated does not experience any like or any dislike and thus he enters nonduality."

The bodhisattva Manikutaraja declared, "It is dualistic to speak of good paths and bad paths. Living in such unconcern, he entertains no concepts of 'path' or 'nonpath.' Understanding the nature of concepts, his mind does not engage in duality. Such is the entrance into nonduality."

The bodhisattva Satyarata declared, "It is dualistic to speak of 'true' and 'false.' When one sees truly, one does not ever see any truth, so how could one see falsehood? Why? One does not see with the physical eye, one sees with the eye of wisdom. And with the wisdom-eye one sees only insofar as there is neither sight nor nonsight. There, where there is neither sight nor nonsight, is the entrance into nonduality."

When the bodhisattvas had given their explanations, they all addressed the crown prince Manjushri: "Manjushri, what is the bodhisattva's entrance into nonduality?"

Manjushri replied, "Good sirs, you have all spoken well. Nevertheless, all your explanations are themselves dualistic. To know no one teaching, to express nothing, to say nothing, to explain nothing, to announce nothing, to indicate nothing, and to designate nothing—that is the entrance into nonduality."

Then, the crown prince Manjushri said to the Licchavi Vimalakirti, "We have all given our own teachings, noble sir. Now, may you elucidate the teaching of the entrance into the principle of nonduality!"

Thereupon, the Licchavi Vimalakirti kept his silence, saying nothing at all.

The crown prince Manjushri applauded the Licchavi Vimalakirti: "Excellent! Excellent, noble sir! This is indeed the entrance into the nonduality of the bodhisattvas. Here there is no use for syllables, sounds and ideas."

When these teachings had been declared, five thousand bodhisattvas entered the door of the dharma of nonduality and attained tolerance of the birthlessness of things.

(*Vimalakirti-nirdesha*)[64] ▲

▼ **EXPOSITION OF THE UNALTERABLE NATURE OF DHARMA**

Subhuti: If the sameness of all dharmas is empty of essential nature, then no dharma does anything to any other. When dharmas have nothing whatever and are nothing whatever, how, then, is it that the bodhisattva on the one side does not swerve from ultimate reality, and on the other does the work of beings, through the four means of conversion?

The Lord: So it is, Subhuti, so it is, as you say. Emptiness does not do anything whatever to anything, nor does it do not anything. If beings on their own could cognize emptiness, then there would be no need for the tathagata's manly effort when he does not swerve from emptiness and yet dissuades beings from the notion of a self, etc., and then through emptiness liberates them from samsara and establishes them in the unconditioned element. And also that unconditioned element is empty.

Subhuti: Of what is it empty?

The Lord: It is empty of all notions. On the other hand, Subhuti, if a magical creation magically creates another magical creation, is there then, perhaps in connection with that an entity which is not emptiness?

Subhuti: No, O Lord. Both these dharmas—the emptiness and the magical creation—are not conjoined or disjoined, they are both empty through emptiness.

The Lord: What do you think, Subhuti, is then the difference between emptiness and magical creation mysteriously concealed?

Subhuti: It is not. And why? Because they both are not apprehended in emptiness, i.e., "this is emptiness' and "this is a magical creation.'

The Lord: There is nothing about the five *skandhas* which is not a magical creation.

Subhuti: If these worldly dharmas are magical creations, are, then, also the supramundane dharmas magical creations, i.e., the four applications of mindfulness, etc. to: their fruits by which the holy men are conceived, i.e., the Streamwinners, etc., to: the tathagata?

The Lord: Since all dharmas are magical creations, each disciple must be a magical creation, each pratyekabuddha, each bodhisattva, each tathagata, each defilement, and each deed. By this method all dharmas are like magical creations.

Subhuti: And again, O Lord, as to this forsaking—as to the fruit of a Streamwinner, etc. to: arhatship, or as to the level of pratyekabuddha, or that of a Buddha, or the forsaking of all defilements with their residues—are these dharmas also magical creations?

The Lord: Any dharmas that there are, as long as they have been produced or stopped, are all magical creations.

Subhuti: What is the dharma which is not a magical creation?

The Lord: The dharma of which there is no production or stopping.

Subhuti: What, then, is that?

The Lord: Nirvana which by its dharmic nature is undeluded.

Subhuti: But the Lord has said that he does not swerve away from emptiness, that it is not apprehended through duality, and that there is no dharma which is not emptiness. Therefore the nirvana which by its dharmic nature is undeluded must be a magical creation.

The Lord: So it is, Subhuti, so it is. All dharmas are empty through their own-being. They have not been made by the disciples, or by the pratyekabuddhas, or by the bodhisattvas, or the tathagatas. But nirvana is the emptiness of own-marks.

Subhuti: How should a person who is a beginner be instructed, how admonished, so that he can cognize the emptiness of own-being?

The Lord: "How is it possible that something was an existent in the past and later on becomes a nonexistent!" There is in it no existent, no nonexistent, no own-being and no other-being. How can there be an emptiness of own-being?

(*The Large Sutra of Perfect Wisdom*)[65] ▲

Perfection of Wisdom

The perfection of wisdom (*prajna-paramita*) is the last and most important of the six perfections (*paramita*) and is to be developed during an arduous and very lengthy career of innumerable lifetimes. It has to be brought to its consummation at the moment the *bodhisattva* enters *nirvana*. The teaching of the perfection of wisdom is found in several *sutras* of variable length. In Tibetan translation these *sutras* fill twenty-five volumes of the canon known as Them spangs-ma.

▼ Manjusri: What are the qualities and what the advantages of a perfection of wisdom which is without qualities? How can one speak of the qualities or advantages of a perfect wisdom which is incapable of doing anything, neither raises up nor destroys anything, neither accepts nor rejects any dharma, is powerless to act and not at all busy, if its own-being cannot be cognized, if its own-being cannot be seen, if it does not bestow any dharma, and does not obstruct any dharma, if it brings about the non-separateness of all dharmas, does not exalt the single oneness of all dharmas, does not effect the separateness of all dharmas, if it is not made, not something to be done, not passed, if it does not destroy anything, if it is not a donor of the dharmas of the common people, of the dharmas of the Arhats, of the dharms of the Pratyekabuddhas, of the dharmas of the bodhisattvas, and not even of the dharmas of a Buddha, and does not take them away, if it does not toil in birth-and-death, nor cease toiling in nirvana, neither bestows nor destroys the dharms of a Buddha, if it is unthinkable and inconceivable, not something to be done, not something to be undone, if it neither produces nor stops any dharmas, neither annhilates them nor makes them eternal, if it neither causes to come nor to go, brings about neither detachment nor non-detachment, neither duality or non-duality, and if, finally, it is nonexistent?

The Lord: Well have you, Manjusri, described the qualities of perfect wisdom. But nevertheless a Bodhisattva should train in just this perfection of wisdom, in the manner of no-training, if he wants to train in, and to accomplish, that concentration of a Bodhisattva which allows him to see all the Buddhas, the Lords, if he wants to see their Buddha-fields, and to know their names, and if he wants to perfect the supreme worship of those Buddhas and Lords, and firmly to believe in and to fathom their demonstration of dharma.

Manjusri: For what reason is this the perfection of wisdom?

The Lord: It is called "perfect wisdom" because it is neither produced nor stopped. And it is so because it is calmly quiet from the very beginning, because there is escape, because there is nothing to be accomplished, and, finally, because of its non-existence. For what is nonexistence, that is perfect wisdom. It is for this reason that one should expect Bodhisattvas to develop perfect wisdom. It is the range of the Bodhisattvas, the great beings, ranging in all dharmas.

(*Saptasatika*)[66] ▲

The Germ of Buddha-Nature

The concept of voidness as the sole inherent quality of existence entailed that it could be viewed as the ultimate. If voidness permeates all that exists, then, so it was argued, it is the only quality that has any claim to ultimate reality, i.e., Buddha-nature. Thus, Buddha-nature as a potentiality rests within all that exists. The technical term "germ of buddha-nature" (*tathagata-garbha*) indicates that each living being has the potential to realize its latent buddhahood. This theory is expounded in the *Ratnagotra-vibhaga-sutra* from which the following excerpt is taken.

▼   All beings are potentially tathagatas:

27 Because the buddha-cognition is contained in the mass of beings,
    Are taken into account because this lineage exists.
    Those who are without the lineage cannot do so.

45 As to its Suchness identical in common people,
   Saints and perfect Buddhas,
   Thus has the Jina's Germ been shown to be in beings,
       by those who have seen the true Reality.

46 But the difference lies in that common people are perverted
       in their views,
   Whereas those who have seen the Truths have undone
       this perversion;
   The tathagats again are unperverted as to what truly is,
   And without intellectual impediments.

46 It is impure in ordinary beings,
   Partly pure and partly impure in the Bodhisattvas,
   And perfectly pure in the tathagatas.

49 Just as space, essentially indiscriminate, reaches everywhere,
   Just to the immaculate element which in its essential nature is
       thought, is present in all.

50 It pervades, as a general mark, the vicious, the virtuous
       and the perfect;
   Just as ether is in all visible forms, be they base, intermediate
       or superior.

It has been said in a sutra: "Therefore, Sariputra, the world of beings is not one thing, and the dharma-body another. The world of beings is just the dharma-body, the dharma-body is just the world of beings. Objectively they are not two. The distinction lies in the words only." And the element of tathagatahood, as it is present in all, is immutable, and cannot be affected by either defilement or purification.

51 In spite of the adventitious faults, and because of the virtues
       essential to its nature.
   The nature of dharma remains immutable, the same in former
       and in subsequent states.

96 Like the Buddha in a faded lotus flower, like honey covered
       by a swarm of bees.
   Like the kernel of a fruit in the husk, like god within impurities,
   Like a treasure hidden in the soil, the fruit in a small seed,
   An image of the Jina in tattered garments.

97 The universal monarch in the vile belly of a woman,
   And like a precious statue covered with dust,
   So is this element established in beings
   Who are covered with the stains of adventitious defilements.

108 Suppose that gold belonging to a man on his travels
   Had fallen into a place full of stinking dirt.

As it is indestructible by nature, it would stay there
For many hundreds of years.

109 A deity, with a pure heavenly eye, would see it there,
And say to people:
"When I have cleansed this gold, the most precious substance of all.
I will bring it back to its precious state."

110 Just so, the great sage, when he has seen the virtue in beings,
Sunk as they are in defilements which are like filth,
In order to cleanse off the mud of these defilements,
Rains down the rain of dharma on all that lives.

118 Suppose that an image of the Jina, made of precious material,
Were covered by a garment, evil-smelling and stinking.
A deity travelling by that way would see it in its neglected state,
Would explain its significance to others so that they might release it.

119 So the Buddha's unattached eye,
Having perceived even in animals the personality of a Sugata,
Though concealed by the taints of manifold defilements,
Shows the means which allow its release.

145 The dharma-body should be known as twofold:
The completely immaculate element of dharma,
And its outpourings, the demonstration of the principle [of dharma],
In its depth and in its variety.

148 Being immutable in its essential nature, lovely, and pure,
To a golden disk that this Suchness been compared.

153 The state of the self-existent can, in the ultimate sense, be approached
only by faith.
For those who have no eyes cannot see the blazing disk of the sun.

154 Nothing should be taken from it, and nothing added on to it;
The real must be seen in its reality, and one who sees the truth
is emancipated.

155 Empty is the element of the adventitious properties which are
distinct from it.
It is not empty of the supreme dharmas, which are properties
indistinct from it.

(*Ratnagotravibhaga* 1)[66] ▲

The Community

To take refuge in the community of Buddhist practitioners is the third pillar on which spiritual progress rests. The community following the Buddhist doctrine is known as the *sangha*. In its widest sense it encompasses monks and nuns, male and female laity. In its narrowest sense it denotes those who made considerable progress on the path to enlightenment; they are the noble ones (Skr. *Arya*). One takes refuge in the *sangha* because the community of fellow practitioners provides social and spiritual support.

The first Buddhists had been converted to Buddha's teaching from their previous faith, a form of early Hinduism or Jainism. In many texts we find accounts about such conversions.

The following excerpt tells about the conversion of Anathapindika, one of the foremost supporters of Buddha Gautama.

▼ "CONVERSION" OF ANATHAPINDIKA AND GIFT OF THE JETA GROVE

The householder Anathapindika, who was the husband of a sister of a banker in Rajagaha, went there on some business at a time when the Order with the Buddha as its head had been invited for the morrow by the banker. And the banker enjoined his slaves and servants to get up early in the morning and cook conjeys, rice, curries and vegetables. So the householder Anathapindika thought to himself: "Formerly, when I used to arrive here this householder put aside all his duties and did nothing but exchange greetings with me, but now he seems excited and is enjoining his slaves and servants to get up early tomorrow and cook various things. Can it be that there is a wedding on foot, or has a great oblation been arranged, or is King Seniya Bimbisara of Magadha invited for the morrow with his troops?" And he asked the banker what was going forward.

"There is neither a wedding, householder, nor has King Seniya Bimbisara been invited with his troops. But a great oblation has been arranged by me: the Order has been invited for the morrow with the Buddha at its head."

> "Householder, did you say Buddha?"
> "Buddha I did say, householder."
> "Householder, did you say Buddha?"
> "Buddha I did say, householder."
> "Householder, did you say Buddha?"
> "Buddha I did say, householder."
> "Householder, did you say Buddha?"
> "Buddha I did say, householder."
> "Even this sound, Buddha, Buddha is hard to come by
>   in the world. Could I go and see this Lord, Arahant,
>   perfect Buddha?"
> "Not now, but tomorrow early."

So the householder Anathapindika lay down with mindfulness so much directed towards the Buddha that he got up three times during the night thinking it was daybreak. As he approached the gateway to the Cool Grove nonhuman beings opened it. But as he was going out from the town, light vanished, darkness appeared; and such fear, consternation, terror arose in him that he wanted to turn back from there. But the yakkha Sivaka, invisible, made this sound heard:

"A hundred elephants, horses or chariots with she-mules,
A hundred thousand maidens adorned with jewelled earrings—
These are not worth a sixteenth part of one length of stride.
Advance, householder; advance, householder.
Advance is better for you, not retreat."

Then the darkness vanished, light appeared so that Anathapindika's fear, consternation and terror subsided.

He then approached the Cool Grove and as the Lord was pacing up and down in the open air he saw him and, stepping down from the place where he had been pacing up and down, he addressed Anathapindika, saying: "Come, Sudatta." He thinking: "The Lord addressed me by name,"inclined his head at the Lord's feet and said he hoped that the Lord was living at ease. The Lord answered:

"Yes, always at ease he lives, the Brahmin, attained to nirvana,
Who is not stained by lusts, cooled, without "basis,"
Having rent all clingings, having averted heart's care,
Tranquil he lives at ease, having won to peace of mind."

Then the Lord talked a talk on various things to the householder Anathapindika, that is to say talk on giving, on moral habit and on heaven; he explained the peril, the vanity, the depravity of pleasures of the senses, the advantage in renouncing them. When the Lord knew that the mind of the householder Anathapindika was ready, malleable, devoid of the hindrances, uplifted, pleased, then he explained to him that teaching on dhamma which the Buddhas have themselves discovered: ill, uprising, stopping, the Way. And as a clean cloth without black specks will easily take dye, even so as he was sitting on that very seat, dhamma-vision, dustless, stainless, arose to the householder Anathapindika, that "whatever is liable to originanation all that is liable to stopping." Then, having seen dhamma, attained dhamma, known dhamma, plunged into dhamma, having crossed over doubt, put away uncertainty and attained without another's help to full confidence in the Teacher's instruction, Anathapindika spoke thus to the Lord:

"It is excellent, Lord. Even as one might set upright what has been upset, or uncover what was concealed, or show the way to one who is astray, or bring an oil lamp into the darkness thinking that those with vision might see forms, even so is dhamma explained in many a figure by the Lord. I myself Lord, am going to the Lord for refuge, to dhamma and to the Order of monks. May the Lord accept me as a lay disciple going for refuge from this day forth for as long as my life lasts.

And, Lord, may the Lord consent to a meal with me on the morrow together with the Order of monks." The Lord consented by becoming silent....

Then the householder Anathapindika, having concluded his business in Rajagaha, set out for Savatthi. On his way he enjoined people, saying: "Masters, build monasteries, prepare dwelling-places, furnish gifts; a Buddha has arisen in the world, and this Lord, invited by me, will come along this road." The people did so. And when the householder Anathapindika had arrived at Savatthi he looked all round it thinking:

"Now, where could the Lord stay that would be neither too far from a village nor too near, suitable for coming and going, accessible to people whenever they want, not crowded by day, having little noise at night, little sound, without folks' breath, secluded from people, fitting for meditation?"

The householder Anathapindika saw Prince Jeta's pleasure grove, neither too far from a village ... fitting for meditation, and he approached Prince Jeta and said: "Young master, give me the pleasure grove to make a monastery."

"The pleasure grove cannot be given away, householder, even for the price of a hundred thousand [coins]."

"The monastery has been bought, young master."

"The monastery has not been bought, householder." They asked the chief ministers of justice whether it had been bought or not, and they said: "When the price was fixed by you, young master, the monastery was bought." So the householder Anathapindika, having gold coins brought out in wagons, spread the Jeta Grove with the price of a hundred thousand. But the gold coins that were brought out the first time were not enough to cover a small open space near the porch. So the householder Anathapindika enjoined the people, saying: "Go back, good people, bring [more] gold coins; I will spread this open space [with them]."

Then Prince Jeta thought to himself: "Now, this can be no ordinary matter inasmuch as this householder bestows so many gold coins," and he spoke thus to Anathapindika:

"Please, householder, let me spread this open space; give it to me, it will be my gift."

Then the householder Anathapindika thinking: "This Prince Jeta is a distinguished, well-known man; surely the faith in this dhamma and discipline of well-known men like this is very efficacious," made over that open space to Prince Jeta. And Prince Jeta built a porch on that open space. The householder Anathapindika had dwelling-places made and cells, porches, attendance-halls, fire halls, huts for what is allowable, privies, places for pacing up and down in, wells, bathrooms, lotus ponds and sheds.

(*Vinaya-pitaka* II, 154–59)[68] ▲

Inauguration of Nuns' Order

Several versions of the subsequent story are preserved in the Pali Canon, each featuring some variations. The following excerpt is taken from the *Vinaya pitaka*, that is, the part of the canon that contains all the rules and regulations pertaining to the monks and nuns. It introduces Pajapati, Buddha's aunt, wet nurse, and stepmother, as asking for admission to the Order. Buddha seems to be disinclined to grant this request. However, Pajapati, together with other women of Buddha's family, are subsequently described exhibiting the appearance of nuns: shaved heads and yellow robes. This causes us to ask whether Pajapati and her fellow nuns were disregarding Buddha's refusal to grant formal admission, which would be an unbelievable disrespect. The story continues to puzzle us when it reports that Buddha's view on this issue was overturned when Ananda intervened on Pajapati's behalf. These issues, together with others, led scholars to question whether the whole story is a later invention. The reason for such invention could be to seek justification as to why the Buddhist community did what no other religious community had yet done, that is, admit women as full members of a religious mendicant order.

Regardless of the outcome of further research on this issue, the account of the inauguration of the nuns' Order had several significant effects on the status and roles of Buddhist nuns: they had to adopt additional rules that put them firmly under the authority of the monks' Order; each nun is junior in rank to even the youngest monk, and, most importantly, the nuns' Order was seen as less prestigious than the monks' Order. The latter situation resulted in a significant economic imbalance, which over time left the nuns' Order impoverished.

From Indian soil the nuns' Order had vanished, certainly prior to the seventh century, while in some Southeast Asian countries it disappeared around the eleventh century. In modern times, fully ordained nuns (*bhikshuni*) exist only in some areas and within certain Buddhist traditions of China, Korea, and Vietnam. In all other countries, Buddhist women can only obtain the rank of a novice. There is now a movement to reinstate full ordination of nuns, but it is met with significant opposition from traditional monks of the Tibetan and Theravada traditions. With a few exceptions, such as the *Fo kuan shan* movement of Taiwan, Buddhist nuns do not enjoy the same prestige or privileges Buddhist monks do, nor are they generally admitted to institutions of Buddhist learning. Often Buddhist nuns are considered nothing more than cheap servants and menial workers.

▼ **ORDINATION OF PAJAPATI THE GREAT**

At one time the Buddha, the Lord, was staying among the Sakyans at Kapilavatthu in the Banyan monastery. Then the Gotamid, Pajapati the Great, approached and greeted the Lord and, standing at a respectful distance, spoke thus to him:

"Lord, it were well that women should obtain the going forth from home into homelessness in this dhamma and discipline proclaimed by the tathagata."

"Be careful, Gotami, of the going forth of women from home into homelessness in this dhamma and discipline proclaimed by the tathagata."

A second and a third time both uttered these words. And Pajapati, thinking that the Lord did not allow the going forth of women, afflicted, grieved, with tearful face and crying, greeted the Lord and departed keeping her right side towards him.

Then the Lord set out for Vesali. And Pajapati too, having had her hair cut off and having donned saffron robes, set out for Vesali with several Sakyan women. Arrived at the Gabled Hall, she stood outside the porch, her feet swollen, her limbs covered with dust, with tearful face and crying. The venerable Ananda saw her, and hearing from her the reason for her distress, told her to wait a moment while he asked the Lord for the going forth of women from home into homelessness. But the Lord answered him as he had answered Pajapati. So Ananda thought: "Suppose that I should now ask the Lord by some other method?" and he spoke thus to the Lord:

"Now, Lord, are women, having gone forth from home into homelessness in this dhamma and discipline proclaimed by the tathagata, able to realize the fruits of stream-winning, of once-returning and of non-returning, and arahantship?"

"Yes, Ananda."

"If so, Lord—and, Lord, the Gotamid, Pajapati the Great, was of great service: she was the Lord's aunt, foster-mother, purse giver of milk, for when the Lord's mother passed away she suckled him—it were well, Lord, that women should obtain the going forth from home into homelessness."

"If, Ananda, the Gotamid, Pajapati the Great, accepts these eight important rules, that may be ordination for her:

"A nun who has been ordained even for a century must greet respectfully, rise up from her seat, salute with joined palms and do proper homage to a monk ordained but that very day.

"A nun must not spend the rains in a residence where there is no monk.

"Every half month a nun should reuqire two things from the order of monks: the date of the observance day, and the coming for the exhortation.

"After the rains a nun must 'invite' before both orders in respect of three matters: what has been seen, heard and suspected [to be an offence].

"A nun, offending against an important rule, must undergo *manatta* discipline for a fortnight before both orders.

"When, as a probationer, she has trained in the six rules for two years, she should seek ordination from both orders.

"A monk must not be abused or reviled in any way by a nun.

"From today admonition of monks by nuns is forbidden, admonition of nuns by monks is not forbidden.

"Each of these rules is to be honoured, respected, revered, venerated, and is never to be transgressed by a nun during her life. If, Ananda, Pajapati accepts these eight important rules, that shall be ordination for her."

When Ananda had told Pajapati this matter, she said:

"Even, Ananda, as a woman or a man when young, of tender years and fond of ornaments, having washed his head, having obtained a garland of lotus or jasmine flowers or of some sweet-scented creeper, should take it in both hands and place it on top of his head—even so do I, honoured Ananda, accept these eight important rules, never to be transgressed during my life."

Then Pajapati approached the Lord and asked him what line of conduct she should follow in regard to the Sakyan women. When the Lord had rejoiced and delighted her with talk on dhamma, she departed; and the Lord said to the monks: "I allow, monks, nuns to be ordained by monks."

These nuns said to Pajapati: "The lady is not ordained, neither are we ordained, for it was laid down by the Lord that nuns should be ordained by monks." Pajapati told the venerable Ananda who told the Lord. He said: "At the time, Ananda, when the eight important rules were accepted by Pajapati, that was her ordination."

Then Pajapati approached the Lord herself and, standing at a respectful distance, said to him:

"Lord, what line of conduct should we follow in regard to those rules of training for nuns which are in common with those for monks?"

"As the monks train themselves, so should you train yourselves in these rules of training."

"And what line of conduct should we follow in regard to those rules of training for nuns which are not in common with those for monks?"

"You should train yourselves in these rules of training according as they are laid down."

(Vinaya-pitaka II, 253 if.)[69] ▲

Decency

The following excerpt renders a story explaining why bathing suits are mandatory for Buddhist nuns. In order to appreciate this story, we must consider how nudity was seen in pre-modern India. Nudity was, and in some remote areas of India still is, a sign of extreme asceticism. If one disrobes oneself of all clothes, which are symbols of one's social class and wealth and enhance one's youth and beauty, one has severed all ties with society—the ultimate act of an ascetic. Thus, to see naked ascetics was a common sight in ancient India. Buddhists resented this practice together with all forms of severe asceticism. It is clear from this story that originally neither Buddha nor his Order had any concerns about the nudity of monks or nuns but that the rules came into place in order to placate laity. Many of the rules defining the monks' and nuns' public behaviour are grounded in meeting the laity's sensitivities.

▼ VISAKHA, THE LAYWOMAN SUPPORTER

After Visakha, Migara's mother, had been roused, rejoiced, gladdened, delighted by the Lord with talk on dhamma, she asked him to consent to accept a meal from her on the morrow together with the order of monks. The Lord consented by becoming silent. Then towards the end of that night heavy rain poured over the four "continents," and the Lord said to the monks: "Monks, even as it is raining in the Jeta Grove, so it is raining over the four continents. Let your bodies get wet with the rain, this is the last great cloud over the four continents."

When the time for the meal had come, Visakha sent a servant woman to the monastery to announce the time. She saw the monks, their robes laid aside, letting their bodies get wet with the rain, but she thought they were Naked Ascetics, not monks. Then the Lord addressed the monks, saying: "Monks, arrange your bowls and robes, it is time for the meal." When Visakha had served and satisfied the order of monks with the Buddha at its head with sumptuous food, solid and soft, she sat down at a respectful distance, and spoke thus to the Lord:

"Lord, I ask for eight boons from the Lord."

"Visakha, tathagatas are beyond granting boons."

"Lord, they are allowable and blameless."

"Speak on, Visakha."

"I, Lord, for life want to give to the order cloths for the rains, food for those coming in [to monasteries], food for those going out, food for the sick, food for those who nurse them, medicine for the sick, a constant supply of conjee, and bathing-cloths for the order of nuns."

"But, having what special reason in mind do you, Visakha, ask the tathagat for the eight boons?"

"Lord, my servant woman told me there were no monks in the monastery, but Naked Ascetics were letting their bodies get wet with the rain. Impure, Lord, is nakedness, it is objectionable. It is for this special reason that for life I want to give the order cloths for the rains.

"And again, an in-coming monk, not accustomed to the roads or resorts for alms, still walks for alms when he is tired. But if he eats my food for those coming in, then when he is accustomed to the roads and resorts for alms he will walk for alms without getting tired.

"And again, an out-going monk, while looking about for food for himself, might get left behind by the caravan, or, setting out tired on a journey, might arrive at the wrong time at the habitation where he wants to go. But if he eats my food for those going out, these things will not happen to him.

"And again, Lord, if an ill monk does not obtain suitable meals, either his disease will get very much worse or he will pass away. But not if he eats my food for the sick.

"And again, Lord, a monk who nurses the sick, looking about for food for himself, will bring back food for the sick after the sun is right up and so he will miss his meal. But, having eaten my food for those who nurse the sick, he will bring back food for the sick during the right time and so he will not miss his meal.

"And again, Lord, if an ill monk does not obtain suitable medicines, either his disease will get very much worse or he will pass away. But this will not happen if he can use my medicine for the sick.

"And again, Lord, conjee was allowed by the Lord at Andhakavinda when he had its ten advantages in mind. I, Lord, having this special reason in mind, want to give for life a constant supply of conjey to the order.

"There was a case where nuns bathed naked together with prostitutes at the same ford of the river Aciravati, and the prostitutes made fun of them, saying: 'Why on earth, ladies, is the Brahma-faring led by you when you are still young? Surely sense-pleasures should be enjoyed? When you are old you can fare the Brahma-faring; and so will you experience both extremes.' The nuns were ashamed. Impure, Lord, is nakedness for women, it is abhorrent and objectionable. I, Lord, having this special reason in mind, want to give for life bathing-cloths for the order of nuns."

"It is very good that you, Visakha, are asking the tathagata for these eight boons. I allow you, Visakha, these eight boons." Then the Lord, on this occasion, having given reasoned talk, addressed the monks, saying: "I allow, monks, cloths for the rains, food for those coming in, for those going out, for the sick, for those who nurse them, medicines for the sick, a constant supply of conjee, bathing-cloths for the order of nuns."

(*Vinaya-pitaka* I, 290–94)[70] ▲

▼ **THE DISCIPLES' TASK**

I, monks, am freed from all snares, both those of devas and those of men. And you monks, are freed from all snares, both those of devas and those of men. Walk, monks, on tour for the blessing of the many folk, for the happiness of the many-folk, out of compassion for the world, for the welfare, the blessing, the happiness of devas and men. Let not two of you go by the same way. Monks, teach dhamma that is lovely at the beginning, lovely in the middle and lovely at the ending. Explain with the spirit and the letter the Brahma-faring completing fulfilled and utterly pure.

There are beings with little dust in their eyes who, not hearing dhamma, are decaying, but if they are learners of dhamma they will grow. And I, monks, will go along to Uruvela, the Camp township, in order to teach dhamma.

(*Vinaya-pitaka* I, 20–21)[71] ▲

▼ ARAHANTS

Ah, happy indeed the arahants! In them no cravings found.
The "I am" conceit is rooted out; confusion's net is burst.
Lust-free they have attained; translucent is the mind of them.
Unspotted in the world are they, Brahma-become, with outflows none.
Comprehending the five groups, pasturing in their seven own mental states,
Worthy of praise, the true men, own sons of the Buddha.
Endowed with the sevenfold gem, trained in the three trainings,
These great heroes follow on, fear and dread overcome.
Endowed with the ten factors, great beings concentrated,
Indeed they are best in the world; no craving's found in them.
Possessed of the adept's knowledge, this compound is their last.
In that pith of the Brahma-faring they depend not on others.
Unshaken by the triple modes, well freed from again becoming,
Attained to the stage of "tamed," they are victorious in the world.
Above, across, below, no lure in them is found.
They roar the lion's roar: "Incomparable are Buddhas in the world."

(*Samyutta-nikaya* III, 83–84)[72] ▲

Selected Voices of Modern Buddhism

Buddhism became gradually known in the West by the late eighteenth century, and by the late nineteenth century scholars were editing large numbers of Buddhist texts and making them available in translations to a wider audience. But it was not until the 1960s and later that the phenomenon of a "Western" or "American" Buddhism aroused scholars' curiosity.[73] By the beginning of the twenty-first century, scholars agree that "modern Buddhism" is a new phase in the history of Buddhism. Some speak even of a "new vehicle," or *Navayana*, that continues the development from Hinayana to Mahayana and Vajrayana.[74] The study of modern Buddhism is now an accepted branch within the study of Buddhism in general.

Modern Buddhism arose from a series of events; some of them happening in the West and some of them in the East. They all took place during the second half of the nineteenth century. The philosophical movement of the European Enlightenment, with its emphasis on reason and humanistic ethics, cast doubts on the truth claims made by traditional religions with which Western people were familiar, i.e., Christianity and Judaism. Some Europeans and Americans responded to this disillusionment with a quest for the supernatural and the occult, while the mainstream culture endorsed the common ideas of the era of Enlightenment. Numerous social circles devoted themselves to the practice of table rapping, communications with the dead, trance, and sightings of ghosts. People in the United States mourned their dead after the Civil War. Finding ways to reach out to them and learning about the fate of those who had been missing led many to experiment with séances and other occult practices. Once the truth claims of Christianity became suspect, interest in "other" religions, such as Buddhism, became a viable option.

Asian Buddhism was severely affected by losing the patronage of premodern monarchies and their wealthy elite when Western powers built their colonies in Asia. With the help of Christian churches, the colonial masters tried to convert the local elite not only to Christianity but also to embrace Western ideas and values. Resentment began to boil up not only among the peasantry and the lower ranks of the urban population but also among those who had received a "Western" education in the missionary schools. In these schools students became acquainted with Western ideas and values as well as methods of communicating and disseminating them through education, youth organisations, and, above all, the printing press. Several gifted Sinhalese from Ceylon, as Sri Lanka was called then, took up the challenge by studying the biblical texts of Christianity in order to demonstrate its inferiority vis-à-vis Buddhism. In 1873 a debate was held between the Buddhist camp, whose leader was the monk Gunananda, and Christian missionaries lead by Reverend De Silva, an Anglican minister. Gunananda presented Buddhism as a humanistic and ethical philosophy that was fully compatible with science and reason. Anagarika Dharmapala, another Sinhalese educated at a missionary school, popularized this view of Buddhism at the World's Parliament of Religions in Chicago in 1893.

The founders of the Theosophical Society, Madam Helena Petrova Blavatsky and Colonel Henry Steel Olcott, were excited to learn about this view of Buddhism and became ardent promoters of a Buddhism that was stripped of all rituals, beliefs in spirits and gods, and the supernatural in general. In their writings they introduced Buddhism as a religion of non-violence and peace, based on reason and compatible with the modern scientific world view. The Theosophical Society, and its members in both the East and West, inaugurated Buddhist youth organizations and schools, but also set up printing presses devoted to spread this revisionist view of Buddhism by claiming that it is the "true" Buddhism, often known as "Protestant" Buddhism.

The cry for a reform of pre-modern Buddhism became prominent in countries that experienced a significant conflict with colonial powers, such as Sri Lanka, Vietnam, and China. In Japan, Buddhists strove to rid their faith from being co-opted by the militaristic imperialism of the Meiji and Showa era. Modern ideas of participant democracy, equality, dignity of all human beings, and the fight against poverty and illiteracy affected in varying degrees Asian reform movements, which in turn affected the Western perception and practice of Buddhism. This web of diverse forces gave shape to what is known as modern Buddhism.

Scholars have identified a number of characteristics of modern Buddhism: in pre-modern times, the individual traditions remained separated from each other, while in modern Buddhism an ecumenical trend became apparent not only by interacting with other Buddhist traditions but also with members of other religions through dialogue and co-celebration. One of the excerpts from the many publications by Tenzin Gyatso, the fourteenth Dalai Lama, illustrates this ecumenical trend. The concept of teacher became redefined when laity—among them women—adopted leading roles in teaching the *dharma*. The excerpt from Karma Lekshe Tsomo addresses the situation of Buddhist nuns living in the West. Democratic structures displaced the old hierarchical patterns of Buddhist institutions and organizations. Above all, Buddhism gained a modern face by integrating a modern ethos and a science-based world view with its own philosophy, by giving priority to the study of texts and to meditation rather than rituals, and by addressing the ills of societies with socially and politically engaged activism. Thich Nhat Hanh, the widely revered Vietnamese Zen master, not only created the term "engaged Buddhism" but also illustrates its meaning within the given excerpt that focuses on the concept of suffering. Some argued that engaged Buddhism is truly a new development that sets modern Buddhism apart from all previous forms of Buddhism. While the bodhisattva of pre-modern Buddhism was a heroic figure who took on the suffering of the world as an individual task, modern engaged Buddhists see suffering as a result of misguided policies and dysfunctional structures, which ought to be addressed with a communal effort.

Colonel Henry Steel Olcott (1832–1907): A Voice of Revisionist Buddhism

Olcott became in his later life the foremost voice in articulating a revisionist form of Buddhism that is often also named Protestant Buddhism because of its many similarities with Victorian Protestantism. Raised as a Presbyterian in New York, he developed a keen interest in occultism in his adult life. As co-founder of the Theosophical Society he saw himself as defender of

Buddhism against activities of the Christian missionaries. Unconsciously perhaps, he adopted many of the missionaries' views and methods of communication by establishing youth organizations, Sunday schools, and printing presses for the dissemination of Buddhist pamphlets. He authored a widely circulating introductory book to Buddhism, *The Buddhist Catechism*, from which the following excerpt is taken:[75]

▼

158 Q How would a Buddhist describe true merit?

A There is no great merit in any merely outward act; all depends upon the inward motive that provokes the deed.

159 Q Give an example.

A A rich man may expend lakhs of rupees in building dāgobas or vihāras, in erecting statues of Buddha, in festivals and processions, in feeding priests, in giving alms to the poor, or in planting trees, digging tanks, or constructing rest-houses by the roadside for travellers, and yet have comparatively little merit if it be done for display, and to make himself praised by men, or for any other selfish motives. But he who does the least of these things with a kind of motive, as from love for his fellow-men, gains great merit. A good deed done with a bad motive benefits others, but not the doer. One who approves of a good deed when done by another shares in the merit, *if his sympathy is real, not pretended*. The same rule as to evil deeds.

170 Q If we were to try to represent the whole spirit of the Buddha's doctrine by one word, which word would we choose?

A Justice.

171 Q Why?

A Because it teaches that every man gets, under the operation of unerring Karma, exactly that reward or punishment which he has deserved, no more and no less. No good deed or bad deed, however trifling, and however secretly committed, escapes the evenly balanced scales of Karma.

172 Q What is Karma?

A A causation operating on the moral, as well as on the physical and other planes. Buddhists say there is no miracle in human affairs: what a man sows that he must and will reap.

179 Q Did the Buddha hold to idol-worship?

A He did not; he opposed it. The worship of gods, demons, trees, etc., was condemned by the Buddha. External worship is a fetter that one has to break if he is to advance higher.

180 **Q** But do not Buddhists make reverence before the statue to the Buddha, his
relics, and the monuments enshrining them?
A Yes, but not with the sentiment of the idolater.

181 **Q** What is the difference?
A Our Pagan brother not only takes his images as visible representations of
the unseen God or gods, but the refined idolater, in worshipping, considers that
the idol contains in its substance a portion of the all-pervading divinity.

182 **Q** What does the Buddhist think?
A The Buddhist reverences the Buddha's statue and the other things you have
mentioned, only as mementos of the greatest, wisest, most benevolent and compassionate man in this world-period (Kalpa). All races and people preserve, treasure up, and value the relics and mementos of men and women who have been
considered in any way great. The Buddha, to us, seems more to be revered and
beloved than any one else, by every human being who knows sorrow.

183 **Q** Has the Buddha himself given us something definite upon this subject?
A From the beginning, he condemned the observance of ceremonies and
other external practices, which only tend to increase our spiritual blindness and
our clinging to mere lifeless forms.

184 **Q** What as to controversies?
A In numerous discourses he denounced this habit as most pernicious. He
described penances for Bhikkhus who waste time and weaken their higher intu-
itions in wrangling over theories and metaphysical subtleties.

186 **Q** Are charms, incantations, the observances of lucky hours, and devil-
dancing a part of Buddhism?
A They are positively repugnant to its fundamental principles. They are the
surviving relics of fetishism and pantheistic and other foreign religions. In the
Brahmajāla Sutta the Buddha has categorically described these and other superstitions as Pagan, mean and spurious.*

190 **Q** Does popular Buddhism contain nothing but what is true and in accord
with science?
A Like every other religion that has existed many centuries, it certainly now
contains untruth mingled with truth; even gold is found mixed with dross. The
poetical imagination, the zeal, or the lingering superstition of Buddhist devotees

---

* The mixing of these arts and practices with Buddhism is a sign of deterioration.
Their facts and phenomena are real and capable of scientific explanation. They are
embraced in the term "magic," but when resorted to for selfish purposes, attract bad
influences about one, and impede spiritual advancement. When employed for harm-
less and beneficent purposes, such as healing the sick, saving life, etc., the Buddha
permitted their use.

have, in various ages and in various lands, caused the noble principles of the Buddha's moral doctrines to be coupled more or less with what might be removed to advantage. ▲

Thich Nhat Hanh (born 1926): Mindfulness and Engaged Buddhism

Thich Nhat Hanh has become one of the foremost voices of modern Buddhism. In his message, he fuses the ancient technique of mindful contemplation (as presented in the *Satipatthana sutta*, see above) with socially engaged activism. Based on the practice of mindfulness and the insight that all existence is interrelated, Thich Nhat Hanh and his followers work toward the good and well-being of the world—true to the vow of a *bodhisattva*.

Thich Nhat Hanh was born in Vietnam under the colonial rule of France. He entered the Buddhist *sangha* in his late teens and was fully ordained in 1949. He complemented his training under a Vietnamese Zen master with studies in philosophy, literature, and foreign languages at Saigon University. At this time he began to work toward reforming the education of Buddhist monks and nuns to meet the challenges of the modern time in general and of Vietnam in particular. With great personal courage, he spoke out against the violence imposed on people by all parties of the Vietnam War and attempted to assist, together with like-minded followers, victims of the war. His poetry and other publications were banned in North as well as South Vietnam. During a visit to the United States and other Western countries, Thich Nhat Hanh talked with political leaders as well as figures of the civil rights movement and spiritual leaders. Fearing that he would be either imprisoned or assassinated upon his return to Vietnam, the Buddhist leaders of Vietnam asked him to seek asylum in France and to work as an expatriate representative for the cause of peace from abroad. In 1968 he opened an office in Paris. He and his fellow monks sought advisory status at the Paris Peace Talks, which in a formal way was denied them. He founded Plum Village in the south of France as a community of mindful practitioners, regardless of whether they are monks, nuns or laity. Through his writings, public speeches, and teachings he advocates the practice of mindfulness to nurture a socially engaged Buddhism.

The following excerpt from *The Heart of the Buddha's Teaching*[76] reflects on the first of the four Noble Truths, suffering. Thich Nhat Hanh reads modern experiences into the ancient text and thus brings the text alive.

▼ TOUCHING OUR SUFFERING

In the Pali version of the *Discourse on Turning the Wheel of the Dharma*, the Buddha told the five monks,

As long as the insight and the understanding of these Four Nobel Truths in their three stages and twelve aspects, just as they are, had not been fully realized, I could not say that in this world with its gods, maras, brahmas, recluses, brahmans, and men, someone had realized the highest awakening. Monks, as soon as the insight and understanding of the Four Nobel Truths in their three stages and twelve aspects, just as they are, had been realized, I could say that in this world with its gods, maras, brahmas, recluses, brahmans, and men, someone had realized the highest awakening.

In the Chinese version of the sutra, the Buddha said,

Monks, the experience of the three turnings of the wheel with regard to each of the Four Truths gives rise to eyes of awakened understanding, and therefore I declare before gods, spirits, shramanas, and brahmans of all times that I have destroyed all afflictions and reached full awakening.

The wheel of the Dharma was put in motion twelve times—three for each of the Four Noble Truths. To understand the Four Noble Truths, not just intellectually but experientially, we have to practise the twelve turnings of the wheel.

The first turning is called "Recognition." We sense that something is wrong, but we are not able to say exactly what it is. We make some effort to escape, but we cannot. We try to deny our suffering, but it persists. The Buddha said that to suffer and not know that we are suffering is more painful than the burden endured by a mule carrying an unimaginably heavy load. We must, first of all, recognize that we are suffering and then determine whether its basis is physical, physiological, or psychological. Our suffering needs to be identified.

Recognizing and identifying our suffering is like the work of a doctor diagnosing an illness. He or she says, "If I press here, does it hurt?" and we say, "Yes, this is my suffering. This has come to be." The wounds in our heart become the object of our meditation. We show them to our doctor, and we show them to the Buddha, which means we show them to ourselves. Our suffering is us, and we need to embrace our fear, hatred, anguish, and anger. "My dear suffering, I know you are there. I am here for you, and I will take care of you." We stop running from our pain. With all our courage and tenderness, we recognize, acknowledge, and identify it.

The second turning of the wheel is called "Encouragement." After recognizing and identifying our pain, we take the time to look deeply into it in order to understand its true nature, which means its causes. After observing our symptoms, the doctor says, "I will look deeply into it. This illness can be understood." It may take him a week to conduct tests and inquire about what we have been eating, our attitudes, how we spend our time, and so on. But he is determined to understand our illness.

The Twelve Turnings of the Wheel

Four Noble Truths	Twelve Turnings
Suffering	*Recognition*: This is suffering. *Encouragement*: Suffering should be understood. *Realization*: Suffering is understood.
Arising of suffering	*Recognition*: There is an ignoble way that has led to suffering. *Encouragement*: That ignoble way should be understood. *Realization*: That ignoble way is understood.
Cessation of suffering (well-being)	*Recognition*: Well-being is possible. *Encouragement*: Well-being should be obtained. *Realization*: Well-being is obtained.
How well-being arises	*Recognition*: There is a noble path that leads to well-being. *Encouragement*: This noble path has to be lived. *Realization*: This noble path is being lived.

Our suffering—depression, illness, a difficult relationship, or fear—needs to be understood and, like a doctor, we are determined to understand it. We practice sitting and walking meditation, and we ask for guidance and support from our friends and, if we have one, our teacher. As we do this, we see that the causes of our suffering are knowable, and we make every effort to get to the bottom of it. At this stage, our practice can still be "set back" (*ashrava*).

The third turning of the wheel is called "Realization" and can be expressed as, "This suffering has been understood." We realize the efforts begun during the second turning. The doctor tells us the name and all the characteristics of our illness. After studying, reflecting upon, and practicing the First Noble Truth, we realize that we have stopped running away from our pain. We can now call our suffering by its specific name and identify all of its characteristics. This alone brings us happiness, joy "without setbacks" (*anashrava*).

Still, after we have successfully diagnosed our ailment, for a time we continue to create suffering for ourselves. We pour gasoline on the first through our words, thoughts, and deed and often don't even realize it. The first turning of the wheel of the Second Noble Truth is the "Recognition": I am continuing to create suffering. The Buddha said, "When something has come to be, we have to acknowledge its presence and look deeply into its nature. When we look deeply, we will discover the kinds of nutriments that have helped it come to be and that continue to feed it."[77] He then elaborated four kinds of nutriments that can lead to our happiness or our suffering—edible food, sense impressions, intention, and consciousness.

The first nutriment is edible food. What we eat or drink can bring about mental or physical suffering. We must be able to distinguish between what is healthful and what is harmful. We need to practice Right View when we shop, cook, and eat. The Buddha offered this example. A young couple and their two-year-old child were trying to cross the desert, and they ran out of food. After deep reflection, the parents realized that in order to survive they had to kill their son and eat his flesh. They calculated that if they ate such and such a proportion of their baby's flesh every day and carried the rest on their shoulders to dry, it would last the rest of the journey. But with every morsel of their baby's flesh they ate, the young couple cried and cried. After he told this story, the Buddha asked, "Dear Friends, do you think the young man and woman enjoyed eating their son's flesh?" "No, Lord, it would not be possible for them to enjoy eating their son's flesh." The Buddha said, "Yet many people eat the flesh of their parents, their children, and their grandchildren and do not know it."[78]

Much of our suffering comes from not eating mindfully. We have to learn ways to eat that preserve the health and well-being of our body and our spirit. When we smoke, drink, or consume toxins, we are eating our own lungs, liver, and heart. If we have children and do these things, we are eating our children's flesh. Our children need us to be healthy and strong.

We have to look deeply to see how we grow our food, so we can eat in ways that preserve our collective well-being, minimize our suffering and the suffering of other species, and allow the earth to continue to be a source of life for all of us. If, while we eat, we destroy living beings or the environment, we are eating the flesh of our own sons and daughters. We need to look deeply together and discuss how to eat, what to eat, and what to resist. This will be a real Dharma discussion.

The second kind of nutriment is sense impressions. Our six sense organs—eyes, ears, nose, tongue, body, and mind—are in constant contact (sparsha) with sense objects, and these contacts become food for our consciousness. When we drive through a city, our eyes see so many billboards, and these images enter our consciousness. When we pick up a magazine, the articles and advertisements are food for our consciousness. Advertisements that stimulate our craving for possessions, sex, and food can be toxic. If after reading the newspaper, hearing the news, or being in a conversation, we feel anxious or worn out, we know we have been in contact with toxins.

Movies are food for our eyes, ears, and minds. When we watch TV, the program is our food. Children who spend five hours a day watching television are ingesting images that water the negative seeds of craving, fear, anger, and violence in them. We are exposed to so many forms, colours, sounds, smells, tastes, objects of touch, and ideas that are toxic and rob our body and consciousness of their well-being. When you feel despair, fear, or depression, it may be because you have ingested too many toxins through your sense impressions. Not only children need to be protected from violent and unwholesome films, TV programs, books, magazines, and games. We, too, can be destroyed by these media.

If we are mindful, we will know whether we are "ingesting" the toxins of fear, hatred, and violence, or eating foods that encourage understanding, compassion, and the determination to help others. With the practice of mindfulness, we will know that hearing this, looking at that, or touching this, we feel light and peaceful, while hearing that, looking at this, or touching that, we feel anxious, sad, or depressed. As a result, we will know what to be in contact with and what to avoid. Our skin protects us from bacteria. Antibodies protect us from internal invaders. We have to use the equivalent aspects of our consciousness to protect us from unwholesome sense objects that can poison us.

The Buddha offered this drastic image: "There is a cow with such a terrible skin disease that her skin is almost no longer there. When you bring her close to an ancient wall or old tree, all the living creatures in the bark of the tree come out, cling to the cow's body, and suck. When we bring her into the water, the same thing happens. Even when she is just exposed to the air, tiny insects come and suck." Then the Buddha said, "This is our situation, also."

We are exposed to invasions of all kinds—images, sounds, smells, touch, ideas—and many of these feed the craving, violence, fear, and despair in us. The Buddha advised us to post a sentinel, namely mindfulness, at each of our sense doors to protect ourselves. Use your Buddha eyes to look at each nutriment you are about to ingest. If you see that it is toxic, refuse to look at it, listen to it, taste it, or touch it. Ingest only what you are certain is safe. The Five Mindfulness Trainings[79] can help very much. We must come together as individuals, families, cities, and a nation to discuss strategies of self-protection and survival. To get out of the dangerous situation we are in, the practice of mindfulness has to be collective.

The third kind of nutriment is volition, intention, or will—the desire in us to obtain whatever it is that we want. Volition is the ground of all our actions. If we think that the way for us to be happy is to become president of a large corporation, everything we do or say will be directed toward realizing that goal. Even when we sleep, our consciousness will continue to work on it. Or suppose we believe that all our suffering and the suffering of our family has been brought about by someone who wronged us in the past. We believe we will only be happy if we inflict harm on that person. Our life is motivated solely by the desire for revenge, and everything we say, everything we plan, is to punish that person. At night, we dream of revenge, and we think this will liberate us from our anger and hatred.

Everyone want to be happy, and there is a strong energy in us pushing us toward what we think will make us happy. But we may suffer a lot because of this. We need the insight that position, revenge, wealth, fame, or possessions are, more often than not, obstacles to our happiness. We need to cultivate the wish to be free of these things so we can enjoy the wonders of life that are always available—the blue sky, the trees, our beautiful children. After three months or six months of mindful sitting, mindful walking, and mindful looking, a deep vision of reality arises in us, and the capacity of being there, enjoying life in the present moment, liberates us from all impulses and brings us real happiness.

One day, after the Buddha and a group of monks finished eating lunch mindfully together, a farmer, very agitated, came by and asked, "Monks, have you seen my cows? I don't think I can survive so much misfortune." The Buddha asked him, "What happened?" and the man said, "Monks, this morning all twelve of my cows ran away. And this year my whole crop of sesame plants was eaten by insects!" The Buddha said, "Sir, we have not seen your cows. Perhaps they have gone in the other direction." After the farmer went off in that direction, the Buddha turned to his Sangha and said, "Dear friends, do you know you are the happiest people on Earth? You have no cows or sesame plants to lose." We always try to accumulate more and more, and we think these "cows" are essential for our existence. In fact, they may be the obstacles that prevent us from being happy. Release your cows and become a free person. Release your cows so you can be truly happy.

The Buddha presented another drastic image: "Two strong men are dragging a third man along in order to throw him into a fire pit. He cannot resist, and finally they throw him into the glowing embers." These strong men, the Buddha said, are our own volition. We don't want to suffer, but our deep-seated habit energies drag us into the fire of suffering. The Buddha advised us to look deeply into the nature of our volition to see whether it is pushing us in the direction of liberation, peace, and compassion or in the direction of suffering and unhappiness. We need to be able to see the kinds of intention-food that we are consuming.

The fourth kind of nutriment is consciousness. Our consciousness is composed of all the seeds sown by our past actions and the past actions of our family and society. Every day our thoughts, words and actions flow into the sea of our consciousness and create our body, mind, and world. We can nourish our consciousness by practising the Four Immeasurable Minds of love, compassion, joy, and equanimity, or we can feed our consciousness with greed, hatred, or ignorance, suspicion, and pride. Our consciousness is eating all the time, day and night, and what it consumes becomes the substance of our life. We have to be very careful which nutriments we ingest.[80]

The Buddha offered another dramatic image to illustrate this: "A dangerous murderer was captured and brought before the king, and the king sentenced him to death by stabbing. 'Take him to the courtyard and plunge three hundred sharp knives through him.' At noon a guard reported, 'Majesty, he is still alive,' and the king declared, 'Stab him three hundred more times!' In the evening, the guard again told the king, 'Majesty, he is not yet dead.' So the king gave the third order: 'Plunge the three hundred sharpest knives in the kingdom through him.'" Then the Buddha said, "This is how we usually deal with our consciousness." Every time we ingest toxins into our consciousness, it is like stabbing ourselves with three hundred sharp knives. We suffer, and our suffering spills out to those around us.

When we practise the first turning of the First Noble Truth, we recognize suffering as suffering. If we are in a difficult relationship, we recognize, "This is a difficult relationship." Our practice is to be with our suffering and take good care of it. When we practice the first turning of the Second Noble Truth, we look deeply into the nature of our suffering to see what kinds of nutriments we have been feeding it. How have we lived in the last few years, in the last few months, that has contributed to our suffering? We need to recognize and identify the nutriments we ingest and observe, "When I think like this, speak like that, listen like this, or act like that, my suffering increases." Until we begin to practice the Second Noble Truth, we tend to blame others for our unhappiness.

Looking deeply requires courage. You can use a pencil and paper if you like. During sitting meditation, if you see clearly a symptom of your suffering, write it down. Then ask yourself, "What kinds of nutriments have I been ingesting that have fed and sustained this suffering?" When you begin to realize the kinds of nutriments you have been ingesting, you may cry. Use the energy of mindfulness all day long to be truly present, to embrace your suffering like a mother holding her baby. As long as mindfulness is there, you can stay with the difficulty. Practice does not mean using only your own mindfulness, concentration, and wisdom. You also have to benefit from the mindfulness, concentration, and wisdom of friends on the path and your teacher. There are things that even a child can see but we ourselves cannot see because we are imprisoned by our notions. Bring what you have written to a friend and ask for his or her observations and insights.

If you sit with a friend and speak openly, determined to discover the roots of your suffering, eventually you will see them clearly. But if you keep your suffering to yourself, it might grow bigger every day. Just seeing the causes of your suffering lessens your burden. Shariputra, one of the Buddha's great disciples, said, "When something takes place, if we look at it deeply in the heart of reality, seeing its source and the food that nourishes it, we are already on the path of liberation." When we are able to identify our suffering and see its causes, we will have more peace and joy, and we are already on the path to liberation.

In the second stage of the Second Noble Truth, "Encouragement," we see clearly that real happiness is possible if we can stop ingesting the nutriments that cause us to suffer. If we know that our body is suffering because of the way we eat, sleep, or work, we vow to eat, sleep, or work in ways that are healthier. We encourage ourselves to put an end to the causes of our suffering. Only by a strong intention not to do things in the same way can we keep the wheel in motion.

Mindfulness is the energy that can help us stop. We investigate the kinds of nutriments we now ingest and decide which ones to continue to eat and which to resist. We sit and look together with our friends, with our family, and as a community. Mindfulness of ingestion, protecting our body and mind, protecting our families, society, and the environment are important topics for us to discuss. When we direct our attention toward our suffering, we see our potential for happiness. We see the nature of suffering and the way out. That is why the Buddha called suffering a holy truth. When we use the world "suffering" in Buddhism, we mean the kind of suffering that can show us the way out.

There are many practices that can help us face our suffering, including mindful walking, mindful breathing, mindful sitting, mindful eating, mindful looking, and mindful listening. One mindful step can take us deep into the realization of beauty and joy in us and around us. Tran Thai Tong, a great meditation master of thirteenth-century Vietnam, said, "With every step, you touch the ground of reality." If you practice mindful walking and deep listening all day long, that is the Four Noble Truths in action. When the cause of suffering has been seen, healing is possible. We vow to refrain from ingesting foods that make us suffer, and we also vow to ingest foods that are healthy and wholesome.

In the third turning to the wheel of the Second Noble Truth, "Realization," we not only vow but w actually stop ingesting the nutriments that create our suffering. Some people think that to end suffering, you have to stop everything— body, feelings, perceptions, mental formations, and consciousness—but that is not correct. The third stage of the Second Noble Truth can be described as, "When hungry, I eat. When tired, I sleep." When someone has realized this stage, she has a certain lightness and freedom. What she wants to do is fully in accord with the mindfulness trainings, and she does nothing to cause herself or other harm.

Confucius said, "At thirty, I was able to stand on my own feet. At forty, I had no more doubts. At fifty, I knew the mandate of Earth and Sky. At sixty, I could do what I wanted without going against the path." The last of the ten ox herding pictures in the Zen tradition is called "Entering the Marketplace with Open Hands." You are free to come and go as you please. This is the action of non-action. Suffering no longer arises. This stage is not something you can imitate. You have to reach this stage of realization within yourself.

At the end of the nineteenth century in Vietnam, Master Nhat Dinh asked the king for permission to retire from being abbot of a national temple so he could live in a mountain hut and take care of his aging mother. Many officials made offerings to the master and begged him to found another temple, but he preferred to live simply, in great peace and joy. One day his mother fell ill and needed fish to eat. He went down to the marketplace, asked some vendors for a fish, and carried it back up the mountain. Onlookers asked, "What is a Buddhist monk doing with a fish?" But someone of Master Nhat Dinh's realization could do as he pleased without going against the precepts. At the third stage of the Second Noble Truth, you only have to be yourself. The form is not important. But be careful! First there has to be genuine insight, genuine freedom. ▲

Women's Voices

In the introductory remarks to this section, it was noted that one of the characteristics of modern Buddhism is the visibility of women as teachers and community leaders. From all continents, modern women have joined one or the other strand of the Buddhist order, as fully ordained nuns (*bhikshuni*) or as renunciants who observe the ten precepts. Some of these nuns have published books and articles reflecting on their own situation within specific contexts. None, however, has reached the impact or publicity of their male counterparts. Thus, while the situation of women within modern Buddhism has improved in comparison to the position they held in pre-modern times, Buddhist women still lag far behind the men in terms of visibility and public status. This should not, however, detract from acknowledging the role women teachers play within their communities.

Karma Lekshe Tsomo, a modern nun

Karma Lekshe Tsomo is perhaps the best-known Buddhist nun in the West due to her publications and her public speaking. She is a significant force within the movement to restore full ordination for women. In the following excerpt, she outlines the difficulties a Western woman will encounter if she decides to live as a nun in a Western country and how a modern Buddhist monastery for nuns should be designed.[81]

▼ LIVING AS A NUN IN THE WEST

As the *Buddhadharma* goes to the West, it sometimes happens that Western people are inspired to lead celibate lives and receive ordination. The wish to become ordained may be a spontaneous impulse of the moment or it may be a reasoned decision based on practical considerations. In either case, there is usually a sincere commitment to the *Dharma* and a desire to devote more time to the practice. Almost all people receive precepts with the best of intentions, yet their lives following ordination take many different turns.

It is hard to visualize the effect that making such a serious commitment will have. Things are never exactly as we imagine. Ordination makes a deep impact upon the mind, often in ways that are inexpressible and imperceptible. Experiences differ, depending largely upon the extent to which we get caught up in judgments, labeling, and expectations. Nevertheless, we wake up the next day with a new perception of ourselves and our relationship to the world. We are faced with new feelings and practical realities that are complex in themselves, being further intensified by the responses of people around us. Even if nothing in particular changes, experiences register in new ways.

While the experience of living as a nun or monk within a loving supportive community will certainly differ from getting ordained and immediately being left completely on one's own, in either case he first teaching of the ordained life is often that we are born alone and die alone. There is no longer anything or anyone to lean on. Essentially the ordained life means relying on the inner experience of the teachings without external props. In a sense, Western people who have been raised to function independently may find it easier to adjust to such a life. The sense of aloneness which persists even in ordained community life is much harder for Asian people to cope with, since they are generally accustomed to a closely interdependent family life. After embarking upon "the homeless life," the monastic community often becomes a surrogate family for them.

The problems encountered by Western people in ordained life more often relate to discipline, emotional conflicts, and physical circumstances. A high percentage return to lay life. If ordained life is so conducive to practice and the people who enter it are so committed to the *Dharma*, what accounts for the high drop-out rate? Clearly, this is a question that requires in-depth research and should not be over-generalized. It is a very personal and individual matter, but few thoughts on the subject may be in order.

Logic tells us that a decision to give up the celibate life may relate to problems in maintaining celibacy. It has become something of a "in" joke in ordained circles that no one gives up their vows due to an overwhelming desire to eat after noon. Some frankly admit to "falling in love." Others become ordained without having satisfactorily explored the limits of relationship and later find curiosity gets the better of them. Some find abstinence restrictive after ordination, though it was never a problem before.

Another problem relates to discipline and culturally conditioned value systems. A valid *Prātimokśa* ordination is necessarily received in a particular *Vinaya* school, which at this point is transmitted through the medium of an Asian Buddhist tradition. The customs concomitant with the traditional lineage may complement individualistic Western lifestyles, but they may also conflict. The latter experience seems to be quite common.

While acknowledging and respecting the tremendous debt owed to Asian cultures, it is obvious that we Western Buddhists need time and space in which to find our own directions. We need to be strict, but not too rigid; to be open and flexible, but not sloppy. We need to learn from Asian Buddhist prototypes without being overwhelmed by Asian cultural components. We want to devise modes of practice which preserve the essence of the Buddha's teachings, yet are compatible with Western civilization. We should strive to preserve the most excellent values of East and West.

Accepting Buddhism does not mean forfeiting the positive aspects of our own religious and cultural heritages; however, becoming a nun or monk does imply adopting genuine Buddhists values authentically. One recommended method is to train closely with respected Asian exponents of monastic discipline during the first years of ordained life. Adjustments to Western cultural and social conditions can then be made on a solid foundation of understanding. Such training is an experience to be treasured. Similar to training in the martial arts, it requires humility and perseverance. While some people cite the hardships of traditional monastic training and the cultural adjustments it requires as reasons for giving up their vows, paradoxically, others cite the lack of such training as a reason. Certainly some experience of traditional training is important for nuns and monks, since they will be instrumental in the process of adapting traditional Buddhist institutions to the Western situation.

There is no doubt that Buddhism is a valuable spiritual path for large numbers of Western people, but is ordination a viable step when there are as yet very few monasteries in the West where they can stay and train? Is living on one's own a realistic alternative? What models should we look to in setting up monastic training centers and what problems can we expect to encounter in the process? Whose job is it to set up such centers and when are they going to get started?

There is a definite consensus on the need for centers where nuns and potential nuns can become accustomed to monastic life. Chaotic environments imply are not conducive to formal meditation practice and disciplined conduct. Living on one's own, isolated from a supportive Sangha and vulnerable to the onslaught of worldly values, can be quite unsettling, especially in the beginning years. Ordained women need monasteries where they can study and attempt to live by the *Vinaya*; lay women need protective surroundings where they can prepare for ordination and can gin experience in monastic values before making a lifelong commitment.

In addition to an intense awareness of the need for training centers, there is a recognition that monasteries for Westerners will differ in some important respects from Asian Buddhist models. Along with this recognition, there is growing concern that meaningful time-honored traditions not be discarded simply on the basis of superficial impressions. Even if they may appear exotic, extraneous, or constraining in the beginning, some traditions have symbolic or psychological significance that can be of great value in the practice. Wisdom and mature judgment are required to discern what will ultimately benefit and what will impede our spiritual growth. Nuns, monks, and others who have undergone many years of formal training have a special responsibility to understand traditions and interpret them for others. They can serve as cultural bridges, helping to bring about a graceful transition from ancient to modern practice.

There are some traditional practices that seem especially apt to arouse resistance—for instance, bowing. It is the custom of bowing to bhikṣus, the first of the eight important rules for *bhikṣuṇīs*, that is most difficult for Western women to countenance. This is understandable; Western people normally have difficulty bowing to anything, especially another human being, whether female or male. The Buddhist custom of bowing to statues of enlightened beings has been widely misinterpreted as "idol worship," causing great misunderstanding since it contravenes one of the ten commandments of the Judaeo-Christian faith. Actually the custom of bowing is meant to demonstrate respect for the enlightenment potential within all living beings, including oneself, and is not a display of worship or subservience at all. Bowing is also used as a practice for engendering humility. In some Buddhist countries the custom of bowing to senior nuns and monks is still widely practised; in others, it is normally reserved for paying reverence to learned or realized masters. It derives from the ancient Indian custom of showing respect to elders; even in contemporary Sri Lanka and India, well-mannered children bow to their parents every morning.

By contrast, Western people do not always naturally engender respect along the lines of seniority. Most are accustomed to making independent decisions, and may resist authority and structures altogether unless they lead to tangible rewards and punishments. The large measure of social, economic, and academic freedom current in Western cultures stimulates individual creativity, even genius, but does little to promote personal discipline. Discipline is frequently labeled suppressive, constrictive, or authoritarian. For those seriously interested in developing self-discipline, therefore, periods of monastic training in traditional Asian monasteries will prove greatly instructive. There are also some monasteries in the West, such as the City of Ten Thousand Buddhas near Ukiah, California, where people may go to train. Eventually, new and creative operational structures will need to be developed which are suitable to the capabilities and temperaments of the members of new monastic communities. Those who display resistance to discipline altogether and an unwillingness to accommodate may simply be unsuited to monastic life.

It is likely that Western Buddhist monasteries will evolve their own models of organization. They may not be run strictly along the lines of Asian monastic institutions, but compatible features can be incorporated form traditional models. The structure of existing meditative communities should be studied and experienced to ascertain which features of each seem most desirable. These can then be implemented on an experimental basis to see which are most workable in the new monastic situation. Some features of traditional structures will be suitable, others can be adapted, some will be rejected, and surely the process of synthesizing will be informative. It would also be good to take a look at the organization of the Christian monastic institutions that have evolved for Western people over many generations.

To my mind, the ideal Western Buddhist monastery should be a sensitive blend of Asian and Western elements that is comfortable for all and still conducive to intensive practice. For example, I would like to see an international, non-sectarian monastery for women grow up somewhere in North America where nuns and prospective nuns could receive training and learn to live by the *Vinaya*. A mediation hall patterned on the Chinese, Japanese, or Korean model, *Vinaya* discipline on the Theravāda mode, and a study program on the Tibetan model, with Western-style private rooms and a vegetarian diet would be a good combination to try. Years of communal living lead me to favor a careful admissions policy and small beginnings. I would like to experiment with a community composed exclusively of women who accept the administrative guidelines set forth in the *Vinaya* texts, and then gradually try to adapt them to Western living conditions.

The concept of such a community would be to incorporate the worthwhile aspects of traditional structures, giving latitude for freedom of expression and a strong element of human warmth. Whether in matters of dress, practice, or monastic organization, there needs to be an adjustment period. Changes in Western societies occur so rapidly these days that expectations run high, both for ourselves and for others. Our push-button background inclines us to be in a great hurry for enlightenment, but achieving perfect awareness requires infinite patience. Taking the ancient guidelines as a basis and receiving commentary on them by great living masters, we can attempt to discover the original essence of the Buddhist teachings and integrate them in ways which are useful in transforming the minds of Western people.

This is definitely a time for women to explore new ways of doing things. At the same time, many people feel the need for preserving the purity of meaningful traditions. Experiencing the beauty of each of the Buddhist traditions helps us to appreciate the beauty of Buddhist culture as a whole. There seems to be a danger, particularly in America, of adapting and rejecting things before they have been sufficiently digested. In recommending a respectful stance toward these ancient cultures, we are not speaking merely from an anthropological point of view; there is something of great historical significance at stake in the transmission of the Dharma to the West. As the first generation of Western Buddhists, we need to conscientiously embody the complete, authentic teachings of each tradition before we can begin to accurately translate them into our own cultural experience. We hope spiritual communities of women will play a special role in the process of religious and cultural transformation. ▲

Cheng Yen (born 1937), a Taiwanese activist and nun

Cheng Yen experienced suffering firsthand when she cared for her seriously ill mother. After the death of both parents, she became a Buddhist nun. Personal experience compelled her to work for the poor, something new in the Buddhist traditions. Two seminal experiences inspired her to dedicate her energy to the poor: the miscarriage of a woman with lots of blood spilled and, interestingly, the example set by Catholic nuns in Taiwan. In 1966 Cheng Yen founded the Buddhist Compassion Relief Foundation that comprised nuns and laywomen. The foundation initially provided clothing and medicine for the poor. Today it is the largest charity in Taiwan, devoting its substantial financial resources to charity, medicine, education, and culture. The following excerpt is an elaboration on "right effort," the sixth step of the Eightfold Noble Path.[82]

▼ THE FOUR PROPER AREAS FOR DILIGENT EFFORTS (SAMYAK-PRADHANA)

1   Put an End to Existing Evil (*Samvara-pradhana*)

Before we learn Buddhism, most of us have wandering minds which lead us to evil thoughts. As soon as we start cultivating our Buddha nature, we need to work diligently to develop appropriate attitudes and methods within ourselves. Our attitudes are of utmost importance; evil thoughts should be eradicated completely as soon as their ugly faces come to mind.

In our daily lives, we cannot get away from all manner of people, places and things. We need to deal with these daily encounters with a steady heart that treats even extraordinary events as if they were commonplace and that loves everyone as equals. Human beings interact with each other through both verbal and body language. In this manner, our words and our attitudes communicate our thoughts. The standard we want to set for ourselves is to be gentle and kind in our words and to always embody a congenial and generous attitude. Of course, we often meet people who speak to us rudely and treat us with little or no respect. Nevertheless, we still need to maintain our own self-dignity and not lower our behavioral standards under any circumstances.

Our goal is not to ask others to change themselves; likewise, our goal is not to inventory their weaknesses. It is wrong to take the words other people let slip out unintentionally and use them to build self-justified resentment and hatred inside ourselves. It is also not worthwhile to feel hurt or angry when other speak rudely to us, because they may just have bad habits of communicating and may not really mean any harm whatsoever. There are also people who look cold and uncaring on the surface, and yet have loving hearts buried inside. We need to avoid stereotyping and judging others by their outward appearances.

It is important to be constantly mindful of our own attitudes and behaviors. Among the ever-changing people, places and things in our daily lives, we need to focus our minds on our own cultivation instead of an ego-based emotions of self-interest, such as resentment, hatred, affection and anger. If we find ourselves feeling resentful, we must eradicate the resentment as quickly as possible. No negligence or laziness can be allowed in this constant process of self-monitoring and correction. This, then, is what is meant by putting an end to existing evil.

2   **Prevent Evil from Arising** (*Prahana-pradhana*)

It is most desirable to always deal with others with a steady heart, one that consistently treats everyone else as we treat ourselves. If we have not yet found ourselves harboring evil thoughts against others, it is important to keep this pure state of mind. Some people treat their acquaintances with kindness and courtesy and get along famously as long as they don't know each other too well. When they become closer and more familiar with each other, they start abandoning gestures of courtesy because they no longer feel the need for them. Soon, conflicts of words and deeds start to arise, and resentment begins to breed. This is why some say, "All hatred begins with love."

This is the reason that we need to maintain our initial attitudes of respect and compromise toward others, no matter how intimately we come to know them. Such is the essence of preventing evil from arising: keeping a loving thought of equality toward all people and maintaining a steady mind which is not excited by extraordinary events. Do not give the seeds of impure and mean-spirited thoughts even the slightest chance to sprout in our minds.

3   **Bring Good into Existence** (*Bhavana-pradhana*)

For those of you have started to learn Buddhism but have not yet thought about doing good deeds, you need to take special care to nurture good thoughts such as compassion.

Once a Tzu Chi commissioner brought along a Tzu Chi member from Taipei to visit our headquarters. This visiting member said to me, "Master, I am very moved by our wonderful Tzu Chi Foundations. We ask people to donate money for good deeds and to fund relief missions. I have found all of these activities extremely meaningful, and I am trying to do as much as I can myself. I would like to join the activities of the Tzu Chi commissioners to rain funds for good causes. But there is one thing that I sincerely ask Master to excuse me from: please do not send me to comfort the sick."

I asked him, "Why do you make this request?"

"I am very loving," he replied, "but I am afraid to spend time with sick people because I fear that they will infect me. Besides, I have heard that commissioners must chant the holy name of Amitabha Buddha for the dead at their bedsides, and I am also very frightened of dead people. Therefore, I ask Master to please accept my request not to participate in these activities."

This member has a loving heart, but he has not developed the ultimate good thought of great compassion for all living beings as if we were all one being. If he were able to treat other patients as if they were his own close relatives, he would automatically understand how to handle himself with these patients. If he could feel with his heart that the dying are actually one with himself, just like close relatives, would he still insist on not getting too close to the dead?

Although many people are loving, they have not yet cultivated loving hearts that treat everyone as themselves, the great compassion for all as one. We need to immediately encourage these people to cultivate good thoughts of great compassion and love for all. Many Tzu Chi commissioners used to be afraid of the sick and the dead. After they joined the Tzu Chi Foundation, they were encouraged by the behavior of other commissioners and their own behavior gradually changed. They would follow others in visiting patients, and would even support and care for these patients with their own hands. They not only accompanied others to chant the holy name of Amitabha Buddha for the dead, they even began changing the clothes of the dead. All of these examples demonstrate that, with proper cultivation and training, it is natural for people to spontaneously develop loving thoughts of equality and unity.

That is why we talk a about bringing good deeds into existence to nurture and grow good thoughts as soon as possible. Life is ever-changing. When, therefore, is there a better time to build good karma and cultivate good thoughts than now? The time for urging others to cultivate loving thoughts, to realize the true path of life and develop the highest consciousness, is also now.

4   **Develop Existing Good Deeds Already Done** (*Anurakkshana-pradhana*)
If other people already have loving hearts, we still need to fervently encourage them to keep these loving hearts forever. We will not settle for loving thoughts and good hearts that only last temporarily. To make the journey of bodhisattva-hood, we urge people to keep a constant, diligent heart. This is the meaning of developing existing good deeds already done. Not only are we practicing the ten meritorious acts, but we can actually move up to the level of practicing bodhisattvahood by diligently cultivating ourselves. ▲

Tenzin Gyatso (born 1935), the Fourteenth Dalai Lama

Tenzin Gyatso was raised and educated in the traditional Tibetan way, preparing incarnated spiritual leaders or *Lamas* for their tasks. When he moved into Indian exile in 1959, he became keenly interested in understanding the modern and Western world. Western diplomatic embassies provided him with crates of books, which he studied with single-minded dedication. Soon he began to publish books on what he considered the essence of Buddhism. His earlier publications followed the traditional Tibetan scholastic way of explaining Buddhism, while in more recent works he has become a major voice in advocating a modern Buddhism.

The first excerpt deals with the first of the Four Noble Truths, suffering, a topic that has been presented here from various vantage points: the rendition of the pre-Mahayana text and Nagarjuna's reflection on it, as well as Thich Nhat Hanh's articulation of the topic of suffering.[83]

The second excerpt reveals the Dalai Lama as a strong advocate of the ecumenical trend within modern Buddhism. The occasion that lead to the book from which the excerpt is taken was the tenth annual John Main Seminar that brought together Christians and Buddhists to explore various contemplative practices. The Dalai Lama interpreted several passages from the Gospels from a Buddhist perspective. In the excerpt, he advocates the need of cooperation and interaction between different faith communities and explores various ways of achieving mutual understanding and respect.[84]

▼ THE FOUR NOBLE TRUTHS

According to popular legend, following his full enlightenment the Buddha remained silent and did not give any teaching for forty-nine days. The first public teaching he gave was to the five ascetics who had been his colleagues when he was leading the life of a mendicant. Having realized that asceticism does not lead to freedom from suffering, the Buddha—then called Siddhārtha Gautama— had given up his penances and parted company with his fellows. His five colleagues had resented what they saw as a betrayal and vowed never to associate with him. For them, this change in Siddhārtha had indicated a failure to sustain his commitment to the life of asceticism. However, when they met him after his enlightenment, they felt spontaneously drawn toward him. It was to these five former colleagues that the Buddha gave his first public teaching at Deer Park in Sarnath.

In this discourse, which became known as the first turning of the wheel of Dharma, the Buddha taught the principles of the Four Noble Truths. As most of you might know, these Four Truths are the truth of suffering, the truth of the origin of suffering, the truth of the cessation of suffering, and the truth of the path leading to this cessation.

According to the sutra concerning the first turning, when the Buddha taught the Four Noble Truths, he taught them within the context of three factors: the nature of the truths themselves, their specific functions, and their effects, or complete attainment. The first factor describes the nature of the individual truths. The second explains the importance of comprehending the specific significance of each for the practitioner: namely, suffering must be recognized, and its origin, eliminated; and the cessation of suffering must be actualized, and the path to cessation, realized. In the context of the third factor, the Buddha explained the ultimate result, or complete attainment, of the Four Noble Truths—that is, the completed recognition of suffering, the completed abandonment of the origin of suffering, and the completed actualization of the path to cessation. I personally find the teaching on the Four Noble truths to be very profound. This teaching lays down the blueprint for the entire body of Buddhist thought and practice, thus setting up the basic framework of an individual's path to enlightenment. I shall elaborate on this further.

What we desire and seek is to have happiness and overcome suffering. This yearning to have happiness and avoid pain and suffering is innate to all of us and needs no justification for its existence or validity. However, happiness and suffering do not arise from nowhere. They arise as consequences of causes and conditions. In brief, the doctrine of the Four Noble Truths states the principle of causality. Keeping this crucial point in mind, I sometimes remark that all of Buddhist thought an practice can be condensed into the following two principles: (1) adopting a world view that perceives the interdependent nature of phenomena, that is, the dependently originated nature of all things and events, and (2) based on that, leading a non-violent and non-harming way of life.

Buddhism advocates the conduct of non-violence on the basis of two simple and obvious promises: (1) as sentient beings, none of us wants suffering; and (2) suffering originates from its causes and conditions. The Buddhist teachings further assert that the root cause of our pain and suffering lies in our own ignorant and undisciplined state of mind. Therefore, if we do not desire suffering, the logical step to take is to refrain from destructive actions, which naturally lead to consequent experiences of pain and suffering. Pain and suffering do not exist in isolation; they come about as the results of causes and conditions. It is in understanding the nature of suffering and its relation to causes and conditions that the principle of dependent origination plays a crucial role. In essence, the principle of dependent origination states that an effect is dependent upon its cause. So, if you don't want the result, you should strive to put an end to its cause.

Within the Four Truths, we find two distinct sets of cause and result operating: suffering is the result, and the origin of suffering is its cause; in like manner, the true cessation of suffering is peace, the result, and the path leading to it is the cause of that peace.

The happiness we seek, a genuine lasting peace and happiness, can be attained only through the purification of our minds. This is possible if we cut the root cause of all suffering and misery our fundamental ignorance. This freedom from suffering, the true cessation, can come about only when we have successfully seen through the illusion created by our habitual tendency to grasp at the intrinsic existence of phenomena and, thereby, gained insight that penetrates into the ultimate nature of reality. To attain this, however, the individual must perfect the three higher trainings. The training in insight, or wisdom, acts as the actual antidote to ignorance and its derivative delusions. However, it is only when training in higher insight is conjoined with a highly developed faculty of single-pointedness of the mind that all of one's energy and mental attention can be focused on the chose object of mediation without distraction. Hence, the training in higher concentration is an indispensable factor in advanced stages of application of the wisdom gained through insight. However, in order for both the trainings in higher concentration and higher insight to be successful, the practitioner must first establish a stable foundation of morality by adopting an ethically sound way of life. ▲

▼ A WISH FOR HARMONY

Spiritual brothers and sister, it is a great joy and privilege for me to have the opportunity to participate in this dialogue and to open the John Main Seminar entitled "The Good Heart." I would like to express my deep appreciation to all those who have helped to organize this event.

I am grateful for the warm words of welcome from the Lady Mayor, and I am very encouraged by her reference to the harmony and understanding that exists among the various communities and religious traditions in this borough, which she described as multicultural, multiethnic, and multireligious. I would like to express my thanks for that.

I met the late Father John Main many years ago in Canada and was impressed to meet a person in the Christian tradition who emphasized meditation as a part of spiritual practice. Today, at the beginning of this Seminar, I think it is very important for us to remember him.

I am also happy to see so many familiar faces and to have the opportunity to meet new and old friends here.

Despite many material advances on our planet, humanity faces many, many problems, some of which are actually of our own creation. And to a large extent it is our mental attitude—our outlook on life and the world—that is the key factor for the future—the future of humanity, the future of the world, and the future of the environment. Many things depend on our mental attitude, both in the personal and public spheres. Whether we are happy in our individual or family life is, in a large part, up to us. Of course, material conditions are an important factor for happiness and a good life, but one's mental attitude is of equal or greater importance.

As we approach the twenty-first century, religious traditions are as relevant as ever. Yet, as in the past, conflicts and crises arise in the name of different religious traditions. This is very, very unfortunate. We must make every effort to overcome this situation. In my own experience, I have found that the most effect method to overcome these conflicts is close contact and an exchange among those of various beliefs, not only on an intellectual level, but in deeper spiritual experiences. This is a powerful method to develop mutual understanding and respect. Through this interchange, a strong foundation of genuine harmony can be established.

So I am always extremely happy to participate in religious dialogue. And I am particularly happy to spend these few days talking with you and practicing my broken English! When I spend a few weeks on retreat in Dharamsala, my residence in

India, I find that my broken English becomes even poorer, so these days of exchange will give me a much-needed opportunity to practice.

Since it is my belief that harmony among different religious traditions is extremely important, extremely necessary, I would like to suggest a few ideas on ways it can be promoted. First, I suggest we encourage meetings among scholars from different religious backgrounds to discuss differences and similarities in their traditions, in order to promote empathy and to improve our knowledge about one another. Secondly, I suggest that we encourage meetings between people from different religious traditions who have had some deeper spiritual experiences. They need not be scholars, but instead genuine practitioners who come together and share insights as a result of religious practice. According to my own experience, this is a powerful and effective means of enlightening each other in a more profound and direct way.

Some of you may have already heard me mention that on a visit to the great monastery at Montserrat in Spain, I met a Benedictine monk there. He came especially to see me—and his English was much poorer than mine, so I felt more courage to speak to him. After lunch, we spent some time alone, face to face, and I was informed that this monk had spent a few years in the mountains just behind the monastery. I asked him what kind of contemplation he had practiced during those years of solitude. His answer was simple: "Love, love, love." How wonderful! I suppose that sometimes he also slept. But during all those years he meditated simply on love. And he was not meditating on just the word. When I looked into his eyes, I saw evidence of profound spirituality and love—as I had during my meetings with Thomas Merton.

These two encounters have helped me develop a genuine reverence for the Christian tradition and its capacity to create people of such goodness. I believe the purpose of all the major religious traditions is not to construct big temples on the outside, but to create temples of goodness and compassion *inside*, in our hearts. Every major religion has the potential to create this. The greater our awareness is regarding the value and effectiveness of other religious traditions, then the deeper will be our respect and reverence toward other religions. This is the proper way for us to promote genuine compassion and a spirit of harmony among the religions of the world.

In addition to encounters among scholars and experienced practitioners, it is also important, particularly in the eyes of the public, that leaders of the various religious traditions occasionally come together to meet and pray, as in the important meeting at Assisi in 1986. This is a third simple yet effective way to promote tolerance and understanding.

A fourth means of working toward harmony among the world's religions is for people of different religious traditions to go on pilgrimages together to visit one another's holy places. A few years ago, I started doing this practice myself in India. Since then, I have had the opportunity to travel as a pilgrim to Lourdes, the

holy place in France, and to Jerusalem. In these places, I prayed with the followers of the various religions, sometimes in silent meditation. And in this prayer and
meditation, I felt a genuine spiritual experience. I hope this will set an example,
serve as a sort of precedent, so that in the future it will be regarded as quite normal for people to join together in pilgrimages to holy sites and share the experience of their different religious backgrounds.

Finally, I would like to come back to the subject of meditation and to my Christian brothers and sisters who practice meditation in their daily lives. I believe this
practice is extremely important. Traditionally in India, there is *samādhi* meditation,
"stilling the mind," which is common to all the Indian religions, including Hinduism,
Buddhism, and Jainism. And in many of these traditions, certain types of *vipaśyanā*,
"analytical meditation," are common as well. We might as why *samādhi*, "stilling
the mind," is so important. Because *samādhi*, or focusing meditation, is the
means to mobilize your mind, to channel your mental energy. *Samādhi* is considered to be an essential part of spiritual practice in all the major religious traditions
of India because it provides the possibility to channel *all* one's mental energy
and the ability to direct the mind to a particular object in a single-pointed way.

It is my belief that if prayer, meditation, and contemplation—which is more
discursive and analytic—are combined in daily practice, the effect on the practitioner's mind and heart will be all the greater. One of the major aims and purposes
of religious practice for the individual is an inner transformation from an undisciplined, untamed, unfocused state of mind toward one that is disciplined, tamed,
and balanced. A person who has perfected the faculty of single-pointedness will
definitely have a greater ability to attain this objective. When meditation becomes
an important part of your spiritual life, you are able to bring about this inner
transformation in a more effective way.

Once this transformation has been achieved, then in following your own
spiritual tradition, you will discover that a kind of natural humility will arise in you,
allowing you to communicate better with people from other religious traditions
and cultural backgrounds. You are in a better position to appreciate the value and
preciousness of other traditions because you have seen this value from within your
own tradition. People often experience feelings of exclusivity in their religious
beliefs—a feeling that one's own path in the only true path—which can create a
sense of apprehension about connecting with others of different faiths. I believe
the best way to counter that force is to experience the value of one's own path
through a meditative life, which will enable one to see the value and preciousness
of other traditions.

In order to develop a genuine spirit of harmony from a sound foundation of
knowledge, I believe it is very important to know the fundamental differences
between religious traditions. And it is possible to understand the fundamental
differences, but at the same time recognize the value and potential of each religious tradition. In this way, a person may develop a balanced and harmonious per-

ception. Some people believe that the most reasonable way to attain harmony and solve problems relating to religious intolerance is to establish one universal religion for everyone. However, I have always felt that we should have different religious traditions because human being possess so many different religious traditions because human beings possess so many different mental dispositions: one religion simply cannot satisfy the needs of such a variety of people. If we try to unify the faiths of the world into one religion, we will also lose many of the qualities and rich-nesses of each particular tradition. Therefore, I feel it is better, in spite of the many quarrels in the name of religion, to maintain a variety of religious traditions. Unfortunately, while a diversity of religious traditions is more suited to serve the needs of the diverse mental dispositions among humanity, this diversity naturally possesses the potential for conflict and disagreement as well. Consequently, people of every religious tradition must make an extra effort to try to transcend intolerance and misunderstanding and seek harmony.

These are a few points that I thought would be useful at the beginning of the Seminar. Now I am looking forward to the challenge of exploring texts and ideas that are not familiar to me. You've given me a heavy responsibility, and I will try my best to fulfill your wishes. I really feel it a great honor and privilege to be asked to comment on selected passages of the Holy Scripture—a scripture I must admit I am not very familiar with. I must also admit that this is the first time I have tried to do such a thing. Whether it will be a success or failure, I don't know! But in any case, I will try my best. Now I'll chant a few verses of auspiciousness and then we will meditate. ▲

Notes

1 Pali was a vernacular used during the sixth century BCE. In its grammatical structure it has a close resemblance to Sanskrit, the classical language of Indian literature.

2 Lord Chalmers, ed. and trans., *Further Dialogues of the Buddha*, vol. 1 (London: Oxford University Press, 1926), 176–77.

3 Ibid., 356.

4 Ibid., 115–22.

5 T.W. Rhys Davids and C.A.F. Rhys Davids, trans., *Dialogues of the Buddha*, pt. 2 (Oxford: Pali Text Society, 1995), 137–38.

6 Ibid., 144–46.

7 Ibid., 146–48.

8 Ibid., 149.

9 Ibid., 154–59.

10 Ibid., 162–64.

11 Ibid., 171–79.

12 Ibid., 179–90.

13 E.H. Johnston, trans., *Buddhacarita*, excerpt II, 31–35 (Delhi: Motilal Banarsidass, 1972).

14 Ibid., IV, 53–56.

15 Ibid., V, 2.

16 Ibid., V, 4–10.

17 Ibid., XIII, 18–22.

18 Ibid., XII, 25–31.

19 Ibid., XIII, 70–72.

20 Ibid., XIV, 49–76.

21 Ibid., XIV, 86–87.

22 The wheels are among the thirty-two signs of a "Great Man" like the Buddha, and point to his universality.

23 Dona asks here whether Buddha is one of the non-human and non-animal beings believed to exist.

24 Edward Conze et al., trans., in *Buddhist Texts through the Ages* (1954; rpt., New York: Harper and Row, 1964), 104–105.

25 Chalmers, ed. and trans., *Further Dialogues*, vol. 1, 121.

26 Conze et al., trans., *Buddhist Texts*, 103.

27 Ibid., 106.

28 Ibid., 112–13.

29 Ibid., 113–14.

30 Ibid., 103.

31 Ibid., 106.

32 Ibid., 140–41.

33 Ibid., 144.

34 Ibid., 144–45.

35 E.K. Dargyay, trans., *Rnying ma 'irgyud 'bum, Further Dialogues of the Buddha*, vol. 1.

36 Chalmers, ed. and trans., *Further Dialogues*, vol. 2, 300.

37 H.V. Guenther, trans., *The Jewel Ornament of Liberation* (Boulder, CO: Shambhala, 1971), 100 [modified].

38 E. Conze, trans., *Buddhist Scriptures*, 70–73.

39 Ibid., 73–77.

40 Conze, trans., *The Perfection of Wisdom in Eight Thousand Lines and Its Verse Summary* (Calcutta: Asiatic Society, 1958), 188.

41 Vidhushekhara Bhattacharga, ed., *Bibliotheca Indica*, 280 (Calcutta: Asiatic Society, 1960), 33–36. Trans. E.K. Dargyay.

42 Chalmers, ed. and trans., *Further Dialogues*, vol. 2, 199–204.

43 Guenther, trans., 92–97.

44 Conze et al., trans., *Buddhist Texts*, 131–32.

45 John R. McRae, *The Northern School and the Formation of Early Ch'an Buddhism* (Honolulu: University of Hawaii Press, 1986), 103.

46 Wing-tsit Chan, *A Source Book in Chinese Philosophy* (Princeton, NJ: Princeton University Press, 1963), 441–42.

47 Guenther, trans., *The Life and Teachings of Naropa* (Oxford: Clarendon Press, 1963), 75.

48 Garma C.C. Chang, trans., *The Hundred Thousand Songs of Milarepa*, vol. 1 (Boulder, CO: Shambhala, 1977), 63.

49 Tanjur Toh, no. 3721.

50 The sutra supposedly adopted its present literary form during the first two centuries of the Christian era.

51 F.M. Mueller, ed. and trans., *Buddhist Mahayana Texts*, Sacred Books of the East, vol. 49 (Delhi: Motilal Banarsidass), 98.

52 Wing-tsit Chan et al., eds., *The Great Asian Religions: An Anthology* (New York: Macmillan, 1969), 278–79.

53 Lam is a spiritual teacher (guru) in Tibetan Buddhism.

54 In tantric Buddhist texts, femininity is a symbol of perfect wisdom. Therefore, the absolute is here referred to with a term in the feminine gender.

55 Dargyay, trans.

56 T.W. Rhys Davids, trans., *The Questions of King Milinda*, Buddhist Sutras, Sacred Books of the East, vol. 11 (Delhi: Motilal Banarsidass, 1965), 146, 148–53.

57 F.J. Streng, trans., *Emptiness: A Study in Religious Meaning* (New York: Abingdon, 1967), 197.

58 T.W. Rhys Davids, trans., *The Questions of King Milinda*, Sacred Books of the East, vol. 36, 181–83.

59 Streng, 217.

60 Charles Prebish and Jane I. Smith, eds., *Introduction to Religions of the East* (Dubuque, IA: Kendall, Hunk, 1974), 74.

61 Conze, trans., *The Perfection of Wisdom*, 213–14.

62 T.W. Rhys Davids, trans., *The Questions of King Milinda*, Sacred Books of the East, vol. 35 (Delhi: Motilal Banarsidass, 1975), 40–45.

63 Conze, trans., *The Perfection of Wisdom*, 111–13.

64 Robert A. Thurman, trans., *The Holy Teaching of Vimalakirti, a Mahayana Scripture* (University Park, PA: Pennsylvania State University Press, 1976), 73–77.

65 Conze, trans., *The Perfection of Wisdom*, 642–43.

66 Conze, trans., *Buddhist Texts*, 150–51.

67 Ibid., 181–84.

68 Ibid., 17–20 (condensed).

69 Ibid., 23–26.

70 Ibid., 26–28 (condensed).

71 Ibid., 33.

72 Ibid., 42.

73 Detailed accounts can be found in Rick Fields, *How the Swans Came to the Lake: A Narrative History of Buddhism in America*, 3rd ed. (Boston: Shambhala, 1992); Heinrich Dumoulin and J. Moraldo, *The Cultural, Political and Religious Significance of Buddhism in the Modern World* (New York: Macmillan, 1976); Christmas Humphreys, *Sixty Years of Buddhism in England (1907-1967): A History and Survey* (London: Buddhist Society, 1968).

74 Christopher S. Queen, *Engaged Buddhism in the West* (Boston: Wisdom Publications, 2000), 2.

75 Henry S. Olcott, *The Buddhist Catechism*, 44th ed. (Adyar, Madras: Theosophical Publishing House, 1947), 37–38, 40–41.

76 New York: Broadway Books, 1999, 28–40.

77 *Samytta Nikaya* II, 47.

78 *Discourse on the Son's Flesh, Samyukta Agama* 373 (*Taisho* 99).

79 See Thich Nhat Hanh, *For a Future to Be Possible: Commentaries on the Five Mindfulness Training*, rev. ed. (Berkeley: Parallax Press, 1998).

80 In the year 255, Vietnamese Meditation Master Tang Hôi taught that our conscious-ness is like the ocean with six rivers of our senses flowing into it. Our mind and our body come from consciousness. They are formed by ourselves and our envi-ronment. Our life can be said to be a manifestation of our consciousness. Because of the food that our consciousness consumes, we are the person we are and our environment is what it is. In fact, the edible foods we take into our body and the foods of sense-impression and intention all end up in our consciousness. Our ignorance, hatred, and sadness all flow back to the sea of consciousness. We should know the kinds of food we feed our consciousness every day. When *vignana* (consciousness) ripens, it brings forth a new form of life, *nama rupa* (mind/body). *Rupa* is our body or physical aspect, and *nama* is our mind or mental aspect. Body and mind are manifestations of our consciousness, and our consciousness is made of these kinds of food. We have to look at the Five Aggregates (*skandhas*) in us— form, feelings, perceptions, mental formations, and consciousness. They are *nama rupa*. The first of the Five Aggregates is *rupa*, the other four are *nama*. They are all products of our *alayavignana*, our store of consciousness.

81 Karma Lekshe Tsomo, "Living as a Nun in the West," in *Sakhyadhita, Daughters of the Buddha*, ed. Karma Lekshe Tsomo (Ithaca, NY: Snow Lion Publications, 1988), 297–303.

82 "The Four Proper Areas for Diligent Efforts (*samyak pradhana*)," in *A Modern Bud-dhist Bible: Essential Readings from East and West*, ed. Donald S. Lopez, Jr. (Boston: Beacon Press, 2002), 228–31.

83 Tenzin Gyatso, the Dalai Lama, *The World of Tibetan Buddhism: An Overview of Its Philosophy and Practice*, trans., ed., and annotated by Geshe Thupten Jinpa (Boston: Wisdom Publications, 1995), 15–18.

84 Tenzin Gyatso, the Dalai Lama, *The Good Heart. A Buddhist Perspective on the Teachings of Jesus*, trans. and annotated by Geshe Thupten Jinpa (Boston: Wisdom Publications, 1996), 38–42.

Sikhism

FOUR

Sikhism

IN THE HISTORY OF RELIGIOUS TRADITIONS, the Sikh tradition stands out as a relatively recent and fascinating phenomenon. The development and maintenance of the tradition is a testimony to the strength of the human spirit in the face of seemingly overwhelming odds. While the Punjab region of northwest India is the cradle of the tradition, Sikhism has not remained an Indian tradition only but has become a world religion with communities and *gurudwaras* throughout the world.

The history of Sikhism stretches from 1469, the birth of Guru Nanak, to the present. The history of the Sikhs can be divided roughly into three periods: the formative period, from the birth of Guru Nanak to the death of the tenth Guru, Gobind Singh, in 1708; the evolution of Sikh institutions and the decline of the faith from 1708 to the middle of the nineteenth century; and a resurgence involving a search for Sikh identity which continues, in some respects, to the present day. Certainly, the beginnings of the tradition must be sought in the formative period in general, and with the teachings of Guru Nanak in particular. While it is debatable that he intended to start a new tradition, clearly his teachings, whether intentional or not, gave rise to a new tradition which, with respect to the pursuit of liberation and the achievement of personal peace and tranquility, regarded itself as superior to the two major religious traditions of north India at the time, the Hindu and Muslim traditions. Nine human gurus followed Nanak as leaders of the community, each with his own contributions to the development of Sikhism.

It is a well-known tradition that, before his death, Guru Gobind Singh declared that guruship for the community would no longer be vested in a

249

person. Rather, guruship would be vested in a book, the *Adi Granth* or *Guru Granth Sahib*. This text has come to be seen as scripture for the Sikh tradition. The position of the text as authoritative scripture is indicated by the two titles for the text. The title *Adi Granth* is meant to indicate that this is the first, or original, book. The title *Guru Granth* is meant to indicate that the book is the guru, but more significantly points to God as the supreme guru and ultimate origin of the teachings contained in the text. The text was initially compiled by the fifth guru, Guru Arjan (1563–1606), and received its final form from the tenth guru, Guru Gobind Singh (1666–1708). In addition to the *Guru Granth* there are other texts or collections that are important in the life of the community. The *Dasam Granth*, probably written by Guru Gobind Singh, has played an important role in the devotional life of the community. The *Janam Sakhis* are collections of anecdotes concerning the life and travels of Nanak, and his encounters with authorities of other traditions during those travels. These anecdotes probably date from the late sixteenth century. The tradition of *rahit namas*, manuals of discipline, has played a crucial role in the process of defining a life of discipline for Sikhs.

Hymns of Guru Nanak

The selections that follow are taken from the *Guru Granth*.[1] They can properly be viewed as hymns. The selections are given the designation of a particular *rag*, or "melody," according to which they are classified in the text. The selections emphasize some of the fundamental beliefs or teachings of the Sikh tradition that have been passed on since the time of Guru Nanak, as well as an awareness of the religious pluralism that characterized the world of Guru Nanak. Guru Nanak's teachings were experientially oriented, emphasizing a path of interiority, of listening to the voice of the divine within or contemplating the name (*Nam*) of God. But this need not be done in isolation from society. Rather, one can experience God and peace in the context of the hustle and bustle of everyday life. In this sense, we have here a householder's religion which says that God can and is to be experienced, that peace is possible in the context of everyday life, not apart from it.

A Conversation

We see here a lengthy conversation between the Yogi Loharipa and Guru Nanak, in which Guru Nanak repeatedly challenges the Yogi's prescriptions for the path to liberation. In his responses, Guru Nanak states that one does not have to separate oneself from society in order to achieve liberation, that one can exercise the necessary discipline in the context of the life of shops, towns, and traders. In the process, Guru Nanak gives us a radical reinterpretation of the requisites of Yoga, a reinterpretation that suggests that true religiosity does not depend on externals. Rather it depends on seeing God in all and cultivating, or listening to, the voice of God within.

▼ RAG RAMKALI

Charpat Yogi Questions

> The sea of life is hard to cross,
> How can we safely reach the other shore?

Nanak Answers

> Thou hast stated the problem correctly,
> What answer then, need I give thee?
> As the lotus flower
> Does not drown in the pool,
> As the duck
> Is not made wet by the pond.
> As the flower thrusts upwards,
> As the duck swims,
> So with the mind intent
> Upon the word of the Guru
> One can safely cross
> The great sea of life,
> Repeating the holy name,
> Living in an aloneness
> Utterly intent,
> Upon the alone,
> In a life of worldly hopes,
> Purging the mind
> Of worldly desires
> Nanak is the slave
> Of the one who graspeth
> The ungraspable
> And maketh others grasp Him.

Loharipa Yogi Pleads

> Know this the way of yoga:
> Shun towns and highways,
> Live in the forests under the trees,
> On roots and wild fruit.
> The yogis must live
> The contemplative life;
> Also for purification

One must visit
The places of pilgrimages.

Nanak Answers to Loharipa

Even while living
In towns and near highways,
Remain alert. Do not covet
Any of the neighbour's goods.
Without the divine name
We cannot attain inner peace
Nor still our inner hunger.
As the Guru has shown
The real life of the city
The real life of its shops
Is a life within us.
We must be traders in truth,
We should eat but little,
We should sleep but little,
This, saith Nanak, is the core
Of the idea of yoga.

Loharipa Expostulates

But yoga is a system
Which I beg thee to adopt,
Its symbols are patched coat,
Earrings, a beggar's wallet.
Out of the six systems,
Adopt this system of yoga,
Out of the twelve yogi sects,
Enter ours, the leading one.
Though thou sayest, only those
Whom God hath enlightened
Have truly grasped God
Control thy mind by my rules
And thou canst attain yoga.

Nanak Answers

My own system is constant,
Contemplation of the word.
My way of wearing earrings:
To discard pride and attachment,
My patched coat and beggar's wallet:
Are seeing God in all things.

Only God can make me free.
The Lord is the truth,
Truth is His name, says the Guru,
He who will may test this.

A Yogi Questions

Why hast thou left thy home,
Why wanderest thou like an hermit?
In what is thy trade?
How settest thou free thy disciples?

Nanak Answers

I left my home to look for a saint;
The desire to see the Lord
Hath made me a hermit.
My trade is in truth,
Through the grace of God
I shall set free my companions.

A Yogi Questions

What is the source of thy knowledge?
To what period belongeth thy system?
Who is thy Guru, and who are thy disciples?
What teaching keepeth thee in detachment?
Tell us all this, my child?

Nanak Answers

With the beginning of the breath of life,
My system began also;
Its source is the wisdom of the true Guru,
The true Guru is the word,
And the human mind is the disciple.
What keepeth me in my detachment
Is meditating on the ungraspable one,
Through the one divine word
God is made real to us,
And the saints destroy the flames,
Of attachment to the little self.

More Questions by a Yogi

How can steel be chewed with waxen teeth?
What drug can cure the disease of pride?
How shall we dress a snow man in fire?
In what cage can the mind rest in peace?

What is it that is everywhere,
With which every mind should be one?
What object of concentration
Can teach the mind to turn wholly to itself?

Nanak Answers

From within, from within,
Make the self as naught as naught;
Root out all feelings of otherness
And become at one with God.
True the world is as hard as steel,
For the stubborn and the self-willed in their folly,
But through the might of the word
This steel can be digested.
Outside thyself and within thyself
Seek only the knowledge of God.
By the blessings of the true Guru
The flames of desires can be destroyed.

(*Rag Ramkali*, verses 4, 5, 7–10, 19, 18, 43–46) ▲

God beyond All Gods

In *Rag Maru* we see an emphasis on God beyond all of the gods of Hinduism, an assertion that god existed before everything we would normally call creation and all human traditions, including religious traditions. In the references to Semitic texts, institutions, and traditions, Guru Nanak shows himself to be aware of traditions such as Christianity and Islam in addition to the variety of Hindu sects and schools. In the reference to the worship of too many gods, we see a gentle criticism of these traditions.

▼ **RAG MARU**

Through uncountable ages,
Complete darkness brooded
Over utter vacancy;
There were no worlds, no firmaments.
The will of the Lord was alone pervasive;
There was neither night nor day, nor sun nor moon
But only God in ceaseless trance.

No air and no water,
No utterance, no source of life,
No beginning or ending, no growth or decay,

No continents, no regions under the earth,
No swelling oceans or winding rivers.

The higher, the middle, the lower planes did not exist,
Eating time did not exist either,
There was neither heaven nor hell.
Since the cycle of birth and death had not begun,
And so there was no upper region of bliss,
No middle region of purgation,
No lowest region of torment.

There were no gods to inhabit the highest heavens,
No Brahma, no Vishnu, no Shiva;
There was the one, the eternal and none besides;
There was neither male nor female
Neither shaping nor begetting,
There was nothing to experience
Either pleasure or pain.

There were no ascetics and no voluptuaries,
No monks and no hermits,
No religious communities of any sort,
No liturgies, no creeds.
There was no one to think of any one,
Except God to think of Himself.
God was His own emanation,
He judged His own worth and rejoiced in His own beauty.

There were not any Vaishnavites, counting their basil beads,
There were no ritual observances or pious forbearances;
Krishna was not, nor were his milkmaids,
Neither were tantras and mantra Shaktis and all their humbug,
Nor was there any flute player.

There were no churches, with their creeds and rites,
There was no maya, the veil of illusion,
That makes dark and defiles;
There were no castes, since there were no births,
There was no predestination to drag us through
The mud of the worldly attachment and death and rebirth
And the worship of too many gods.

There were no living bodies and souls,
There was nothing and no one to accept or deny the truth:

The great Gorakh and Machindera did not exist.
There was no subject for contemplation,
No object of knowledge,
Nothing to trace the genesis of,
Nothing to sit judgment on.

There were no divisions of caste or rank, no sectarian antagonisms,
No idols nor temples, nor creeds of particular nations,
There were no clashing forms of prayer and worship,
Nor any to worship or pray.

There were no mullas or qazis or hadjis;
No sufis and no disciples of the Sufis,
No proud kings, nor their subjects,
Nor masters either, nor slaves.
There did not exist either the cult based on adoring worship of Vishnu
Nor that based on Shiva, the passive male,
And Shakti, the active female:
There was neither friendship nor sexual appetite;
God was both creditor and debtor then,
Such being His pleasure.

There had not been inscribed the Vedas,
Nor the scriptures of the Semitics,
None read a gospel at dawn, an epistle at sunset,
Only the unspeakable spoke of Himself to Himself.
Only the unknowable of Himself had His knowledge.

When He so willed, He shaped the universe;
The firmament He spread without a prop to support it.
He created the high gods, Brahma, Vishnu and Shiva.
And Maya the goddess, the veil of illusion,
Who maketh truth dark and increaseth worldly attachment.
To some, to a chosen few, the Guru revealeth the Lord's word.
The Lord creates and He watcheth His creation;
He made the heavenly bodies,
Our universe in the endless space,
Above, below and around it.
And out of the unmanifested, unmovable ground of His being,
To us and in us, He made Himself manifest.
None knoweth the Lord's beginning nor His end,
The true Guru revealeth but this secret:
Nanak, those whom the knowledge of the Lord

Maketh to wonder,
Are caught into His truth,
Since singing His glory,
They become aware of His wonder.

• • •

Where self exists,
God is not;
Where God exists,
There is no self.
Sage, probe this mystery,
Of the immanence of the Lord in all that is,
Without the grace of the Guru
We could not know this essence of truth.

When we encounter the true teacher,
And when the little self dies,
Doubt and fear die with it,
And the pains of birth, death and rebirth,
The Guru's teaching is the highest wisdom
Since it shows us where our liberator is.
Nanak repeats: "I am that. That is I."
The three worlds are included in that formula.

(Rag Maru, 43, 44) ▲

Relationship with the Divine

In the references to the awakening of nature in spring, the bee as a messenger of love, the longing for the home of one's childhood, and the separation of husband and wife, we see Guru Nanak's emphasis on a "felt" relationship with the divine. The hymn moves from an emphasis on the pangs of separation to the possibility and joy of union with the divine and closes with Guru Nanak's emphasis on interiority—God is to be known within.

▼ **RAG TUKHARI**

Chet (March–April)

It is the month of Chet,
It is spring. All is seemly,
The beautiful honey-bee can be seen,
In the flower bedecked woodland,
The home of my childhood days.
But there is sorrow of separation in my soul,

Longingly I wait for the Lord;
If the husband comes not home, how can a wife
Find peace of mind?

The sorrow of separation wastes away my body,
The koel calls in the mango groves,
Its notes are full of joy,
But there is a sorrow in my soul.
The honey-bee hovers about the blossoming bough,
A messenger of love and hope.
But O Mother of mine, it is like death to me,
For there is sorrow in my soul,
How shall I find peace and blessedness?

Spake the Guru:
Blessed peace would be attained in Chet,
If the Lord comes and meets the wife.

Vaisakh (April–May)

Beauteous Vaisakh,
When the bough adorns itself anew,
The wife awaits her Lord;
Her eyes fixed on the door,
"Come my Love, come have compassion for me,
Thou, my Love, alone can help me cross,
The turbulent waters of life; come home.
Without Thee I am as worthless as a shell,
Cast Thou Thine eyes upon me.
O who can make me worthy of Thee?
Who can make me win Thy love?
Who has seen my love?
Who can show Him to me?"

Spake the Guru:
Thou hast not far to go for the Lord,
Know Him within thee, thou art His mansion.
If thy body and soul yearn for the Lord,
The Lord shall love thee;
And Vaisakh appears beautiful;
If thy mind is imbued with the Lord
In Vaisakh you will meet the Lord you love.

(*Rag Tukhari* 45) ▲

Rahit Namas

Important in the development of Sikhism, particularly for the process of defining a Sikh, is the tradition of the *rahit namas*. A *rahit* is a code of conduct or path while the *namas* are the manuals in which the codes appear. As the latter term *namas* indicates, there is more than one such manual. Arguably, the code of conduct finds its origin in the inauguration of the khalsa by Gobind Singh in 1699. Those who wished to be members of the khalsa were expected to submit to a code, the most obvious element of which was adherence to the five Ks. In the years following Gobindh Singh, several codes of conduct appeared, all attempting to define what appropriate Sikh conduct is.

Early in the twentieth century, the Singh Sabha, a reform movement begun in 1873, initiated the process of compiling a new *rahit nama*, one that would remove outdated aspects of earlier *rahit namas* and that would find broad acceptance among Sikhs. The result was the *Sikh Rahit Maryada*, which appeared in 1950. As the excerpt below indicates,[2] a fundamental aspect of the *Sikh Rahit Maryada* is to define who a Sikh is in terms of personal discipline, belief, relationship to the community of Sikhs, relationship to other religious communities, and the ceremonies that are to be observed at important points in the life of a Sikh.

▼ SIKH RAHIT MARYADA

A Sikh is any person who believes in God (Akal Purakh); in the ten Gurus (Guru Nanak to Gobind Singh); in Sri Guru Granth Sahib, other writings of the ten Gurus, and their teachings; in the Khalsa initiation ceremony instituted by the tenth Guru; and who does not believe in any other system of religious doctrine.

A Sikh should rise early (3 a.m. to 6 a.m.) and having bathed he should observe *nam japan* by meditating on God. Each day a Sikh should read or recite the order known as the "Daily Rule" (*nit-nem*). The daily rule comprises the following portions of the scripture: Early morning (3 a.m.–6 a.m.) *Japji, Jap,* and the *Ten Savayyas* (5.1).... In the evening at sunset: Sodar Rahiras (5.2).... At night before retiring: *Sohila* (5.3). At the conclusion of the selections set down for early morning and evening (*Sodar Rahiras*) the prayer known as Ardas must be recited (5.4).

The influence of the Gurus' word is best experienced in a religious assembly (*sangat*). Each Sikh should therefore join in sangat worship, visiting gurdwaras and drawing inspiration from the sacred scripture in the sangat's presence. In each gurdwara, the Guru Granth Sahib should be opened daily.... The Guru Granth Sahib must be treated with great reverence while it is being opened, read, or closed.

When it is to be opened it should be laid under a canopy in a place which is clean and tidy. It should be set on a stool or lectern over which a clean cloth covering has been spread. Cushions should be used to support it while it is open and a mantle should be provided for covering it when it is not being read. A whisk should be provided for use when it is open.... Shoes must be removed before entering the gurdwara. Feet, if unclean, should be washed.... Whenever a Sikh enters a gurdwara, his first duty must be to bow before the Guru Granth Sahib, touching the floor with his forehead.... No Sikh may sit bareheaded in the presence of the sangat or an opened Guru Granth Sahib....

The only works which may be sung as kirtan in a sangat are those which are recorded in the sacred scriptures (1.2–3) or the commentaries on sacred scripture composed by Bhai Gurdas and Bhai Nand (1.4).

A practice to be commended is for each Sikh regularly to read right through the entire contents of the Guru Granth Sahib, planning his daily instalments in such a way that he completes the task in four weeks (or whatever period may be convenient for him).... An unbroken reading of the Guru Granth Sahib (*akhand path*) may be held in time of distress or to mark an occasion of particular joy. Such a reading takes approximately forty-eight hours, the actual reading continuing without interruption.

Karah Prasad [sanctified food], which has been prepared in the prescribed manner may be brought to the gurdwara for distribution. The prescribed method for preparing karah prasad is as follows. Equal portions (by weight) of wholemeal flour, sugar (the best available) and ghee should be mixed in a clean (iron) vessel while passages from the sacred scriptures are sung or recited.

Each Sikh should live and work in accordance with the principles of Gurmat. Gurmat may be defined as follows:

(a) To worship only the one supreme God (*Akal Purakh*), spurning all other gods and goddesses;

(b) To accept as the means of deliverance only the ten Gurus, the Guru Granth Sahib, and the works of the ten Gurus;

(c) To believe that the same spirit was successively incarnated in the ten individual Gurus;

(d) To reject caste distinctions and untouchability; magical amulets, mantra, and spells; auspicious omens, days, times, planets, and astrological signs; the ritual feeding of Brahmans to sanctify or propitiate the dead; oblation for the dead; the superstitious waving of lights; (traditional) obsequies; fire sacrifices; ritual feasting or libations; sacred tufts of hair or ritual shaving; fasting for particular phases of the moon; frontal marks; sacred threads and sanctified rosaries; worshipping at tombs, temples, or cenotaphs; idol worship; and all other such superstitions;

(g) A knowledge of Gurmukhi is essential for Sikhs (1.2[10]);

(i) Do not cut a child's hair;

(r) When Sikhs meet they should greet each other by saying, "Vaheguru ji ka Khalsa, Vaheguru ji ki fateh" [Hail to the Guru's Khalsa! Hail to the victory of the Guru!]. This is the correct form for both men and women;

(s) A Sikh must wear a kachh (4.5[43]) and a turban. Apart from these garments he may wear whatever he chooses. The turban is optional for women.

Sikh Rahit Maryada includes rubrics for a birth and naming ceremony, marriage, Khalsa initiation, and cremation. The birth and naming ceremony is conducted as follows:

Following the birth of a child in a Sikh home, the family and relatives should visit their gurdwara as soon as the mother is able to rise and bathe. (There is no particular period fixed for this purpose.) They should take karah prasad with them or arrange to have it prepared on their behalf. While they are in the gurdwara they should celebrate the event and give thanks by singing such hymns as Guru Arjan's "God has broken every barrier" (*Sorath* raga), and his "God has sent this wondrous gift" (*Asa raga*) (5.7.3). If a complete reading of the Guru Granth Sahib has been undertaken [to mark the occasion] the concluding ceremony should be performed [at this time]. A passage should be chosen at random and the officiating granthi should propose a name, beginning with the same letter as the first word of the randomly chosen shabad. If the suggested name meets with the sangat's approval it shall be the name bestowed on the child. To a boy's name "Singh" should be added, and to a girl's name "Kaur."

After the six prescribed stanzas of *Anand Sahib* have been read, the child's birth is celebrated with an appropriate *Ardas and the distribution of karah prasad.*

Sikh marriages are solemnized in accordance with an order known as the Anand rite (5.7.6).

At the time of the actual marriage, the congregation should assemble in the presence of the Guru Granth Sahib and kirtan should be sung, either by professional singers (*ragi*) or the congregation. The bride and bridegroom should be seated in front of the Guru Granth Sahib, the bride on the groom's left. Having first secured the consent of the assembled sangat, the Sikh (either man or woman) who is to conduct the marriage ceremony should instruct the couple to stand, together with their parents or guardians, and should then recite the *Ardas* with which the ceremony begins.

The officiant should then instruct the couple in the teachings of the Gurmat concerning the duties of marriage.... To signify their assent to these injunctions, the couple should bow before the Guru Granth Sahib. The bride's father or senior relative should then place in her hand the hem of one of the garments worn by the bridegroom. The person serving as reader then sings the *Lavan* hymn, Guru Ram Das's *Suhi Chhant*.[2] After each of the four stanzas, the couple walk around the Guru Granth Sahib, the bridegroom followed by the bride, who continues to hold his hem. While they are thus proceeding around the Guru Granth Sahib either the ragis or the entire congregation repeat the appropriate stanza. After completing each of the first three rounds, the couple bow before the Guru Granth Sahib and then stand erect to hear the next stanza. Following the fourth round they bow and resume their seats. The ragis or others appointed for this particular purpose then sing the first five stanzas and the last stanza of *Anand Sahib*.

The ceremony finally concludes with *Ardas* and the serving of karah prasad.

The order for the conduct of funeral ceremonies includes the following instructions.

When a death takes place there should be no excessive lamenting, no beating of breasts or grief-stricken wailing. The best method of reconciling oneself to the will of God is to read the sacred scriptures or repeat God's name…. A corpse should be bathed and clad in clean garments, complete with all five Ks (4.5[43]). It should be laid on a bier and *Ardas* (5.4) should be recited. The bier should then be carried to the cremation ground to the accompaniment of appropriate hymns. At the cremation ground a funeral pyre should be erected and before consigning the body to the flames, *Ardas* should be recited. The corpse should then be laid on the pyre, and the pyre should be lit by a son, some other relative, or a close friend. The assembled sangat should meanwhile sit some distance away and sing hymns appropriate to a funeral (5.7.7)…. When the pyre is well ablaze, *Kirtan Sohila* should be recited (5.3), followed by *Ardas*.

After the cremation, a reading of the Guru Granth Sahib should be initiated on behalf of the departed soul, either in the house of the deceased or in a neighbouring gurdwara. When the funeral pyre has cooled, the body's ashes, together with any remaining bones, should be gathered and should either be cast into running water or buried at the place of cremation. No memorial should be erected to mark the spot where the cremation took place.

The manual concludes the section on "personal discipline" with an exhortation to perform seva, or "service."

Seva is a fundamental feature of Sikhism. Gurdwara maintenance provides a means of inculcating this essential virtue. Common examples are the sweeping of a gurdwara, serving water to members of the sangat or fanning them, serving food in the gurdwara dining hall (*langar*), and cleaning the shoes [of worshippers].

The Guru's *langar* serves two purposes. It inculcates the spirit of *seva* in Sikhs; and it breaks down false notions of status and caste. Anyone may eat in the *langar*, regardless of his status or caste. When all take their places in the same line [to receive their food] there should be no discrimination on the basis of national-ity, caste, or religion. The only qualification is that the food which is given to ini-tiated members of the Khalsa (4.5[34]) must be served from a separate dish. ▲

Notes

1 Trilochan Singh et al., trans., *Selections from the Sacred Writings of the Sikhs*, 3rd ed. (London: George Allen and Unwin, 1973), 99–108.
2 W.H. McLeod, trans. and ed., *Textual Sources for the Study of Sikhism* (Manchester: Manchester University Press, 1984), 79–83.

Early Chinese Thought

FIVE

Early Chinese Thought

NORMALLY WHEN ONE THINKS OF ANCIENT CHINA, one thinks of traditions such as Daoism/Taoism and Confucianism. However, as recent archeological evidence has suggested, significant civilizations, indeed significant religious traditions, existed long before the time of Confucius. The archeological finds suggest that prehistoric China dates back as much as 5,000 years ago. According to the traditional Chinese view, Chinese dynastic history begins with the Xia/Hsia dynasty, which supposedly ruled China prior to 1766 BCE. Before the Xia, China was purportedly ruled by three sage kings, Yao, Shun, and Yu. Life under the three sage kings was thought to have been ideal, so much so that one sees appeals to the ideal time of the sage kings in later thinkers such as Confucius. The formative period of Chinese civilization is usually thought to be the period under the rule of the Shang Dynasty (approximately 1766–1122 BCE).

It is here that we see the development of beliefs and ideas that carry over to later periods and thinkers. For example, the Shang had a conception of a supreme deity ruling over a realm inhabited by a host of spirits in much the same way that the Shang rulers ruled over their subjects. It was thought that the spirits of departed ancestors went to this realm and continued to influence life on earth. The idea of a supreme god was taken over by the Zhou/Chou dynasty (approximately 1122–249 BCE), only to be given the name Tian/T'ien, or Heaven. Closely connected to the belief in Heaven was the idea of the Mandate of Heaven, possibly a development of the early Zhou period. Involved in this idea is the belief that the earthly ruler receives his mandate, or the legitimacy to rule, from Heaven. He maintains this

mandate only so long as he rules according to the Will of Heaven, governing in the interests of all. If he becomes a tyrant, he loses the mandate. The
Zhou rulers justified their defeat of the Shang by way of appeal to the Mandate of Heaven. The idea of the Will of Heaven also finds its way into the
Analects of Confucius.

Archeological evidence indicates that the belief in and practice of divination (perhaps as old as the fourth millennium BCE) was widespread during the period of the Shang. The purpose of divination was primarily to
foretell the future; it was mostly used by the court for advice from the supernatural order in matters of state. Materials used were shells and bones that
were heated. The resulting cracks were seen as clues that could be interpreted by an expert to provide advice for whatever question was being asked.
In addition to bones, milfoil stalks were also used. In this case, the stalks would
be thrown and the resulting configurations would be interpreted by the
diviner. It is commonly thought that the *Yijing/I-ching*, or *Book of Changes*,
a manual to be used to harmonize one's life with the Dao/Tao, is based on
the practice of divination.

The selections that follow are taken from texts called the Confucian
Classics. These are five in number: the *Book of Changes* (*Yijing*), the *Book of
History* (*Shujing/Shu-ching*), the *Book of Poetry* (*Shijing/Shih-ching*), the *Classic of Rites* (*Lijing/Li-ching*), and the *Spring and Autumn Annals* (*Qunqiu/Ch'un-
ch'iu*). The characterization of these texts as Confucian Classics refers to the
belief that Confucius edited them, added appendices, and in the case of the
Spring and Autumn Annals, authored them. Whether or not Confucius had
a hand in editing these texts, the tradition points to the value given to these
texts as windows to beliefs and practices before the time of Confucius. They
are, arguably, texts that provide an insight into the concerns and beliefs
that characterized Chinese society prior to the birth of the Confucian and
Daoist traditions: arguably, given the history of these texts. They have been
edited and reinterpreted throughout Chinese history. Indeed, many books,
including Confucian texts, were destroyed under the Qin/Ch'in dynasty
(221–206 BCE). The Confucian canon, including the Classics, was reconstructed and re-edited during the time of Han rule.

Book of Historical Documents

The *Book of Historical Documents*[1] is in effect, government documents made
up of speeches by rulers and ministers, narratives of events, and statements
relating to principles of government. Traditionally they have been seen as
documents relating to the era of the sage kings. Scholars question this relationship just as they question Confucius's role in editing the *Book of History*.

Nonetheless, the text is an important one in the sense that it provides a glimpse into concerns and beliefs prior to the time of Confucius. Indeed, one sees here ideas that are also found in the *Analects*. In the selections that follow, we see references to the decree of Heaven, the idea that Heaven responds to affairs on earth, particularly the actions of rulers, and belief in the Age of the Sage Kings from whom rulers are to take their cue for humane government. References to the princes of the Zhou indicate that we have here a justification of the overthrow of the Shang through an appeal to the Mandate of Heaven.

▼   In the fifth month, on the day Ting-hae, the king arrived from Yen, and came to the honoured city of Chow. The duke of Chow said, "The king speaks to the following effect, 'Ho! I make an announcement for you of the four kingdoms and many other regions. Ye who were the officers and people of the prince of Yin, I have dealt very leniently as regards your lives, as ye all know. You kept reckoning greatly upon some decree of Heaven, and did not keep with perpetual awe before your thoughts the preservation of your sacrifices.

'God sent down correction on Hea, but the sovereign only increased his luxury and sloth, and would not speak kindly to the people. He proved himself on the contrary dissolute and dark, and would not yield for a single day to the leading of God;—this is what you have heard. He kept reckoning on the decree of God in his favour, and would not promote the means of the people's support. By great inflictions of punishment also, he increased the disorder of the States of Hea. The first cause of his evil course was the internal misrule, which made him unfit to deal well with the multitudes. Nor did he seek at all to employ men whom he could respect, and who might display a generous kindness to the people, but he daily honoured the covetous and cruel, who were guilty of cruel tortures in the cities of Hea. Heaven on this sought a true lord for the people, and made its distinguishing and favouring decree light on T'ang the Successful, who punished and destroyed the sovereign of Hea. Heaven's refusal of its favour to Hea was decided, and it was because the righteous men among your many regions were not permitted to continue long in their posts of enjoyment, and the many officers whom Hea respected were quite unable to maintain an intelligent preservation of the people in the enjoyment of their lives, but on the contrary aided one another in oppression, so that of the hundred ways of promoting prosperity they could not advance one.

'In the case indeed of T'ang the Successful, it was because he was the choice of your many regions that he superseded Hea and became the lord of the people. He paid careful attention to the essential virtues of a sovereign, in order to stimulate the people, and they on their part imitated him, and were stimulated. From him down to the emperor Yih, the sovereigns all made their virtue illustrious, and were cautious in the use of punishments;—thus also exercising a stimulating influence over the people. When they, having examined the evidence in criminal cases, put to death those chargeable with many crimes, they exercised the same influence; they did so also, when they liberated those who were not purposely guilty. But when the throne came to your late sovereign, he could not with the good will of your many regions continue in the enjoyment of the favouring decree of Heaven.'"

"Oh! the king speaks to the following effect, 'I announce and declare to you of the many regions, Heaven had no set purpose to do away with the sovereign of Hea, or with the sovereign of Yin. But it was the case that your ruler, being in possession of your many regions, abandoned himself to great excess, and reckoned on the favouring decree of Heaven, making trifling excuses for his conduct. And so in the case of the sovereign of Hea;—his schemes of government were not of a tendency to secure his enjoyment of the empire, so that Heaven sent down ruin on him, and the chief of your State entered into the line of his succession. Indeed, it was the case that the last sovereign of your Shang was luxurious to the extreme of luxury, while his schemes of government showed neither purity nor progress, so that Heaven sent down such ruin on him.

'The wise, not thinking, became foolish, and the foolish, by thinking, became wise. Heaven for five years waited kindly and forbore with the descendant of T'ang, to see if he would indeed prove himself the true ruler of the people, but there was nothing in him deserving to be regarded. Heaven then sought among your many regions, making a great impression by its terrors to stir up one who might look reverently to it; but in all your regions, there was not one deserving of its regard. There were, however, our kings of Chow, who treated well the multitudes of the people, and were able to sustain the burden of virtuous government, and to preside over all services to spirits and to Heaven. Heaven thereupon instructed them, and increased their excellence, made choice of them, and gave them the decree of Yin to rule over your many regions.'"

(*Book of Historical Documents, Numerous Regions* 1–19) ▲

▼   The duke of Chow spake to the following effect, "Prince Shih, Heaven, unpitying, sent down ruin on Yin; Yin has lost its appointment, and the princes of our Chow have received it. I do not dare, however, to say, as if I knew it, 'The foundation will ever truly abide in prosperity. (If Heaven aid sincerity,—)' Nor do I dare to say, as if I knew it 'The final end will issue in our misfortunes.' Oh! you have said, O prince, 'It depends on ourselves.' I also do not dare to rest in the favour of God, never forecasting at a distance the terrors of Heaven in the present time when there is no murmuring or disobedience among the people;—the issue is with men. Should our present successor to his fathers prove greatly unable to reverence Heaven and the people, and so bring to an end their glory, could we in our families be ignorant of it? The favour of Heaven is not easily preserved. Heaven is hard to be depended on. Men lose its favouring appointment because they cannot pursue and carry out the reverence and brilliant virtue of their fore-fathers.

(*Book of Historical Documents, Prince Shih* 1–4) ▲

Book of Odes

The *Book of Odes*,[2] or the *Book of Poetry*, is a collection of some three hundred poems dating from the early Zhou period. It is a book of folk songs on themes such as love and songs relating to court life. As in the case of the *Book of History*, this text was supposedly edited by Confucius, who is said to have selected these poems from a larger body of poetry. Most of the poems are thought to date from the early Zhou period. In the following selections we see references to the importance of rituals, the importance of addressing and making offerings to the ancestors, the belief in the Mandate of Heaven, and a justification for the ascendancy of the House of Zhou.

▼   **ANCESTORS AND THE LORD ON HIGH**

Abundant is the year, with much millet and much rice,
And we have tall granaries,
With hundreds of thousands and millions of units.
We make wine and sweet spirits
And offer them to our ancestors, male and female,
Thus to fulfill all the rites,
And bring down blessings to all.

(*Book of Odes*, ode no. 279, "Abundant Is the Year")

Heaven produces the teeming multitude;
As there are things, there are their specific principles [tse].
When the people keep to their normal nature,
They will love excellent virtue.
Heaven, looking down upon the House of Chou
Sees that its light reaches the people below,
And to protect the Son of Heaven,
Gave birth to Chung Shan-fu [to help him].

(*Book of Odes*, ode no. 260, "The Teeming Multitude")

They [descendants of Yin] became subject to Chou
Heaven's Mandate is not constant.
The officers of Yin were fine and alert.

They assist at the libation in our capital.
In their assisting in the libation,
They always wear skirted robes and close caps [peculiar to Yin].
Oh, you promoted servants of the king,
Don't you mind your ancestors!
Don't you mind your ancestors!
Cultivate your virtue.
Always strive to be in harmony with Heaven's Mandate.
Seek for yourselves the many blessings.
Before Yin lost its army,
Its kings were able to be counterparts to the Lord on High.
In Yin you should see as in a mirror
That the great mandate is not easy (to keep).

(Book of Odes, ode no. 235, "King Wen") ▲

Book of Changes

One of the most influential works from China, the *Book of Changes* is a manual of divination attributed to the ancient sages.[3] Its earliest parts are likely the product of the Zhou period, while some parts may be as late as the Qin or early Han periods. The text as we have it is made up of hexagrams, or combinations of broken and unbroken lines placed on top of each other. Each hexagram has a name and an attached commentary that requires interpretation. The unbroken lines represent the *yang* force and the broken lines represent the *yin* force. The text is, therefore, based on the idea of the constant interplay of the *yin* and *yang*, and understanding this interplay in order to harmonize one's life with the *dao*. Consulting the manual involved the use of heated bones and, later, milfoil stalks, thrown to the ground. The patterns of broken and unbroken lines derived from this practice would be matched to the appropriate hexagram and the commentary attached to the hexagram would be applied to the concern brought by the petitioner. The commentaries or appendices have traditionally been attributed to Confucius, but that tradition is questioned by modern scholarship. The *Book of Changes* has functioned as both a book of divination and a book of wisdom. We see elements of the latter in the excerpt below, particularly in the references to understanding the way of Heaven in order that the sage might model his actions after the actions of heaven.

▼ CH'IEN/THE CREATIVE

_____ *above Ch'ien the Creative, Heaven*
=====
===== *below Ch'ien the Creative, Heaven*
=====

The first hexagram is made up of six unbroken lines. These unbroken lines stand for the primal power, which is light-giving, active, strong, and of the spirit. The hexagram is consistently strong in character, and since it is without weakness, its essence is power or energy. Its image is heaven. Its energy is represented as unrestricted by any fixed conditions in space and is therefore conceived of as motion. Time is regarded as the basis of this motion. Thus, the hexagram includes also the power of time and the power of persisting in time, that is, duration.

The power represented by the hexagram is to be interpreted in a dual sense—in terms of its action on the universe and of its action on the world of men. In relation to the universe, the hexagram expresses the strong, creative action of the Deity. In relation to the human world, it denotes the creative action of the holy man or sage, of the ruler or leader of men, who through his power awakens and develops their higher nature.

> *The Judgment*
> The Creative works sublime success,
> furthering through perseverance.

According to the original meaning, the attributes [sublimity, potentiality of success, power to further, perseverance] are paired. When an individual draws this oracle, it means that success will come to him from the primal depths of the universe and that everything depends upon his seeking his happiness and that of others in one way only, that is, by perseverance in what is right.

The specific meanings of the four attributes became the subject of speculation at an early date. The Chinese word here rendered by "sublime" means literally "head," "origin," "great." This is why Confucius says in explaining it: "Great indeed is the generating power of the creative; all beings owe their beginning to it. This power permeates all heaven." For this attribute inheres in the other three as well.

The beginning of all things lies still in the beyond in the form of ideas that have yet to become real. But the Creative furthermore has power to lend form to these archetypes of ideas. This is indicated in the word success, and the process is represented by an image from nature: "The clouds pass and the rain does its work, and all individual beings flow into their forms."

Applied to the human world, these attributes show the great man the way to notable success: "Because he sees with great clarity causes and effects, he completes the six steps at the right time and mounts toward heaven on them at the right time, as though on six dragons." The six steps are the six different positions given in the hexagram, which are represented later by the dragon symbol. Here it is shown that the way to success lies in apprehending and giving actuality to the way of the universe [tao], which, as a law running through end and beginning, brings about all phenomena in time. Thus each step attained forthwith becomes a preparation for the next. Time is no longer a hindrance but the means of making actual what is potential.

The act of creation having found expression in the two attributes sublimity and success, the work of conservation is shown to be a continuous actualization and differentiation of form. This is expressed in the two terms "furthering" [literally, "creating that which accords with the nature of a given being"] and "persevering" [literally, "correct and firm"]. "The course of the Creative alters and shapes beings until each attains its true, specific nature, then it keeps them in conformity with the Great Harmony. Thus does it show itself to further through perseverance."

In relation to the human sphere, this shows how the great man brings peace and security to the world through his activity in creating order: "He towers high above the multitude of beings, and all lands are united in peace."

Another line of speculation goes still further in separating the words "sublime," "success, "furthering," and "perseverance," and parallels them with the four cardinal virtues in humanity. To sublimity, which, as the fundamental principle, embraces all the other attributes, it links love. To the attribute success are linked the mores, which regulate and organize the expressions of love and thereby make them successful. The attribute furthering is correlated with justice, which creates the conditions in which each receives that which accords with his being, that which is due him and which constitutes his happiness. The attribute perseverance is correlated with wisdom, which discerns the immutable laws of all that happens and can therefore bring about enduring conditions. These speculations, already broached in the commentary called *Wen Yen*, later formed the bridge connecting the philosophy of the "five stages [elements] of change," as laid down in the Book of History (Shu Ching) with the philosophy of the Book of Changes, which is based solely on the polarity of positive and negative principles. In the course of time this combination of the two systems of thought opened the way for an increasingly intricate number symbolism.

> *The Image*
> The movement of heaven is full of power.
> Thus the superior man makes himself strong
> and untiring.

Since there is only one heaven, the doubling of the trigram Ch'ien, of which heaven is the image, indicates the movement of heaven. One complete revolution of heaven makes a day, and the repetition of the trigram means that each day is followed by another. This creates the idea of time. Since it is the same heaven moving with untiring power, there is also created the idea of duration both in and beyond time, a movement that never stops nor slackens, just as one day follows another in an unending course. This duration in time is the image of the power inherent in the Creative.

With this image as a model, the sage learns how best to develop himself so that his influence may endure. He must make himself strong in every way, by consciously casting out all that is inferior and degrading. Thus he attains that tirelessness which depends upon consciously limiting the fields of his activity.

(The *I Ching*, or *Book of Changes*) ▲

Notes

1 Readings taken from *Study Aids for World Religions*, vol. 1 (Hamilton: McMaster University, Department of Religion), C6–C7.
2 Readings taken from Wing-tsit Chan, trans. and comp., *A Sourcebook in Chinese Philosophy* (Princeton: Princeton University Press, 1963), 5–7.
3 Readings taken from the *I Ching*, or *Book of Changes*, 3rd ed., Richard Wilhelm, trans., rendered into English by Cary F. Baynes. Bollingen Series XIX (Princeton: Princeton University Press, 1967), 3–7.

Confucian Thought

SIX

Confucian Thought

THE CONFUCIAN TRADITION has arguably been the dominant tradition of thought throughout much of Chinese history. While Confucius's teachings had relatively little impact during his own lifetime, these teachings were preserved by a community of disciples after his death in 479 BCE. A central figure in keeping the teachings alive in the years after the death of Confucius was Mencius (Mengzi/Meng-tzu). Although not a direct disciple of Confucius, his admiration for Confucius and his writing did much to popularize the teachings of the Master in the tumultuous years that led to the end of the Zhou dynasty. A younger contemporary of Mencius, Xunzi/Hsun-tzu, took Confucius's thought in a direction opposed to that of Mencius, but his influence on the tradition was not as great as was the influence of Mencius. The tradition received a serious setback with the establishment of the Qin dynasty in 221 BCE. The first emperor of the dynasty decreed the destruction of books and had many Confucian scholars executed. As a result, many Confucian texts were destroyed. Confucian fortunes changed with the establishment of the Han dynasty in 206 BCE. Under the early Han, a Confucian system of administration and a system of competitive examinations designed to prepare men for governmental service, and based on the study of the Confucian Classics, was implemented. This system of Confucian education remained the foundation of Chinese education until the early part of the twentieth century.

Following the collapse of the Han in 220 CE, the Confucian tradition was overshadowed by the growth of Buddhism, which prospered from the anarchy that followed the collapse of the Han. A revival of sorts, known as neo-Confucianism, occurred under the rule of the Tang/T'ang (617–907 CE) and the Song/Sung (960–1279 CE). The revival was an attempt not only to revive interest in the original sources but also to meet head-on the influence and popularity of Buddhism and Daoism.

As this brief overview implies, what was considered the canon (those texts regarded as foundational for the tradition) changed over time. The canon of early Confucianism is known as the Five Classics: the *Book of Changes* (*Yijing*), the *Book of History* (*Shujing*), the *Book of Poetry* (*Shijing*), the *Classic of Rites* (*Lijing*), and the *Spring and Autumn Annals* (*Qunqui*). These texts became the basis for the Confucian system of education established in the Han period. In the Song period neo-Confucian scholars reformulated Confucian thought on the basis of the Four Books: the *Analects* (*Lunyu*) which contains sayings of and anecdotes about Confucius, the *Book of Mencius, The Great Learning*, and *The Doctrine of the Mean*. The latter two were extracted from the *Book of Rites* (*Liji/Li Chi*), part of the corpus of the *Classic of Rites* (*Lijing*).

Confucius

As has already been pointed out, tradition has it that Confucius edited the Five Classics. While this tradition is rejected by modern scholarship, it does underline what appears to be Confucius's view of himself as a transmitter of traditions essential for right living and good government. This is the central concern of Confucius's teachings, a concern that undoubtedly points to the chaotic character of the time in which he lived.

Confucius (the Latin version of his name, Kongfuzi/K'ung Fu-tzu) was born in the state of Lu (in today's Shandong province). The traditional date for his birth is 551 BCE. This places Confucius in the latter half of the Zhou period, sometimes referred to as the period of the warring states. Although his family was poor, he did receive an education. After a short stint in the bureaucracy of the state of Lu, he started his own school and made something of a name for himself as a scholar. As a result he was given a position as magistrate (the position has been variously described as police commissioner or minister of justice). His tenure in this position was short-lived. He left the state of Lu in a vain search for a ruler who would take seriously the kinds of reforms Confucius thought essential for good government. After some years (the number ranges from ten to thirteen) he returned to his home state to teach. He died in 479 BCE at the age of seventy-three.

The ideas of Confucius, as they are expressed in the *Analects*, have to do with the proper ordering of society, beginning with the family and extending outwards to larger society and government. The concern for the proper ordering of society had much to do with the time in which Confucius lived, the period of the warring states. This was, to say the least, a period of turmoil and insecurity, and the Zhou rulers were not powerful enough to do much about the chaos. It is to this situation that Confucius turned his attention in the belief that the social order could be set right, that a society of peace, order, and prosperity was possible, and that this could be had through implementing the "right" way.

The Analects

The *Analects* is generally acknowledged to be one of few reliable sources on Confucius.[1] There is, however, some scholarly debate over how much of the *Analects* can be attributed to Confucius and his disciples. The earliest segment (the first ten chapters) is thought to have been compiled after the death of Confucius, by disciples of his immediate disciples. This means that the earliest section dates from about one hundred years after the death of Confucius. The rest may represent two successive additions, with chapters eleven to fifteen representing the first addition and chapters sixteen to twenty representing the second.

The *Analects* contain sayings of Confucius, conversations with followers, and anecdotes about Confucius. As is indicated above, the concern is with right living in the context of family, society, and government. Confucius evidently believed that it was possible to establish a society of peace, order, and harmony. Such a society had once been in existence during the period of the sage kings. Accordingly, in his conversations, Confucius made appeals to a golden age, the time of the sage kings, arguing that right living, particularly for rulers, meant living according to the principles and virtues exemplified by the sage kings. In this respect Confucius did not see himself as a reformer, but as a transmitter of tradition. The following selections are arranged according to concepts that Confucius thought to be essential for a society of order, peace and harmony.

▼ THE CONCEPTS OF TIAN/T'IEN AND THE "MANDATE OF HEAVEN" IN THE ANALECTS

The Master said, At fifteen I set my heart upon learning. At thirty, I had planted my feet firm upon the ground. At forty, I no longer suffered from perplexities. At fifty, I knew what were the biddings of Heaven. At sixty, I heard them with docile ear. At seventy, I could follow the dictates of my own heart; for what I desired no longer overstepped the boundaries of right. (*Analects* 2:4)

Wang-sun Chia asked about the meaning of the saying,

> Better pay court to the stove
> Than pay court to the Shrine.

The Master said, It is not true. He who has put himself in the wrong with Heaven has no means of expiation left. (*Analects* 3:13)

Ssu-ma Niu grieved, saying, Everyone else has brothers; I alone have none. Tzu-hsia said, I have heard this saying, "Death and life are the decree of Heaven; wealth and rank depend upon the will of Heaven. If a gentleman attends to business and does not idle away his time, if he behaves with courtesy to others and observes the rules of ritual, then all within the Four Seas are his brothers." How can any true gentleman grieve that he is without brothers? (*Analects* 12:5)

Kung-po Liao spoke against Tzu-lu to the Chi Family. Tzu-lu Ching-po informed the Master saying, I fear my master's mind has been greatly unsettled by this. But in the case of Kung-po Liao, I believe my influence is still great enough to have his carcass exposed in the marketplace. The Master said, if it is the will of Heaven that the Way shall prevail, then the Way will prevail. But if it is the will of Heaven that the Way should perish, then it must needs perish. What can Kung-po Liao do against Heaven's will? (*Analects* 14:38)

Master K'ung said, There are three things that a gentleman fears: he fears the will of Heaven, he fears great men, he fears the words of the Divine Sages. The small man does not know the will of Heaven and so does not fear it. He treats great men with contempt, and scoffs at the words of the Divine Sages. (*Analects* 16:8) ▲

▼ THE CONCEPT OF REN/JEN IN THE ANALECTS

Master Yu said, Those who in private life behave well towards their parents and elder brothers, in public life seldom show a disposition to resist the authority of their superiors. And as for such men starting a revolution, no instance of it has ever occurred. It is upon the trunk that a gentleman works. When that is firmly set up, the Way grows. And surely proper behaviour towards parents and elder brothers is the trunk of Goodness? (*Analects* 1:2)

Wealth and rank are what every man desires; but if they can only be retained to the detriment of the Way he professes, he must relinquish them. Poverty and obscurity are what every man detests; but if they can only be avoided to the detriment of the Way he professes, he must accept them. The gentleman who ever parts company with Goodness does not fulfill that name. Never for a moment does a gentleman quit the way of Goodness. He is never so harried but that he cleaves to this; never so tottering but that he cleaves to this. (*Analects* 4:5)

The Master said, I for my part have never yet seen one who really cared for Goodness, nor one who really abhorred wickedness. One who really cared for Goodness
would never let any other consideration come first. One who abhorred wickedness would be so constantly doing Good that wickedness would never have a
chance to get at him. Has anyone every managed to do Good with his whole
might even as long as the space of a single day? I think not. Yet I for my part have
never seen anyone give up such an attempt because he had not the strength to
go on. It may well have happened, but I for my part have never seen it. (*Analects*
4:6)

The Master said, Shen! My Way has one [thread] that runs right through it. Master Tseng said, Yes. When the Master had gone out, the disciples asked, saying
What did he mean? Master Tseng said, Our Master's Way is simply this: Loyalty,
consideration. (*Analects* 4:15)

Tzu-kung said, If a ruler not only conferred wide benefits upon the common
people, but also compassed the salvation of the whole State, what would you say
of him? Surely, you would call him Good? The Master said, It would no longer be
a matter of "Good." He would without doubt be a Divine Sage. Even Yao and Shun
could hardly criticize him. As for Goodness—you yourself desire rank and standing; then help others to get rank and standing. You want to turn your own merits to account; then help others to turn theirs to account—in fact, the ability to take
one's own feelings as a guide—that is the sort of thing that lies in the direction of
Goodness. (*Analects* 6:28)

Jan Yung asked about Goodness. The Master said, Behave when away from home
as though you were in the presence of an important guest. Deal with the common
people as though you were officiating at an important sacrifice. Do not do to others what you would not like yourself. Then there will be no feelings of opposition
to you, whether it is the affairs of a State that you are handling or the affairs of a
Family.
    Jan Yung said, I know that I am not clever; but this is a saying that, with your
permission, I shall try to put into practice. (*Analects* 12:2)

The Master said, One who has accumulated moral power (*te*) will certainly also possess eloquence; but he who has eloquence does not necessarily possess moral
power. A Good Man will certainly also possess courage; but a brave man is not necessarily Good. (*Analects* 14:5)

The Master said, He whose wisdom brings him into power, needs Goodness to
secure that power. Else, though he get it, he will certainly lose it. He whose wisdom brings him into power and who has Goodness whereby to secure that

power, if he has not dignity wherewith to approach the common people, they will not respect him. He whose wisdom has brought him into power, who has Goodness whereby to secure that power and dignity wherewith to approach the common people, if he handle them contrary to the prescriptions of ritual, is still a bad ruler. (*Analects* 15:32)

The Master said, When it comes to Goodness one need not avoid competing with one's teacher. (*Analects* 15:3)

The Master said, Yu, have you ever been told of the Six Sayings about the Six Degenerations? Tzu-lu replied, No, never. [The Master said] Come, then; I will tell you. Love of Goodness without love of learning degenerates into silliness. Love of wisdom without love of learning degenerates into utter lack of principle. Love of keeping promises without love of learning degenerates into villainy. Love of uprightness without love of learning degenerates into harshness. Love of courage without love of learning degenerates into turbulence. Love of courage without love of learning degenerates into mere recklessness. (*Analects* 17:8)

Tzu-hsia said,

> One who studies widely and with set purpose,
> Who questions earnestly, then thinks for himself
> about what he had heard—
> such a one will incidentally achieve Goodness. (*Analects* 19:6) ▲

▼ THE CONCEPT OF LI IN THE ANALECTS

Master Yu said, In the usages of ritual it is harmony that is prized; the Way of the Former Kings from this got its beauty. Both small matters and great depend upon it. If things go amiss, he who knows the harmony will be able to attune them. But if harmony itself is not modulated by ritual, things will still go amiss. (*Analects* 1:12)

The Master said, [the good man] does not grieve that other people do not recognize his merits. His only anxiety is lest he should fail to recognize theirs. (*Analects* 1:16)

The Master said, Govern the people by regulations, keep order among them by chastisements, and they will flee from you, and lose all self-respect. Govern them by moral force, keep order among them by ritual and they will keep their self-respect and come to you of their own accord. (*Analects* 2:3)

Meng I Tzu asked about the treatment of parents. The Master said, Never disobey! When Fan Ch'ih was driving his carriage for him, the Master said, Meng asked me about the treatment of parents and I said, Never disobey! Fan Ch'ih said, In what sense did you mean it? The Master said, While they are alive, serve them according to ritual. When they die, bury them according to ritual and sacrifice to them according to ritual. (*Analects* 2:5)

Duke Ting [died 495 BCE] asked for a precept concerning a ruler's use of his ministers and a minister's service to his ruler. Master K'ung replied saying, a ruler in employing his ministers should be guided solely by the prescriptions of his ritual. Ministers in serving their ruler, solely by devotion to his cause. (*Analects* 3:19)

Duke Ching of Ch'i asked Master K'ung about government. Master K'ung replied saying, Let the prince be a prince, the minister a minister, the father a father and the son a son. The Duke said, How true! For indeed when the prince is not a prince, the minister not a minister, the father not a father, the son not a son, one may have a dish of millet in front of one and yet not know if one will live to eat it. (*Analects* 12:11)

Fan Ch'ih asked the Master to teach him about farming. The Master said, You had much better consult some old farmer. He asked to be taught about gardening. The Master said, You had much better go to some old vegetable-gardener. When Fan Ch'ih had gone out, the Master said, Fan is no gentleman! If those above them love ritual, then among the common people none will dare to be disrespectful. If those above them love right, then among the common people none will dare to be disobedient. If those above them love good faith, then among the common people none will dare depart from the facts. If a gentleman is like that the common people will flock to him from all sides with their babies strapped to their backs. What need has he to practice farming? (*Analects* 13:4)

Tsai Yu asked about the three years' mourning, and said he thought a year would be quite long enough: "If gentlemen suspend their practice of the rites for three years, the rites will certainly decay; if for three they make no music, music will certainly be destroyed. [In a year] the old crops have already vanished, the new crops have come up, the whirling drills have made new fire. Surely a year would be enough?"

The Master said, Would you then [after a year] feel at ease in eating good rice and wearing silk brocades? Tsai Yu said, Quite at ease. [The Master said] If you would really feel at ease, then do so. But when a true gentleman is in mourning, if he eats dainties, he does not relish them, if he hears music, it does not please him, if he sits in his ordinary seat, he is not comfortable. That is why he abstains from these things. But if you would really feel at ease, there is no need for you to abstain.

When Tsai Yu had gone out, the Master said, How inhuman Yu is! Only when a child is three years old does it leave its parents' arms. The three years' mourning is the universal mourning everywhere under Heaven. And Yu—was he not the darling of his father and mother for three years? (*Analects* 17:21)

The Master said, He who does not understand the will of Heaven cannot be regarded as a gentleman. He who does not know the rites cannot take his stand. He who does not understand words, cannot understand people. (*Analects* 20:3)

▲

Mencius

As we have pointed out in the introduction to Confucius, the survival of the work of Confucius is a result of the devotion and work of a community of disciples. Mencius played no small role in the preservation of the tradition. To be sure he added his own ideas to that tradition. Mencius was born in approximately 372 BCE, almost a century after the death of Confucius, and died in 289 BCE. Important to note is the fact that Mencius, like Confucius, lived in the period of the warring states. If anything, the chaos of his time was worse than it had been at the time of Confucius. Like Confucius, it was to this situation that he spoke, drawing upon the teachings of the master as Mencius understood them. His ideas are contained in a book entitled the *Book of Mencius*. This may not be his own work, but may rather be the work of his disciples.

Mencius's thought has often been referred to as idealistic Confucianism. This suggests that while his ideas are based on the teachings of Confucius, he gave to these teachings his own stamp, developing them in much fuller fashion than the ideas developed in the *Analects*. His dependence on Confucius is evident in his insistence on Confucian virtues, particularly the virtue of *ren/jen*. His idealism is evident in his view of human nature, that human nature is intrinsically or originally good in that the human being is born with the beginnings of goodness or compassion. The human being, then, has a natural inclination to goodness. These beginnings can be developed to produce the Confucian virtues, qualities that are necessary for right living and that are conducive to the development of a society of peace and harmony. The following selections from the *Book of Mencius*[2] deal primarily with Mencius's view of human nature.

▼ **THE BOOK OF MENCIUS**

Book Six, Part I

6A:1   Kao Tzu said, "Human nature is like the willow tree, and righteousness is like a cup or a bowl. To turn human nature into humanity and righteousness is like turning the willow into cups and bowls." Mencius said, "Sir, can you follow the nature of the willow tree and make the cups and bowls, or must you violate the nature of the willow tree before you can make the cups and bowls? If you are going to violate the nature of the willow tree in order to make cups and bowls, then must you also violate human nature in order to make it into humanity and righteousness? Your words, alas! would lead all people in the world to consider humanity and righteousness as calamity [because they required the violation of human nature]!"

6A:2   Kao Tzu said, "Man's nature is like whirling water. If a breach in the pool is made to the east it will flow to the east. If a breach is made to the west it will flow to the west. Man's nature is indifferent to good and evil, just as water is indifferent to east and west." Mencius said, "Water, indeed, is indifferent to the east and west, but is it indifferent to high and low? Man's nature is naturally good just as water naturally flows downward. There is no man without this good nature; neither is there water that does not flow downward. Now you can strike water and cause it to splash upward over your forehead, and by damming and leading it, you can force it uphill. Is this the nature of water? It is the forced circumstance that makes it do so. Man can be made to do evil, for his nature can be treated in the same way."

6A:3   Kao Tzu said, "What is inborn is called nature." Mencius said, "When you say that what is inborn is called nature, is that like saying that white is white?" "Yes." "Then is the whiteness of the white feather the same as the whiteness of snow? Or, again, is the whiteness of snow the same as the whiteness of white jade?" "Yes." "Then is the nature of a dog the same as the nature of an ox, and is the nature of an ox the same as the nature of a man?"

6A:4   Kao Tzu said, "By nature we desire food and sex. Humanity is internal and not external, whereas righteousness is external and not internal." Mencius said, "Why do you say that humanity is internal and righteousness external?" "When I see an old man and respect him for his age, it is not that the oldness is within me, just as, when something is white and I call it white, I am merely observing its external appearance. I therefore say that righteousness is external." Mencius said, "There is no difference between our considering a white horse to be white and a white man to be white. But is there no difference between acknowledging the age of an old horse and the age of an old man? And what is it that we call righteousness, the fact that a man is old or the fact that we honor his old age?" Kao Tzu said, "I love my own younger brother but do not love the younger brother of, say, a man from the state of Ch'in. This is because I am the one to determine that pleasant feeling. I therefore say that humanity comes from within. On the other hand, I respect the old men of the state of Ch'u as well as my own elders. What determines my pleasant feeling is age itself. Therefore I say that righteousness is external." Mencius said, "We love the roast meat of Ch'in as much as we love our own. This is even so with respect to material things. Then are you going to say that our love of roast meat is also external?"

6A:5　　Meng Chi Tzu asked Kung-tu Tzu, "What does it mean to say that right-eousness is internal?" Kung-tu Tzu said, "We practise reverence, and therefore it is called internal." "Suppose a fellow villager is one year older than your older brother. Whom are you going to serve with reverence?" "I shall serve my brother with reverence." "In offering wine at a feast, to whom will you offer first?" "I shall offer wine to the villager first." Meng Chi Tzu said, "Now you show reverence to one but honor for age to the other. What determines your actions certainly lies without and not within." Kung-tu Tzu could not reply and told Mencius about it. Mencius said, "If you ask him whether he will serve with reverence his uncle or his younger brother, he will say that he will serve with reverence his uncle. Then you ask him, in case his younger brother is acting at a sacrifice as the representative of the deceased, then to whom is he going to serve with reverence? He will say he will serve the younger brother with reverence. Then you ask him 'Where is your reverence for your uncle?' He will then say, '[I show reverence to my younger brother] because he represents the ancestral spirit in an official capacity.' You can then likewise say, '[I show reverence to the villager] because of his position.' Ordinarily, the reverence is due the elder brother, but on special occasions it is due the villager." When Chi Tzu heard this, he said, "We show reverence to uncle when reverence is due him, and we show reverence to the younger brother when rev-erence is due him. Certainly what determines it lies without and does not come from within." Kung-tu Tzu said, "In the winter we drink things hot. In the sum-mer we drink things cold. Does it mean that what determines eating and drink-ing also lies outside?"

6A:6　　Kung-tu Tzu said, "Kao Tzu said that man's nature is neither good nor evil. Some say that man's nature may be made good or evil, therefore when King Wen and King Wu were in power the people loved virtue, and when Kings Yu and Li were in power people loved violence. Some say that some men's nature is good and some men's nature is evil. Therefore even under (sage-emperor) Yao there was Hsiang [who daily plotted to kill his brother], and even with a bad father Ku-sou, there was [a most filial] Shun (Hsiang's brother who succeeded Yao), and even with (wicked king) Chou as nephew and ruler, there were Viscount Ch'i of Wei and Prince Pi-kan. Now you say that human nature is good. Then are those people wrong?" Mencius said, "If you let people follow their feelings (orig-inal nature), they will be able to do good. This is what is meant by saying that human nature is good. If man does evil, it is not the fault of his natural endowment. The feeling of commiseration is found in all men; the feeling of shame and dislike is found in all men; the feeling of respect and reverence is found in all men; and the feeling of right and wrong is found in all men. The feeling of commiseration is what we call humanity; the feeling of shame and dislike is what we call righteous-ness; the feeling of respect and reverence is what we call propriety (*li*); and the feeling of right and wrong is what we call wisdom. Humanity, righteousness, propriety, and wisdom are not drilled into us from outside. We originally have them with us. Only we do not think [to find them]. Therefore it is said, 'Seek and you will find it, neglect and you will lose it.' [Men differ in the development of their endowments], some twice as much as others, some five times, and some to an incalculable degree, because no one can develop his original endowment to the fullest extent. The *Book of Odes* says, 'Heaven produces the teeming multitude. As there are things there are their specific principles. When the people keep their normal nature they will love excellent virtue.' Confucius said, 'The writer of this poem indeed knew the Way (Tao). Therefore as there are things, there must be their specific principles, and since people keep to their normal nature, therefore they love excellent virtue."'

6A:7 Mencius said, "In good years most of the young people behave well. In bad years most of them abandon themselves to evil. This is not due to any difference in the natural capacity endowed by Heaven. The abandonment is due to the fact that the mind is allowed to fall into evil. Take for instance the growing of wheat. You sow the seeds and cover them with soil. The land is the same and the time of sowing is also the same. In time they all grow up luxuriantly. When the time of harvest comes, they are all ripe. Although there may be a difference between the different stalks of wheat, it is due to differences in the soil, as rich or poor, to the unequal nourishment obtained from the rain and the dew, and to differences in human effort. Therefore all things of the same kind are similar to one another. Why should there be any doubt about men? The sage and I are the same in kind. Therefore Lung Tzu said, 'If a man makes shoes without knowing the size of people's feet, I know that he will at least not make them to be like baskets.' Shoes are alike because people's feet are alike. There is a common taste for flavor in our mouths. I-ya was the first to know our common taste for food. Suppose one man's taste for flavor is different from that of others, as dogs and horses differ from us in belonging to different species, then why should the world follow I-ya in regard to flavor? Since in the matter of flavor the whole world regards I-ya as the standard, it shows that our tastes for flavor are alike. The same is true of our ears. Since in the matter of sounds the whole world regards Shih-k'uang as the standard, it shows that our ears are alike. The same is true of our eyes. With regard to Tzu-tu, none in the world did not know that he was handsome. Any one who did not recognize his handsomeness must have no eyes. Therefore I say there is a common taste for flavor in our mouths, a common sense for sound in our ears, and a common sense for beauty in our eyes. Can it be that in our minds alone we are not alike? What is it that we have in common in our minds? It is the sense of principle and righteousness (*i-li* moral principles). The sage is the first to possess what is common in our minds. Therefore moral principles please our minds as beef and mutton and pork please our mouths."

6A:8   Mencius said, "The trees of the Niu Mountain were once beautiful. But can the mountain be regarded any longer as beautiful since, being in the borders of a big state, the trees have been hewed down with axes and hatchets? Still with the rest given them by the days and nights and the nourishment provided them by the rains and the dew, they were not without buds and sprouts springing forth. But then the cattle and the sheep pastured upon them once and again. That is why the mountain looks so bald. When people see that it is so bald, they think that there was never any timber on the mountain. Is this the true nature of the mountain? Is there not [also] a heart of humanity and righteousness originally existing in man? The way in which he loses his originally good mind is like the way in which the trees are hewed down with axes and hatchets. As trees are cut down day after day, can a mountain retain its beauty? To be sure, the days and nights do the healing, and there is the nourishing air of the calm morning which keeps him normal in his likes and dislikes. But the effect is slight, and is disturbed and destroyed by what he does during the day. When there is repeated disturbance, the restorative influence of the night will not be sufficient to preserve (the proper goodness of the mind). When the influence of the night is not sufficient to preserve it, man becomes not much different from the beast. People see that he acts like an animal, and think that he never had the original endowment (for goodness). But is that his true character? Therefore with proper nourishment and care, everything grows, whereas without proper nourishment and care, everything decays. Confucius said, "Hold it fast and you preserve it. Let it go and you lose it. It comes in and goes out at no definite time and without anyone's knowing its direction.' He was talking about the human mind."

6A:10   Mencius said, "I like fish and I also like bear's paw. If I cannot have both of them, I shall give up the fish and choose the bear's paw. I like life and I also like righteousness. If I cannot have both of them, I shall give up life and choose righteousness. I love life, but there is something I love more than life, and therefore I will not do anything improper to have it. I also hate death, but there is something I hate more than death, and therefore there are occasions when I will not avoid danger. If there is nothing that man loves more than life, then why should he not employ every means to preserve it? And if there is nothing that man hates more than death, then why does he not do anything to avoid danger? There are cases when a man does not take the course even if by taking it he can preserve his life, and he does not do anything even if by doing it he can avoid danger. Therefore there is something men love more than life and there is something men hate more than death. It is not only the worthies alone who have this moral sense. All men have it, but only the worthies have been able to preserve it." ▲

Xunzi

A rival to Mencius was the Confucian Xunzi, who lived from approximately 300–238 BCE. He witnessed the demise of the house of Zhou. His ideas were much less optimistic than were Mencius's, perhaps a reflection of his own awareness that the idealism of thinkers like Mencius had not produced the kind of ideal society that Mencius thought possible. Nonetheless, he took seriously the teachings of Confucius, particularly the emphasis on virtue and education to produce virtue.

Xunzi's thought is often referred to as realistic Confucianism and is contained in a book called the *Xunzi*. As the term "realism" indicates, Xunzi offered a different interpretation of Confucian thought than did Mencius. Arguing directly against Mencius, Xunzi took the position that the human being is by nature evil. In making this claim, he was not suggesting that goodness (the development of Confucian virtues) is not possible. Rather, his position was that the human being's natural inclination was toward selfishness rather than goodness or compassion, and that it is this selfishness that has to be overcome to produce the Confucian virtues. The following selections are taken from the *Xunzi* and reflect Xunzi's arguments against Mencius over the understanding of human nature.

▼ THE XUNZI

The Nature of Man Is Evil (chap. 23)[3]

The nature of man is evil; his goodness is the result of his activity. Now, man's inborn nature is to seek for gain. If this tendency is followed, strife and rapacity result and deference and compliance disappear. By inborn nature one is envious and hates others. If these tendencies are followed, injury and destruction result and loyalty and faithfulness disappear. By inborn nature one possesses the desires of ear and eye and likes sound and beauty. If these tendencies are followed, lewdness and licentiousness result, and the pattern and order of propriety and righteousness disappear. Therefore to follow man's nature and his feelings will inevitably result in strife and rapacity, combine with rebellion and disorder, and end in violence. Therefore there must be the civilizing influence of teachers and laws and the guidance of propriety and righteousness, and then it will result in deference and compliance, combine with pattern and order, and end in discipline. From this point of view, it is clear that the nature of man is evil and that his goodness is the result of activity.

Crooked wood must be heated and bent before it becomes straight. Blunt metal must be ground and whetted before it becomes sharp. Now the nature of man is evil. It must depend on teachers and laws to become correct and achieve propriety and righteousness and then it becomes disciplined. Without teachers and laws, man is unbalanced, off the track, and incorrect. Without propriety and righteousness, there will be rebellion, disorder, and chaos. The sage-kings of antiquity, knowing that the nature of man is evil, and that it is unbalanced, off the track, incorrect, rebellious, disorderly, and undisciplined, created the rules of propriety and righteousness and instituted laws and systems in order to correct man's feelings, transform them, and direct them so that they all may become disciplined and conform with the Way (Tao). Now people who are influenced by teachers and laws, accumulate literature and knowledge, and follow propriety and righteousness are superior men, whereas those who give rein to their feelings, enjoy indulgence, and violate propriety and righteousness are inferior men. From this point of view, it is clear that the nature of man is evil and that his goodness is the result of his activity.

Mencius said, "Man learns because his nature is good." This is not true. He did not know the nature of man and did not understand the distinction between man's nature and his effort. Man's nature is the product of Nature; it cannot be learned and cannot be worked for. Propriety and righteousness are produced by the sage. They can be learned by men and can be accomplished through work. What is in man but cannot be learned or worked for is his nature. What is in him and can be learned or accomplished through work is what can be achieved through activity. This is the difference between human nature and human activity. Now by nature man's eye can see and his ear can hear. But the clarity of vision is not outside his eye and the distinctness of hearing is not outside his ear. It is clear that clear vision and distinct hearing cannot be learned. Mencius said, "The nature of man is good; it [becomes evil] because man destroys his original nature." This is a mistake. By nature man departs from his primitive character and capacity as soon as he is born, and he is bound to destroy it. From this point of view, it is clear that man's nature is evil.

By the original goodness of human nature is meant that man does not depart from his primitive character but makes it beautiful, and does not depart from his original capacity but utilizes it, so that beauty being [inherent] in his primitive character and goodness being [inherent] in his will are like clear vision being inherent in the eye and distinct hearing being inherent in the ear. Hence we say that the eye is clear and the ear is sharp. Now by nature man desires repletion when hungry, desires warmth when cold, and desires rest when tired. This is man's natural feeling. But now when a man is hungry and sees some elders before him, he does not eat ahead of them but yields to them. When he is tired, he dares not seek rest because he wants to take over the work [of elders]. The son yielding to or taking over the work of his father, and the younger brother yielding to or taking over the work of his older brother—these two lines of action are contrary to original nature and violate natural feeling. Nevertheless, the way of filial piety is the pattern and order of propriety and righteousness. If one follows his natural feeling, he will have no deference or compliance. Deference and compliance are opposed to his natural feelings. From this point of view, it is clear that man's nature is evil and that his goodness is the result of his activity.

Someone may ask, "If man's nature is evil, whence come propriety and righteousness?" I answer that all propriety and righteousness are results of the activity of sages and not originally produced from man's nature. The potter pounds the clay and makes the vessel. This being the case, the vessel is the product of the artisan's activity and not the original product of man's nature. The artisan hews a piece of wood and makes a vessel. This being the case, the vessel is the product of the artisan's activity and not the original product of man's nature. The sages gathered together their ideas and thoughts and became familiar with activity, facts, and principles, and thus produced propriety and righteousness and instituted laws and systems. This being the case, propriety and righteousness, and laws and systems are the products of the activity of the sages and not the original products of man's nature.

As to the eye desiring color, the ear desiring sound, the mouth desiring flavor, the heart desiring gain, and the body desiring pleasure and ease—all these are products of man's original nature and feelings. They are natural reactions to stimuli and do not require any work to be produced. But if the reaction is not naturally produced by the stimulus but requires work before it can be produced, then it is the result of activity. Here lies the evidence of the difference between what is produced by man's nature and what is produced by his effort. Therefore the sages transformed man's nature and aroused him to activity. As activity was aroused, propriety and righteousness were produced, and as propriety and righteousness were produced, laws and systems were instituted. This being the case, propriety, righteousness, laws, and systems are all products of the sages. In his nature, the sage is common with and not different from ordinary people. It is in his effort that he is different from and superior to them.

It is the original nature and feelings of man to love profit and seek gain. Suppose some brothers are to divide their property. If they follow their natural feelings, they will love profit and seek gain, and thus will do violence to each other and grab the property. But if they are transformed by the civilizing influence of the pattern and order of propriety and righteousness, they will even yield to outsiders. Therefore, brothers will quarrel if they follow their original nature and feeling but, if they are transformed by righteousness and propriety, they will yield to outsiders.

People desire to be good because their nature is evil. If one has little, he wants abundance. If he is ugly, he wants good looks. If his circumstances are narrow, he wants them to be broad. If poor, he wants to be rich. And if he is in a low position, he wants a high position. If he does not have it himself, he will seek it outside. If he is rich, he does not desire more wealth, and if he is in a high position, he does not desire more power. If he has it himself, he will not seek it outside. From this point of view, [it is clear that] people desire to be good because their nature is evil.

Now by nature a man does not originally possess propriety and righteousness; hence he makes strong effort to learn and seeks to have them. By nature he does not know propriety and righteousness; hence he thinks and deliberates and seeks to know them. Therefore, by what is inborn alone, man will not have or know propriety and righteousness. There will be disorder if man is without propriety and righteousness. There will be violence if he does not know propriety and righteousness. Consequently by what is inborn alone, disorder and violence are within man himself. From this point of view, it is clear that the nature of man is evil and that his goodness is the result of his activity.

Mencius said, "The nature of man is good." I say that this is not true. By goodness at any time in any place is meant true principles and peaceful order, and by evil is meant imbalance, violence, and disorder. This is the distinction between good and evil. Now do we honestly regard man's nature as characterized by true principles and peaceful order? If so, why are sages necessary and why are propriety and righteousness necessary? What possible improvement can sages make on true principles and peaceful order?

Now this is not the case. Man's nature is evil. Therefore the sages of antiquity, knowing that man's nature is evil, that it is unbalanced and incorrect, and that it is violent, disorderly, and undisciplined, established the authority of rulers to govern the people, set forth clearly propriety and righteousness to transform them, instituted laws and governmental measures to rule them, and made punishment severe to restrain them, so that all will result in good order and be in accord with goodness. Such is the government of sage-kings and the transforming influence of propriety and righteousness.

But suppose we try to remove the authority of the ruler, do away with the transforming influence of propriety and righteousness, discard the rule of laws and governmental measure, do away with the restraint of punishment, and stand and see how people of the world deal with one another. In this situation, the strong would injure the weak and rob them, and the many would do violence to the few and shout them down. The whole world would be in violence and disorder and all would perish in an instant. From this point of view, it is clear that man's nature is evil and that his goodness is the result of his activity.

The man versed in ancient matters will certainly support them with evidences from the present, and he who is versed in [the principles of] Nature will certainly support them with evidences from the world of men. In any discussion, the important things are discrimination and evidence. One can then sit down and talk about things, propagate them, and put them into practice. But now Mencius said that man's nature is good. He had neither discrimination nor evidence. He sat down and talked about the matter but rose and could neither propagate it nor put it into practice. Is this not going too far? Therefore if man's nature is good, sage-kings can be done away with and propriety and righteousness can be stopped. But if his nature is evil, sage-kings are to be followed and propriety and righteousness are to be greatly valued. For bending came into existence because there was crooked wood, the carpenter's square and ruler came into existence because things are not straight, and the authority of rule is instituted and propriety and righteousness are made clear because man's nature is evil. From this point of view, it is clear that man's nature is evil and that his goodness is the result of his activity. Straight wood does not depend on bending to become straight; it is straight by nature. But crooked wood must be bent and heated before it becomes straight because by nature it is not straight. Now, the nature of man is evil. It has to depend on the government of sage-kings and the transforming influence of propriety and right-eousness, and then all will result in good order and be in accord with goodness. From this point of view, it is clear that man's nature is evil and that his goodness is the result of his activity. ▲

Neo-Confucians

Confucian influence reached its height in Chinese society during the Han dynasty, which lasted from 202 BCE to approximately 220 CE. This was not an unbroken rule for it was challenged for a short period in the common era (9–23 CE). Consequently one can refer to the former and the later Han peri-ods. With the collapse of the Han, Confucian influence waned. The Han period was followed by a lengthy period of disunity and strife. It was not until the short-lived Sui dynasty (589–618 CE) that China was reunited. During the time of the Sui, Tang rule (618–906 CE), and Song rule (960–1279 CE), China saw the ascendancy and development of Buddhist schools of thought. The Song period also saw the revival of Confucian thought. While attempts to reform Confucian thought precede the Song period, it was during the Song period that Confucian thought and Confucian centres of learning chal-lenged Buddhist intellectual centres. The revival of Confucian thought dur-ing this period is generally referred to as Neo-Confucianism. As the term indicates, there is a dependence in this development on Confucian thought, particularly the thought of Confucius and Mencius. But in order to compete successfully with Buddhist thought, a new interpretation had to be offered, one that read into the Classics elements of Buddhism and Daoism. The two major Neo-Confucian developments in the Song dynasty were the School of Principle or Reason and the School of Intuition or Mind. In both, one can see not only an attempt to remain true to the humanist emphases of Con-fucius and Mencius, but also a desire to incorporate metaphysical and spec-ulative aspects of Daoism and Buddhism.

Zhu Xi/Chu Hsi

Zhu Xi (1130–1200 CE) is known as the great synthesizer of the School of Principle or Reason. He was perhaps the most influential thinker among neo-Confucians. Evidence of this can be seen in the fact that his commentaries on the *Four Books* became central for a reformed Confucian educational and examination system. He taught that there is an immaterial and immutable principle inherent in all things, giving them their essence. The human being, too, has an inherent principle. This is one's true nature that can be understood through investigation. Through investigation and cultivation one's conduct can be brought into harmony with one's true being or principle. The result is perfection or enlightenment.[4]

▼   *Question*: The Great Ultimate is not a thing existing in a chaotic state before the formation of Heaven and earth, but a general name for the principles of Heaven and earth and the myriad things. Is that correct?

Answer: The Great Ultimate is merely the principle of Heaven and earth and the myriad things. With respect to heaven and earth, there is the Great Ultimate in them. With respect to the myriad things, there is the Great Ultimate in each and every one of them. Before Heaven and earth existed, there was assuredly this principle. It is the principle that through movement generates the yang. It is also this principle that through tranquility generates the yin. [49:8b–9a]

Question: [In your commentary on Chou Tun-yi's *T'ung shu*], you said: "Principle is a single, concrete entity, and the myriad things partake of it as their reality. Hence each of the myriad things possesses in it a Great Ultimate." According to this theory, does the Great Ultimate not split up into parts?

Answer: Fundamentally there is only one Great Ultimate, yet each of the myriad things has been endowed with it and each in itself possesses the Great Ultimate in its entirety. This is similar to the fact that there is only one moon in the sky but when its light is scattered upon rivers and lakes, it can be seen everywhere. It cannot be said that the moon has been split. [49:10b–11a]

The Great Ultimate is not spatially conditioned; it has neither corporeal form nor body. There is no spot where it may be placed. When it is considered in the state before activity begins, this state is nothing but tranquility. Now activity, tranquility, yin and yang are all within the realm of corporeality. However, activity is after all the activity of the Great Ultimate and tranquility is also its tranquility, although activity and tranquility themselves are not the Great Ultimate. This is why Master Chou Tun-yi spoke only of that state as Non-ultimate. While the state before activity begins cannot be spoken of as the Great Ultimate, nevertheless the principle of pleasure, anger, sorrow, and joy are already inherent in it. Pleasure and joy belong to yang and anger and sorrow belong to yin. In the initial stage the four are not manifested, but their principles are already there. As contrasted with the state after activity begins, it may be called the Great Ultimate. But still it is diffi-cult to say. All this is but a vague description. The truth must be genuinely and earnestly realized by each individual himself. [49:11a–b]

Someone asked about the Great Ultimate.

Answer: The Great Ultimate is simply the principle of the highest good. Each and every person has in him the Great Ultimate and each and every thing has in it the Great Ultimate. What Master Chou called the Great Ultimate is an appel-lation for all virtues and the highest good in Heaven and earth, man and things. [49:11b]

The Great Ultimate is similar to the top of a house or the zenith of the sky, beyond which point there is no more. It is the ultimate of principle. Yang is active and yin is tranquil. In these it is not the Great Ultimate that acts or remains tran-quil. It is simply that there are the principles of activity and tranquility. Principle is not visible; it becomes visible through yin and yang. Principle attaches itself to yin and yang as a man sits astride a horse. As soon as yin and yang produce the five agents, they are confined and fixed by physical nature and are thus differen-tiated into individual things each with its nature. But the Great Ultimate is in all of them. [49:13a]

Wang Yangming/Wang Yang-Ming

The School of Mind or Intuition culminated in the thought of Wang Yang-ming (1472–1529 CE).[5] In protest against Zhu Xi's emphasis on investigation of things and their inherent principles, and the prolonged study of Confu-cian Classics, he asserted that the mind contains all things and is one with the moral law of the universe. It manifests itself in innate knowledge, the orig-inal substance of the mind. One's task is to remain true to this innate knowl-edge by following its promptings without the obscuring effects of selfishness and rationalization.

▼

I [Hsu Ai] did not understand the teacher's doctrine of the unity of knowledge and action and debated over it back and forth with Huang Tung-hsien and Ku Wei-hsien without coming to any conclusion. Therefore I took the matter to the teacher. The teacher said: Give an example and let me see. I said: For example, there are peo-ple who know that parents should be served with filial piety and elder brothers with respect, but they cannot put these things into practice. This shows that knowledge and action are clearly two different things.

The teacher said: The knowledge and action you refer to are already separated by selfish desires and no longer knowledge and action in their original substance. There have never been people who know but do not act. Those who are supposed to know but do not act simply do not yet know. When sages and worthies taught people about knowledge and action, it was precisely because they wanted them to restore this original substance, and not just to have them behave like that and be satisfied. Therefore the *Great Learning* points to true knowledge and action for people to see, saying [they are] "like loving beautiful colors and hating bad odors" [VI]. Seeing beautiful colors appertains to knowledge, while loving beautiful colors appertains to action. However, as soon as one sees a beautiful color, he has already loved it. Smelling a bad odor appertains to knowledge, while hating a bad odor appertains to action. However, as soon as one smells a bad odor, he has already hated it. It is not that he smells it first and then makes up his mind to hate it. A person with his nose stopped up does not smell the bad odor even if he sees a malodorous object before him, and so he does not hate it. This amounts to not knowing bad odor. Suppose we say that so-and-so knows filial piety and brotherly respect before they can be said to know them. It will not do to say that they know filial piety and brotherly respect simply because they show them in words. Or take one's knowledge of pain. Only after one has experienced pain can one know pain. The same is true of cold or hunger. How can knowledge and action be separated? I have said that knowledge is the crystallization of the will to act and action is the task of carrying out that knowledge; knowledge is the beginning of action and action is the completion of knowledge. ▲

Notes

1   Readings taken from *Study Aids for World Religions*, vol. 1 (Hamilton: McMaster University, Department of Religion), C7–C12.
2   Readings taken from Wing-tsit Chan, *A Source Book in Chinese Philosophy* (Princeton: Princeton University Press, 1963), 51–57.
3   Ibid., 128–32.
4   Readings taken from Wm. Theodore de Bary, ed., *Sources of Chinese Tradition*, vol. 1 (New York: Columbia University Press, 1960), 484–85.
5   Ibid., 523–24.

Daoist/Taoist
Thought

SEVEN

Daoist/Taoist Thought

WHILE THE FOCUS OF DAOIST THOUGHT is on the term *dao/tao*, the Daoist tradition by no means has a corner on the term. Indeed, Confucius used the term to refer to the way, that is, cultivating the virtues that will lead to the development of the *junzi/chun-tzu*, the superior person. Daoists objected to the Confucian understanding of the *dao* and, in opposition, proposed a more mystical and metaphysical understanding of the concept. For them, the *dao* is the source of all being, a reality that must be understood intuitively so that one can align one's life with the movement of the *dao*.

Like Confucian thought, the tradition of Daoist thought emerged in the tumultuous years of the period of the warring states. Tradition has it that Daoism begins with Laozi/Lao Tzu, supposedly a sixth-century BCE figure, and the text he authored, the *Daodejing/Tao Te Ching*. While that tradition has been questioned by modern scholarship, it is fair to say that the *Daodejing* and the *Zhuangzi/Chuang Tzu* form the basis for the development of philosophical Daoism and have also played a role in the development of religious Daoism.

As the distinction between philosophical and religious Daoism suggests, the tradition is not all of one piece. Rather we have here interacting traditions that have evolved over time in response to developments in Chinese social, political, and religious life. The fundamental texts for philosophical Daoism were written in the period of the warring states in response to issues that also concerned Confucius. Both texts received considerable attention and reinterpretation in Daoist protest movements that developed in response to the chaos and disunity that followed the collapse of the Han dynasty.

Religious Daoism has its origins in the shamanistic and divination practices of early China, and in the concerns for longevity or immortality that
were well established by the time of the late Zhou period. These practices and
concerns came to be associated with Daoist terminology at least as early as
the Han period. The concern for, and interest in, longevity was instrumental in promoting the development of the Chinese alchemical traditions,
both outer and inner alchemy. The second half of the Han period saw the
emergence of messianic Daoist movements promising healing through rituals, and a utopian vision of the future. One of these movements, the Heavenly Masters movement, continues to the present day. The concerns for
longevity and healing coalesced with the belief in a pantheon of popular
deities whose powers were thought to be available through proper rituals and
meditation. The interest in longevity and healing points to the belief that
it is somehow possible to transcend the limitations of the physical body, an
idea that becomes a significant feature of religious Daoism. What makes
these developments Daoist is not only the use of Daoist terminology but also
the claim that these developments owe their inspiration to Laozi and
Zhuangzi.

The Daoist Canon, the *Daozang/Tao Tsang*, emerging over time through
these various strands of Daoism, is vast and complex. Although it was first
organized in the fifth century CE, it continued to grow after this time and now
comprises over one thousand volumes. Regarded as divine revelations to
Daoist adepts, the texts of the canon deal with a variety of subjects, such as
inner and outer alchemy, secret names of gods, talismans and incantations,
rituals, diet, sexual techniques, and breath-yoga. Tucked away in this array
of texts are the *Daodejing*, the *Zhuangzi*, and the Confucian Classic, the *Yijing*.

Daodejing

Traditionally the *Daodejing* (also referred to as the *Laozi*) has been attributed to the sage Laozi, and traditionally Laozi has been seen as an older
contemporary of Confucius. However, the view accepted by most scholars
is that the text is the work of a number of Daoist scholars who lived in the
latter half of the Zhou period, perhaps even after the time of Zhuangzi. The
Daodejing is a short text comprising eighty-one poems, the power of which
lies in their evocative and enigmatic character.

Like the *Analects,* the text is concerned with the creation of a peaceful
harmonious society. The means suggested, however, are quite different from
the means suggested by Confucius. Rather than emphasizing education for
the sake of cultivating virtue, the *Daodejing* emphasizes harmony with the
dao, the primordial principle from which everything issues and to which

everything returns. The *Daodejing* does not reject the Confucian virtues but insists that these arise naturally from harmony with the *dao*. The nature of the *dao* and the means to achieve harmony with the *dao* is the subject matter of the following poems taken from the *Daodejing*.[1]

▼ **DAODEJING**

1   The Tao (Way) that can be told of is not the eternal Tao;
    The name that can be named is not the eternal name.
    The Nameless is the origin of Heaven and Earth;
    The named is the mother of all things.
    Therefore let there always be non-being so we may see their subtlety,
    And let there always be being so we may see their outcome.
    The two are the same,
    But after they are produced, they have different names.
    They both may be called deep and profound [*hsuan*].
    Deeper and more profound,
    The door of all subtleties!

2   When the people of the world all know beauty as beauty,
    There arises the recognition of ugliness.
    When they all know the good as good,
    There arises the recognition of evil.
    Therefore:
    Being and non-being produce each other;
    Difficult and easy complete each other;
    Long and short contrast each other;
    High and low distinguish each other;
    Sound and voice harmonize with each other;
    Front and back follow each other.
    Therefore the sage manages affairs without action [*wu-wei*]
    And spreads doctrines without words.
    All things arise, and he does not turn away from them.
    He produces them, but does not take possession of them.
    He acts, but does not rely on his own ability.
    He accomplishes his task, but does not claim credit for it.
    It is precisely because he does not claim credit that his accomplishment
        remains with him.

3   Do not exalt the worthy, so that the people shall not compete.
    Do not value rare treasures, so that the people shall not steal.
    Do not display objects of desire, so that the people's hearts shall not
        be disturbed.

Therefore in the government of the sage,
He keeps their hearts vacuous [hsu],
Fills their bellies,
Weakens their ambitions,
And strengthens their bones,
He always causes his people to be without knowledge [cunning] or desire,
And the crafty to be afraid to act.
By acting without action, all things will be in order.

4　Tao is empty [like a bowl],
It may be used but its capacity is never exhausted.
It is bottomless, perhaps the ancestor of all things.
It blunts its sharpness,
It unties its tangles.
It softens its light.
It becomes one with the dusty world.
Deep and still, it appears to exist forever.
I do not know whose son it is.
It seems to have existed before the Lord.

6　The spirit of the valley never dies.
It is called the subtle and profound female.
The gate of the subtle and profound female
Is the root of Heaven and Earth.
It is continuous, and seems to be always existing.
Use it and you will never wear it out.

7　Heaven is eternal and Earth everlasting.
They can be eternal and everlasting because they do not exist
　　for themselves,
And for this reason can exist forever.
Therefore the sage places himself in the background, but finds himself
　　in the foreground.
He puts himself away, and yet he always remains.
Is it not because he has no personal interests?
This is the reason why his personal interests are fulfilled.

8　The best [man] is like water.
Water is good; it benefits all things and does not compete with them.
It dwells in [lowly] places that all disdain.
This is why it is so near to Tao.
[The best man] in his dwelling loves the earth.
In his heart, he loves what is profound.

In his associations, he loves humanity.
In his words, he loves faithfulness.
In government, he loves order.
In handling affairs, he loves competence.
In his activities, he loves timeliness.
It is because he does not compete that he is without reproach.

9   To hold and fill to overflowing
          Is not as good as to stop in time.
     Sharpen a sword-edge to its very sharpest,
          And the [edge] will not last long.
     When gold and jade fill your hall,
          You will not be able to keep them.
     To be proud with honor and wealth
          Is to cause one's own downfall.
     Withdraw as soon as your work is done.
     Such is Heaven's Way.

14   We look at it and do not see it;
          Its name is The Invisible.
     We listen to it and do not hear it;
          Its name is The Inaudible.
     We touch it and do not find it;
          Its name is The Subtle [formless].
     These three cannot be further inquired into,
     And hence merge into one.
     Going up high, it is not bright, and coming down low, it is not dark.
     Infinite and boundless, it cannot be given any name;
     It reverts to nothingness.
     This is called shape without shape,
     Form [hsiang] without object.
     It is The Vague and Elusive.
     Meet it and you will not see its head.
     Follow it and you will not see its back.
     Hold on to the Tao of old in order to master the things of the present.
     From this one may know the primeval beginning [of the universe].
     This is called the bond of Tao.

18   When the great Tao declined,
     The doctrines of humanity [Jen] and righteousness [i] arose.
     When knowledge and wisdom appeared, There emerged great hypocrisy.
     When the six family relationships are not in harmony,
     There will be the advocacy of filial piety and deep love to children.

When a country is in disorder,
There will be praise of loyal ministers.

19   Abandon sageliness and discard wisdom;
Then the people will benefit a hundredfold.
Abandon humanity and discard righteousness;
Then the people will return to filial piety and deep love.
Abandon skill and discard profit;
Then there will be no thieves or robbers.
However, these three things are ornament [wen] and not adequate.
Therefore let people hold on to these:
Manifest plainness,
Embrace simplicity,
Reduce selfishness,
Have few desires.

25   There was something undifferentiated and yet complete,
Which existed before heaven and earth.
Soundless and formless, it depends on nothing and does not change.
It operates everywhere and is free from danger.
It may be considered the mother of the universe.
I do not know its name; I call it Tao.
If forced to give it a name, I shall call it Great.
Now being great means functioning everywhere.
Functioning everywhere means far-reaching.
Being far-reaching means returning to the original point.
Therefore Tao is great.
Heaven is great.
Earth is great.
And the king is also great.
There are four great things in the universe, and the king is one of them.

28   He who knows the male [active force] and keeps to the female
        [the passive force or receptive element]
Becomes the ravine of the world.
Being the ravine of the world,
He will never depart from eternal virtue,
But returns to the state of infancy.
He who knows the white [glory] and yet keeps to the black [humility],
Becomes the model for the world.
Being the model for the world,
He will never deviate from eternal virtue,
But returns to the state of the Ultimate of Nonbeing.

He who knows glory but keeps to humility,
Becomes the valley of the world.
Being the valley of the world,
He will be proficient in eternal virtue,
And returns to the state of simplicity [uncarved wood].
When the uncarved wood is broken up, it is turned into concrete things
     [as Tao is transformed into the myriad things].
But when the sage uses it, he becomes the leading official.
Therefore the great ruler does not cut up.

34 The Great Tao flows everywhere.
It may go left or right.
All things depend on it for life, and it does not turn away from them.
It accomplishes its task, but does not claim credit for it.
It clothes and feeds all things but does not claim to be master over them.
Always without desires, it may be called The Small.
All things come to it and it does not master them; it may be called
     The Great.
Therefore [the sage] never strives himself for the great, and thereby
     the great is achieved.

38 The man of superior virtue is not [conscious of] his virtue,
And in this way he really possesses virtue.
The man of inferior virtue never loses [sight of] his virtue,
And in this way he loses his virtue.
The man of superior virtue takes no action, but has no ulterior motive
     to do so.
The man of inferior virtue takes action, and has an ulterior motive
     to do so.
The man of superior humanity takes action, but has no ulterior motive
     to do so.
The man of superior righteousness takes action, and has an ulterior motive
     to do so.
The man of superior propriety takes action,
And when people do not respond to it, he will stretch his arms and
     force it on them.
Therefore, only when Tao is lost does the doctrine of virtue arise.
When virtue is lost, only then does the doctrine of humanity arise.
When humanity is lost, only then does the doctrine of righteousness arise.
When righteousness is lost, only then does the doctrine of propriety arise.
Now, propriety is a superficial expression of loyalty and faithfulness,
     and the beginning of disorder.

Those who are the first to know have the flowers [appearance] of Tao
    but are the beginning of ignorance.
For this reason the great man dwells in the thick [substantial], and does
    not rest with the thin [superficial].
He dwells in the fruit [reality], and does not rest with the flower
    [appearance].
Therefore he rejects the one, and accepts the other.

63 Act without action.
    Do without ado.
    Taste without tasting.
    Whether it is big or small, many or few, repay hatred with virtue.
    Prepare for the difficult while it is still easy.
    Deal with the big while it is still small.
    Difficult undertakings have always started with what is easy,
    And great undertakings have always started with what is small.
    Therefore the sage never strives for the great,
    And thereby the great is achieved.
    He who makes rash promises surely lacks faith.
    He who takes things too easily will surely encounter much difficulty.
    For this reason even the sage regards things as difficult,
    And therefore he encounters no difficulty. ▲

Zhuangzi

As in the case of Laozi, there is considerable controversy about the man and
the work named after him. He is thought to have been a contemporary of
Mencius. The dates given for him are 369 to 286 BCE, but these dates are
not at all certain. Almost nothing is known about the man. Traditionally
the text—the *Zhuangzi*—was thought to have been composed sometime
after the *Daodejing*, but scholars have suggested that the text may predate the
Doadejing.

    Zhuangzi shares with the *Daodejing* the concerns for harmony with the
Dao. He does not, however accept the concern to create an ideal society, a
utopia. Rather, his concern is with the transcendent freedom of the individual and the means to achieve that freedom. Here we are confronted not
with poetry but with stories that have to do with the freedom that arises from
harmony with the *dao*.

▼ **THE GREAT TEACHER** (chap. 6)[2]

He who knows the activities of Nature (*Tien*, Heaven) and the activities of man is perfect. He who knows the activities of Nature lives according to Nature. He who knows the activities of man nourishes what he does not know with what he does know, thus completing his natural span of life and will not die prematurely half of the way. This is knowledge at its supreme greatness.

However, there is some defect here. For knowledge depends on something to be correct, but what it depends on is uncertain and changeable. How do we know that what I call Nature is not really man and what I call man is not really Nature?

Furthermore, there must be the pure man before there can be true knowledge. What is meant by a pure man? The pure man of old did not mind having little, did not brag about accomplishments, and did not scheme about things. If [the opportunity] had gone, he would not regret, and if he was in accord [with his lot in life] he did not feel satisfied with himself. Being of this character, he could scale heights without fear, enter water without getting wet, and go through fire without feeling hot. Such is the knowledge that can at last ascend to Tao.

The pure man of old slept without dreams and awoke without anxiety. He ate without indulging in sweet tastes and breathed deep breaths. The pure man draws breaths from the great depths of his heels, the multitude only from their throats. People defeated [in argument] utter words as if to vomit, and those who indulge in many desires have very little of the secret of Nature.

The pure man of old knew neither to love life nor to hate death. He did not rejoice in birth, nor did he resist death. Without any concern he came and without any concern he went, that was all. He did not forget his beginning nor seek his end. He accepted [his body] with pleasure, and forgetting [life and death], he returned to [the natural state]. He did not violate Tao with his mind, and he did not assist nature with man. This is what is meant by a pure man.

Such being the pure man, his mind is perfectly at ease. His demeanor is natural. His forehead is broad. He is as cold as autumn but as warm as spring. His pleasure and anger are as natural as the four seasons. He is in accord with all things, and no one knows the limit thereof. Therefore the sage, in employing an army, can destroy a country without losing the affection of the people. His benefits may be extended to ten thousand generations without any [partial] love for any man.

Therefore he who takes special delight in understanding things is not a sage. He who shows [special] affection [to anyone] is not a man of humanity (*jen*, love). He who calculates opportunity is not a worthy person. He who does not see through benefits and injuries is not a superior man. He who seeks fame and thus loses his own nature is not learned. And he who loses his own nature and thus misses the true way is not one who can have others do things for him. Such men as Hu Puchieh (who drowned himself rather than accept the throne from Yao), Wu

Kuang (who also drowned himself instead of accepting the throne from T'ang), Po-i and Shu-ch'i (who, as citizens of the Shang, refused to eat the grains of the Chou and chose to starve to death), the viscount of Chi (who pretended to be mad and became a slave because the wicked King Chou did not accept his advice), Hsu Yu (a recluse who painted his body and pretended to be mad), Chi T'o (who drowned himself when he heard that Wu Kuang had declined the throne and King T'ang might offer it to him), and Shen-t'u Ti (of the Shang, who drowned himself), did things as others would have them do, took delight in what others would delight, and did not take delight in what would be delightful to themselves.

The pure man of old was righteous but impartial, and humble but not subservient. He was naturally independent but not obstinate. His humility was manifest but not displayed. Smiling, he seemed to be happy. He acted as if he had to. His countenance improved further and further in richness, and his virtue rested more and more in the [highest good]. His efforts seemed to be those of the common people, but his loftiness could not be restrained. Deep and profound, he seemed to be like a closed door [unfathomable]. Without any attachment, he seemed to have forgotten what he said. He considered law as part of the nature [of government and not of his making], ceremonies as an aid [wanted by people themselves], knowledge as a [product of] time, and virtue as people's observance. To regard law as part of the nature of government means to be broadminded when it comes to killing. To regard ceremonies as an aid to people themselves means that they prevail in the world [like conventions]. To regard knowledge as a product of time means to respond to events as if they had to be. And to regard virtue as people's observance means that it is comparable to the fact that anyone with two feet can climb a hill, but people think that a pure man makes diligent effort to do so. Therefore what he liked was one and what he did not like was also one. That which was one was one and that which was not one was also one. He who regards all things as one is a companion of Nature. He who does not regard all things as one is a companion of man. Neither Nature nor man should overcome the other. This is what is meant by a pure man.

Life and death are due to fate [ming, destiny] and their constant succession like day and night is due to Nature, beyond the interference of man. They are the necessary character of things. There are those who regard Heaven as their father and love it with their whole person. How much more should they love what is more outstanding than Heaven [that is, self-transformation itself]? There are those who regard the ruler as superior to themselves and would sacrifice their lives for him. How much more should they sacrifice for what is more real than the ruler (Nature)?

When the springs are dried up, the fishes crowd together on the land. They moisten each other with the dampness around them and keep one another wet by their spittle. It is better for them to forget each other in rivers and lakes. Rather than praise (sage-emperor) Yao and condemn (wicked king) Chieh, it is better to forget both and to transform their ways [which give rise to conventional standards of right and wrong].

The universe gives me my body so I may be carried, my life so I may toil, my old age so I may repose, and my death so I may rest. To regard life as good is the way to regard death as good. A boat may be hidden in a creek or a mountain in a lake. These may be said to be safe enough. But at midnight a strong man may come and carry it away on his back. An ignorant person does not know that even when the hiding of things, large or small, is perfectly well done, still something will escape you. But if the universe is hidden in the universe itself then there can be no escape from it. This is the great truth of things in general. We possess our body by chance and we are already pleased with it. If our physical bodies went through ten thousand transformations without end, how incomparable would this joy be! Therefore the sage roams freely in the realm in which nothing can escape but all endures. Those who regard dying a premature death, getting old, and the beginning and end of life as equally good are followed by others. How much more is that to which all things belong and on which the whole process of transformation depends (that is, Tao)?

• • •

Tzu-ssu, Tzu-yu, and Tzu-lai were conversing together, saying, "Whoever can make non-being the head, life the backbone, and death the buttocks, and whoever knows that life and death, and existence and non-existence are one, that man shall be our friend." The four looked at each other and smiled, completely understood one another, and thus became friends.

Soon afterward Tzu-yu fell ill and Tzu-ssu went to see him. "Great is the Creator!" said the sick man. "See how he (or it) has made me crumbled up like this!" His back was hunched and his backbone was protruding. His internal organs were on the top of his body. His cheeks were level with his navel. His shoulders were higher than his head. The hair on top of his head pointed up toward the sky. The yin and yang (passive and active cosmic forces) in him were out of order, but his mind was at ease as though nothing had happened. He limped and walked quickly to the well and looked at his reflection, and said, "Alas! The Creator has made me crumbled up like this!"

"Do you dislike it?" asked Tzu-ssu.

"No," said Tzu-yu, "why should I dislike it? Suppose my left arm is transformed into a cock. With it I should herald the dawn. Suppose my right arm is transformed into a sling. With it I should look for a dove to roast. Suppose my buttocks were transformed into wheels and my spirit into a horse. I should mount them. What need do I have for a chariot? When we come, it is because it was the occasion to be born. When we go, it is to follow the natural course of things. Those who are contented and at ease when the occasion comes and live in accord with the course of Nature cannot be affected by sorrow or joy. This is what the ancients called release from bondage. Those who cannot release themselves are so because they are bound by material things. That material things cannot overcome Nature, however, has been a fact from time immemorial. Why, then, should I dislike it?"

Soon afterward Tzu-lai fell ill, was gasping for breath and was about to die. His wife and children surrounded him and wept. Tzu-li went to see him. "Go away," he said. "Don't disturb the transformation that is about to take place." Then, leaning against the door, he continued, "Great is the Creator! What will he make of you now? Where will he take you? Will he make you into a rat's liver? Will he make you into an insect's leg?"

Tzu-lai said, "Wherever a parent tells a son to go, whether east, west, south, or north, he has to obey. The yin and yang are like man's parents. If they pressed me to die and I disobeyed, I would be obstinate. What fault is theirs? For the universe gave me the body so I may be carried, my life so I may toil, my old age so I may repose, and my death so I may rest. Therefore to regard life as good is the way to regard death as good.

"Suppose a master foundryman is casting his metal and the metal leaps up and says, 'I must be made into the best sword (called *mo-yeh*).' The master foundryman would certainly consider the metal as evil. And if simply because I possess a body by chance, I were to say, 'Nothing but a man! Nothing but a man!' the Creator will certainly regard me as evil. If I regard the universe as a great furnace and creation as a master foundryman, why should anywhere I go not be all right! When the body is formed, we sleep. With it visibly there, we wake."

Tzu Sang-hu, Meng Tzu-fan, and Tzu Ch'in-chang were friends. They said to each other, "Who can live together without special effort to live together and help each other without any special effort to help each other? Who can ascend to heaven, roam through the clouds, revolve in the realm of the infinite, live without being aware of it, and pay no attention to death?" The three looked at each other and smiled, completely understood each other, and thus became friends.

After a short while of silence, Tzu Sang-hu died. Before he was buried, Confucius had heard about it and sent (his pupil) Tzu-kung to take part in the funeral. One of the friends was composing a song and the other was playing a lute and they sang in harmony, saying "Alas! Sang-hu. Alas! Sang-hu. You have returned to the true state but we still remain here as men!"

Tzu-kung hurried in and said, "I venture to ask whether it is in accord with the rules of propriety to sing in the presence of a corpse."

The two men looked at each other, laughed, and said, "How does he know the idea of rules of propriety?" Tzu-kung returned and told Confucius, asking him, "What sort of men are those? There is nothing proper in their conduct, and they looked upon their bodies as external to themselves. They approached the corpse and sang without changing the color of countenance. I don't know what to call them. What sort of men are they?"

"They travel in the transcendental world," replied Confucius, "and I travel in the mundane world. There is nothing common between the two worlds, and I sent you there to mourn! How stupid! They are companions of the Creator, and roam in the universe of one and original creative force (*ch'i*). They consider life as a burden like a tumor, and death as the cutting off of an abscess. Such being their views, how do they care about life and death or their beginning and end? To them life is but a temporary existence of various elements in a common body which they borrow. They are unaware of their livers and gall (emotions) and oblivious of their ears and eyes (sensation). They come and go, and begin and end and none will know when all these will stop. Without any attachment, they stroll beyond the dusty world and wander in the original state of having no [unnatural] action (*wu-wei*). How can they take the trouble to observe the rules of propriety of popular society in order to impress the multitude?"

Tsu-kung asked, "If that is the case, which world would you follow?"

"I am Nature's prisoner," said Confucius. "But let me share something with you."

Tzu-kung said, "May I ask which is your world?"

Confucius said, "Fishes attain their full life in water and men attain theirs in the Tao. Those fish which attain a full life in water will be well nourished if a pool is dug for them, and those men who attain a full life in the Tao will achieve calmness of nature through inaction. Therefore it is said, 'Fishes forget each other (are happy and at ease with themselves) in rivers and lakes and men forget each other in the workings of Tao.'" ▲

Religious Daoism

While works such as the *Daodejing* and the *Zhuangzi* are usually referred to as texts of philosophical Daoism, their emphasis on a long and serene life and spiritual freedom was significant in the development of religious Daoism, a tradition made up of a variety of developments. A significant aspect of religious Daoism has been the search for longevity or immortality. Fundamental for this search was the belief that the forces of decay that one normally observes in the body could be stopped and reversed. Among important early thinkers of this development was Ge Hong/Ko Hung (263–343 CE), who articulated the fundamental ideas of religious Daoism: immortality, internal and external alchemy, and merit. The following excerpts[3] from Ge Hong emphasize these ideas.

▼ THE BELIEF IN IMMORTALS

Someone asked: Is it really possible that spiritual beings and immortals (*hsien*) do not die?

Pao-p'u Tzu said: Even if we had the greatest power of vision, we could not see all the things that have corporeal form. Even if we were endowed with the sharpest sense of hearing, we could not hear all the sounds there are. Even if we had the feet of Ta-chang and Hsu-hai [expert runners], what we had already trod upon would not be so much as what we have not. And even if we had the knowledge of [the sages] Yu, I, and Ch'i-hsieh, what we know would not be so much as what we do not know. The myriad things flourish. What is there that could not exist? Why not the immortals, whose accounts fill the historical records? Why should there not be a way to immortality.

Thereupon the questioner laughed heartily and said: Whatever has a beginning necessarily has an end, and whatever lives must eventually die.... I have only heard that some plants dry up and wither before frost, fade in color during the summer, but do not flower, or wither and are stripped of leaves before bearing fruit. But I have never heard of anyone who enjoys a life span of ten thousand years and an everlasting existence without end. Therefore people of antiquity did not aspire to be immortals in their pursuit of knowledge, and did not talk of strange things in their conversations. They cast aside perverse doctrines and adhered to what is natural. They set aside the tortoise and the crane [symbols of immortality] as creatures of a different species, and looked upon life and death as morning and evening....

Pao-p'u answered: ... Life and death, beginning and end, are indeed great laws of the universe. Yet the similarities and differences of things are not uniform. Some are this way and some are that. Tens of thousands of varieties are in constant change and transformation, strange and without definite pattern. Whether things are this way or that, and whether they are regular or irregular in their essential or subsidiary aspects, cannot be reduced to uniformity. There are many who say that whatever has a beginning must have an end. But it is not in accord with the principle [of existence] to muddle things together and try to make them all the same. People say that things are bound to grow in the summer, and yet the shepherd's purse and the water chestnut wilt. People say that plants are bound to wilt in the winter, and yet the bamboo and the cypress flourish. People say that whatever has a beginning will have an end, and yet Heaven and earth are unending. People say that whatever is born will die, and yet the tortoise and the crane live forever. When the yang is at its height, it should be hot, and yet summer is not without cool days. When the yin reaches its limit, it should be cold, and yet even a severe winter is not without brief warm periods....

Among creatures none surpasses man in intelligence. As creatures of such superior nature, men should be equal and uniform. And yet they differ in being virtuous or stupid, in being perverse or upright, in being fair or ugly, tall or short, pure or impure, chaste or lewd, patient or impatient, slow or quick. What they pursue or avoid in their interests and what their eyes and ears desire are as different as Heaven and earth, and as incompatible as ice and coals. Why should you wonder at the fact that immortals are different and do not die like ordinary people?... But people with superficial knowledge are bound by what is ordinary and adhere to what is common. They all say that immortals are not seen in the world, and therefore they say forthwith that there cannot be immortals. [2;1a–4a]

Among men some are wise and some are stupid, but they all know that in their bodies they have a heavenly component (*hun*) and an earthly component (*p'o*) of the soul. If these are partly gone, man becomes sick. If they are completely gone, man dies. If they are partially separated from the body, the occult expert has a means to retain and restrict them. If they are entirely separated, there are principles in the established rites to recall them. These components of the soul as entities are extremely close to us. And yet, although we are born with them and live with them throughout life, we never see or hear them. Should one say that they do not exist simply because we have not seen or heard them? [2:12a]

[From *Pao-p'u Tzu* 2:1a–4a; 12a] ▲

▼ ALCHEMY

The immortals nourish their bodies with drugs and prolong their lives with the application of occult science, so that internal illness shall not arise and external ailment shall not enter. Although they enjoy everlasting existence and do not die, their old bodies do not change. If one knows the way to immortality, it is not to be considered so difficult. [2:3b–4a]

Among the creatures of nature, man is the most intelligent. Therefore those who understand [creation] slightly can employ the myriad things, and those who get to its depth can enjoy [what is called in the *Lao Tzu*] "long life and everlasting existence" [chap. 59]. As we know that the best medicine can prolong life, let us take it to obtain immortality, and as we know that the tortoise and the crane have longevity, let us imitate their activities to increase our span of life.... Those who have obtained Tao are able to lift themselves into the clouds and the heavens above and to dive and swim in the rivers and seas below. [3:1a, 5a]

Pao-p'u Tzu said: I have investigated and read books on the nourishment of human nature and collected formulas for everlasting existence. Those I have perused number thousands of volumes. They all consider cinnabar [after it has been turned into mercury] and gold fluid to be the most important. Thus these two things represent the acme of the way to immortality.... The transformations of the two substances are the more wonderful the more they are heated. Yellow gold does not disintegrate even after having been smelted a hundred times in the fire, and does not rot even if buried in the ground until the end of the world. If these two medicines are eaten, they will strengthen our bodies and therefore enable us not to grow old nor to die. This is of course seeking assistance from external substances to strengthen ourselves. It is like feeding fat to the lamp so it will not die out. If we smear copperas on our feet, they will not deteriorate even if they remain in water. This is to borrow the strength of the copper to protect our flesh. Gold fluid and reconverted cinnabar, however, upon entering our body, permeate our whole system of blood and energy and are not like copperas which helps only the outside. [4:1a–3a]

It is hoped that those who nourish life will learn extensively and comprehend the essential, gather whatever there is to see and choose the best. It is not sufficient to depend on cultivating only one thing. It is also dangerous for people who love life to rely on their own specialty. Those who know the techniques of the *Classic of the Mysterious Lady* and the *Classic of the Plain Lady* [books on sexual regimen no longer extant] will say that only the "art of the chamber" will lead to salvation. Those who understand the method of the breathing exercises will say that only the permeation of the vital power can prolong life. Those who know the method of stretching and bending will say that only physical exercise can prevent old age. And those who know the formulas of herbs will say that only medicine will make life unending. They fail in their pursuit of Tao because they are so onesided. People of superficial knowledge think they have enough when they happen to know of only one way and do not realize that the true seeker will search unceasingly even after he has acquired some good formulas. [6:4a]

[From *Pao-p'u Tzu* 2:3b–4a; 3:1a, 5a; 4:1a–3a; 6:4a] ▲

▼ **THE MERIT SYSTEM**

Furthermore, as Heaven and earth are the greatest of things, it is natural, from the point of view of universal principles, that they have spiritual power. Having spiritual power it is proper that they reward good and punish evil. Nevertheless their expanse is great and their net is wide-meshed. There is not necessarily an immediate response [result] as soon as this net is set in operation. As we glance over Taoist books of discipline, however, all are unanimous in saying that those who seek immortality must set their minds to the accumulation of merits and the accomplishment of good work. Their hearts must be kind to all things. They must treat others as they treat themselves, and extend their humaneness (*jen*) even to insects. They must rejoice in the fortunes of men and pity their suffering, relieve the destitute and save the poor. Their hands must never injure life, and their mouths must never encourage evil. They must consider the success and failure of others as their own. They must not regard themselves highly, nor praise themselves. They must not envy those superior to them, nor flatter dangerous and evil-minded people. In this way they may become virtuous and blessed by Heaven; they may be successful in whatever they do, and may hope to become immortal.

If, on the other hand, they hate good and love evil; if their words do not agree with their thoughts; if they say one thing in people's presence and the opposite behind their backs; if they twist the truth; if they are cruel to subordinates or deceive their superiors; if they betray their task and are ungrateful for kindness received; if they manipulate the law and accept bribes; if they tolerate injustice but suppress justice; if they destroy the public good for their selfish ends; if they punish the innocent, wreck people's homes, pocket their treasures, injure their bodies, or seize their positions; if they overthrow virtuous rulers or massacre those who have surrendered to them; if they slander saints and sages or hurt Taoist priests; if they shoot birds in flight or kill the unborn in womb or egg; if in spring or summer hunts they burn the forests or drive out the game; if they curse spiritual beings; if they teach others to do evil or conceal their good deeds or endanger others for their own security; if they claim the work of others as their own; if they spoil people's happy affairs or take away what others love; if they cause division in people's families or disgrace others in order to win; if they overcharge or underpay; if they set fire or inundate; if they injure people with trickery or coerce the weak; if they repay good with evil; if they take things by force or accumulate wealth through robbery or plunder; if they are unfair or unjust, licentious, indulgent, or perverted; if they oppress orphans or mistreat widows; if they squander inheritance and accept charity; if they cheat or deceive; if they love to gossip about people's private affairs or criticize them for their defects; if they drag Heaven and earth into their affairs and rail at people in order to seek vindication; if they fail to repay debts or play fair in the exchange of goods; if they seek to gratify their desires without end; if they hate and resist the faithful and sincere; if they disobey orders from above or do not respect their teachers; if they ridicule others for doing good; if they destroy people's crops or harm their tools so as to nullify their utility, and do not feed people with clean food; if they cheat in weights and measures; if they mix spurious articles with genuine; if they take dishonorable advantage; if they tempt others to steal; if they meddle in the affairs of others or go beyond their position in life; if they leap over wells or hearths [which provide water and fire for food]; if they sing in the last day of the month [when the end should be sent off with sorrow] or cry in the first day of the month [when the beginning should be welcomed with joy]; if they commit any of these evil deeds; it is a sin.

The Arbiter of Human Destiny will reduce their terms of life by units of three days or three hundred days in proportion to the gravity of the evil. When all days are deducted they will die. Those who have the intention to do evil but have not carried it out will have three-day units taken just as if they had acted with injury to others. If they die before all their evil deeds are punished, their posterity will suffer for them. [6:5b–7a]

Someone asked: Is it true that he who cultivates the way [to become an immortal] should first accomplish good deeds?

Pao-p'u Tzu answered: Yes, it is true. The middle section of the Yu-ch'ien ching says: "The most important thing is to accomplish good works. The next is the removal of faults. For him who cultivates the way, the highest accomplishment of good works is to save people from danger so they may escape from calamity, and to preserve people from sickness so that they may not die unjustly. Those who aspire to be immortals should regard loyalty, filial piety, harmony, obedience, love, and good faith as their essential principles of conduct. If they do not cultivate moral conduct but merely devote themselves to occult science, they will never attain everlasting life. If they do evil, the Arbiter of Human Destiny will take off units of three hundred days from their allotted life if the evil is great, or units of three days if the evil is small. Since [the punishment] depends on the degree of evil, the reduction in the span of life is in some cases great and in other cases small. When a man is endowed with life and given a life span, he has his own definite number of days. If his number is large, the units of three hundred days and of three days are not easily exhausted and therefore he dies later. On the other hand, if one's allotted number is small and the offences are many, then the units are soon exhausted and he dies early."

The book also says: "Those who aspire to be terrestrial immortals should accomplish three hundred good deeds and those who aspire to be celestial immortals should accomplish 1,200. If the 1,199th good deed is followed by an evil one, they will lose all their accumulation and have to start all over. It does not matter whether the good deeds are great or the evil deed is small. Even if they do no evil but talk about their good deeds and demand reward for their charities, they will nullify the goodness of these deeds although the other good deeds are not affected." The book further says: "If good deeds are not sufficiently accumulated, taking the elixir of immortality will be of no help." [3:7b–8a, 10a–b] ▲

The Alchemical Tradition

Interest in the alchemical tradition, particularly inner alchemy, or in Daoist adepts for that matter, is not confined to ancient China nor to the domain of males, as the following treatise indicates. In general, the position of women in classical China was inferior to that of men. After all, the hierarchical structure of Confucian society was patriarchically oriented. Some presentations of the *yin* and the *yang* supported such a structure. The *Book of Changes*, for example, regarded Heaven, represented as *yang*, as superior to earth, represented as *yin*. Nonetheless, the feminine principle and female adepts do play a significant role in the development of China's religious traditions. There is both textual and archeological evidence for the existence of female deities in ancient China. Female deities have played, and continue to play, a significant role in popular religion. More significantly, the Daoist canon includes stories of female adepts, women who were able to transcend societal barriers and to become recognized as sages nd immortals in their own right. For example, Ge Hong's fourth-century *Biographies of Spirit Immortals* includes the story of "The Lady of Great Mystery," who is said to have mastered the secrets of immortality. Sun Buer, a Daoist adept from the twelfth century, composed texts on the techniques of immortality for women. *Spiritual Alchemy for Women*[4] was written in 1899 for Cao Zhenjie in recognition of her great knowledge. As the title of the treatise and the discussion of mediation techniques and energy channels indicate, the alchemy involved belongs to the "inner" alchemical tradition, in effect, a spiritualization of the outer alchemical tradition which emphaizes Daoist yogic techniques designed to nourish and unite the yin and yang in order to nourish the life force within.

▼ SPIRITUAL ALCHEMY FOR WOMEN

In the science and essence of life, men and women are the same—there is no discrimination. In sum, what is important is perfect sincerity and profound single mindedness. An ancient document says, "Only perfect sincerity in the world is capable of ruling." A classic says, "The perfection of single mindedness is that whereby one may heed the order of life."

In general, what is most essential at the beginning of this study is self-refinement. Self-refinement is a matter of mind and breathing resting on each other. This means that the mind rests on the breathing and the breathing rests on the mind.

What is most important in this is harmony. Harmony is in balance, balance is in harmony. Are they one or two? The union of balance and harmony is called the go-between.

With the harmonious attunement of the go-between, there is natural mutual love between mind and breathing; there is mutual attraction, mutual inspiration, mutual expiration. Continuing uninterrupted, do not forget, yet do not force.

Lao-tzu said, "The single-minded energy is most supple, able to be like an infant." This is the perfection of true harmony.

The Master of the Jade Moon, a spiritual alchemist, said, "When husband and wife meet in old age, their feelings are naturally affectionate."

A classic says, "Tie them into one whole, mix them in one place, make them into one piece, force them in one furnace."

The same classic also says, "Cow and bull go together with each other, sun and moon are in the same place; positive and negative charges merge, metal and fire commingle."

The reality behind all these sayings is spirit and energy being together, which means mind and breathing being together.

Spirit is essence, energy is life. That is what is meant by the classic saying, "The root of essence is rooted in mind; the stem of life stems from breathing."

It is necessary to know that creative evolution only takes place when spirit and energy are joined into one. The joining of the two into one is the reversion of the two modes—yin and yang—back into one totality.

This is called the twin cultivation of essence and life.

The twin cultivation of essence and life is a matter of keeping the mind and breathing together, not letting them separate even for a moment.

Therefore, an ancient alchemist said that, "firing the medicine to produce the elixir" means driving the energy by the spirit, thereby attaining the Tao.

In daily practice it is essential to embrace the breathing steadily with the mind and embrace the mind steadily with the breathing. When you have done this for a time, once you reach even balance you naturally become very stable and concentrated. You plunge into a profound trance where there is no sky and no earth, where you forget about everything, including your own body.

This stage is the experience referred to by the classic saying, "Knowing the white, keep the black, and illumination of spirit will come of itself." You seem to feel body and mind revitalized and supple, with unusual buoyancy and well being.

One alchemist said that in this state you are like someone without the power of speech eating honey, unable to tell of its sweetness.

Another alchemist said, "Almost imperceptible, the first transformation of yin and yang—heaven and earth, full of living energy, suddenly revolve. Therein is a bit of fine scenery—how can this work be put into words?"

This time is what is known as "the primordial energy coming from the void of space."

As one alchemist said, "The winter solstice is midnight, where you find the celestial mind has no change, where creative energy first stirs, before myriad things are born."

This is what is referred to in alchemical texts as Living Midnight.

One alchemist said of this, "Gather energy quickly when winter comes."

Another said, "Gathering means gathering without trying to gather, which means splitting open the primordial indefinite."

This "splitting open the primordial indefinite" refers to the time of ultimate emptiness and perfect quietude. To empty oneself to the ultimate extent and preserve quietude to perfection is known as returning to *Earth*, the spiritually receptive mode.

Earth the receptive is associated with the southwest: It is known as "the region where the medicine is produced," "the land of primordial non-differentiation," and "the opening of the Mysterious Female."

An alchemist called seeker of the Fundamental said, "If you want to look for the primordial seed of realization, you must seek out undifferentiated wholeness to set up the foundation."

Understanding Reality, the classic of spiritual alchemy, says, "If you want to attain the immortality of the open spirit, you must set the foundation of the Mysterious Female. Once the foundation is set up, the open spirit does not die. Then how can the person die?"

The aforementioned self-refinement, setting up the foundation, and gathering the great primal medicine, are all the same for men and women. Therefore it is said, "The great Way does not make a distinction between men and women; yin and yang, in their various combinations are all the same." After this I'll talk more about temporal difference.

In his *Secret of Feminine Alchemy*, Liu I-ming says, "There is a true secret about starting practice. The operation is as different for men and women as sky from sea. The principle for men is refinement of energy, the expedient for women is refinement of body."

Men begin practice with the attention in the lower abdomen, just below the navel. Women start work with the attention between the breasts.

Immortal Sister Zhang, one of the great Taoist women, was initiated long ago by Lu Yan, one of the ancestors of spiritual alchemy. Lu told her, "After midnight and before noon, settle the breathing and sit. As the energy passes through the midspine and on through the brain, gaining the power of energy, contemplate the self."

Lu also said, "You must find the ancestor of your own house. Thunder in the earth rumbles, setting in motion rain on the mountain. Wait until washing; and the yellow sprouts emerge form earth. Grab the golden essence of vitality and lock it tightly. Fire metal and wood to produce the dragon and tiger."

In general, it is necessary to refine oneself thoroughly before one will have autonomy. Also one must take the positive energy of heaven and earth day after day, and concentrate to clear the mind hour after hour, before the effects of the practice will be experienced. It may take one or two months, or perhaps three or four months. The length of time depends only on the depth of one's work.

While carrying out the work it may happen that women feel there is energy in the opening between the breasts that thrusts out, divides and goes into the breasts, right through the nipples, which then erect. This is what alchemical classics call the living midnight when the medicine is produced.

One alchemist said, "Suddenly at midnight there is a peal of thunder, and ten thousand doors, a thousand gates, open one after another. If you perceive that there is form within nothingness, I will admit you have seen the original human being in person."

When the work reaches this point, the hundred energy channels in the body are in harmony, while their critical apertures, the passes where energy can accumulate, are all opened. In truth, each pulse fills the chest, all is spring.

Now to explain Lu Yan's initiatory statement to Immortal Sister Zhang. "After midnight and before noon" refers to the fact that the midnight hour is best for finding reality. People who practice quiet sitting usually do it late at night or early in the morning.

To "settle the breathing" means to tune the breath so that it is even. In sitting," two people sit with unified attention placed between them. With mutual concentration, pure attention is embraced. With pure attention in the center, a unified energy flows, thus pressing tightly on the midspine, and going through the brain.

This is what is referred to as the reversal of the Yellow River, meaning the opening of the spiritual energy channel.

"Gaining energy, contemplate the Self." The "self" here is a metaphor for pure positive energy, and the self has been refined into an incorruptible immortal of absolute unity. This is what alchemical classics refer to as absolute unity containing true energy.

"Find the ancestor of your own house" means seeking out the very beginning of the living body receiving energy, finding the primordial point of original generative energy.

"Thunder in the earth rumbles, setting in motion rain on the mountain." This is the same as the saying, "The white clouds pay court to the palace on high, ambrosia pours on the polar mountain.

"Wait until washing, and the yellow sprouts emerge from earth." Waiting means waiting for the right time, washing means washing the mind and refining oneself. This is what is meant by the alchemical term "perfumed steaming." As for "yellow sprouts" yellow is the color of the earth, sprouts are the life potential. Emerging from the earth means that the experience is like when myriad things grow in spring, and the whole earth is renewed.

At this time the positive energy goes all the way to heaven, in the form of a fiercely blazing fire, resembling the flaming wind. Quickly gather it up and send it into the central chamber, in the center of the torso. This is why Yu Lan said, "Grab the golden essence and lock it up tightly."

Another alchemist said, "Hold the golden essence fast, draw it carefully on, send it into the field of elixir."

As for "Fire metal and wood to produce the dragon and tiger," this refers to the perfection of the sense and essence of consciousness, the first sprouting of the Tao.

To sum up, it is just a matter of having people draw their attention to the inner sense of the real mind, carrying the work through the natural cycle. The dragon and tiger mean the ascent and descent of bipolar energy.

If you work diligently, as one alchemist said, "When that one point of energy returns of itself and sinks into the body, it turns into year-round spring. A bit of white cloud brings a waft of fragrance; each time the rain passes, all is refreshed. Unconscious like a drunkard all day long, free and at ease, just keeping 'the spring within the hollow.' When the essence of negativity throughout the body has been stripped away, it turns into a mass of pure positive gold."

The work after this is the same for women as for men. Overall, in the secrets of the spiritual alchemy for women, these words alone should be the quickest route. Lu Yan did not hoard his celestial treasure, but divulged it all at once. It is a pity that people do not recognize it.

Yet it should be realized that expressions such as "below the navel" and "between the breasts" are both representational. Do not look for them as having physical form.

A classic says, "Clinging to this body is not the Way. Shunning this body is also wrong."

It is also said, "The whole body, inside and out, is all dark."

It is also said, "Looking right before your eyes, you don't recognize the real, much less what is important therein."

The developmental process is subtle and necessitates personal transmission and mental reception from a true teacher. Only when you have understood it do you have a place to start.

An alchemist said, "How can the personal transmission be explained on paper? Do not mislead yourself by blind guesswork." ▲

Notes

1 Readings taken from Wing-tsit Chan, *A Source Book in Chinese Philosophy*, (Princeton: Princeton University Press, 1963), 139–44, 146, 148–49, 152, 154, 157, 158, 169.
2 Ibid., pp. 191–94, 196–99.
3 Readings taken from Wm. Theodore de Bary, ed., *Sources of Chinese Tradition*, vol. 1 (New York: Columbia University Press, 1960), pp. 258–64.
4 Thomas Cleary, trans. and ed., *Immortal Sisters: Secrets of Taoist Women* (Boston: Shambhala, 1989), 94–99.

Chinese Communist Thought

EIGHT

Chinese Communist Thought

PERHAPS THE MOST SIGNIFICANT EVENT in modern China, particularly for its ramifications for religious traditions, was the emergence of Mao Zedong/Mao Tse-tung as leader of the Chinese Communist Party and the eventual victory of the Communists in 1949. Given its Marxist underpinnings, the opposition of the Maoist regime to China's ancient traditions is not surprising. Confucianism was attacked as reactionary, Buddhist temples and monasteries were closed, and Daoism was seen largely as superstition. According to Maoist ideology, the need for religions and religious institutions would disappear with the establishment of a utopian society. This, obviously, has not happened: there is no utopian society and religions and their institutions have disappeared. Traditional beliefs based on the concepts of the *dao* and *yin* and *yang* have not died away, nor have Confucian family values. Indeed, in recent years attacks on Confucius and Confucian values have been reversed, and institutionalized Daoism has experienced something of a resurgence. In effect, the Chinese Communist experiment can be read as a failed attempt to replace the old traditions with a new state religion, one that borrowed from tradition while criticizing tradition. The following excerpts point to the persistence of tradition in the thought of Mao himself.

Mao Zedong

It may perhaps seem strange to treat Mao as part of religious development in China. The following excerpts should make clear how this is possible. In Mao Zedong the philosopher, we find a very deliberate attempt to replace the existing ideologies, be they Buddhist, Confucian, Taoist, or Christian, with Marxist-Leninist ideology, which is regarded as the fountainhead of all truth. The overthrow of old authority systems and superstitions is emphasized in the first excerpt,[1] taken from a report written by Mao in 1927 to highlight the revolutionary potential of the peasantry. The second excerpt, written during the Yenan period of the Communist revolution, underlines the necessity of having theory and practice properly balanced. The Party, of course, was to be the arbiter for what was and was not a correct balance. Mao asserted that knowing correctly and changing the world in accordance with correct knowledge would eventually lead to absolute truth, indeed to the liberation of the world from untruth. The similarity to establishing a kind of kingdom of god on earth is unmistakable. The third excerpt includes a poem written by Mao. In his commentary on the poem (minus the references) Jordan Paper makes a compelling case for seeing in the poem the unmistakable expression of Daoist ideals.

▼ OVERTHROWING THE CLAN AUTHORITY OF THE ELDERS AND ANCESTRAL TEMPLES, THE THEOCRATIC AUTHORITY OF THE CITY GODS AND LOCAL DEITIES AND THE MASCULINE AUTHORITY OF THE HUSBANDS

A man in China is usually subject to the domination of three systems of authority: (1) the system of the state (political authority), ranging from the national, provincial, and county government to the township government; (2) the system of the clan (clan authority), ranging from the central and branch ancestral temples to the head of the household; and (3) the system of gods and spirits (theocratic authority), including the system of the nether world ranging from the King of Hell to the city gods and local deities, and that of supernatural being ranging from the Emperor of Heaven to all kinds of gods and spirits. As to women, apart from being dominated by the three systems mentioned above, they are further dominated by men (the authority of the husband). These four kinds of authority— political authority, clan authority, theocratic authority, and the authority of the husband—represent the whole ideology and institution of feudalism and patriarchy, and are the four great cords that have bound the Chinese people and particularly the peasants. We have already seen how the peasants are overthrowing the political authority of the landlords in the countryside. The political authority of the landlords is the backbone of all other systems of authority. Where it has already been overthrown, clan authority, theocratic authority, and the authority of the husband are all beginning to totter. Where the peasant association is powerful, the clan elders and administrators of temple funds no longer dare oppress members of the clan or embezzle the funds. The bad clan elders and administrators have been overthrown as local bullies and bad gentry. No ancestral temple dare any longer, as it used to do, inflict cruel corporal and capital punishments like "beating," "drowning," and "burying alive." The old rule that forbids women and poor people to attend banquets in the ancestral temple has also been broken. On one occasion the women of Paikwo, Hengshan, marched into their ancestral temple, sat down on the seats and ate and drank, while the grand patriarchs could only look on. At another place the poor peasants, not admitted to the banquets in the temples, swarmed in and ate and drank their fill, while the frightened local bullies, bad gentry, and gentlemen in long gowns all took to their heels.

Theocratic authority begins to totter everywhere as the peasant movement develops. In many places the peasant associations have taken over the temples of the gods as their offices. Everywhere they advocate the appropriation of temple properties to maintain peasant schools and to defray association expenses, calling this "public revenue from superstition." Forbidding superstition and smashing idols has become quite the vogue in Liling. In its northern districts the peasants forbade the festival processions in honor of the god of pestilence. There were many idols in the Taoist temple on Fupo hill, Lukow, but they were all piled up in a corner to make room for the district headquarters of the Kuomintang, and no peasant raised any objection. When a death occurs in a family, such practices as sacrifice to the gods, performance of Taoist or Buddhist rites, and offering of sacred lamps are becoming rare. It was Sun Hsiaoshan, the chairman of the peasant association, who proposed all this, so the local Taoist priests bear him quite a grudge. In the Lungfeng Nunnery in the North Third district, the peasants and school teachers chopped up the wooden idols to cook meat. More than thirty idols in the Tungfu Temple in the South district were burnt by the students together with the peasants; only two small idols, generally known as "His Excellency Pao," were rescued by an old peasant who said, "Don't commit a sin!" In places where the power of the peasants is predominant, only the older peasants and the women still believe in gods, while the young and middle-aged peasants no longer do so. Since it is the young and middle-aged peasants who are in control of the peasant association, the movement to overthrow theocratic authority and eradicate superstition is going on everywhere.

As to the authority of the husband, it has always been comparatively weak among the poor peasants, because the poor peasant women, compelled for financial reasons to take more part in manual work than women of the wealthier classes, have obtained more right to speak and more power to make decisions in family affairs. In recent years rural economy has become even more bankrupt and the basic condition for men's domination over women has already been undermined. And now, with the rise of the peasant movement, women in many places have set out immediately to organize the rural women's association; the opportunity has come for them to lift up their heads, and the authority of the husband is tottering more and more every day. In a word, all feudal and patriarchal ideologies and institutions are tottering as the power of the peasants rises. In the present period, however, the peasants' efforts are concentrated on the destruction of the landlords' political authority. Where the political authority of the landlords is already completely destroyed, the peasants are beginning their attacks in the other three spheres, namely, the clan, the gods, and the relationship between men and women. At present, however, such attacks have only just "begun" and there can be no complete overthrow of the three until after the complete victory of the peasants' economic struggle. Hence at present our task is to guide the peasants to wage political struggles with their utmost strength, so that the authority of the landlords may be thoroughly uprooted. An economic struggle should also be started immediately in order that the land problem and other economic problems of the poor peasants can be completely solved.

The abolition of the clan system, of superstitions, and of inequality between men and women will follow as a natural consequence of victory in political and economic struggles. If we crudely and arbitrarily devote excessive efforts to the abolition of such things, we shall give the local bullies and bad gentry a pretext for undermining the peasant movement by raising such slogans of counter-revolutionary propaganda as "The peasant association does not show piety towards ancestors," "The peasant association abuses the gods and destroys religion," and "The peasant association advocates the community of women." Clear proof has been forthcoming recently at both Siangsiang in Hunan and Yangsin in Hupeh, where the landlords were able to take advantage of peasant opposition to the smashing of idols. The idols were set up by the peasants, and in time they will pull them down with their own hands; there is no need for anybody else prematurely to pull down the idols for them. The agitational line of the Communist Party in such matters should be: "Draw the bow to the full without letting go the arrow, and be on the alert." The idols should be removed by the peasants themselves, and the temples for martyred virgins and the arches for chaste and filial widowed daughters-in-law should likewise be demolished by the peasants themselves; it is wrong for anyone else to do these things for them.

In the countryside I, too, agitated among the peasants for abolishing superstitions. What I said was:

"One who believes in the Eight Characters hopes for good luck; one who believes in geomancy hopes for the beneficial influence of the burial ground. This year the local bullies, bad gentry, and corrupt officials all collapsed within a few months. Is it possible that till a few months ago they were all in good luck and all under the beneficial influence of their burial grounds, while in the last few months they have all of a sudden been in bad luck and their burial grounds all ceased to exert any beneficial influence on them?

"The local bullies and bad gentry jeer at your peasant association, and say: 'How strange! It has become a world of committeemen; look, you can't even go to the latrines without meeting one of them!' Quite true, in the towns and in the villages, the trade unions, the peasant association, the Kuomintang, and the Communist Party all have their committee members—it is indeed a world of committeemen. But is this due to the Eight Characters and the burial grounds? What a strange thing! The Eight Characters of all the poor wretches in the countryside have suddenly changed for the better! And their burial grounds have suddenly started to exert a beneficial influence!

"The gods? They may quite deserve our worship. But if we had no peasant association but only the Emperor Kuan and the Goddess of Mercy, could we have knocked down the local bullies and bad gentry? The gods and goddesses are indeed pitiful; worshiped for hundreds of years, they have not knocked down for you a single local bully or a single one of the bad gentry!

"Now you want to have your rent reduced. I would like to ask: How will you go about it? Believe in the gods, or believe in the peasant association?" These words of mine made the peasants roar with laughter. ▲

▼   ON PRACTICE[2]

The Marxists hold that man's social practice alone is the criterion of the truth of his knowledge of the external world. In reality, man's knowledge becomes verified only when, in the process of social practice (in the process of material production, of class struggle, and of scientific experiment), he achieves the anticipated results. If man wants to achieve success in his work, that is, to achieve the anticipated results, he must make his thoughts correspond to the laws of the objective world surrounding him; if they do not correspond, he will fail in practice. If he fails he will derive lessons from his failure, alter his ideas, so as to make them correspond to the laws of the objective world, and thus turn failure into success; this is what is meant by "failure is the mother of success" and "a fall into the pit, a gain in your wit."

The theory of knowledge of dialectical materialism raises practice to the first place, holds that human knowledge cannot be separated the least bit from practice, and repudiates all incorrect theories which deny the importance of practice or separate knowledge from practice. Thus Lenin said, "Practice is higher than (theoretical) knowledge because it has not only the virtue of universality, but also the virtue of immediate reality.

• • •

Apart from their genius, the reason why Marx, Engels, Lenin, and Stalin could work out their theories is mainly their personal participation in the practice of the contemporary class struggle and scientific experimentation; without this no amount of genius could bring success. The saying "a scholar does not step outside his gate, yet knows all the happenings under the sun" was mere empty talk in the technologically undeveloped old times; and although this saying can be realized in the present age of technological development, yet the people with real firsthand knowledge are those engaged in practice, and only when they have obtained "knowledge" through their practice, and when their knowledge, through the medium of writing and technology, reaches the hands of the "scholar" can the "scholar" know indirectly "the happenings under the sun."

If a man wants to know certain things or certain kinds of things directly, it is only through personal participation in the practical struggle to change reality, to change those things or those kinds of things, that he can come into contact with the phenomena of those things or those kinds of things; and it is only during the practical struggle to change reality, in which he personally participates, that he can disclose the essence of those things or those kinds of things and understand them.

• • •

Thus the first step in the process of knowledge is contact with the things of the external world; this belongs to the stage of perception. The second step is a synthesis of the data of perception by making a rearrangement or a reconstruction; this belongs to the stage of conception, judgment, and inference. It is only when the perceptual data are extremely rich (not fragmentary or incomplete) and are in correspondence to reality (not illusory) that we can, on the basis of such data, form valid concepts and carry out correct reasoning.

Here two important points must be emphasized. The first, a point which has been mentioned before, but should be repeated here, is the question of the dependence of rational knowledge upon perceptual knowledge. The person is an idealist who thinks that rational knowledge need not be derived from perceptual knowledge. In the history of philosophy there is the so-called "rationalist" school which admits only the validity of reason, but not the validity of experience, regarding reason alone as reliable and perceptual experience as unreliable; the mistake of this school consists in turning things upside down. The rational is reliable precisely because it has its source in the perceptual, otherwise it would be like water without a source or a tree without roots, something subjective, spontaneous, and unreliable. As to the sequence in the process of knowledge, perceptual experience comes first; we emphasize the significance of social practice in the process of knowledge precisely because social practice alone can give use to man's knowledge and start him on the acquisition of perceptual experience from the objective world surrounding him. For a person who shuts his eyes, stops his ears, and totally cuts himself off from the objective world, there can be no knowledge to speak of. Knowledge starts with experience—this is the materialism of the theory of knowledge.

The second point is that knowledge has yet to be deepened, the perceptual stage of knowledge has yet to be developed to the rational stage—this is the dialectic of the theory of knowledge. It would be a repetition of the mistake of

"empiricism" in history to hold that knowledge can stop at the lower stage of perception and that perceptual knowledge alone is reliable while rational knowledge is not. This theory errs in failing to recognize that, although the data of
perception reflects certain real things of the objective world (I am not speaking
here of idealist empiricism which limits experience to so-called introspection),
yet they are merely fragmentary and superficial, reflecting things incompletely
instead of an essence. To reflect a thing in its totality, to its essence and its inherent laws, it is necessary, through thinking, to build up a system of concepts and
theories by subjecting the abundant perceptual data to a process of remodeling
and reconstructing—discarding the crude and selecting the refined, eliminating
the false and retaining the true, proceeding from one point to another, and going
through the outside into the inside; it is necessary to leap from perceptual knowledge to a rational knowledge. Knowledge which is such a reconstruction does not
become emptier or less reliable; on the contrary, whatever has been scientifically
reconstructed on the basis of practice in the process of knowledge is something
which, as Lenin said, reflects objective things more deeply, more truly, more fully.
As against this, the vulgar plodders, respecting experience yet despising theory,
cannot take a comprehensive view of the entire objective process, lack clear direction and long-range perspective, and are self-complacent with occasional successes
and peephole views. Were those persons to direct a revolution, they would lead
it up a blind alley.

The dialectical-materialist theory of knowledge is that rational knowledge
depends upon perceptual knowledge and perceptual knowledge has yet to be
developed into rational knowledge. Neither "rationalism" nor "empiricism" in philosophy recognizes the historical or dialectical nature of knowledge, and although
each contains an aspect of truth (here I am referring to materialist rationalism and
empiricism, not to idealist rationalism and empiricism), both are erroneous in
the theory of knowledge as a whole. The dialectical-materialist process of knowledge from the perceptual to the rational applies to a minor process of knowledge
(e.g., knowing a single thing or task) as well as to a major one (e.g., knowing a
whole society or a revolution).

But the process of knowledge does not end here. The statement that the
dialectical-materialist process of knowledge stops at rational knowledge, covers
only half the problem. And so far as Marxist philosophy is concerned, it covers only
the half that is not particularly important. What Marxist philosophy regards as the
most important problem does not lie in understanding the laws of the objective
world and thereby becoming capable of explaining it, but in actively changing
the world by applying the knowledge of its objective laws. From the Marxist
viewpoint, theory is important, and its importance is fully shown in Lenin's statement: "Without a revolutionary theory there can be no revolutionary movement." But Marxism emphasizes the importance of theory precisely and only

because it can guide action. If we have a correct theory, but merely prate about it, pigeon-hole it, and do not put it into practice, then that theory, however good, has no significance.

Knowledge starts with practice, reaches the theoretical plane via practice, and then has to return to practice. The active function of knowledge not only manifests itself in the active leap from perceptual knowledge to rational knowledge, but also—and this is the more important—in the leap from rational knowledge to revolutionary practice. The knowledge which enables us to grasp the laws of the world must be redirected to the practice of changing the world, that is, it must again be applied in the practice of production, in the practice of the revolutionary class struggle and revolutionary national struggle, as well as in the practice of scientific experimentation. This is the process of testing and developing theory, the continuation of the whole process of knowledge.

• • •

But generally speaking, whether in the practice of changing nature or of changing society, people's original ideas, theories, plans, or programs are seldom realized without any change whatever. This is because people engaged in changing reality often suffer from many limitations: they are limited not only by the scientific and technological conditions, but also by the degree of development and revelation of the objective process itself (by the *fact* that the aspects and essence of the objective process have not yet been fully disclosed). In such a situation, ideas, theories, plans, or programs are often altered partially and sometimes even wholly along with the discovery of unforeseen circumstances during practice. That is to say, it does happen that the original ideas, theories, plans, or programs fail partially or wholly to correspond to reality and are partially or entirely incorrect. In many instances, failures have to be repeated several times before erroneous knowledge can be rectified and made to correspond to the laws of the objective process, so that subjective things can be transformed into objective things, viz., the anticipated results can be achieved in practice. But in any case, at such a point, the process of man's knowledge of a certain objective process at a certain stage of its development is regarded as completed....

It often happens, however, that ideas lag behind actual events; this is because man's knowledge is limited by a great many social conditions. We oppose the diehards in the revolutionary ranks whose ideas, failing to advance with the changing objective circumstances, manifest themselves historically as "right" opportunism. These people do not see that the struggles arising from contradictions have already pushed the objective process forward, while their knowledge has stopped at the old stage. This characterizes the ideas of all die-hards. With their ideas divorced from social practice, they cannot serve to guide the chariot-wheels of society; they can only trail behind the chariot grumbling that it goes too fast, and endeavor to drag it back and make it go in the opposite direction.

We also oppose the phrase-mongering of the "leftists." Their ideas are ahead of a given stage of development of the objective process: some of them regard their fantasies as truth; others, straining to realize at present an ideal which can only be realized in the future, divorce themselves from the practice of the majority of the people at the moment and from the realities of the day and show themselves as adventurist in their actions. Idealism and mechanistic materialism, opportunism, and adventurism, are all characterized by a breach between the subjective and the objective, by the separation of knowledge from practice. The Marxist-Leninist theory of knowledge, which is distinguished by its emphasis on social practice as the criterion of scientific truth, cannot but resolutely oppose these incorrect ideologies. The Marxist recognizes that in the absolute, total process of the development of the universe, the development of each concrete process is relative; hence, in the great stream of absolute truth, man's knowledge of the concrete process at each given stage of development is only relatively true. The sum total of innumerable relative truths is the absolute truth.

• • •

To discover truth through practice, and through practice to verify and develop truth. To start from perceptual knowledge and actively develop it into rational knowledge, and then, starting from rational knowledge, actively direct revolutionary practice so as to remold the subjective and the objective world. Practice, knowledge, more practice, more knowledge; the cyclical repetition of this pattern to infinity, and with each cycle, the elevation of the content of practice and knowledge to a higher level. Such is the whole of the dialectical materialist theory of knowledge, and such is the dialectical materialist theory of the unity of knowing and doing. ▲

Mao the Poet

The *wenren* (*wen* = person), or literati, the traditional elite, stood between two opposite ideals: *ren* and *ziran*.... *Ren* (etymologically: man and two), usually translated "benevolence," means the ultimate in social responsibility. *Ren* was the ideal of the *rujia* (usually but incorrectly translated as "Confucianism" and *ru* alone as "scholar"), the dominant ideology of state and clan religion combined, as interpreted by Kongfuzi and those who nominally followed him. *Ziran* (literally: "of itself," "spontaneity") expresses both the ideal of nature (as opposed to human artifice) and individuality or personal freedom. *Ziran* is one, if not the basic, tenet of the daojia (usually translated as "Daoism" but nonetheless distinct from *daojiao*—Daoist religious institutions per se—albeit the two are considerably interrelated).

Mao Zedong (Mao Tse-tung) hardly requires an introduction. Although of peasant background, Mao received a traditional education (against his father's will). Even when attending normal school (1913–1918), he received training in classical prose, a skill that he cultivated. Throughout his life, he practised calligraphy and wrote poetry in the classical style. Although it is unlikely he would have used the term to describe himself, he was a *wenren*. In inclination and occupation, he fully maintained the dominant elite ideal, service to others (*ren*): "party" and "people" replacing "clan" and "state" as objects of service.

Among Mao's published poems, one is exceptional in regard to the sentiments expressed. The following translation is overly literal in order to indicate the parallel structure of the middle lines.

▼ ASCENDING MOUNT LU³

Single mountain peak floats beside Great River [Yangtze];
Briskly ascend four hundred verdant switchbacks.
Coldly look toward ocean, see world—
Warm wind blowing rain from sky to river.
Clouds hanging over Nine Tributaries, yellow crane hovers;
Waves descend toward Three Wu, white mist rises.
Magistrate Tao not know what place gone—
Perhaps at Peach Blossom Spring ploughing a field? ▲

The poem is in the Tang (seventh to tenth centuries) eight-line regulated verse form, a highly structured poetic genre, little of which can be indicated in translation. In this genre, the poem is divided into two quatrains with the import of the entire poem in the last couplet. The first quatrain provides the setting; the second, the meaning. The fifth and sixth lines oppose rising and descending.

The "yellow crane" here has two closely related meanings, each well known through a number of poems, including those of China's most famous poet, Li Bo (701–762). In one, Li Bo mentions a Yellow Crane Tower by the Yangtze, a name derived from its primary meaning as a familiar of the *xian* (shaman/Daoist adept). This sense of the "yellow crane" is found in another poem by Li Bo. In turn Li Bo's use of the term derives from the poetry of Ruan Ji (210–63). The Yellow Crane Tower was built to commemorate the place where, according to legend, a person attained *xian*hood, flying off on a yellow crane. Mao referred to the tower in an early (1927) poem, "Tower of the Yellow Crane."

"White mist" has been a variant of "white cloud," a symbol of shamanic ascent, since it is first found in the *Zhuangzi*. From the time of the *Chuci* (fourth-century BCE text), it has come to serve as a poetic (or visual in painting) metaphor for a euphoric state, ranging from the mystic experience to the simple ecstasy of freedom. Although the two lines could be read some-what differently, its meaning is certain when we realize that Bao Zhao (421–465), one of China's most important medieval poets, wrote a poem with the same title which contains the following lines:

> We will mount the road of feathered men
> And merge forever with smoke and mist.

By using Bao Zhao's title, Mao is clearly referring to the older poem, especially the two lines on which he write a variation.

"Magistrate Tao" refers to the famous poet, Tao Qian (Yuanming, 365–427), who is the traditional epitome of a Daoist poet, an individual who rejects the dominant social ideals to live a life of rusticity, nature, and mystic experience. His home was a village at the south foot of Mount Lu. The key word here is *magistrate*, because it is unusual to refer to him in that manner. Tao held that position only once for a brief period, and he gave up the position and refused to hold others. "Peach Blossom Spring" is the title of his well-known allegory which describes the social ideal of the *Zhuangzi*: an isolated egalitarian village where food, shelter, and leisure time are in sufficiency but not excess.

In his poem, Mao is expressing a longing for freedom: freedom from responsibility, from cares, from office. He does so through the traditional mode, through a literary expression of the Daoist ideal. For Mao, Daoism (as a set of *daojia* concepts, not a *daojiao* system of doctrines) meant an alternative to the dominant ideology. This Daoism was understood as an aesthetic sensibility expressed through poetry and painting, as well as a mode of living (retirement).

Notes

1 Readings taken from Wm. Theodore de Bary, ed., *Sources of Chinese Tradition*, vol. 2 (New York: Columbia University Press, 1960), 210–14.
2 Ibid., 243–48.
3 Jordan Paper, *The Spirits Are Drunk* (Albany: State University of New York Press, 1995), 159–62.

Shinto

NINE

Shinto

"SHINTO" MEANS "THE WAY OF THE KAMI" and was coined to differentiate what were thought to be indigenous Japanese beliefs and traditions from foreign imports such as Buddhist and Confucian thought. The term refers to myths, beliefs, and practices which were thought to have their origin in ancient Japan. Central to Shinto is the belief in and worship of the *kami* from whom the life of the universe is said to arise and through whom this life is maintained. The *kami* are recognized through prayer and ritual activity. Through such activity, human beings acknowledge their dependence on the *kami* and ask the *kami* for help, maintenance, and good fortune. The selections that follow are taken from successive periods in the development of Shinto, a development in which we see the emergence of the Sun Goddess as the chief deity, the growing importance of ritual, attempts to purify Shinto, the establishment of Shinto as the national faith, and the eventual disestablishment of Shinto.

The Ancient Mythology

Ancient myths and beliefs were eventually committed to writing, although this happened fairly late in Japanese history. The results were two texts, the *Kojiki* (Record of Ancient Matters), and the *Nihongi/Nihon Shoki* (Chronicles of Japan), both dating from the early eighth century CE. As the titles suggest, these texts are, in part, political and historical documents relating to the early history of Japan, particularly the eventual recognition of the Yamato family or clan as the carrier and preserver of the heritage of the land.

But, they are also repositories of ancient Japanese beliefs, the myths or legends that have to do with the creation of Japan, the role of the *kami* in that process, and the ascendancy of Amaterasu to a position of supremacy among the *kami*. The excerpts[1] also provide us with an insight to the multivalent nature of the term *kami*. While this is usually understood as meaning gods (thus the translation of Shinto as the way of the gods), it has a much broader reference than gods or goddesses with superhuman powers. Divinity is resident in many things including natural phenomena, animals, and human beings.

▼ THE AGE OF THE KAMI

The Five Separate Heavenly Deities Come into Existence

At the time of the beginning of heaven and earth, there came into existence in Takama-no-Para a deity named Ame-No-Mi-Naka-Nusi-No-Kami; next, Taka-Mi-Musubi-No-Kami; next, Kami-Musubi-No-kami. These three deities all came into existence as single deities, and their forms were not visible.

Next, when the land was young, resembling floating oil and drifting like a jellyfish, there sprouted forth something like reed-shoots. From these came into existence the deity Umasi-Asi-Kabi-Piko-Di-No-Kami; next, Ame-No-Toko-Tati-No-Kami. These two deities also came into existence as single deities, and their forms were not visible.

The five deities in the above section are the Separate Heavenly Deities.

The Seven Generations of the Age of the Gods Come into Existence

Next there came into existence the deity Kuni-No-Toko-Tati-No-Kami; next, Toyo-Kumo-No-No-Kami. These two deities also came into existence as single deities, and their forms were not visible.

Next there came into existence the deity named U-Pidi-Ni-No-Kami; next, his spouse Su-Pidi-Ni-No-Kami. Next, Tuno-Gupi-No-Kami; next, his spouse Iku-Gupi-No-Kami. Next, Opo-To-No-Di-No-Kami; next, his spouse Opo-To-No-Be-No-Kami. Next, Omo-Daru-No-Kami; next, his spouse Aya-Kasiko-Ne-No-Kami. Next, Izanagi-No-Kami; next, his spouse Izanami-No-Kami.

The deities in the above section, from Kuni-No-Toko-Tati-No-Kami through Izanami-No-Kami, are called collectively the Seven Generations of the Age of the Gods.

Izanagi and Izanami Are Commanded to Solidify the Land. They Create Onogoro Island

At this time the heavenly deities, all with one command, said to the two deities Izanagi-No-Mikoto and Izanami-No-Mikoto:

"Complete and solidify this drifting land!"

Giving them the Heavenly Jeweled Spear, they entrusted the mission to them.

Thereupon, the two deities stood on the Heavenly Floating Bridge and, lowering the jeweled spear, stirred with it. They stirred the brine with a churning-churning sound, and when they lifted up [the spear] again, the brine dripping down from the tip of the spear piled up and became an island. This was the island Onogoro.

Izanagi and Izanami Marry and Bear Their First Offspring

Descending from the heavens to this island, they erected a heavenly pillar and a spacious palace.

At this time [Izanagi-no-mikoto] asked his spouse Izanami-No-Mikoto, saying:

"How is your body formed?"

She replied saying:

"My body, formed though it be formed, has one place which is formed insufficiently."

Then Izanagi-No-Mikoto said:

"My body, formed though it be formed, has one place which is formed to excess. Therefore, I would like to take that place in my body which is formed to excess and insert it into that place in your body which is formed insufficiently, and [thus] give birth to the land. How would this be?"

Izanami-No-Mikoto replied, saying:

"That will be good."

Then Izanagi-No-Mikoto said:

"Then let us, you and me, walk in a circle around this heavenly pillar and meet and have conjugal intercourse."

After thus agreeing, [Izanagi-no-mikoto] then said:

"You walk around from the right, and I will walk around from the left and meet you."

After having agreed to this, they circled around; then Izanami-No-Mikoto said first:

"*Ana-ni-yasi, how good a lad!*"

Afterwards, Izanagi-No-Mikoto said:

"*Ana-ni-yasi, how good a maiden!*"

After each had finished speaking, [Izanagi-no-mikoto] said to his spouse:

"It is not proper that the woman speak first."

Nevertheless, they commenced procreation and gave birth to a leech-child. They placed this child into a boat made of reeds and floated it away.

Next, they gave birth to the island of Apa. This also is not reckoned as one of their children.

Izanagi and Izanami, Learning the Reason for Their Failure, Repeat the Marriage Ritual

Then the two deities consulted together and said:

"The child which we have just borne is not good. It is best to report [this matter] before the heavenly deities."

Then they ascended together and sought the will of the heavenly deities. The heavenly deities thereupon performed a grand divination and said:

"Because the woman spoke first, [the child] was not good. Descend once more and say it again."

Then they descended again and walked once more in a circle around the heavenly pillar as [they had done] before.

Then Izanagi-No-Mikoto said first:

"Ana-ni-yasi, how good a maiden!"

Afterwards, his spouse Izanami-No-Mikoto said:

"Ana-ni-yasi, how good a lad!"

The story continues with the account of how Izanami died giving birth to fire and descended to the underworld. Her spouse, Izanagi, followed her to the impure underworld, unsuccessfully trying to bring her back to life; this episode is sometimes compared with the Greek story of Orpheus. When Izanagi escaped from the underworld he purified himself, thereby creating many deities, including Ama-Terasu.

Izanagi Entrusts Their Missions to the Three Noble Children

At this time Izanagi-No-Mikoto, rejoicing greatly, said:

"I have borne child after child, and finally in the last bearing I have obtained three noble children."

Then he removed his necklace, shaking the beads on the string so that they jingled, and giving it to Ama-Terasu-Opo-Mi-Kami, he entrusted her with her mission, saying:

"You shall rule Takama-No-Para."

The name of this necklace is Mi-Kura-Tana-No-Kami.

Next he said to Tuku-Yomi-No-Mikoto, entrusting him with his mission:

"You shall rule the realms of the night."

Next he said to Take-Paya-Susa-No-Wo-No-Mikoto, entrusting him with his mission:

"You shall rule the ocean."

Piko-po-no-ninigi-no-mikoto Is Commanded to Descend from the Heavens and Rule the Land. Saruta-biko meets him to serve as his guide

Then Ama-Terasu-Opo-Mi-Kami and Taka-Ki-No-Kami commanded the heir apparent Masa-Katu-A-Katu-Kati-Paya-Pi-Ame-No-Osi-Po-Mimi- No-Mikoto, saying:

"Now it is reported that the pacification of the Central Land of the Reed Plains has been finished. Therefore, descend and rule it, as you have been entrusted with it."

Then the heir apparent Masa-Katu-A-Kati-Paya-Pi-Ame-No-Po-Mimi-No-Mikoto replied, saying:

"As I was preparing to descend, a child was born; his name is Ame-Nigisi-Kuni-Nigisi-Ama-Tu-Piko-Piko-Po-No-Ninigi-No-Mikoto. This child should descend."

This child was born of his union with the daughter of Taka-Ki-No-Kami, Yorodu-Pata-Toyo-Aki-Tu-Si-Pime-No-Mikoto, who bore Ame-No-Po-Akari-No-Mikoto; next, Piko-Po-No-Ninigi-No-Mikoto. (Two deities)

Whereupon, in accordance with his words, they imposed the command upon Piko-Po-No-Ninigi-No-Mikoto:

"Toyo-Asi-Para-No-Midu-Po-No-Kuni has been entrusted to you as the land you are to rule. In accordance with the command, descend from the heavens!"

Then, as Piko-Po-No-Ninigi-No-Mikoto was about to descend from the heavens, there appeared in the myriad heavenly crossroads a deity whose radiance shone above through Takama-No-Para and below through the Central Land of the Reed Plains.

Then Ama-Terasu-Opo-Mi-Kami and Taka-Ki-No-Kami commanded Ame-No-Uzume-No-Kami, saying:

"Although you are a graceful maiden, you are [the type of] deity who can face and overwhelm [others]. Therefore go alone and inquire: 'Who is here on the path of my offspring descending from the heavens?'"

When she inquired, the reply was:

"I am an earthly deity named Saruta-Biko-No-Kami. I have come out because I have heard that the offspring of the heavenly deities is to descend from the heavens, and I have come forth to wait that I might serve as his guide." ▲

Early and Medieval Shinto[2]

The *Nihongi*, although written in the eighth century and therefore belonging to the medieval period, provides a wealth of insight into the early history of Japan and early developments in Shinto. In the first excerpt from the *Nihongi*, we see the establishment of the worship of Kami Omononushi or, the Kami of Yamato, as well as other *kami*, in response to natural calamities and political instability. It would not be amiss to see in this excerpt a rationalization for the ascendancy of the Yamato clan in the religious and political affairs of Japan. In the second excerpt, we see the eventual enshrinement of the Sun Goddess at the Ise shrine. In the remaining excerpts from the *Nihongi* we see an emphasis on the need to continue the worship of the *kami* to maintain harmony in the land. Interestingly, this is put in terms of keeping the *yin* and *yang* forces in harmony, an obvious influence from

Chinese thought traditions. The remaining excerpts from the Nihongi speak to the need for purification. Both veneration of the *kami* and periodic purification become central elements of worship in Shinto.

▼ THE NIHONGI

Enshrinement of the Sun Goddess and the Kami of Yamato

During the reign of the tenth legendary emperor, Sujin, there were many people who wandered away from their homes, and there were also some rebellions. The situation was such that the imperial virtue alone could not control the nation. Therefore, the emperor was penitent from morning till night, asking for divine punishment of the kami of heaven and earth upon himself. Prior to that time the two kami, the Sun Goddess and the Kami of Yamato were worshipped together within the imperial palace. The emperor, however, was afraid of their potencies and did not feel at ease living with them. Therefore, he entrusted Princess Toyosukiiri to worship the Sun Goddess at the village of Kasanui in Yamato, where a sacred shrine was established. Also he commissioned Princess Nunakiiri to worship the Kami of Yamato.

(*Nihongi* [Chronicles of Japan], bk. 5, 6th year)

[Then] the emperor stated, "I did not realize that numerous calamities would take place during our reign. It may be that the lack of good rule might have incurred the wrath of the kami of heaven and earth. It might be well to inquire the cause of the calamities by means of divination." The emperor therefore assembled the eighty myriads of kami and inquired about this matter by means of divination. At that time the kami spoke through the kami-possession of Princess Yamatototohi-momoso, "Why is the emperor worried over the disorder of the nation? Doesn't he know that the order of the nation would be restored if he properly venerated me?" The emperor asked which kami was thus giving such an instruction, and the answer was: "I am the kami who resides within the province of Yamato, and my name is Omononushi-no-kami." Following the divine instruction, the emperor worshiped the kami, but the expected result did not follow. Thus the emperor cleansed himself and fasted as well as purifying the palace, and addressed himself to the kami in prayer, asking, "Is not our worship sufficient? Why is our worship not accepted? May we be further instructed in a dream as the fulfillment of your divine favor toward us."

That night a noble man who called himself Omononushi-no-kami appeared and spoke to the emperor in his dream, "The emperor has no more cause to worry over the unsettled state of the nation. It is my divine wish to be worshiped by my child, Otataneko, and then the nation will be pacified immediately." Upon learning the meaning of the dream, the emperor was greatly delighted and issued a proclamation throughout the country to look for Otataneko, who was subsequently found in the district of Chinu and was presented to the court. Whereupon the emperor asked Otataneko as to whose child he was, and the answer was: "My father's name is the Great Kami Omononushi. My mother's name is Princess Iku-tamayori." The emperor then said, "Now prosperity will come to us." Thus, Otataneko was made the chief priest in charge of the worship of the great Kami Omononushi. After that the emperor consulted divination as to the desirability of worshiping other kami, and found it desirable to do so. Accordingly he paid homage to the eighty myriads of kami. Thereupon the pestilence ceased and peace was restored in the nation, and good crops of the five kinds of grain made the peasantry prosperous.

(Nihongi, 7th year)

The Enshrinement of the Sun Goddess at Ise

[The Eleventh legendary emperor, Suinin,] proclaimed, "Our predecessor (Emperor Sujin), had complete oversight of the government and venerated the heavenly and earthly kami. Moreover, he disciplined himself and lived reverently each day. Therefore, people enjoyed prosperity and the nation was peaceful. And now, during our reign, how can we be negligent of the worship of the heavenly and earthly kami?"

Accordingly, the Sun Goddess, who had been cared for by Princess Toyosuki-iri, was now entrusted to Princess Yamato. Thereupon Princess Yamato visited various places, looking for the permanent settling place of the Sun Goddess, and finally reached the province of Ise. At this time, the Sun Goddess instructed Princess Yamato, saying, "The province of Ise, whose divine wind blows, is washed by successive waves from the Eternal Land. It is a secluded and beautiful place, and I wish to dwell here." Thus, in compliance with the divine instruction, a shrine [which became the most important Shinto shrine] was erected in honor of the Sun Goddess in the province of Ise, and at the same time an Abstinence Palace was established along the river Isuzu where the Sun Goddess originally descended from heaven.

(Nihongi, bk. 6, 35th year)

Prince Shotoku's Proclamation for the Worship of Kami

[In 607 during the reign of Empress Suiko, r. 592–628] the following edict was issued [by the Prince Regent Shotoku, 573–621]: "We are told that our imperial ancestors, in governing the nation, bent humbly under heaven and walked softly on earth. They venerated the kami of heaven and earth, and established shrines on the mountains and by the rivers, whereby they were in constant touch with the power of nature. Hence the winter (yin, negative cosmic force) and summer (yang, positive cosmic force) elements were kept in harmony, and their creative powers blended together. And now during our reign, it would be unthinkable to neglect the veneration of the kami of heaven and earth. May all the ministers from the bottom of their hearts pay homage to the kami of heaven and earth."

(*Nihongi*, bk. 12, 15th year)

The Reform of the Taika (645–650 CE)

[In 645, Emperor Kotoku, r. 645–654] together with the empress dowager and the crown prince summoned all the ministers to gather together under a great plan-era tree, and commanded them to take the following oath: "We solemnly declare to the kami of heaven and earth that heaven covers us and earth upholds us, and that there is only one imperial way. In recent years, however, the principle which regulates the relationship between throne and subjects was violated, so that the guilty subjects had to be eliminated by us with assistance from heaven. Now all of us realize the truth in our hearts to the effect that from this time onward there shall be no administration other than that of the emperor, and that the subjects shall not act contrary to the will of the sovereign. Should we violate this oath, we would invite the heavenly and earthly curse, and would be slain by demons."

(*Nihongi*, bk. 25 Taika, 1st year)

[Two years later, the following edict was issued:] "According to the way of the kami the Sun Goddess commanded her divine descendants to rule the nation. Accordingly, this nation from its inception has been governed by the sovereigns. Indeed from the time of the first august emperor this nation under heaven maintained order and no one questioned it. In recent years, however, the names of the kami and the emperors came to be distorted and are claimed by the clan chieftains and local barons. No wonder the minds of the people lost coherence, and it became difficult to govern the nation. Therefore at this time when we are destined to rule according to the way of the kami, we must first compel the people to realize these things in order to govern properly the nation and the people. Then, we shall issue a series of edicts, one today and another tomorrow."

(*Nihongi*, Taika, 3rd year)

[In the year 650] the governor of the province of Anato presented a white pheasant to the emperor. Whereupon Great Minister Kose offered the following words of salutation: "We, the ministers and functionaires of the government offer our congratulations to Your Majesty. The appearance of a white pheasant in the western province is a sure sign that Your Majesty is ruling the nation with serene virtue. May Your Majesty continue to provide peaceful rule of the four corners [of Japan] for a thousand autumns and ten thousand years. In turn, it is our humble wish to serve Your Majesty with utmost fidelity." Having completed the salutation the Great Minister made repeated obeisances. Then the emperor declared, "We know that heaven gives good omens as a response to the good rule of the sage king. Not only such birds and animals as the phoenix, unicorn, white pheasant, and white crow but also herbs and trees have been chosen by Heaven and Earth as instruments of good omens. One can understand why sage kings have received such favorable omens, but why should we, the unworthy one, merit it? This is due, we are certain, to the work of those who assist us, the ministers, clan chieftains, government officials, and provincial governors, who meticulously abide by the rules and regulations with utmost fidelity. This being so, we trust that all of you, from the ministers down to the functionaries of various offices, venerate the kami of heaven and earth with pure hearts, and endeavor to bring about the prosperity of the nation in response to the good omen."

(*Nihongi*, Hakuchi, 1st year)

Drought and the Great Purification Rite

[In the year 676, during the reign of Emperor Temmu, r. 673–686], a great drought took place. Thus, the imperial emissaries were dispatched in various directions to make offerings and pray to all the kami, and even the Buddhist priests were solicited to pray to the [Buddhas]. But there was still no rain, and the five grains did not grow; thereby the peasantry was starving. The emperor also propitiated the Wind Kami of Tatsuta Shrine and the Great Kami of Abstinence of Hirose Shrine.

Meanwhile a star of seven or eight feet in length appeared in the eastern sky. Then the emperor proclaimed, "Let a great purification rite be held in every section of the land. In each province its governor should provide one horse and one piece of cloth to be used for the ritual. Also the official of each district should supply one sword, one deerskin, one mattock, one small sword, one sickle, one set of arrows, and one sheaf of rice in the ear, whereas each household must offer a bundle of hemp for this purpose." It was further decreed that "all sentences of death, confiscation, and banishment shall be mitigated one degree. Other sentences of minor degree, such as banishing the guilty from one area to another within the same province, whether or not they have been arrested, except these who have already been banished, shall be pardoned." On this day the emperor also commanded that living animals and birds be turned loose.

(*Nihongi*, bk. 29, 5th year)

Gleanings from Ancient Sources

The *Kogo shui* (Gleanings from Ancient Sources), from which the following excerpts are taken, was written in 806–807 by Imbe-no-Hironari. The Imbe clan to which the writer obviously belonged was one of several ancient priestly clans or guilds. While the document contains aspects of the ancient mythology found in the *Kojiki*, it is also a defence of the prerogatives of the priesthood, particularly those of the Imbe clan. In these excerpts we see references not only to the rights and duties of priestly clans, particularly the Nakatomi, Imbe, and Sarume clans, but also to the need for shrines as places where the *kami* could dwell and be venerated. Shrines have historically been the most visible expression of Shinto. As these excerpts indicate, the priesthood was, to a great extent, responsible for the proper veneration of the *kami*.

▼ **SHINTO PRIESTHOOD**

We are told that in old days there was no writing in Japan, whereby everybody, noble and humble, old and young memorized ancient traditions and transmitted them orally from one generation to the next. Since the introduction of the art of writing from China, however, people have become frivolous and do not seem to like to discuss ancient matters. Meanwhile, with the passage of time traditional accounts have undergone certain changes, and very few nowadays seem to be aware of the original accounts. Fortunately, by the imperial command I have been given this opportunity to write down for the benefit of the throne some of the ancient traditions which have been handed down in my family.

(Kogo shui 1:545)

[In the days of the first legendary emperor Jimmu], after the imperial forces conquered their foes throughout the nation, the imperial palace was established at Kashiwara in the province of Yamato. At that time, Prince Ame no Tomi ("heavenly wealth") was commissioned to build the palace, securing timber from the mountains, grounding the palace pillars into the nethermost rock-bottom and raising the palace beams to reach the Plain of High Heaven. Prince Ame no Tomi was also commissioned, with the assistance of the various branches of the Imbe clan, to produce such sacred treasures as mirrors, jewels, spears, shields, cotton and hemp cloths.

(Kogo shui 1:550)

Then, in accordance with the commandment of the two heavenly ancestral kami, [the Kami of High Generative Force and the Sun Goddess], a sacred site was established inside the palace compound for the worship of [various] kami. Prince Hi no Omi, chieftain of the Kume clan, was placed in charge of the palace gates, while Prince Nigihayahi with the members of the Mononobe clan were placed in charge of swords and shields. When all the preparations were done, Prince Ame no Tomi, with the assistance of the members of the Imbe clan, placed the sacred mirror and sacred sword, which are the imperial regalia, in the main hall of the palace, and, after hanging the jewels and presenting offerings, recited the liturgy for bringing good fortune to the imperial palace. It was followed by the solemn service for the guardian kami of the palace gates.

(Kogo shui 1:551)

In those days the distinction between the emperor and the kami was not so sharply made, so that it was taken for granted that they dwell together in the same palace. Also, the properties of the kami and those of the emperor were not differentiated, and both were kept in the sacred treasure house which was kept under the supervision of the Imbe clan. It was by the imperial command that Prince Ame no Tomi and other families under his rule were to make great offerings to the kami, and Prince Ame no Taneko, [the chieftain of the Nakatomi clan], was to conduct the ceremony to cleanse both the heavenly and earthly sins and defilements. Accordingly, a sacred enclosure was built on Mount Tomi, where Prince Ame no Tomi presented offerings and recited sacred liturgy (norito) to thank the heavenly kami for the blessings bestowed on the emperor. From that time onward, it became the hereditary duties of the Nakatomi and the Imbe clans to be in charge of the divine worship, while the Sarume clan was charged with the sacred dance and pantomime. Other clans were also given respective duties in the court.

(Kogo shui 1:551)

During the reign of the [tenth legendary emperor, Sujin, r. 97–33 BC], the sovereign, who was awed by the potency of the kami, did not feel right to dwell with them in the same palace. Thus, he commissioned the Imbe clan to produce the mirror and the sword for his own protection. It is to be noted that the mirror and the sword thus made have been used as the symbol of imperial dignity at the time of the enthronement ever since. At any rate, Emperor Sujin established the sacred site at the village of Kasanui in the province of Yamato in honor of the Sun Goddess and the sacred sword and appointed his daughter, Princess Toyo-suki-iri, to be the chief priestess there. The emperor also established "heavenly" and "earthly" shrines and set aside lands and houses in order to maintain worship of the 800 myriads of kami. The practice of offering portions of what is secured in hunting by men as well as the practice of offering handicraft by women were initiated at this time. This explains why we still use the skins of bear and deer, stags' horns and clothes as offerings in the worship of the kami of heaven and earth.

(Kogo shui 1:55, 1–52)

In the days of the [eleventh legendary emperor, Suinin, r. 29 BC–CE 70] his daughter, Princess Yamato, was appointed to serve as the high priestess of the Sun Goddess. A shrine was established for the Sun Goddess, following her wish, in the province of Ise, and an "abstinence palace" was also built [there] for the dwelling of the imperial high priestess.

(Kogo shui 1:552)

In the days of Emperor [Kotoku, r. 645–654], the chieftain of the Imbe, named Sakashi, was made the chief official governing Shinto priests, and he was put in charge of the census registration of imperial princes and princesses, court rituals, marriage of high government officials, divinations for the throne and the govern-ment. Under his supervision, the summer and winter ceremonies of divination were established in the court. Unfortunately, his descendants were not capable of car-rying on the competent leadership exercised by Sakashi, and thus the prestige of the Imbe family has declined to this day.

(Kogo shui 1:553)

During the reign of Emperor [Temmu, r. 673–686], the hereditary family titles were reclassified into eight ranks, based on the services rendered by those families to the government during his reign, but not based on the services rendered by their ancestors at the time when the grandson of the Sun Goddess descended from heaven. Accordingly, the Nakatomi was given the second highest rank and the sword which signifies this rank, while the Imbe was given only the third rank and a smaller sword which signifies this rank.

(Kogo shui 1:553) ▲

It was in the [early eighth century] that the first record of the kami was established, but it was far from being complete. Besides, ceremonials for the worship of the kami were not very well regulated. Only [in the middle of the eighth century] was a more complete record of the kami compiled. By that time, however, the Nakatomi took advantage of their influence and registered arbitrarily even the remote shrines if they had connections with the Nakatomi, whereas they excluded some of the greater shrines which had no connections with them. Furthermore, let me write down some of the items which also have been overlooked by the authorities. They are as follows:

It is well known that the sacred sword called the "grass mowing sword" is one of the heavenly symbols of the imperial dignity, and that it has supernatural potency. And yet the Atsuta Shrine which is the dwelling place of this sacred sword has not as yet been honored properly by receiving annual offerings from the court.

Veneration of ancestors is supremely important in our proprieties. For this reason the emperor at the occasion of enthronement pays homage to the kami of heaven, mountains, rivers, as well as other kami. Chief among the kami is the Sun Goddess, the ancestress of the imperial clan, whose supremacy over other kami cannot be questioned. It is a regrettable matter that now the offerings of the Min-istry of Shinto Affairs are first offered to other kami before they are presented to the shrine of the Sun Goddess at Ise.

The third matter which must be mentioned is the fact that from the time of the Plain of High Heaven the ancestors of the Nakatomi and the Imbe clans served the Sun Goddess and that the ancestress of the Sarume clan also propiti-ated the Sun Goddess [when the latter hid herself in the heavenly rock-cave]. In other words, the duties of the three clans—the Nakatomi, the Imbe, and the

Sarume—are inseparable. And yet, today the priestly offices of the Ise Shrine are entrusted only to the Nakatomi clan, excluding the Imbe and the Sarume clans.

(*Kogo shui* 1:553)

Similarly, the ceremony for quieting the emperor's spirit was originally performed by the [ancestress of the Sarume clan], and this function should have been inherited by the members of this clan. Nowadays, however, the members of other clans are assigned to perform this rite, which is contrary to time-honored custom.

In accordance with the tradition from the age of kami, the staff of the Ministry of Shinto Affairs ought to include the members of the Nakatomi, the Imbe, the Sarume, the Kagami-tsukuri (mirror makers), the Tamatsukuri (jewel makers), the Tate-nui (shield makers), and other clans. However, today the staff of the ministry include only the members of two or three clans, such as the Nakatomi and the Imbe, while members of other qualified clans are excluded. It is lamentable to see that the descendants of the kami decrease and are doomed to disappear.

(*Kogo shui* 1:554) ▲

The *Engi Shiki* (Institutes of the Engi Period)[3]

The *Engi Shiki* is a collection of books dating from approximately 927 CE. While aspects of the prayers, ceremonies, and festivals found in the *Engi Shiki* no doubt derive from an earlier period, the contents provide an insight into developments in Shinto in the tenth century. By the tenth century, considerable systemization has taken place in Shinto practices. This can be seen is the recording and systematization of festivals and ritual prayers in the following excerpts. Important in the ritual prayer is the reference to the mythology that forms the basis of Shinto.

Classification of Festivals

The great food festival celebrated upon an emperor's succession is regarded as the high grade festival. The middle grade festivals include those of the early spring festival, the monthly service of thanksgiving, the divine testing of the new crop, the harvest festival, and the festival of the kami enshrined at Kamo. [All others, such as] the great abstaining, the service to the kami of the wind, the prayers for freedom from sickness, the festival of the Isakawa Shrine of the Yamato Province, and so on, are regarded as the low-grade festivals.

Regular Festivals

The second month
- Early spring festival: Prayers for harvest are offered to 3,132 kami,

among whom 737 kami are worshiped by the officials of the Ministry of Shinto, while 2,395 kami are worshiped by provincial officials.
- Festival of the thunder kami.
- Festival of the four kami enshrined at Kasuga at Nara.
- The festival of the four kami enshrined at Oharano.

The third month
- Prayers for freedom from sickness [addressed to the kami of the Omiwa Shrine and the kami of the Sai Shrine].

The fourth month
- Festival of the three kami of the Isakawa Shrine [of the Yamato province].
- The great abstaining festival of [the female kami of food of] the Hirose Shrine.
- The festival of the two wind kami of the Tatsuta Shrine [praying for protection of crops from storm].

The sixth month
- Prayers for the health of the emperor [offered daily during the first eight days of the sixth month].
- Service of divination.
- The festival of the gate of the imperial palace.
- The great exorcism of the last day of the sixth month.
- Fire pacifying festival [to prevent fire in the palace].
- Service to the kami of the crossroads [outside the capital].

The ninth month
- The divine tasting of the new crop at the grand shrine of Ise. Veneration of the kami by the high priestess (or female diviner) [at the shrine of the Shinto Ministry]. Veneration of the kami by the priestess [who prays for the protection] of the imperial gates.

The eleventh month
- The festival of the new crop [in which the emperor, together with seventy-one kami enshrined at various places, takes wine and food made from rice].
- Soul-pacifying festival.
- The harvest festival.

The twelfth month
- Service for the (emperor's) soul-pacifying.

▼ **SHINTO RITUAL PRAYERS**

He says [referring to the sovereign, in whose behalf a priest of the Nakatomi clan or a diviner of the Urabe clan recites]:

Hear all of you assembled—imperial and royal princes, nobles and officials.

Hear all of you assembled that on the occasion of the great exorcism of the sixth month of the current year, various offences and defilements incurred by the functionaries of the government offices, including those attendants who wear the scarf, the sash, the quiver and the sword, as well as those attendants of the attendants, will be cleansed and purified. Thus He speaks.

Hear all of you assembled that the ancestral kami of the sovereign dwelling in the Plain of High Heaven commanded the gathering of the 800 myriads of kami for consultation, and then declared, "Our august grandchild is commissioned to rule and pacify the country of the Plentiful Reed Plains of the Fresh Ears of Grain (Japan)." Following this commission, the unruly kami [of the land of Japan] were either pacified or expelled, and even the rocks, trees, and leaves which had formerly spoken were silenced, and thus enabling the august grandchild (Ninigi) to descend from the heavenly rock-seat, dividing the myriad layers of heavenly clouds, and reach the entrusted lands.

Thus pacified, the land became the Great Yamato or the country of the Sun-seen-on-high, where the palace pillars were deeply grounded in the rock below and the palace beams were built to reach the Plain of High Heaven for the dwelling of the august grandchild, who, living in the shadow of heaven and sun, ruled the peaceful nation. With the increase of the descendants of the heavenly kami, however, various offences were committed by them. Among them, the offences of destroying the divisions of the rice fields, covering up the irrigation ditches, opening the irrigation sluices, sowing the seeds over the seeds planted by others, planting pointed rods in the rice fields, flaying living animals or flaying them backwards, emptying excrements in improper areas, and the like, are called the "offences to heaven," whereas the offences of cutting the living or the dead skin, suffering from white leprosy or skin excrescences, violating one's own mother or daughter, step-daughter or mother-in-law, cohabiting with animals, allowing the defilements by creeping insects, the thunder or the birds, killing the animals of others, invoking evils on others by means of witchcraft, and the like, are called the "offences to earth," and are differentiated from the "offences to heaven."

When these offences are committed, the chief of the Nakatomi priestly clan is commanded, in accordance with the ritual performed in the heavenly palace [of the Sun Goddess], to cut off the bottom and the ends of a sacred tree and place them in abundance as offerings on divine seats, and also to cut off the bottom and ends of sacred sedge reeds and slice them into thin pieces, and then to recite the potent words of the heavenly ritual prayers. When this ritual is performed properly, the heavenly kami will hear the words of petition by opening up the heavenly rock door and by dividing the myriad layers of heavenly clouds, while [at the same time] the earthly kami will hear the words of petition by climbing up to the peaks of high and low mountains and by pushing aside the mists of the high and the low mountains.

When the heavenly and the earthly kami thus hear the ritual prayers, all the offences will be gone from the court of the august grandchild as well as from the four quarters of the land under the heaven, just as the winds of morning and evening blow away the morning and evening mists, as the anchored large ship is untied and is pushed out into the ocean, or as the dense bushes are cut off at the bottom by sharp sickles. Indeed, all offences and defilements will be purified and will be carried to the ocean from the peaks of the high and low mountains by the princess whose name is "Descent into the Current," the kami dwelling in the currents of the rapid stream which surges down the hillside.

When the offences are thus taken to the ocean, the princess named "Swift Opening," the kami who lives in the meeting place of eight hundred currents of the brine, will swallow them up.

When the offences are thus swallowed up, the kami who dwells at the breath-blowing-gate called the "Lord Breath-blowing-gate" will blow them away into the nether-world.

When the offences are thus blown away, the princess named "Swift Wanderer," the kami who dwells in the netherworld, will wander away with them and lose them.

And when the offences are thus lost, it is announced that from this day onward there is no offence remaining among the officials of the sovereign's court and in the four quarters of the land under heaven, while the horses with their ears turned toward the Plain of High Heaven stand listening.

Hear all of you assembled that all the offences have been cleansed and purified on the great exorcism celebrated in the dusk on the last day of the sixth month of the current year.

Oh, you diviners of the four provinces, leave here carrying the offences to the great rivers, and cast them away by the rite of purification. Thus he speaks. ▲

Kitabatake Chikafusa (1263–1354)

The Shinto represented by Kitabatake Chikafusa[4] is one of many movements and interpretations that appeared during Japan's medieval period. The following excerpt is taken from *The Records of Legitimate Succession of the Divine Sovereigns*. As the title indicates this was, in part, a political document written at a time when the country was divided between two contending courts. Kitabatake wrote the document to support the claims of the southern court. Aside from this, it is an important theological document providing an interpretation of Shinto in the context of the influence of Confucian and Buddhist thought. While he does not reject foreign ideas and theories (indeed, he incorporates a good deal of Buddhist and Indian thought), he nonetheless attempts to show the superiority and uniqueness of Shinto. In this sense the syncretism represented by Kitabatake represents an interesting counter-point to the syncretism represented by Ryobu or Dual Shinto in which the *kami* were seen as manifest traces of original Buddhist sources or divinities.

▼ The Records of Legitimate Succession of Divine Sovereign

Japan is the divine country. The heavenly ancestor it was who first laid its founda-tions, and the Sun Goddess left her descendants to reign over it forever and ever. This is true only of our country, and nothing similar may be found in foreign lands. That is why it is called the divine country.

The Names of Japan

In the Age of the Gods, Japan was known as the "ever-fruitful land of reed-covered plains and luxuriant rice fields." This name has existed since the creation of heaven and earth. It appeared in the command given by the heavenly ancestor Kunitokotachi to the Male Deity and the Female Deity. Again, when the Great God-dess Amaterasu bequeathed the land to her grandchild, that name was used; it may thus be considered the primal name of Japan. It is also called the country of the great eight islands. This name was given because eight islands were produced when the Male Deity and the Female Deity begot Japan. It is also called Yamato, which is the name of the central part of the eight islands. The eighth offspring of the deities was the god Heavenly-August-Sky-Luxuriant-Dragon-fly-Lord-Youth [and the land he incarnated] was called O-yamato, Luxuriant-Dragon-fly-Island. It is now divided into forty-eight provinces. Besides being the central island, Yam-ato has been the site of the capital through all the ages since Jimmu's conquest of the east. That must be why the other seven islands are called Yamato. The same is true of China, where All-Under-Heaven was at one time called Chou because the dynasty had its origins in the state of Chou, and where All-Within-the-Seas was called Han when the dynasty arose in the territory of Han.

The word Yamato means "footprints on the mountain." Of old, when heaven and earth were divided, the soil was still muddy and not yet dry, and people passing back and forth over the mountains left many footprints; thus it was called Yama-to—"mountain footprint." Some say that in ancient Japanese *to* meant "dwelling" and that because people dwelt in the mountains, the country was known as Yama-to—"mountain dwelling."

In writing the name of the country, the Chinese characters Dai-Nippon and Dai-Wa have both been used. The reason is that, when Chinese writing was intro-duced to this country, the characters for Dai-Nippon were chosen to represent the name of the country, but they were pronounced as "Yamato." This choice may have been guided by the fact that Japan is the Land of the Sun Goddess, or it may have thus been called because it is near the place where the sun rises....

Japan's Position Geographically

According to the Buddhist classics, there is a mountain called Sumeru which is surrounded by seven gold mountains. In between them is the Sea of Fragrant Waters, and beyond the gold mountains stretch four oceans which contain the four continents. Each continent is in turn composed of two smaller sections. The southern continent is called Jambu (it is also known as Jambudvipa, another form of the same name) from the name of the jambu-tree. In the center of the southern continent is a mountain called Anavatapta, at the summit of which is a lake. A jambu-tree grows beside this lake, seven *yojanas* in circumference and one hundred *yojanas* in height. (One *yojana* equals forty *li*; one *li* equals 2,160 feet.) The tallest of these trees grows in the center of the continent, and gives it its name. To the south of Anavatapta are the Himalayas and to the north are the Pamirs. North of the Pamirs is Tartary; south of the Himalayas is India. To the northeast is China, and to the northwest, Persia. The continent of Jambu is seven thousand *yojanas* long and broad; that is, 280,000 *li*. From the eastern sea to the western sea is 90,000 *li*; from the southern sea to the northern sea is also 90,000 *li*. India is in the very center, and is thus the central land of Jambu; its circumference is likewise 90,000 *li*. However big China may seem, when compared with India it is only a remote, minor country. Japan is in the ocean, removed from China. Gomyo Sojo of Nara and Saicho of Hiei designated it as the Middle Country, but should not that name refer to the island of Chamara, which lies between the northern and southern continents? When, in the *Kegon Sutra*, it states that there is a mountain called Kongo [Diamond], it refers to the Kongo Mountain in modern Japan, or so it is believed. Thus, since Japan is a separate continent, distinct from both India and China and lying in a great ocean, it is the country where the divine illustrious imperial line has been transmitted.

Japan's Position Chronologically

The creation of heaven and earth must everywhere have been the same, for it occurred within the same universe, but the Indian, Chinese, and Japanese traditions are each different. According to the Indian version, the beginning of the world is called the "inception of the kalpas." (A kalpa has four stages—growth, settlement, decline, and extinction—each with twenty rises and falls. One rise and fall is called a minor kalpa; twenty minor kaplas constitute a middle kalpa, and four middle kalpas constitute a major kapla.) A heavenly host called "Light-Sound" spread golden clouds in the sky which filled the entire Brahmaloka. Then they caused great rains to fall, which accumulated on the circle of wind to form the circle of water. It expanded and rose to the sky, where a great wind blew from it foam which it cast into the void; this crystallized into the palace of Brahma. The water gradually receding formed the palaces of the realm of desire, Mount Sumeru, the four continents, and the Iron Enclosing Mountain. Thus the countless millions of worlds came into existence at the same time. This was the kalpa of creation. (These countless millions of worlds are called the three-thousand-great-thousand worlds.)

The heavenly host of Light-Sound came down, were born, and lived. This was the kalpa of settlement. During the kalpa of settlement there were twenty rises and falls. In the initial stage, people's bodies shone with a far-reaching effulgence, and they could fly about at will. Joy was their nourishment. No distinction existed between the sexes. Later, sweet water, tasting like cream and honey, sprang from the earth. (It was also called earth-savor.) One sip of it engendered a craving for its taste. Thus were lost the godlike ways, and thus also was the light extinguished, leaving the wide world to darkness. In retribution for the actions of living creatures, black winds blew over the oceans, bearing before them on the waves the sun and the moon, to come to rest half-way up Mount Sumeru, there to shine forth on the four continents under the heavens. From that time on there were the day and the night, the months, and the seasons. Indulgence in the sweet waters caused men's faces to grow pale and thin. Then the sweet waters vanished, and vegetable food (also called earth-rind) appeared, which all creatures ate. Then the vegetable food also vanished, and wild rice of multiple tastes was provided them. Cut in the morning, it ripened by evening. The eating of the rice left dregs in the body, and thus the two orifices were created. Male and female came to differ, and this led to sexual desire. They called each other husband and wife, built houses, and lived together. Beings from the Light-Sound Heaven who were later to be born entered women's wombs, and once born became living creatures.

Later, the wild rice ceased to grow, to the dismay of all creatures. They divided the land and planted cereals, which they made their food. Then there were those who stole other people's crops, and fighting ensued. As there was no one to decide such cases, men got together and established a Judge-King whom they called kshatriya (which means landowner). The first king bore the title of People's Lord [*Minshu*]. He enjoyed the love and respect of the people because he ruled the country with laws which embodied the ten virtues. The realm of Jambu was prosperous and peaceful with no sickness or extremes of cold or heat. Men lived so long that their years were almost without number. Successive descendants of People's Lord ruled the land for many years, but as the good laws gradually fell into abeyance, the life-span decreased until it was only 84,000 years. People were eighty feet tall. During this period there was a king, the wheels of whose chariot rolled everywhere without hindrance. First the precious Golden Wheel came down from heaven and appeared before the king. Whenever the king went abroad, the wheel rolled ahead of him, and the lesser rulers evinced their welcome and homage. No one dared do otherwise. He reigned over the four continents and enjoyed all treasures—elephants, horses, pearls, women, lay-Buddhists, and military heroes. He who is possessed of these Seven Treasures is called a Sovereign of the

Golden Wheel. There followed in succession [sovereigns of] Silver, Copper, and Iron Wheels. Because of the inequality of their merits, the rewards also gradually diminished. The life-span also decreased by one year each century, and human stature was similarly reduced by one foot a century. It was when the life-span had dropped to 120 years that Shakya Buddha appeared. (Some authorities say that it was when the life-span was 100 years. Before him three Buddhas had appeared.)

When the life-span has been reduced to a bare ten years, the so-called Three Disasters will ensue, and the human species will disappear almost entirely, leaving a mere 10,000 people. These people will practice good deeds, and the life-span will then increase and the rewards improve. By the time that a life-span of 20,000 years is reached, a King of the Iron Wheel will appear and rule over the southern continent. When the lifespan reaches 40,000 years, a King of the Copper Wheel will appear and rule over the eastern and southern continents. When the life-span reaches 60,000 years, a King of the Silver Wheel will appear and rule over three continents, the eastern, western, and southern. When the lifespan reaches 84,000 years, a King of the Golden Wheel will appear and rule over all four continents. The rewards in his reign will be those mentioned above. In his time a decline will again set in, followed by the appearance of Maitreya Buddha. There are then to follow eighteen other rises and falls....

In China, nothing positive is stated concerning the creation of the world even though China is a country which accords special importance to the keeping of records. In the Confucian books nothing antedates King Fu-hsi. In other works they speak of heaven, earth, and man as having begun in an unformed, undivided state, much as in the accounts of our Age of the Gods. There is also the legend of King P'an-ku, whose eyes were said to have turned into the sun and the moon, and whose hair turned into grasses and trees. There were afterwards sovereigns of Heaven, sovereigns of Earth, and sovereigns of Man, and the Five Dragons, followed by many kings over a period of 10,000 years.

The beginnings of Japan in some ways resemble the Indian descriptions, telling as it does of the world's creation from the seed of the heavenly gods. However, whereas in our country the succession to the throne has followed a single undeviating line since the first divine ancestor, nothing of the kind has existed in India. After their first ruler, King People's Lord, had been chosen and raised to power by the populace, his dynasty succeeded, but in later times most of his descendants perished, and men of inferior genealogy who had powerful forces became the rulers, some of them even controlling the whole of India. China is also a country of notorious disorders. Even in ancient times, when life was simple and conduct was proper, the throne was offered to wise men, and no single lineage was established. Later, in times of disorder, men fought for control of the country. Thus some of the rulers rose from the ranks of the plebeians, and there were even some of barbarian origin who usurped power. Or, some families after generations of service as ministers surpassed their princes and eventually supplanted them. There have already been thirty-six changes of dynasty since Fu-hsi, and unspeakable disorders have occurred.

Only in our country has the succession remained inviolate, from the beginning of heaven and earth to the present. It has been maintained within a single lineage, and even when, as inevitably has happened, the succession has been transmitted collaterally, it has returned to the true line. This is due to the ever-renewed Divine Oath, and makes Japan unlike all other countries.

It is true that the Way of the Gods should not be revealed without circumspection, but it may happen that ignorance of the origins of things may result in disorder. In order to prevent that disaster, I have recorded something of the facts, confining myself to a description of how the succession has legitimately been transmitted from the Age of the Gods. I have not included information known to everyone. I have given the book the title of *The Records of the Legitimate Succession of the Divine Sovereigns.* ▲

Shinto Resurgence[5]

In Kitabatake's thought we see articulated the view that Japan is unlike other countries in that it is based on an unbroken lineage established by Amaterasu. What makes the state strong is its adherence to the principles of Shinto. The idea that Shinto is fundamental to good government and that it should be the foundation of the Japanese state grows in significance from the fifteenth century to the establishment of Shinto as the state religion in the nineteenth century. This period has often been referred to as the period of the revival of Shinto. In the excerpts that follow we see a gradual shift from the assimilation of Buddhist and Confucian ideas with Shinto to the outright rejection of any dependence on imported traditions.

Ichijo Kanera (1402–1481)

In this excerpt from Ichijo we see an emphasis on the foundations of good government. As did Kitabatake, Ichijo asserted that this foundation must be Shinto. This meant, of course, Shinto as understood and interpreted by him. In his first principle, the veneration of the *kami*, we see not only the assertion that Japan's foundation is based on the activities of the *kami* but also an emphasis on the importance of the shrine and the activities of the priesthood. The principles also include respect for the law of the Buddha (but not to the detriment of acting on behalf of one's subjects) and the importance of virtues such as integrity, justice, dignity, honesty, and loyalty. The emphasis on virtue must surely be informed by his knowledge of Confucian thought. In articulating the principle for good rule, Ichijo shows himself to be knowledgeable about Shinto, Buddhist, and Confucian thought.

▼ **Main Outlines of the Shodan Jiyo (Principles of Good Rule)**

[First] is the importance of venerating the kami. Our nation is a divine nation. After the separation of heaven and earth, the seven generations of the heavenly kami, followed by the five generations of earthly kami, initiated all the activities on earth. The sovereigns as well as their subjects, both noble and humble, are all descendants of the kami. The fact that the Ministry of Shinto Affairs was considered the first in importance among the one hundred offices of the government, and that the activities of the government begin each year with the repair of Shinto shrines and celebration of worship services, indicates the extent to which the kami are venerated. For instance, on the occasion of the New Year festival, which is celebrated on the fourth of the second month of each year, offerings are presented to the 3,132 kami in order to avoid calamities and to pray for good harvest for the year. There are other important festivals for which the imperial emissaries present offerings to the kami. These festivals are celebrated by the court, not for the benefit of the sovereigns themselves but for all their subjects. Since the kami do not accept unworthy worship, the emperor being the master of one hundred kami takes supreme charge of all the worship of the kami of the nation. There are, of course, some shrines for which provincial and local officials are in charge, and there are also certain kami who favor the worship offered by their descendants, such as the kami of Iwashimizu Hachiman who are worshiped by the members of the Minamoto family, the kami of the Kasuga Shrine by the Fujiwara, and the kami of the Kitano Shrine by the Sugawara family. In addition, there are the eight shrines which enshrine the spirits of those who for political reasons or otherwise have died unnatural deaths. They were not the kami who descended from heaven, but in order to prevent them from haunting the people their descendants were given government ranks and have been entrusted with the worship of these shrines. As to the repair of the shrines, there should be no negligence. While the Grand Shrine of Ise alone has been designated to be rebuilt in every twenty-first year, other shrines should be repaired according to their needs from time to time. Unfortunately, for the past ten-odd years due to the disorder of the nation many shrines have become dilapidated and the worship of the kami has been neglected. [Under these circumstances,] it is useless for the officials to offer prayers privately. Rather, they should repair the shrines and diligently attend to the worship of the kami. If they do so with pure heart, the kami are bound to impart blessings.

[Second] is the importance of respecting the Law of the Buddha, because the law of the sovereign, and also the teaching of the Buddha is the same as the teaching of the Chinese classics. As far as Buddhism is concerned, it was originally the one teaching of the Buddha but came to be divided into the eight sects. It must be noted that only in Japan have these eight traditions of Buddhism been preserved intact. Thus, [those who rule the nation] ought to be concerned with the preservation of all eight traditions. Which tradition is to be adhered to depends on the destiny and sentiment of different persons. More important than following the Buddhist discipline is for the emperor to be benevolent to the people and to restore the dignity of the imperial court, and for the shogun (generalissimo, commanding general) to be concerned with the arts of the warrior and to eliminate the anxieties on the part of the people. It would be a mistake for the emperor and the shogun to be excessively devout to Buddhism at the expense of their more important duties. It is well known that the merciful bodhisattva made a vow to accept the suffering of the people on their behalf. It would be difficult for the rulers of the nation—to do exactly what the bodhisattva vowed to do, but to be diligent day and night in governing the nation is just as significant as the bodhisattva's act of vowing to accept the sufferings of all creatures or as benevolent as the way of the ancient Chinese sage kings. Even if a ruler should build a temple and give a feast to the monks, if they should be motivated from impure desire and involve hardships of the populace, such acts might bring worldly fame but would not become the good seed for enlightenment. It is well to remember that a poor woman's offering of a single lantern is more meritorious than a millionaire's offering of one thousand lanterns. As to the priests, their desire to spread their own sect is understandable. But, should they persuade the ignorant men and women and develop partisanship, perform sorcery, and disturb the daily activities of the people, they should be considered devils in the eyes of the Law of the Buddha and enemies to the law of the sovereign, and thus should be reprimanded strictly according to the rule [of the shogun]. One should never forget that the prosperity of various Buddhist sects today owes much to the hidden virtues of various prelates of old days, who considered it the blessing of Buddha as much as the sovereign to be permitted to renounce the world and enter the priesthood.

[Third] is the principle of integrity for the position of constable. The position of constable was established [in 1185 by Minamoto Yoritomo, the founder of the Kamakura Shogunate], as the military governor, which in effect was the deputy of the shogunate in various provinces. From then till now there have been some constables who have abided by the law, never indulging in activities other than those which are their duties, loyal to their masters and benevolent to the people, and known for their integrity and virtues. Unfortunately, today it is a common practice for them to ignore the will of their superiors, fail to appreciate the wisdom of their subordinates, steal other people's territories by force, and accumulate wealth according to their selfish desires. In so doing, they invite the criticism and enmity of others. One can understand the constables' desire to have a large number of retainers, but they often pay inordinate amounts to persons [who in turn have no sense of integrity]. Such retainers stick to their master only so long as it is profitable for them to do so, but desert their master when he really needs them. Every person would like to have both fame and profit, but be it remembered that profit lasts only for a short period of time while fame is a

matter to be counted for generations to come. A real warrior is willing to die to preserve his fame, whereas one who risks a bad name would consider riches more precious than his own life. We learn from the priest Jichin that everything we do must
be based on reasonableness. Being ordinary mortals everyone fails to follow reasonableness at one time or another, but those who refuse to correct their mistakes
and shortcomings are doomed to invite great misfortune for themselves.

[Fourth] is the principle of selecting just persons for the position of the magistrate.

[Fifth] is the principle of selecting the right personal attendants with such qualities as honesty, loyalty, selfishness, courage, learning, and willingness to risk
their lives to remonstrate with their master over his mistakes.

[Last] is the principle of dignity and power needed for the ruler of the nation.
[That is to say, a person with real dignity and power is sensitive to reasonableness
and does not demonstrate his influence by force.] His influence should be felt naturally by people around him and eventually spread to distant places. A ruler with
dignity and power should not neglect small things, otherwise he would not
accomplish great things. Above all, he should follow the way of humaneness.

> (*Shinko gunsho ruiju* [Classified collection of Japanese
> classics, newly edited edition], 21:36–45)

Kumazawa Banzan (1619–1691)

Kumazawa Banzan was a samurai reformer who emphasized self-understand-
ing and self-discipline. His education, as the following excerpt indicates,
was a thoroughly Confucian one. As a self-confessing Confucian he emphasized individual merit as opposed to hereditary privilege. Such emphases
were seen with alarm, and as a result he was attacked by the conservatives
of his day. His ideas and example, particularly his emphasis on self-discipline,
became an inspiration for the leaders of the Meiji Restoration in 1868. In
the following excerpt, he refers to himself as a Confucian and shows himself to be keenly aware of the influence of Buddhism in Japan. Of interest is
not only his interweaving of Shinto and Confucian ideas but also his criticism of Buddhism and its negative influence on Japan's rulers and proper
rule.

▼ SELECTIONS FROM THE COLLECTION OF LETTERS

Question: I think you are right in stating that it is senseless to criticize Buddhism, and that one should rather endeavor to [cultivate] one's own virtues. [If we
should follow your principle,] there may not be any rivalry, but might it not result
in the danger [or crime] of asserting the fundamental unity of the three teachings
(Confucianism, Buddhism, and Shinto)?

Answer: I do not understand how one can talk falsely about the unity when there is no unity [among the three teachings]. Besides, unity is usually followed by disunity. Even within Buddhism there are quarrels based on different views. [On the other hand,] if each other's differences are kept so as to avoid quarrels, there will be no problem. [After all,] Buddhists are children of Heaven and Earth. We [Confucianists] are also children of Heaven and Earth. All persons are in this sense brothers, only divided according to their views and professions. If one stresses the view of Confucianism, the other would stress the view of Buddhism, and there will be debates [as to which one is right and which one is wrong.] However, if our association is based solely on our [basic] brotherly [love], there will be no room for quarrels.

(*Shugi washo* [Collected essays on private matters], chap. 1, 18)

Question: I understand that worship is to be performed by persons of appropriate status, [so that in China] the Son of Heaven offers worship to heaven and earth, the three lights (sun, moon, and stars), and famous mountains and great rivers of the empire, the feudal lords offer worship to famous mountains and great rivers of the state, and the descendants of the sages and worthies are entrusted with the worship of their ancestors. In other words, there are ranks of high officials, knights, and common people. Why, then, in Japan do people regardless of their differences in status and sex pay homage to the Sun Goddess, who should properly be worshiped only by the emperor and not even by the feudal lords. I fail to understand how people, noble [and humble] as well as old [and young], follow such improper practices.

Answer: As you rightly point out, in China only those who have acquired propriety offer worship; otherwise, worship might be polluted by selfish desires and also by evil magic. Furthermore, it is believed that it is senseless for people to offer prayers if they had sinned against Heaven. Thus, the Chinese hold that one has to be emancipated from the illusion of serving parents [merely as human parents] and that one should consider parents as nothing but noble deities. It follows, then, that men being the children of the deities house the deities in their own bodies, and that they share the same spirit with heavenly deities. And, inasmuch as the virtues of heavenly deities are humanity, righteousness, propriety, and wisdom, they are expected to serve heaven with propriety in order to receive blessings. If they act against the way of heaven, they will have misfortunes.

Japan, on the other hand, is the nation of the kami. While ancient Japan might have not attained propriety, it was permeated by the influence and virtues of the kami, so that people did not do evil deeds because they felt as if the kami were present [in this world]. When they paid homage to the kami, their selfish desires disappeared [and they became free from] evil magic. In so doing, they acted according to the way of Heaven, being filial to parents and loyal to the lords. However, the difference between China and Japan is based on the differences of time and place. For example, nowadays the sovereign [cannot be approached directly by the lowly populace]. But Emperor Yao provided a drum [in front of the palace] and declared that if farmers, artisans, or merchants wished to speak directly to him they should strike the drum and the emperor would come out to listen to them. Thus, people were made to feel as if they were speaking to their own parents. In the days when the Sun Goddess ruled, she being full of divine virtues treated the nation as her child, and like Yao and Shun she was close to the lowly populace. It is due to her legacy, which was intended to remain as an example to later generations, that her palace with thatched roof has been preserved [at the Grand Shrine of Ise]. Moreover, now that she has moved up to the divine status, [she is free to live among common people], so that anybody can approach her. In other words, the Sun Goddess, not only during the time of her direct reign but also [until ten thousand ages to come] continues to dispense bright virtues as the sun and moon illuminate the world. When one pays homage to her, or even when one recalls her like a saintly teacher, one receives divine assistance abundantly.

(Shu-gi washo, vol. 2, 38)

Question: According to an old saying, the law of the sovereign and the Law of the Buddha resemble the two wheels of the same chariot. If this were so, was Japan before the introduction of the Law of the Buddha like a one-wheeled chariot, only with the law of the sovereign?

Answer: What was known as the way of the kami during the divine age and what is called the way of the true king are one and the same in substance. Now, as to the analogy of the two wheels, it referred to the civil (literary) and military (defense) arts of the great way which is the principle of ruling the world. Before the wheel of the Law of the Buddha existed, in the age of the heavenly and earthly kami and in the age of the early human sovereigns, the great way was followed whereby people were blessed with good rule. After the expansion of the Law of the Buddha, the sovereign neglected the wheel of the military arts in favor of Buddhism, so that the way of the true king declined because of the loss of the virtues of wisdom, humaneness, and courage. And, since there cannot be true civil arts without the military arts, the imperial house lost the rule of the nation. Then, the military families, [which took over the rule of the nation,] neglected the wheel of the civil arts in favor of Buddhism, so that the way of the true king declined because of the loss of the virtues of wisdom, humaneness, and courage. And, since there cannot be true civil arts without the military arts, the imperial house lost the rule of the nation. Then, the military families, [which took over the rule of the nation,] neglected the wheel of the civil arts in favor of Buddhism. But, since the military without the civil arts is the way of a barbarian and not of the superior man, the rule by the military families was bound to be defective. Some say that the Law of Buddha, being the way of ascetics, transcends others. If it were so, it should stay above Shinto, the way of the kami, and [Confucianism], the way of man, instead of posing itself as one of the two wheels, [the other being either Shinto or Confucianism].

(*Shugigaisho* [Collected essays on public matters], chap. 1)

Question: I fail to understand why the Grand Shrine of Ise despises Buddhism and does not allow Buddhist monks to enter its sacred compound. The Sun Goddess, being the kami long before the establishment of Buddhism, had no reason to despise it.

Answer: You must be aware of the fact that the imperial court is called the "forbidden territory," which implies a place where persons of [questionable character] are not allowed to enter. The Grand Shrine of Ise, [being more strict than the imperial court,] should not allow not only Buddhist priests but all persons of [questionable character], as it was the case with the imperial court. Later, when some of the emperors became enamored with Buddhism, Buddhist clerics were allowed to enter the imperial court. However, the old rule has been preserved at Ise until the present time. In this connection, I might mention that according to the divine oracle given to Princess Yamato, the Sun Goddess made it very clear that she rejected Buddhism on the ground that it would harm the way of the kami and ruin the way of the true king. Upon learning his account, any one born in Japan, even if he happens to be lured into Buddhism through temporary delusion, ought to repent. On the other hand, we must recognize the fact that many persons have gone into the Buddhist priesthood for economic reasons. Thus, unless the great way is put into effect and rectifies [the present lamentable situation], even [those Buddhist priests] who are inwardly unhappy cannot do anything else.

(*Shugigaisho*, chap. 2) ▲

Motoori Norinaga (1730–1801)

Motoori Norinaga is known as one of the leaders of the Shinto Revival, along with Kamo Mabuchi (1697–1769) and Hirata Atsutane (1776–1843). In Motoori we see an outright assertion of the superiority of Japan as the only place in which the true way has been transmitted. In his works he repudiates any dependence on foreign traditions. Foreign countries may have had the truth at one time, but this has since been lost. In the interests of promoting pure Shinto, he published a critical edition of the *Kojiki*, reviving an interest in the text through his work. In the excerpts that follow we see an obvious emphasis on the mythology of the *Kojiki*, particularly the assertion of the superiority of the Sun Goddess as a universal deity.

▼ SUMMARY OF THE TAMAKUSHIGE (JEWELED COMB BOX)

In this world there is only one true way [for man to live], and as such it knows, in principle, no national boundaries. In reality, however, this true way has been correctly transmitted only in Japan whereas it has been lost since ancient times in foreign countries. To be sure, in other countries various ways have been advocated, each claiming to be the true way. But these are branch ways, so to speak, and not the main correct way. Such branch ways may here and there resemble the true way, [but they cannot be confused with the true way].

In order to consider the one true way, we must first understand the [underlying] principle of the total structure of this world. That is to say, everything in this cosmos as well as all the deities were produced by the creative spirit of the two kami, namely, the Kami of High Generative Force and the Kami of Divine Generative Force. Without such divine creative spirit the development of the human race and the growth of other creatures would not have been possible. Needless to say, it was due to this divine creative spirit that Izanagi and Izanami were able to produce lands, animate, and inanimate beings and kami at the beginning of the divine age. The operation of the creative spirit is so mysterious that it is beyond human comprehension. But, because the correct truth has not been transmitted there, people in some foreign countries have attempted to explain the principles of heaven and earth and myriad other things in terms of yin (negative cosmic force) and yang (positive cosmic force), the Eight Trigrams, and the Five Elements. But such explanations are false views based on speculations of human knowledge, and as such are contrary to the correct principle.

(*Motoori Norinaga zenshu* [Complete works of
Motoori Norinaga], 546–47)

It is to be recalled that when Izanami died, Izanagi, greatly grieved, followed her to the nether world. And as he returned to this world, Izanagi cleansed himself in order to purge himself of the defilements of the nether world. While he was thus purifying himself, the Sun Goddess was born, and it was by her father's divine order that she was made to rule permanently the Plain of High Heaven. The Sun Goddess is no other than the sun of heaven itself which illuminates the world now. Then, the Sun Goddess sent her grandson (Ninigi) to rule Japan with the divine commission that the throne which his descendants would occupy would prosper forever. This divine commission is the basic foundation of all the principles of this world. Therefore, those who are interested in the true way must first inquire what had taken place during the divine age and then they would understand the principles [of the world]. It is to be noted that what takes place during the divine age is found in ancient legends, which were not told by any one person but have been transmitted orally [from the divine age] and were subsequently recorded in the *Kojiki* and the *Nihongi* (The chronicles of Japan). While the accounts of these two books are so clear that there can be no room for doubt, many interpreters of these divine scriptures in later generations advanced false interpretations, presumably based on mysterious oral transmission [outside the scriptures]. Or, some scholars [of our country] have been influenced only by the foreign logic and failed to believe in the [sacred events] of the divine age. Some of them, not realizing that all the principles of the world had been already provided in the events of the divine age, cannot understand the legitimacy of the ancient legends of our country. Because of their sole dependence on the theories of foreign countries, they interpret falsely whatever does not agree with the views of foreign countries. Some of them would go so far as to say that the Plain of High Heaven refers to the capital on earth and has nothing to do with heaven, and that [the Sun Goddess], being the great ancestress of our imperial dynasty, was nothing but a sacred person living in this nation and thus is not the sun in heaven. These interpretations are erroneous theories, derived from private opinions of some scholars who distorted and belittled the ancient legends of Japan in order to harmonize them by coercion to foreign logic. In so doing they lost the great fundamentals, and their views are contrary to the meaning of the divine scriptures.

(*Motoori Norinaga zenshu* 4:547–48)

We must bear in mind that there is no line which divides heaven and earth, and that the Plain of High Heaven is situated above all countries. And, since the Sun Goddess rules heaven and illuminates every corner of heaven and earth, thus without her blessing no country on earth can exist even for a single day or single hour. In short, she is the most precious kami in this world. Unfortunately, foreign countries, which have lost the ancient accounts of the divine age, have no way of knowing that the Sun Goddess is to be venerated, and they reduce, based on the speculation of human knowledge, the movements of sun and moon to the activities of yin and yang. In China, the Heavenly Deity is regarded as the most precious, supreme being, whereas in other countries some other deities are venerated. But such deities were concocted by mere speculations and given certain names, but what is known as the Heavenly Deity or the Way of Heaven has no reality. It is lamentable that foreign countries venerate such beings who are unreal, not knowing of the Sun Goddess, while we must be grateful to know the legacy of the Sun Goddess, thanks to the ancient legends of the divine age which have been correctly transmitted. Indeed, our country, being literally the homeland where the Sun Goddess was born, is destined to be the great center of all other nations. It is impossible to cite all the reasons why our nation is superior to foreign countries. However, we must first point out the unrivalled quality of rice crops, which are most important for the preservation of human life, produced in our country. This being the case, you might infer other reasons [for the supremacy of Japan]. Unfortunately, however, those who were born in this country have come to take it for granted, and fail to think of the blessing of imperial kami when they eat rice every morning and every evening.

(Motoori Norinaga zenshu 4:548–49)

More important is the heritage of the imperial family, which being the descendants of the Sun Goddess, is destined to survive undisrupted for generations until the end of the world as proclaimed in the divine commission [given by the Sun Goddess]. The fact that the divine commission [has been fulfilled in actuality] makes it evident that the ancient legends of the divine age are not false. Other countries may boast their own ways as though they alone were noble countries, but the fact that their respective imperial dynasties, which are the foundations of nations, have been broken frequently indicates clearly that their claims are not based on the truth. Yet, other countries consider Japan solely as a small island nation beyond the ocean and never seem to realize that the real true way has been preserved there. More tragic are those [Japanese scholars] who have been enamored with the deceptive theories of foreign countries, so that they too regard Japan only as a small nation, never dreaming that the true way has been transmitted in such a small nation. In reality, the value of anything cannot be judged by its size. For example, our country, though small in size, has a higher density than other countries, and judging by the numerical strength of people our country may be regarded as a large country, unequaled in its richness and bravery.

(Motoori Norinaga zenshu 4:549–50)

It goes without saying that every event in this world is willed by the kami. There are various kinds of kami, noble and humble, good and evil, and just and unjust. Among the events there are some which may be regarded as unreasonable or unjust; these are operated by evil kami, such as the events which cause troubles to the nation and harm to the people. The evil kami is the one who came out of the nether world with the great kami Izanagi when he [returned from there and] purified himself. Although the heavenly kami attempt to overcome the power of the evil kami, they cannot always restrain him. There are certain reasons, established already during the divine age, why evil is mingled with good, as recorded in the *Kojiki* and *Nihongi*. I have elaborated on this point in my *Commentary on the Kojiki*.

(Motoori Norinaga zenshu 4:552)

As to the nether world, I might mention one or two things such as that it is situated at the bottom of the earth, and that it is an unclean and undesirable place, to which all the dead are destined to go. Everyone in this world, both noble and humble, and good and bad, must go to the nether world when they die. This is a sad fact and is seemingly unreasonable. But, inasmuch as it has been preordained for mysterious reasons, according to the true legend of the divine age, we should not speculate on it with our limited human knowledge. We should accept the fact that when one dies, he has to part with his wife and children, wealth, and everything else which is dear to him, and once he goes to the unclean nether world he will never be able to return. This being the case, there is nothing sadder than death in this world. And yet, there are various teachings in the foreign countries which advocate that death is not lamentable and that there are various kinds of future life depending on one's goodness or badness or degrees of spiritual discipline while on earth. Under the influence of such [foreign] teachings, there are some people who pretend not to be sad when death occurs or those who write certain poems or passages to the effect that they have attained enlightenment before death. These teachings, however, are deceitful fabrications, contrary to the human sentiment and the true principle. Because death is a sad affair, even the great kami Izanagi cried like a child when his spouse passed away, and he followed her even to the nether world. This is an honest human sentiment, and everyone must feel that way. Our ancestors, before they came under the influence of foreign ideas, accepted the simple truth that all the dead are destined to go to the nether world, so that there was nothing else for them to do except to cry and mourn. Unfortunately, foreigners, not knowing that evil is caused by evil kami, attempted to find a rational explanation for seemingly unreasonable phases of life and invented such theories as the moral law of cause and effect or destiny which has been preordained by Heaven.

(*Motoori Norinaga zenshu* 4:552–54) ▲

Hirata Atsutane (1776–1843)

Hirata Atsutane continues, in his writing, the emphasis that we see in Motoori on the superiority of Shinto. In this, like Motoori, he appeals to the ancient mythology. However, we see in Hirata even more severe criticism of foreign traditions than we do in Motoori Norinaga. He seems to reserve his harshest criticism for Confucians and Buddhists, regarding their influence as polluting and calling for them to leave the country if they are not satisfied with the way of the *kami*.

▼ MAIN OUTLINES OF THE ZOKUSHINTO TAII (A SUMMARY OF PSEUDO-SHINTO)

In this world, there are often different expressions referring to the same thing, while, on the other hand, the same designations are often used to refer to different things. Among the examples of the same designation referring to different things, the most conspicuous is the case of Shinto which might be minutely divided into twelve or thirteen traditions. Even if we classify Shinto on the basis of major differences, there are at least five traditions, which must be kept in mind by those who aspire to the true study.

(*Hirata Atsutane zenshu* [Complete works of Hirata Atsutane], vol. 1,
"Zoku-Shinto taii" [Summary of Pseudo-Shinto], 2)

Firstly, as I stated in my work, *The Summary of the Ancient Way (Kodo taii)*, true Shinto follows the tradition initiated by the two creator kami, the Kami of High Generative Force and the Kami of Divine Generative Force, which was inherited by the two kami, Izanagi and Izanami, whose union begot everything in this world as well as all kami including the Sun Goddess. When Ninigi, the grandson of the Sun Goddess, descended from heaven, he received the commission from the Sun Goddess to the effect that her descendants were to rule the world from generation to generation. Accordingly, the successive sovereigns, following the divine commission without asserting their own ideas, have ruled the nation which is to last as long as heaven and earth exist. It is this tradition which has been called Shinto, as evidenced by the edict (647) of Emperor Kotoku, stating, "Our nation has always been ruled according to the will of the Sun Goddess who entrusted it to her divine descendants," In this edict the expression, kannagara, is used, and this expression is interpreted in the *Chronicles of Japan* to mean "to follow the way of the kami," or again "to possess the way of the kami." This indeed expresses clearly the intent of the ancient way, which is what we call Shinto. It must be pointed out that the way of the kami does not imply anything unusual. It simply means that the sovereigns are to abide by the divine commission faithfully, and that we too, inasmuch as we originally came out of the creative spirit of the kami, are endowed with the way of the kami. It implies therefore that we have the innate capacity to venerate the kami, the sovereign, and our parents, to show benevolence to our wives and children, and to carry out other obligations which are taught by Confucian scholars. To live according to these [kami-given virtues] without distorting them is nothing but to follow the way of the kami. Thus, the sovereign is to rule the nation, following this way, while it is the duty of all subjects to abide by the will of the sovereign. In this respect, no one, here including the scholars of Confucianism and Buddhist priests, can be exempted from the way of the kami. Those who are not satisfied with it had better not live in this country.

(*Hirata Atsutane zenshu* 2–3)

[The second usage of the term] Shinto is mentioned in the *Chronicles of Japan* in describing Emperor Yomei (r. 586–587) as having "believed in the law of the Buddha and venerated the Way of the Kami." The [second] meaning of this term is the broad designation of the cultic activities regarding the kami, such as worship, prayer, and the rite of purification, which to be sure are ultimately rooted in Shinto, but this is greatly different from the first meaning of the term, namely, *kan-*

nagara, just as the branches and leaves are different from their main trunk. The second meaning of the term Shinto is often confused with the first, even by many so-called Shintoists of later generations simply because [the *Chronicles of Japan*] mentioned this term side by side with the Law of the Buddha. Thus, those who call themselves scholars of Shinto today, not knowing what the true Shinto is, equate Shinto only with such things as the rite of purification and prayer.

(*Hirata Atsutane zenshu* 3)

The third meaning of the term Shinto is found in [one of the Chinese classics] which uses it to refer to the way of heaven such as the principles of the four seasons and the growth of plants. In this sense, the Chinese character, *shen* (*shin* or *kami* in Japanese), does not mean anything so specific as a kami who has real substance. It must be kept in mind that when the Chinese characters were introduced to Japan, many ancient Japanese concepts were matched to the written characters, some of which were appropriate whereas others were not. In the case of the kami of our nation for which the character *shen* was used, it was half correct and half wrong. In reality, the Chinese used the expression, *shen*, to refer to the mysterious way of heaven and nature. However, nowadays the ancient matters are interpreted through the literal meaning of the written characters, which is a great mistake and causes confusing ideas. For example, Dazai Yayemon wrote that Shinto originally existed in the way of Chinese sages because the expression, the way of *shen*, was first used in [one of the Chinese classics]. For the most part, Japanese] Confucian scholars are very foolish. Particularly, this man Dazai has a twisted mind and is determined to slander our nation and thus advanced such a false theory.

(*Hirata Atsutane zenshu* 3–5)

The fourth and fifth meanings of the term Shinto are used by "Dual or Two-sided Shinto" (*Ryobu Shinto*) [which is the Buddhist dominated system of Buddhist-Shinto amalgamation], and the "Unique Shinto" (*Yuiitsu Shinto*) [which advocates the unity of Shinto, Buddhism, and Confucianism, even though it considers Shinto as basic], respectively. The notion of ryobu was never meant to refer to Shinto and Buddhism. It refers to the two realms of the universe, called the "Realm of Diamond Element" and the "Realm of Matrix Repository," in the Shingon Buddhism systematized by Kukai (774–835). But the tradition of Dual Shinto modified this notion of the two realms and concocted the system of Buddhist-Shinto amalgamation by deceiving people with the theory that the kami are the manifestations of the Buddha [in Japan] and that the Buddha is the original nature of the kami. Dual Shinto claims to have synthesized all the good elements, and discarded the undesirable elements, of Shinto, Buddhism, and Confucianism. But [Motoori Norinaga] refuted this claim in his work, *The Jeweled Bamboo Basket* (*Tama katsuma*), and stated that Dual Shinto is predominantly Buddhist with certain features of Confucianism, but that it has not appropriated the intent of the way of the kami, and only mentions certain names of the kami. It is neither Buddhism nor Confucianism; it goes without saying that it is not the way of the kami.

(*Hirata Atsutane zenshu* 5–6) ▲

The Disestablishment of State Shinto[6]

The resurgence of Shinto and the attempt to purge it from any dependence on imported traditions, particularly on the part of those who argued for a pure Shinto, reached its height during the Meiji Restoration. Shinto was proclaimed as the sole basis for government. The governing principles of the country were to be reverence for the *kami* and reverence for the imperial throne. Obeisance at Shinto shrines was recommended for all subjects as a patriotic duty. State Shinto, as this development has come to be called, took on a highly patriotic and militaristic colouring, eventually coming to be associated with Japan's entry into World War II. After the defeat of Japan, the Allied Powers attempted to sever the official relationship between Shinto and government through an order issued to the Japanese government. It is noteworthy that in the Imperial Edict that follows, the Emperor declared the ideas that he is manifest god and that the Japanese race is superior as fictitious.

▼   **Orders from the Supreme Commander for the Allied Powers to the Japanese Government**

15 December 1945
Memorandum for: Imperial Japanese Government
Through: Central Liaison Office, Tokyo

Subject: Abolition of Governmental Sponsorship, Support, Perpetuation, Control, and Dissemination of State Shinto (*Kokka Shinto, Jinja Shinto*)

1. In order to free the Japanese people from direct or indirect compulsion to believe or profess to believe in a religion or cult officially designated by the state, and
    In order to lift from the Japanese people the burden of compulsory financial support of an ideology which has contributed to their war guilt, defeat, suffering, privation, and present deplorable condition, and
    In order to prevent recurrence of the perversion of Shinto theory and beliefs into militaristic and ultra-nationalistic propaganda designed to delude the Japanese people and lead them into wars of aggression, and

In order to assist the Japanese people in a rededication of their national life to building a new Japan based upon ideals of perpetual peace and democracy, It is hereby directed that:

a) The sponsorship, support, perpetuation, control, and dissemination of Shinto by the Japanese national, prefectual, and local governments, or by public officials, subordinates, and employees acting in their official capacity are prohibited and will cease immediately.

b) All financial support from public funds and all official affiliation with Shinto and Shinto shrines are prohibited and will cease immediately.

   i. While no financial support from public funds will be extended to shrines located on public reservations or parks, this prohibition will not be construed to preclude the Japanese Government from continuing to support the areas on which such shrines are located.

   ii. Private financial support of all Shinto Shrines which have been previously supported in whole or in part by public funds will be permitted, provided such private support is entirely voluntary and is in no way derived from forced or involuntary contributions.

c) All propagation and dissemination of militaristic and ultra-nationistic ideology in Shinto doctrines, practices, rites, ceremonies, or observances, as well as in the doctrines, practices, rites, ceremonies and observances of any other religion, faith, sect, creed, or philosophy, are prohibited and will cease immediately.

d) The Religious Functions Order relating to the Grand Shrine of Ise and the Religious Functions Order relating to State and other Shrines will be annulled.

e) The Shrine Board (*Jingi-in*) of the Ministry of Home Affairs will be abolished, and its present functions, duties, and administrative obligations will not be assumed by any other governmental or tax-supported agency.

f) All public educational institutions whose primary function is either the investigation and dissemination of Shinto or the training of a Shinto priesthood will be abolished and their physical properties diverted to other uses. Their present functions, duties, and administrative obligations will not be assumed by any other governmental or tax-supported agency.

g) Private educational institutions for the investigation and dissemination of Shinto and for the training of priesthood for Shinto will be permitted and will operate with the same privileges and be subject to the same controls and restrictions as any other private educational institution having no affiliation with the government; in no case, however, will they receive support from public funds, and in no case will they propagate and disseminate militaristic and ultra-nationalistic ideology.

h) The dissemination of Shinto doctrines in any form and by any means in any educational institution supported wholly or in part by public funds is prohibited and will cease immediately.

   i. All teachers' manuals and text-books now in use in any educational institution supported wholly or in part by public funds will be censored, and all Shinto doctrine will be deleted. No teachers' manual or text-book which is published in the future for use in such institutions will contain any Shinto doctrine.

   ii. No visits to Shinto shrines and no rites, practices, or ceremonies associated with Shinto will be conducted or sponsored by any educational institution supported wholly or in part by public funds.

i) Circulation by the government of "The Fundamental Principles of the National Structure" (*Kokutai no Hongi*), "The Way of the Subject" (*Shinmin no Michi*), and all similar official volumes, commentaries, interpretations, or instructions on Shinto is prohibited.

j) The use in official writings of the terms "Greater East Asia War" (*Dai Toa Senso*), "The Whole World under One Roof' (*Hakko Ichi-u*), and all other terms whose connotation in Japanese is inextricably connected with State Shinto, militarism, and ultra-nationalism is prohibited and will cease immediately.

k) God-shelves (*kamidana*) and all other physical symbols of State Shinto in any office, school institution, organization, or structure supported wholly or in part by public funds are prohibited and will be removed immediately.

l) No official, subordinate, employee, student, citizen, or resident of Japan will be discriminated against because of his failure to profess and believe in or participate in any practice, rite, ceremony, or observance of State Shinto or of any other religion.

m) No official of the national, prefectural, or local government, acting in his public capacity, will visit any shrine to report his assumption of office, to report on conditions of government, or to participate as a representative of government in any ceremony or observance. ▲

▼ **Imperial Edict**

Facing now a new year, we recall how, at the beginning of the Meiji Era, Emperor Meiji deigned to hand down the Charter Oath in Five Articles as the policy of the state.

He declared:

1. Conference shall be inaugurated widely, and all things shall be settled by public discussion.

2. Upper and lower classes shall be of one mind, and governmental administration shall be carried out vigorously.

3. Each and every person, in one and the same manner, beginning with the civil and military authorities and extending to all the masses, shall have opportunity to realize his aspirations, that the human spirit be not frustrated.

4. The evil practices of former times shall be broken down, and everything shall be founded on the just and equitable principles of nature.

5. Knowledge shall be sought throughout the world, that the foundations of imperial rule may be strengthened.

His majesty's wishes were impartial and just. What can we add to them? We herewith renew the oath and resolve on the promotion of the welfare of the nation. At all costs we must pattern our actions according to the spirit of the Charter Oath, we must leave behind the evil practices of former years, we must foster the will of the people, raise up government and people, and carry through in the spirit of peace, we must enrich education and strengthen the foundations of culture, and thus undertake the advancement of the life of the people and the establishment of a new Japan.

Cities and towns, large and small, that have sustained the ravages of war, the sufferings of an afflicted people, the stagnation of industry, the lack of food, the growing trend of unemployment—all this wounds the heart. Yet we doubt not that if our countrymen [waga kokumin], by squarely facing the ordeals of the present and by firmly resolving to seek civilization through peace, bring this resolution to good issue, then not only for our country but also for all mankind a bright future will open up.

Moreover, we know that the spirit of love of home and the spirit of love of country are especially strong in our nation. Now in truth is the time for expanding this and for putting forth sacrificial efforts for the consummation of the love of mankind. When we reflect on the results of the long-continued war which has ended in our defeat [haiboku], we fear that there is danger that our people find the situation hard to bear and that they sink to the depths of discouragement. As the winds of adversity gradually heighten, there is peril in the weakening of moral principles and the marked confusion of thought that they bring.

We stand together with you our countrymen. Our gains and losses have ever been one. We desire that our woe and weal should be shared. The bonds between us and our countrymen have been tied together from first to last by mutual trust and affection. They do not originate in mere myth and legend. They do not have their basis in the fictitious ideas that the emperor is manifest god [akitsu mikami] and that the Japanese people are a race superior to other races and therefore destined to rule the world.

In order to alleviate the trials and sufferings of the people, my government will exhaust all means for devising every kind of plan and program. At the same time, it is our wish that our countrymen should trample disaster underfoot and rise above it, and that they should go forward bravely in making good the suffering of the present and in building up industry and civilization. In the development of the characteristics of tolerance and mutual forgiveness, in mutual dependence and assistance, in the unity of the civil life of our country—in these things there is well revealed the true worth of our supreme tradition, for which we are not ashamed. We doubt not that herein is the reason why in truth our countrymen can make a tremendous contribution to the happiness and progress of mankind. ▲

Notes

1 Readings taken from H. Byron Earhart, *Religion in Japanese Experience, Sources and Interpretations* (Encino and Belmont, CA: Dickenson Publishing, 1974), 14–18.
2 Readings taken from Wing-tsit Chan et al., comps., *The Great Asian Religions: An Anthology* (London: Macmillan, 1969), 239–46.
3 Ibid., 262–66.
4 Readings taken from Wm. Theodore de Bary, ed., *Sources of Japanese Tradition*, vol. I (New York: Columbia University Press, 1964), 268–74.
5 Readings taken from Wing-tsit Chan, et al., *The Great Asian Religions: An Anthology*, 292–301.
6 Readings taken from H. Byron Earhart, *Religion in Japanese Experience: Sources and Interpretations*, 28–34.

New Religions

TEN

New Religions

SINCE THE 1800S, Japan has experienced the growth of new religions, many of which became popular and grew rapidly in organization and numbers following World War II. While these traditions are usually referred to as new, it should be noted that some have been in existence for more than a century. A case in point is Sokagakkai, a movement that traces its inspiration to the thirteenth-century founder of Nichiren Buddhism. In general these movements were characterized by charismatic founders whose teachings tended to be syncretistic and aimed at everyday concerns. Two such movements are Tenrikyo and Sokagakkai. Tenrikyo, founded by Miki Nakayama (1798–1887), shows traces of Shinto and shamanism. Sokagakkai, founded by Makiguchi Tsunebaro (1871–1944), takes its inspiration from the Lotus Sutra as this was understood and interpreted by Nichiren.

Tenrikyo

▼ THE LIFE OF THE FOUNDRESS[1]

"I am the Creator, the true and real God. I have the preordination for this Residence. At this time I have appeared in this world in person to save all mankind. I ask you to let Me have your Miki as My living Temple."

Quite unprepared for such a revelation, her husband Zenbei was much surprised to hear it, and so were all those present, his family, relatives, and the exorcist Ichibei who was at prayer. Needless to say, they had never heard of such a god as "the true and real God," so that they could not give a ready consent to the demand to offer Miki as the Temple God. While at a loss what to do, Zenbei remembered a series of quite strange happenings which occurred one after another during the last year. It started on October 26, 1837, when the eldest son Shuji, who was then seventeen years old, was sowing barley as usual in the field with his mother. Meanwhile, he suddenly began to suffer from a severe pain in the left leg, so severe that he wished to return and barely managed to get home.... Of course, Shuji, who was the dearest son to his parents, was at once put under medical treatment, but it did not seem to have any effect upon him. Being advised to send for an exorcist and to have him pray, they sent a servant to the exorcist Ichibei in Nagataki village and asked him to exorcise the pain of Shuji. Then miraculously the pain left him, but the next day it began to attack him again. Again they sent a servant to Ichibei to have him exorcise Shuji and then the pain stopped again. But on the next day it was the same again. On the third day the pain left him at last, and he was well for about twenty days, when again his leg began to ache severely. Now Zenbei went in person to Ichibei in Nagataki village, and was given the advice to hold a ritual of exorcism called *yosekaji* at home. So coming back, Zenbei, calling in Ichibei and Soyo of the Magata village, held the ritual in the household. Ichibei offered an earnest prayer and tried to practise a curing with Soyo as the medium, who stood still, in her hands two sacred staffs from which cut-paper was hanging. Then the pain in the leg suddenly left Shuji. But in about half a year, he began to suffer from the pain once more. So he held the ritual of *yosekaji*, and he got well. However, he felt the pain again. Thus he repeated it as many as nine times a year.

Meanwhile, the ninth year of Tempo came, and it was at ten in the evening of the 23rd of October, when the three of the family began to have a severe pain respectively, Shuji in the leg, Miki in the loins, and Zenbei in the eyes. They at once sent for Ichibei, who was found to have been at the house of a family named Inuri in the same village on that day. Ichibei came and was surprised to find things quite serious. He was asked to offer incantations and prayers as soon as possible, but unfortunately he was not prepared for it. So that night he went back and early the next morning he came again to perform incantations, and sent for Soyo who was to become the medium, but she was out and nobody knew where she was. There was no other way but to have Miki stand with the sacred staffs in her hands and to offer prayers and incantations through her. Now Ichibei offered his prayers in earnest. Zenbei, reflecting back upon the outline of the happenings in that way, could not but feel that there was something behind it all.

However, they could in no way give a ready consent to the demand put under the name of the original God, so he made up his mind to reject the demand, saying that there were many children to be brought up, and that he was so busy as a village official that he could not afford to offer Miki as the Temple of God, and that if he was a god who would save people in the world, he was requested to descend elsewhere, because there were many other good places as well.

At that time Miki was forty-one years old, and Zenbei fifty-one, both of whom were in the prime of life as householders. The eldest son Suji was eighteen, the eldest daughter Masa fourteen, the third daughter Haru eight, the youngest Kokan was yet no more than two, counting in the Japanese way. Rejected thus, the pains of Miki became even greater, and the original God would not draw back. In such a situation, praying being compelled to stop, he consulted with the relatives who were staying at the house, and the relatives and friends who were called together that day, but no one would persuade him to accede to the demand.

So Zenbei came near Miki who was sitting at the ritual place, and refused compliance with the demands on the grounds that his children were all too young, and that Miki was a householder who could not be spared. At the reply, however, Miki assumed the more solemn attitude, saying rather soothingly and persuadingly, "It is no wonder that you fear so much, but the day will come in twenty or thirty years when you would all be convinced of the justice of My demand." But Zenbei and the others repeated the rejection, saying that they could never wait for so long as twenty or thirty years, so they wished Him to draw back at once. At the reply, Miki began to assume a wild appearance, the sacred staffs in her hands flung up, and the paper on the staffs was torn. So, putting their heads together about what they should do, they refused again and again, but the original God would not draw back. They were compelled to keep consulting day and night for three days, during which they refused repeatedly, and then the voice of the original God said, "If you should refuse, this house shall be destroyed."

At his sharp and harsh words, Zenbei and the other people were frightened into deep silence once more, while Miki, who from the beginning had taken no meal, sitting upright and solemn with the sacred staffs in her hands, urged the people to accede to the demand. If it should continue like this, what would become of her? Zenbei began to be anxious about her fearing for the worst, and at the same time to feel the possibility of being convinced. For however troubled he might be, he could not but find in the words of God wishing to save the world some truth convincing enough to him.

So Zenbei made up his mind to act upon his resolution, and gave his answer with a firm determination, to offer Miki willingly as the Temple of God. It was 8 o'clock in the morning of October 26, the ninth year of Tempo.

As soon as the reply was made, Miki became pacified, and at the same time Miki Nakayama became the Temple of *Tsuki-Hi*, God the Parent. The mind of God the Parent entered the body of Miki, and She came to establish the ultimate teaching of saving the people of the world.

As we are taught in the Ofudesaki:

"What I think now is spoken through Her mouth. Human is the mouth that speaks, but Divine is the mind that thinks within.

Listen attentively to Me! It is because I have borrowed Her mouth, while I have lent My mind to Her"....

The mouth of the Foundress is not different from that of an ordinary person, but the words spoken through the lips are those of God the Parent, and it is God the Parent Himself that is speaking through the mouth of the Foundress. Her outward appearance is quite similar to that of an ordinary person, but it is the mind of *Tsuki-Hi*, God the Parent, that dwells in Her body. Therefore the teachings which were later given through the lips, through the pen, through action, and through wonderful salvation, are the very ones directly given by God the Parent....

The Foundress first urged the family that they should be reduced to poverty. The Foundress not only taught the family the need of being reduced to poverty, but She Herself set an example by giving away Her property which She had brought to the family when She married, and then clothes of family members and food.

When we part with things, and wipe out our worldly desires, we shall have our mind brightened, and then the path to the life of *yokigurashi* will be opened up. But that was not all the Foundress urged, She went so far as to urge the family to take down the main house....

In this way the Foundress went through a hard time for as long as fifteen years. Fifteen years after the opening of the way of faith, that is, on February 22, in the sixth year of Kaei, Her husband Zenbei passed away, at the age of sixty-six, the Foundress was then fifty-six. Though in the deep sorrow, just as God the Parent ordains, the youngest daughter Kokan who was seventeen years old, went to Osaka to promulgate the holy name of Tenri-O-no-Mikoto to the world. Miss Kokan walked to Osaka accompanied by several attendants, and taking up their lodging in an inn near the Dotonbori street, she promulgated the holy name of God the Parent, chanting "*Namu*, Tenri-O-no-Mikoto" in the crowded streets beating wooden clappers. It was the first mission of our religion to the world. Soon after the main house of the Nakayama family found a buyer in a village to the north from Shoyashiki. When the house was taken down, the Foundress served to the helpers *sake* and some food, saying, "I want to set about My task of building a new world. I wish you to celebrate My enterprise with me." The helpers were all deeply impressed with Her cheerful attitude of mind, saying, "it is natural to feel sad when one takes down one's house. We have never seen or heard of such a cheery taking down of a house."...

While she was passing through such a narrow path of faithful life with bright spirit, filled with the parental affection of whole-hearted saving of mankind, She came to be famous first as the god of easy delivery, as is often said, "*obiya* (the grant of easy delivery) and *hoso* (the smallpox healing) are the opening of universal salvation." It began with the easy delivery granted to the third daughter Haru, when she had been staying with the Foundress to give birth to her first baby. Among the villagers, a woman named Yuki Shimizu was the first to be given the grant.

As the rumor of wonderful easy delivery was spread all over Yamato Province, there began to appear in the country a large number of worshippers, who crowded about Her with such devotion as to call Her a living deity of delivery....

Soon after, the Foundress taught the words and gesture of the "*tsu-tome*" or service for the first time:

"Sweep away all evils and save us, O, Parent, Tenri-O-no-Mikoto." It was on this occasion that the gesture was first adopted in the service. For up to that time, the service had been performed by repeating the name of God the Parent, "*Namu*, Tenri-O-no-Mikoto; *Namu*, Tenri-O-no-Mikoto," clapping the wooden clappers. '*Namu*' means *Tsuki-Hi*, the Parent.

Since then the form of service was brought to perfection, that is, in the third year of Meiji, the Foundress taught the second and fourth sections of the Mikagura-uta, and in the eighth year of Meiji, the accompanying words and gesture of *kagura teodori* were almost completed, and then the eleven kinds of gesture were taught, and at last in the fifteenth year of Meiji, the present words of the service were completed. ▲

Soka Gakkai

▼ THE OBJECTIVE OF THE SOKAGAKKAI

The objective of the Sokagakkai lies, first of all, in teaching the individual how to redevelop his character and enjoy a happy life, and in showing all mankind how eternal peace can be established, through the supreme Buddhism, the religion of mercy and pacifism. Through this supreme religion, a person can escape from poverty and live a prosperous life, if only he works in earnest; a man troubled with domestic discord will find his home serene and happy; and a man suffering from disease will completely recover his health and be able to resume his work. Through the power of the Gohonzon, a mother worried with her delinquent son will see him reform, and a husband who is plagued with a neurotic wife can have her return to normalcy. We often hear of a man whose business is failing and who, after being converted to Nichiren Shoshu, has a brilliant idea, or makes a contact with an unexpected customer and begins to prosper again.

Most people are afflicted with various problems—either spiritual, physical or material, but everyone who believes in the Gohonzon (the object of worship in Nichiren Shoshu) can solve any problem and achieve a happy life. Men who are timid or irritable can gradually become normal before they become aware of the change in their character.

The true intention of the Daishonin is to save the whole world through the attainment of each individual's happiness in life. Consequently, members of the Sokagakkai are actively trying to make, first of all, the Japanese people realize this great Buddhism as soon as possible. But there is no nationality in religion. Nichiren Daishonin made a wonderful prediction about seven hundred years ago to the effect, "As the Buddhism of Sakyamuni found its way to Japan from India by way of China, conversely, Our Buddhism will return from Japan to India by way of China."

Without a doubt, the Buddhism of the Daishonin will spread all over the East in the near future, and finally throughout the whole world. World peace as well as the welfare of individual nations can be achieved only when the true religion is made the basic thought. If you take this Buddhism as the guiding principle of your daily lives, the happiness of the individual will be closely reflected in the prosperity of the society in which you live.

Each country can achieve prosperity without any harm to, or discord with, any other country. This is the spirit of Kosen-rufu (propagation of Nichiren Daishonin's teachings) and the Nichiren Shoshu Sokagakkai is positively striving to achieve this sublime purpose.

Members' Daily Activities

The Sokagakkai's objective is to make all people happy. To achieve this, the members themselves enjoy happiness through their practice of Buddhism and at the same time introduce the immense blessings of the Gohonzon to others. The Sokagakkai promotes various activities so that each individual member can deepen his faith and also help the unhappy.

Gakkai members' most fundamental activities are Gongyo, daily prayer, and Shakubuku, introducing the True Buddhism to non-believers.

The practice of Gongyo is indispensable for all Gakkai members. Neglecting it would be the same as living without eating! At the same time, the practice of Shakubuku for agonized and troubled people is also indispensable. Thus, Gongyo and Shakubuku are the fundamental practices for believers and at the same time the source of the unfathomable blessings of the Gohonzon.

Another important Gakkai activity for general members is the *Zadankai*, discussion meetings, where they talk freely with other members and with non-believers who attend the meetings for the first time. This helps the members to enrich their knowledge of the True Buddhism.

The study of Buddhism is also encouraged, as well as *Tozankai*, pilgrimage to Taisekiji, which is also an important activity for members.

Members can enjoy the immense delight of having faith in Nichiren Shoshu through these various activities.

Gongyo, Daily Worship

The most important of all the activities of the Sokagakkai members is practising Gongyo in the morning and evening. [Sokagakkai] President Ikeda spoke of the importance of Gongyo as follows:

"Suppose a man has an excellent TV set. He cannot enjoy interesting programs unless he turns it on. No matter how precious a book a man may have, he cannot gain any knowledge from it unless he opens it.

"In a like manner, you cannot gain any blessings from the DaiGohonzon unless you practise Gongyo. Earnest prayer to the Gohonzon is the only true source of all your acts in life, the origin of the vital life-force, the root of your study in Buddhism, and the mainspring of your blessed life."

In the early stages of faith, every member is apt to neglect Gongyo for he feels the time required is too long, or often he stops Gongyo when he has a visitor because he feels embarrassed to be seen at prayer. As every member has joined the Sokagakkai to gain happiness, he should keep his faith untiringly and never be swayed by external hindrances or difficulties which may try to disturb his faith.

Shakubuku, Introduction to True Buddhism

Shakubuku literally means to correct one's evil mind and to convert it to good. It results from the delight of believing in Nichiren Daishonin's Buddhism and from the heartfelt wish for helping the unhappy through Buddhism.

Shakubuku is rooted in humanity, and by practising Shakubuku, one can enjoy the great blessings of the Gohonzon. The most conspicuous blessings one can receive by practising Shakubuku are lively spirit and vigorous life-force. Shakubuku is the source of the Gohonzon's blessings and strong vitality.

Shakubuku should be carried out for the purpose of helping people from misery and misfortune.

There are many who are not helped by politics, money or the arts. Such people, whether or not they are conscious of it, are seeking the Gohonzon to change their karma. This is the revelation of the Buddhist mercy which comes from earnest practice. It is natural for believers to devote themselves to the salvation of all mankind, if they but realize the unfathomable mercy of the True Buddha.

It is desirable for members to practise Shakubuku for people who, being ignorant of the True Buddhism, are simply opposed to having faith in it. When one looks back upon the days before he was converted to Nichiren Shoshu, he will realize that he also had been more or less opposed to it. After being converted to this religion, however, he found his view of life to be false, and was awakened to the need to march forward on the highway to happiness. This fact well testifies to the necessity of Shakubuku for non-believers.

Zadankai Discussion Meetings

Zadankai, discussion meetings, are held daily wherever the Sokagakkai members live. Meetings are held every day with 20–30 members or sometimes even more than 50 attending. They talk about the True Buddhism and encourage one another so that all attendants deepened their faith. To the non-believers who attend the meeting, members try to explain fully how True Buddhism can improve human life. Naturally, the discussion meeting is filled with a cheerful atmosphere and hope for constructing a brighter future.

Discussion meetings, a traditional activity of the Sokagakkai, have been conducted since the days of first president Tsunesaburo Makiguchi. In those days, his home was the meeting place. In the days of second president Josei Toda, also, it was through discussion meetings that he embarked on the reconstruction of the Sokagakkai.

President Ikeda promoted all his Gakkai activities around the traditional *Zadankai*. He also made it a rule to read the Gosho (the collection of Nichiren Daishonin's works) for those present. Thus the foundation for the Sokagakkai's development into its present position was established by the three successive presidents with the discussion meetings as its foundation.

Some might think it easier to promote the propagation of a religion through propaganda—for example, by holding large-scale meetings rather than *Zadankai* which are attended by only a limited number of persons. In reality, however, the small discussion meetings are the best and the surest way for propagating the True Buddhism. One will clearly understand this if he considers that the fantastic advance of the Sokagakkai stemmed from the *Zadankai*. ▲

Notes

1 Readings taken from H. Byron Earhart, *Religion in Japanese Experience: Sources and Interpretations* (Encino and Belmont, CA: Dickenson, 1974), 238–49.

Glossary

Permissions

ahimsa (Sanskrit) non-harming, non-violence

akshara (Sanskrit) letter of the Sanskrit alphabet

arahat see *arhant*

arhant (Sanskrit) "noble one," a Buddhist saint who has realized nirvana through the help of a Buddha (Hinayana), a Buddhist saint who has penetrated the doctrinal truth and is absorbed in deep meditation, but who has yet to achieve unrestricted compassion and omniscience in order to achieve nirvana (Mahayana)

ashrama (Sanskrit) the [four] stages of life in Hinduism

asrava (Sanskrit) influx of karma (Jainism), the mind-contaminating influences

asura (Sanskrit) demi-gods similar to the Titans in classical mythology

atman (Sanskrit) the true self, soul, soul monad

bhakti (Sanskrit) devotion

bhavana (Sanskrit) "cultivation of the mind" in Buddhism; the term identifies the various methods to discipline, control, and focus the mind

bhikkhu (Pali *bhikku*, Sanskrit *bhiksu*) the Buddhist monk who lives from alms given to him

bodhi (Sanskrit) enlightenment as realization of final truth

bodhicitta (Sanskrit) "mind of enlightenment" as the characteristic of a bodhisattva, that is to devote all one's efforts to the realization of enlightenment for the benefit of all sentient beings

391

bodhisattva (Sanskrit) "a person committed to achieve enlightenment," the historical Buddha before his enlightenment, a person before the realization of buddhahood, the ideal of Mahayana

bo[dhi] tree, a fig tree under which the Buddha sat when he achieved enlightenment

brahmacari (Sanskrit) a student of the *Samhitas* and dedicated to *brahman*; later, the first stage of a holy life

brahmacairya (Sanskrit) celibate and "pure" life of a religious person

buddha (Sanskrit) the Enlightened One, the Awakened One, honorific title of the founder of Buddhism

devi (Sanskrit) goddess

dhamma see *dharma*

dharma (Sanskrit) Hinduism: "ordained duties"

dharma (Sanskrit; Pali *dhamma*) in Buddhism: (1) the doctrine; (2) the truth; (3) element-like entities which form clusters which the unenlightened person perceives as "things" and "living beings"

dharma shastra (Sanskrit) genre of legal literature

duhkha (Sanskrit *duhkha*, Pali *dukkha*) "suffering," the first noble truth in Buddhism, better translated as unsatisfaction

guru (Sanskrit) spiritual teacher

i (Chinese) righteousness, Confucianism

jina (Sanskrit) "conqueror," a name given to the Buddhas because of their conquest of the world of suffering and wrong views, and to the Jaina *Tirthankaras* because of their transcending the river of suffering

kalaratri (Sanskrit) the cosmic night at the end of an aeon, frequently identified with Durga

kami (Japanese) divine beings of Shintoism

karman (Sanskrit) act, ritual, future effect of one's deeds

khanda (Sanskrit) section of a book

koti (Sanskrit) ten millions

lama (Tibetan *bla ma*) = Sanskrit *guru*

li (Chinese) unit to measure distance, equivalent to a mile

li (Chinese) ritual, proper behaviour, propriety as the moral guideline in Confucianism

maharatri (Sanskrit) the night in which the world is totally destroyed

mara (Sanskrit) personification of forces adverse to the achievement of enlightenment in Buddhism

ming (Chinese) fate, destiny

moharatri (Sanskrit) the night at the end of this world

moksha (Sanskrit) in Hinduisin, liberation from the world

mukti (Sanskrit) release from earthly bonds

nembutsu (Japanese) the Japanese contracted pronunciation of *namo Amith-abha-Buddhaya*, "Veneration to Buddha Amitabha," the main practice of the followers of the Pure Land School

nirvana (Sanskrit; Pali *nibbana*) "the blowing out" of ignorance, passion, and hatred (Theravada), the obtaining of omniscience as a true understanding of reality (Mahayana), the goal of Buddhism which designates the end of the cycle of death and rebirth

parinirvana (Sanskrit) the final nirvana when the body-sustaining karmic forces come to an end

prajna (Sanskrit; Pali *panna*) wisdom, the third component of the Buddhist path, consisting of listening, reasoning, and contemplating the dharma which leads to enlightenment

qi/ch'i (Chinese) creative force

ren/jen (Chinese) man, humanity, humaneness, basic principle in Confucianism

rishi (Sanskrit) ancient seer who "sees" the Veda and puts them into human words

saha (Sanskrit) the world of humans

samsara (Sanskrit) the endless cycle of death and rebirth which constitutes this world

sangha (Sanskrit) the Buddhist community consisting of monks, nuns, male and female lay people; in a stricter sense the sangha consists of those individuals who have made significant progress on the path to enlightenment

shila (Sanskrit; Pali *sila*) ethics

shramana (Sanskrit) wandering ascetic

shruti (Sanskrit) "learning which is heard," the Vedas as sacred scripture of Hinduism

shunya (Sanskrit; Pali *sunna*) "void" of inherent being, the characteristic of all things which are impermanent, unsatisfactory and without a self identity

siddhanta (Sanskrit) doctrinal system, tenet

skandha (Sanskrit; Pali *khandha*) five aggregations which are the constituents of each sentient being: form and colour, emotions, perceptions, predispositions, and consciousness

smriti (Sanskrit) "that which is remembered," a vast body of semi-canonical Hindu texts

sugata (Sanskrit) a title for a Buddha

sukhavati (Sanskrit) the "Pure Land," a realm created through Buddha Amitabha's meditation with conditions most conducive to the studying of the dharma *sutra* (Sanskrit; Pali *sutta*) "thread," short stanzas suitable for memorization

svadha (Sanskrit) originally a libation of melted butter poured into the sacred fire for the ancestors; later the word replaced the actual offering

svaha (Sanskrit) an exclamatory expression which concludes prayers; similar to amen

tian/t'ien (Chinese) "heaven" as primary moral force governing the course of the world as well as the conduct of virtuous people; nature in Taoism

tathagata (Sanskrit) "who has come like those before," an expression used by the historical Buddha to refer to himself after he had obtained enlightenment

tathata (Sanskrit) suchness, a term of Buddhist philosophy defining true reality

tripitaka (Sanskrit; Pali *tipitaka*) "three baskets," the three collections of texts which constitute the Buddhist canon

varna (Sanskrit) "colour," caste

vashatkara (Sanskrit) the *hotar*'s incantation when the *adhvaryu* throws the offerings into the sacred fire

wen (Chinese) "ornament" as accidental features

wuwei/wu-wei (Chinese) "no action," prime concept of Taoism as avoiding actions which are against the natural flow of things

xiang/hsiang (Chinese) form, Taoism

xu/hsu (Chinese) vacuous, Taoism

xuan/hsuan (Chinese) the deep and profound, identifying the primordial base of existence in Taoism

yang (Chinese) the principle of the bright, dry, hot, day, summer, sun, outside, and the male, complement of yin

yin (Chinese) the principle of the dark, wet, cold, night, winter, moon, inside, and female, complement of yang

PERMISSIONS

The editors and publisher gratefully acknowledge permission to reprint copyright material from the following sources:

The Buddhacarita, or Acts of the Buddha, E.H. Johnston, trans. (Delhi: Motilal Banarsidass, 1972). Excerpt, II, 31–35; IV, 53–56; V, 2, 4–10; XIII, 18–22, 25–31, 70–72; XIV, 49–76, 86–87. Reprinted with the permission of Motilal Banarsidass.

The Buddhhist Catechism, 44th ed., Henry S. Olcott (Adyar, Chennai: Theosophical Publishing House, 1947), pp. 37–38, 40–41. Reprinted with permission of Theosophical Publishing House, Adyar, Chennai 600 020, India. Copyright © The Theosophical Publishing House, Adyar, Chennai–600 020, India. http://www.ts-adjar.org.

Buddhist Mahayana Texts, F.M. Mueller, ed., trans. (1894; rpt. Delhi: Motilal Banarsidass, 1965). Excerpt, vol. 49, p. 98. Reprinted with the permission of Motilal Banarsidass.

Buddhist Scriptures, Edward Conze, trans. (Harmondsworth: Penguin Classics, 1959). Copyright © Edward Conze, 1959. Excerpt, pp. 70–77. Reproduced by permission of Penguin Books Ltd.

Buddhist Sutras, T.W. Rhys Davids, trans. (1881; rpt. Delhi: Motilal Banarsidass, 1965). Excerpt, vol. II, pp. 146, 148–53. Reprinted with the permission of Motilal Banarsidass.

Buddhist Texts through the Ages, Edward Conze, et al., trans. (1954; rpt. New York: Harper and Row, 1964). Reprinted with the permission of Bruno Cassirer Ltd.

The Devotional Poems of Mirabai, A.J. Alston, trans. (Delhi: Motilal Banarsidass, 1980). Excerpt, nos. 4, 5, 7, 63, 66–70. Reprinted with the permission of Motilal Banarsidass.

Emptiness: A Study in Religious Meaning, by Frederick J. Streng (New York: Abingdon Press, 1967). Excerpt, pp. 197, 215–17. Ch. 25, vv. 9, 24 revised by the author. Reprinted with the permission of Frederick J. Streng.